LOUIS LOUCHEUR
AND THE SHAPING OF MODERN FRANCE
1916–1931

Louis Loucheur
and the Shaping of Modern France
1916–1931

Stephen D. Carls

———

Louisiana State University Press / Baton Rouge and London

Copyright © 1993 by Louisiana State University Press
All rights reserved
Manufactured in the United States of America
First printing
02 01 00 99 98 97 96 95 94 93   5 4 3 2 1

Designer: Glynnis Phoebe
Typeface: Trump Mediaeval
Typesetter: Precision Typographers, Inc.
Printer and binder: Thomson-Shore, Inc.

Library of Congress Cataloging-in-Publication Data

Carls, Stephen Douglas.
    Louis Loucheur and the shaping of modern France, 1916–1931 /
Stephen D. Carls.
        p.   cm.
    Includes bibliographical references and index.
    ISBN 0-8071-1787-0
    1. Loucheur, Louis, 1872–1931. 2. Politicians—France—Biography.
3. Industrialists—France—Biography. 4. France—Economic
conditions—1918–1945. 5. France—Politics and
government—1914–1940. I. Title.
HC272.5.L68C37   1993
338.944'0092—dc20
    [B]   92-40840
                                                          CIP

A portion of this book appeared previously in slightly different form as "Louis Loucheur and the Economic Mobilization of France During World War I," in *Proceedings of the Twelfth Annual Meeting of the Western Society for French History*, 1985, pp. 208–17. Letters by Louis Loucheur are quoted with the permission of Annie Michelin, Claude Sarrade-Loucheur, and Marc Sarrade-Loucheur.

The paper in this book meets the guidelines for permanence and durability of the Committee on Production Guidelines for Book Longevity of the Council on Library Resources. ♾

To my parents,
Ernest and Eleanor Carls,
and my wife,
Catherine

CONTENTS

ILLUSTRATIONS

Preface

"Tuesday, December 12, 1916 . . . 9:30 p.m. . . . The die is cast."[1] When Louis Loucheur, a prewar industrialist turned wartime munitions manufacturer, used those words in his diary in reaction to his nomination as undersecretary of state in a newly created armaments ministry, he had no idea just how permanently the event he was recording would alter his long-range plans. Yet what he wrote shows an awareness that the unexpected turn had thrust his life toward an unknown fate. The risk may have been routine for the bold entrepreneur, however. Loucheur's entry into public life had not resulted from any carefully laid political plans but stemmed from a government need for his technical expertise in munitions production at a time when France was facing a production crisis. Though he experienced difficulties with more tradition-bound officials after joining the armaments ministry, he became one of the key government administrators during the remainder of the war, in virtue of his understanding of the nature of total war, his gift for efficiency and organization, and his knowledge of new technologies. The long-term impact of his appointment in 1916 became apparent after the war. Instead of returning to the private sector, he stayed in politics, where he did much to shape the economic and social policies of France until his death in 1931. It is his years of public service, from 1916 to 1931, that will be the primary focus of this study.

When the First World War broke out in the summer of 1914, it was widely believed that the conflict would be over in weeks and that the economic impact would be slight. None of the belligerents were pre-

1. Louis Loucheur, *Carnets secrets, 1908–1932*, ed. Jacques de Launay (Brussels, 1962), 26. Loucheur employed the Caesarean Latin "Alea jacta est" in his diary.

pared for the military stalemate they were to encounter. In France, where the early fighting brought about the loss of an important segment of heavy industry and cut off the sources of certain indispensable raw materials, the government reacted to the munitions crisis that fall by organizing private industry for armaments production. Although the government at first relied upon the free-market system, its control over the economy gradually increased, owing to the complexity of total war, until its influence extended to most vital areas. It was the war's economic side that brought Loucheur into the armaments ministry in late 1916. By war's end, he, as minister of armaments, oversaw a production network of more than 1.5 million people.

After the war, Loucheur soon emerged as Premier Georges Clemenceau's chief economic adviser, and in that capacity, as well as in his position as minister of industrial reconstruction, he exerted considerable influence on domestic economic policy in 1919. His activities during that year also involved international politics, for he was an important participant at the Paris peace conference and in discussions related to Allied postwar economic cooperation.

Nor did Loucheur's contributions to French economic policy end when the Clemenceau government collapsed in early 1920. First elected to the Chamber of Deputies in late 1919, Loucheur was outspoken in expressing his views on the economy in parliament throughout the 1920s. As the minister of the liberated regions (January, 1921–January, 1922), minister of commerce (March, 1923–June, 1923, and July, 1926), minister of finance (November and December, 1925), minister of labor and health (June, 1928–February, 1930), national economics minister (December, 1930, and January, 1931), and member of the French delegation to the League of Nations (1924–1929), Loucheur had many opportunities to engage in economic decision making domestically and internationally. His interests embraced social issues: he played a pivotal role in developing and applying legislation concerning low-income housing as well as in preparing a social-insurance program for workers.

Loucheur was an early figure of the new managerial-technical class known as technocrats, whose movement really began to make headway in France during and after World War II. He stressed many technocratic ideas, including efficiency, business consolidation, vigorous economic expansion, increased government involvement by technical experts, mass production, and economic modernization of a kind that would allow France to compete in international markets with Britain, the

United States, and Germany.[2] He stated one of his primary themes of 1919 dramatically when, in February, he called on all the French to participate in a "hymn to production." Certainly his education at the Ecole Polytechnique was critical in planting his zeal for modernization; the prestigious engineering school influenced many who were enthusiastic about renovating France's productive plant. Related to Loucheur's technocratic outlook was his problem-solving approach to economic emergencies. His pragmatism was conspicuous both during and after the war.

Another aspect of Loucheur's viewpoint was his general commitment to economic liberalism, though he questioned some of the liberal economic practices the Third Republic pursued prior to World War I. During those years there were strong tendencies toward gradual economic change as against potentially disruptive rapid growth; the state participated in the economic system, but by and large it restricted its role to maintaining a balance between the static and dynamic sectors by means of protective tariffs and upholding the market economy by periodically intervening to mend weaknesses.[3] Because of the seeming success of the economic policy before the war, it is not surprising that at the cessation of hostilities many in the business world began to demand an end to the government's emergency controls and a return to business as usual. Loucheur too was anxious to restore France to commercial freedom as quickly as possible and began dismantling parts of the government's wartime control apparatus soon after the November armistice. He wanted the state to remain involved in the economy only on a selective basis. But he was also eager to modify prewar economic policy, for during the war he had seen firsthand a national industrial plant that was in many respects backward, poorly organized, and inefficient. He knew that France needed economic renewal to be a major economic power, and he believed that the

2. See Richard Kuisel, *Ernest Mercier: French Technocrat* (Berkeley and Los Angeles, 1967), vii–ix. Kuisel writes, "The typical French technocrat seeks economic modernization—meaning economic expansion, the scientific utilization of resources, and an organized national economy directed by technicians. Yet economic and political streamlining alone does not satisfy him for he also wants to see society infused with the values of efficiency, productivity, and expertise, and in this way urges a radical transformation of traditional values." Kuisel also focuses on French technocracy in "Technocrats and Public Economic Policy: From the Third to the Fourth Republic," *Journal of European Economic History*, II (1973), 53–99.

3. See Richard Kuisel, *Capitalism and the State in Modern France: Renovation and Economic Management in the Twentieth Century* (Cambridge, Eng., 1981), 8–20.

government could play a key role in promoting the changes he considered essential. Loucheur hoped that by infusing economic liberalism with modernizing concepts, such as limited state participation in certain industries, he could assure France's future industrially. Although he had to deal with domestic and international constraints upon the industrial renovation he sought, he was a decisive force behind the realization of some central goals of the modernizers during the initial postwar decade.

In the international sphere, Loucheur advocated close European cooperation. For example, as early as 1919 he proposed a European steel cartel that would have included Germany. And in the mid- and late 1920s he intensified his efforts to raise the level of European economic cooperation by sponsoring an international economic conference in Geneva and supporting private groups and government leaders favorable to some kind of European union.

In the following pages, the reader will learn how a private munitions manufacturer became one of the most powerful government officials in France during the war, and how he occupied a pivotal position in the Allied victory over the Central Powers and in the development of France's postwar economic and social policies. In spite of the paucity of evidence regarding a number of questions, it is hoped that the book will enlarge insight into the controversies that have surrounded Loucheur's name since he embarked upon his public service career in 1916.

The book owes much to the support and assistance of other scholars. First of all, I wish to thank Kim Munholland, of the University of Minnesota, for introducing me to the subject of Louis Loucheur and for sharing his ideas over several years on how to improve my study. He later gave support to my successful effort to obtain the endorsement of the First Books Program of the American Historical Association. Also a key person in the early phases of this study was Austin Caswell, of Indiana University, who gave generously of his time in helping me obtain source materials and in making comments on the text. In recent years my manuscript has profited from critical readings by Dan Silverman, of Pennsylvania State University, and Stephen Schuker, of the University of Virginia. Both made valuable recommendations for strengthening the text stylistically, factually, and interpretively. I want to add, however, that any errors of interpretation and fact are entirely mine, and I accept full responsibility for them.

My research also benefited from the willingness of several people in France to share information about Loucheur. The late Simone Loucheur, the daughter of Louis Loucheur, graciously granted me an interview in 1977, as did Paul Huvelin, the son-in-law of Alexandre Giros, and Robert Guillain, a secretary to Loucheur at the League of Nations in the late 1920s. Important too was the cooperation I received from the Sarrade-Loucheur family. The late Jacques Sarrade-Loucheur, Louis Loucheur's grandson, was a great source of encouragement and assistance. He not only shared experiences he had had with his grandfather but he also gave me access to family documents. Other members of the family likewise showed support for the endeavor.

I received valuable assistance from the staffs of archives in France, Britain, the United States, and Switzerland. The number who facilitated my work with their expertise is many. I wish to express my gratitude to all of them for their professional concern and numerous acts of kindness. Several library staffs were also of particular importance to the realization of my undertaking. The librarians at Sterling College and Union University worked indefatigably to obtain materials I needed. The library staffs of the University of Minnesota and the Bibliothèque Nationale were always cooperative in my search for materials.

A sabbatical and other forms of assistance from Sterling College did much to advance my project, as did professional support from Union University. I also received a McMillan travel grant from the University of Minnesota and a grant from the Southern Regional Education Board. I want to express my deep appreciation to all of these sources for their aid.

Finally, a special thank-you is due my family. My wife, Catherine, whom I met early in my research on Loucheur, has shown boundless patience through many years. By helping in translation, offering scholarly criticism, and often adjusting her schedule to meet mine, she has made numerous sacrifices, both personal and professional. Her encouragement and support were decisive in bringing my manuscript to fruition. I also want to thank my three children—Philip, Elizabeth, and Paul—for tolerating my frequent absence from their daily life, and my parents and my father-in-law, Victor Maire, for faithfully cheering me on.

ABBREVIATIONS

AANV   Archives de l'Assemblée Nationale, Versailles

ADN   Archives du Département du Nord, Lille

AN   Archives Nationales, Paris

APP   Archives de la Préfecture de Police, Paris

AS   Archives du Sénat, Paris

BIT   Bureau International du Travail, Geneva

HHPL   Herbert Hoover Presidential Library, West Branch, Iowa

HI   Hoover Institution on War, Revolution, and Peace, Stanford, California

LNA   League of Nations Archives, Geneva

MAE   Archives du Ministère des Affaires Etrangères, Paris

MF   Archives du Ministère des Finances, Paris

PRO   Public Record Office, London

SHA   Service Historique de l'Armée de Terre, Vincennes

Louis Loucheur
and the Shaping of Modern France
1916–1931

I

THE FORMATIVE YEARS

Louis Loucheur began his career as an industrialist before the First World War. The French have looked back on the belle époque as a time during which the country achieved a "happiness" never duplicated since. In the two generations following the Franco-Prussian War of 1870–1871, France not only enjoyed political stability but also experienced considerable economic growth, which in the final prewar years amounted to a boom.[1]

In part because of the tremendous business success that Loucheur enjoyed before the war, his outlook reflected the economic liberalism that typified the prevailing approach to economic questions. Liberals in those years were suspicious of any significant state participation in the economy; they argued that the market system should operate unimpaired by state regulation or interference. Still, if liberal doctrine served as a general guide, the Third Republic did not follow its precepts strictly. In the 1890s, for example, the republic adopted a protectionist tariff policy so that producers could survive whether competitive or not. The state sought above all to maintain a balance between the various sectors of the French economy. As Richard Kuisel notes, "Whenever the republic intervened in this era it was to protect the balanced economy or to meet some misfortune. Rarely, if ever, did it act to promote economic expansion, plan development, or advance economic democracy. Discriminatory taxes defended independent shopkeepers against the inroads of aggressive chain retailers and department stores; fiscal practice helped small farmers and small firms survive; other measures sheltered,

---

1. Gordon Wright, *France in Modern Times* (2nd ed.; Chicago, 1974), 269–70.

subsidized, and salvaged hard-pressed sectors."[2]   The relative success of the French economy in the years immediately preceding the war reinforced the commitment to an economic liberalism in which the state acted as a protector and defender.

Loucheur rose, largely through his own efforts, from a family of modest means to a position of considerable wealth. In 1919, when he stood for the Chamber of Deputies, he liked to invoke his origins as a self-made man. "I come . . . from the people," he stressed. And he suggested that other "children of the masses" could emulate his success.[3] In some ways, Loucheur offers a French parallel to the American characters Horatio Alger created in the second half of the nineteenth century.

Loucheur was born in Roubaix, a textile town in the department of the Nord, on August 12, 1872. The only son among four children of a struggling architect, he was reared a Catholic. He attended a religious primary school and then continued his studies at the Lycée de Lille. After two years of preparatory studies, he won a scholarship to the prestigious Ecole Polytechnique in 1890. Loucheur was fascinated by geometry and at the Polytechnique independently demonstrated two difficult theorems concerning epicycles; they came to be called the Loucheur theorems. Just before the end of his studies, his determination was severely tested when his father died and his mother was injured in a train accident. Loucheur, who was in the midst of his last set of exams, was shaken, but he mustered the emotional strength to persevere in his exams and to graduate with a respectable class standing. His resolve on that occasion prefigured qualities he was to display during other crises. The Polytechnique gave him rationalistic, problem-solving experience that shaped his later action in both business and government.[4]

While at the Polytechnique, Loucheur formed a bond with Alexandre Giros, who was later to play a crucial role in his business career. The two had adjoining rooms and study seats during their second year of studies, and the long-enduring friendship that began between them in the fall of 1891 was reinforced when the two young men later roomed

2. Richard Kuisel, *Capitalism and the State in Modern France: Renovation and Economic Management in the Twentieth Century* (Cambridge, Eng., 1981), 16. For Kuisel's overall argument about this, see pp. 1–30.

3. *Le Progrès du Nord* (Lille), November 10, 1919, p. 1.

4. Fernand Motte, "Discours," in *Louis Loucheur*, without recorded editor (Les Moulineaux, n.d.), 25–27; Simone Loucheur, Interview, June 17, 1977; Kuisel, *Capitalism and the State*, 26–27.

together at Vincennes, during their military service under the command of Captain Ferdinand Foch.[5]

Primarily on the basis of his credentials as a Polytechnician or "X," Loucheur was upon discharge offered a job at 1,800 francs ($360) a year as a construction engineer with the Chemins de Fer du Nord, which was then headed by another "X," Albert Sartiaux.[6] Loucheur's supple mind and engineering skills caught the attention of his superiors, as it was to do repeatedly in the years ahead. He was soon supervising the enlargement of the rail station Paris-Nord, and when that project reached its completion more quickly than planned, his future with the rail line seemed assured.[7]

Through friends, Loucheur, dazzled by life in Paris, obtained an invitation to a dance at the home of Henri Lenicque, whose family was part of the Parisian bourgeoisie. Loucheur, though conscious of the distance between his provincial origins and the occasion, left Lenicque's daughter Suzanne with what she described as an "impression of loyalty ... of security that was ... rather ... attractive."[8] Loucheur married her in November, 1896, and they eventually had two daughters, Marthe and Simone. One reason the young Parisienne was contented in marrying Loucheur was that his railway post did not require him to do much traveling. But their situation changed in 1899, when Loucheur's friend Giros offered him a partnership in a construction firm. By accepting that, Loucheur arrived at a turning point in his career.[9]

Giros and Loucheur had taken different professional paths after their year of military service. Giros' first position was with the Compagnie des Forges de Champagne, and he then spent three years working for a large construction firm. Eager for independence, he began his own business and after some difficult months obtained his first contract through family connections. When other contracts followed, he con-

5. Alexandre Giros, "Allocution prononcée par M. Alexandre Giros," in *Louis Loucheur*, without recorded editor (Les Moulineaux, n.d.), 54; Motte, "Discours," 27.

6. *X* is the term used for students at and graduates of the Ecole Polytechnique.

7. Louis Loucheur, *Carnets sècrets, 1908–1932*, ed. Jacques de Launay (Brussels, 1962), 6; Motte, "Discours," 27–28; Giros, "Allocution prononcée," 55.

8. Simone Loucheur, "Histoire familiale," in Simone Loucheur Papers, in family possession, Paris.

9. *Ibid.*; Motte, "Discours," 28; Giros, "Allocution prononcée," 55. Giros is less precise about the date for the beginning of their partnership, stating that it was in either 1899 or 1900.

templated a bright future and made an extremely generous offer to Loucheur. The partnership he proposed was to have an initial capital investment of forty thousand francs, all of it coming from him, with Loucheur contributing an equal sum only when his finances permitted. Until Loucheur could make his investment, the profits were to be divided two-thirds for Giros and one-third for Loucheur. The Société Giros et Loucheur, which the two friends formed, was soon known by its telegraphic code name Girolou. Within six months, Loucheur had funds to establish equality with Giros in the division of profits.[10]

Girolou at first specialized in projects of reinforced concrete, but the company's activities spread quickly to include the construction of hydroelectric systems, electrical power distribution grids, and urban and rural rail networks. The potential of reinforced concrete and electricity—both recent technological developments—impressed the two entrepreneurs before it did most of their contemporaries, and they knew how to capitalize on the future that was opening before them. They were fortunate in their timing, for they began their enterprise during an economic upswing that has often been described as Europe's second industrial revolution. Technological acceleration relied upon the company's construction capabilities, which found application throughout France and beyond, in Tunisia and Algeria.[11]

Loucheur's personal qualities helped him achieve business success. Above all, he possessed remarkable vision. As one of his employees commented, "He had a synthetic mind that literally 'saw' into the future. . . . In 1905, the distribution of electrical current among users was a local, at most a regional, affair. Loucheur understood that, with an improvement in technology, a national network of intercommunication would inevitably be created. The foundation of his business policies was to unite neighboring networks as far as possible so that they could bolster and support one another."[12] He also proved decisive, and willing to take risks, and he ventured into rapidly developing areas of business at a time when much of French industry was encrusted by tradition and

10. Giros, "Allocution prononcée," 55; Motte, "Discours," 29.

11. Giros, "Allocution prononcée," 55; David Landes, *The Unbound Prometheus: Technological Change and Industrial Development in Western Europe from 1750 to the Present* (London, 1969), 235; Loucheur, *Carnets secrets*, 8–9; Louis Loucheur, *Tramways départementaux de la Creuse: Propositions de MM. A. Giros et Loucheur, avril, 1911* (Auxerre, 1911), 4.

12. Philippe Girardet, *Ceux que j'ai connus* (Paris, 1952), 114.

skeptical of innovation. A contemporary remarked, "The boldness of [Girolou's] ideas, which are supported by the data of modern technology, is revealed in the use of materials viewed with disfavor by the conventional and empirical tradition."[13] Loucheur's exceptional organizational ability was confirmed when, during the war, he succeeded in swiftly converting peacetime factories for the mass production of shells and again when, after the 1918 armistice, he in eight days created a plan for reconversion of war production plants. His organizational skill in part reflected his talent for choosing capable men and delegating significant responsibilities. He rarely entrusted responsibilities to someone who proved unable to fulfill them. Loucheur's "trampoline method" consisted in clearly defining the task at hand and then letting the project director determine the means for achieving it. What counted for him were results, and he judged his subordinates on that criterion alone.[14]

Girolou's success owed much to the compatibility of its two founders, notwithstanding their differing personalities. Loucheur—dynamic, impulsive, energetic, impatient, bold, and direct—perfectly complemented the calmer, more patient, and more reflective Giros, and the synergy between them imparted a balance and harmony to their business.[15]

As new commercial possibilities involving large sums of money arose, Giros and Loucheur decided to limit Girolou to financial procurement, research, and planning, and to establish a separate firm for actual construction. In July, 1908, they established the Société Générale d'Entreprises (SGE), which enjoyed immediate profitability.[16] Giros later recalled, "Success never stopped during the six years before the war. Important contracts awarded to us in France and the colonies launched the firm's reputation."[17]

With Loucheur the driving force, expansion followed on an international scale: the new company took on projects in Turkey, Russia, Morocco, Italy, and Spain. In Turkey, the SGE joined with other French firms in embarking in 1910 on the construction of three thousand kilometers of roads as well as the repair of another six thousand kilometers. The contract, worth more than a hundred million francs, was the largest Lou-

13. Motte, "Discours," 29.
14. Girardet, Ceux que j'ai connus, 112, 115.
15. Paul Huvelin, Interview, July 20, 1977.
16. Motte, "Discours," 29; Giros, "Allocution prononcée," 55–56.
17. Giros, "Allocution prononcée," 56.

cheur's firm had participated in. An additional new company, the Routes de Constantinople, had charge of the projects, with Loucheur a member of its board of directors. Loucheur discerned still another opportunity in the Ottoman Empire. In the spring of 1911 he became associated with the Société Ottomane d'Electricité de Constantinople, for which the SGE worked under contract. But the Turks became embroiled in war, first with Italy, in 1911, and then with other Balkan states, in 1912. The work of the Routes de Constantinople ended abruptly, although the operations of the electricity firm continued uninterrupted. In view of the unsettled situation in Turkey, Loucheur and the SGE turned their attention increasingly to Russia, where the firm was the major provider of financial backing for a public-works project in 1913. Later the SGE landed a contract to build the main electrical generating station for St. Petersburg, but work on it came to a halt when the war began.[18]

Not surprisingly, Loucheur's wide-ranging activity led to contact with French government officials.[19] For example, he went to Berlin in September, 1911, before his company moved into Morocco, to confer with the French ambassador Jules Cambon. They discussed political conditions between France and Germany in Morocco, where an international crisis was seething. The visit brought Loucheur into contact with Premier Joseph Caillaux, to whom, upon returning to France, he delivered a letter from Cambon. Caillaux was seeking an understanding with Germany on a business basis. In addition, Loucheur's visit to Berlin may have let him make contact with Aristide Briand, a socialist who had abandoned the movement in 1906 to accept a ministerial post and who had just finished a term as premier; the evidence for that encounter is fragmentary, however.[20]

Loucheur also struck up a friendship with Joseph Noulens, the finance minister in René Viviani's government in 1914, when war broke out. Loucheur's diary entries in the summer of 1914 confirm the intimacy between them. They discussed the military situation, and Lou-

18. Loucheur, *Carnets secrets*, 11–12, 14, 18; Loucheur, *Tramways départementaux*, 4.

19. An intriguing question here is the extent to which political connections may have helped in securing contracts for Loucheur's company. In view of Loucheur's contacts with prominent French politicians and the number and importance of projects his company obtained abroad, it seems likely that political influence was involved. Evidence that might confirm this possibility—such as documents in the archives of the Société Générale d'Entreprises—was unavailable to the author, however.

20. Loucheur, *Carnets secrets*, 12–13.

cheur followed with great interest Noulens' emergency financial measures. The rapport of the two men endured during the war, when Noulens went off to Petrograd as ambassador, and after it, when Loucheur used his influence to help secure Clemenceau's appointment of Noulens as minister of agriculture.[21]

Before the war, Loucheur established through his business activities other important contacts and friendships with men on whom he would later draw for his staff at the armaments ministry. One of those men was Albert Petsche, a fellow "X" and the manager of a public utility syndicate. Loucheur and Petsche worked together on several public utility ventures, among them the creation of the Energie Electrique de la Région Parisienne and the Energie Electrique du Nord-Est Parisien. As a member of Loucheur's cabinet in the armaments ministry after 1916, Petsche would collaborate in overseeing the production and importation of coal. In 1914, Petsche's syndicate, which became known as the Messine group, joined in the formation of a new company headed by Loucheur to electrify the government rail lines. Another Polytechnician, Ernest Mercier, represented the Messine group in the new company. Loucheur and Mercier too became friendly, and Mercier also joined Loucheur's ministry during the war.[22]

In short, by 1914, Loucheur, operating within the context of French economic liberalism, had established a business concern of international scope. In the process, he had demonstrated qualities that set him apart, including an openness to modern industrial techniques, an emphasis on efficiency, a willingness to take risks, and an aggressive commitment to expansion. Just as important, he had through his far-flung business interests established political contacts that would later stand him in good stead. As a result, he already had some familiarity with the inner workings of government by the time the war began. Notably, Loucheur had developed decisive friendships with various graduates of the Ecole Polytechnique. Although he did not restrict his associations to "X"s in the course of his political career, the esprit de corps that existed among Polytechnicians clearly determined his preferences respecting collaborators and friends.

21. *Ibid.*, 14, 17; Joseph Noulens to Louis Loucheur, October 1, 1917, in Louis Loucheur Papers, Box 9, Folder 2, HI; Joseph Noulens to Louis Loucheur, May 8, 1919, in Louis Loucheur Papers, II/N, O; *Le Temps* (Paris), July 24, 1919, p. 2.

22. Richard Kuisel, *Ernest Mercier: French Technocrat* (Berkeley and Los Angeles, 1967), 3–4, 6; Ernest Mercier, *Albert Petsche, 1860–1933* (Paris, n.d.), 31, 36–37.

2

FROM MUNITIONS MAKER TO
GOVERNMENT OFFICIAL, 1914–1916

———————

At the outbreak of hostilities in 1914, the general belief was that the war would be over quickly. Millions of men left their regular occupations to participate in the anticipated battles, and economic activities in the belligerent states came to a virtual standstill. That the economic interruption was a deliberate decision is evidence that the people in power expected a short conflict, for the economic and social life of the warring nations could not survive long with the mobilized forces removed from the productive system. But the battle of the Marne, which stopped the German advance toward Paris, and the "race to the sea" that ensued, changed the complexion of the struggle. Trenches and a war of attrition replaced the initial war of movement, and both the Entente Powers—or the Allies—and the Central Powers, led by Germany, settled in for what appeared to be a lengthy conflict. Suddenly the home front began to look extremely important, especially since munitions supplies were practically exhausted. In the economic mobilization that followed, France was particularly handicapped, because it had been deprived of a vital part of its heavy industry and coal when the German offensive wheeled through the country's northeastern corner.[1]

France reacted to the changed military situation with urgency, and among its new priorities was a rapid increase in munitions production. In artillery, for example, French army headquarters—the GQG—requested on September 17 that the production of shells for the 75-mm.

———

1. Theodore Ropp, *War in the Modern World* (Rev. ed.; New York, 1962), 239–43; Marc Ferro, *The Great War, 1914–1918* (Boston, 1973), 118; Kuisel, *Capitalism and the State*, 31.

gun, the backbone of French weaponry at the time, be raised from fourteen thousand to forty thousand per day. Shortly thereafter, the order rose to a hundred thousand. Since the state munitions plants were unable to meet such increases, the government turned to private industry for assistance.[2]

The other belligerent powers also experienced serious munitions shortages early in the war. The British faced mounting needs in the fall and winter of 1914–1915 as the size of their army expanded and ammunition consumption far outstripped original estimates. The government pressed private manufacturers to produce ever larger quantities, but after years of government parsimony, the British munitions industry lacked the ability to raise output rapidly. To assist, the government made large sums available to the industry, and it also took steps to enhance the state's coordination and control of the effort, culminating in the creation of a munitions ministry in the late spring of 1915. By that point, Britain's munitions industry had increased production considerably, although output still fell far short of the military's declared needs.[3]

In France, the responsibility for organizing wartime production lay with the minister of war, Alexandre Millerand. A former socialist by then associated with the parliamentary Right, Millerand had returned to the ministry of war at the onset of hostilities, after an initial term in 1912–1913. He met with leading industrialists on September 20, 1914, to lay the foundations for French wartime munitions manufacture. The decision reached was to divide the private munitions industries into regions, each headed by an industrial "group chief." Any order would go directly to the group chief who would allocate it among the plants in his region. This measure let the private industrial sector construct its own edifice and operate it independently of the state. The organizing of groups began in the days after the September accord, and Millerand, eager to maintain direct contact with the industrialists, set up weekly meetings with representatives of industry.[4]

Loucheur was among those who responded to the government's call

2. Frédéric Reboul, *Mobilisation industrielle* (2 vols.; Paris, 1925), I, 116.

3. David French, *British Economic and Strategic Planning, 1905–1915* (London, 1982), 133–69.

4. Robert Pinot, *Le Comité des Forges de France au service de la nation* (Paris, 1919), 149–50, 187–88; Gerd Hardach, "La Mobilisation industrielle en 1914–1918: Production, planification et idéologie," trans. Dora Fridenson and Evelyne Shalgian, in *1914–1918: L'Autre Front*, ed. Patrick Fridenson (Paris, 1977), 91.

for help. Mobilized as an artillery lieutenant when the war broke out, he at the beginning served as a liaison officer between the field armies and the state arsenals, but in the fall he returned to the civilian sector, and for the next two years he produced munitions as a private manufacturer.[5] In these years the groundwork for his emergence on the French political scene was laid, for almost immediately he gained a reputation in government circles as innovative and dynamic. When France faced a serious heavy-artillery crisis in early 1916, Loucheur improved his standing with government officials by offering a bold plan to increase production. Thus, at the formation of an armaments ministry in late 1916 to strengthen French munitions production, Loucheur was a prime candidate for a powerful post within it.

In anticipation of the government's need for substantial quantities of shells after the battle of the Marne, Loucheur, following the suggestion of a friend and business associate, Lazare Lévy, came up with a plan to produce them on a large scale using American equipment and unskilled labor. He, at the invitation of his colonel—and accompanied by Lévy—went to Bordeaux, the relocated seat of government, to present his ideas and request financial backing for them. The war ministry expressed some suspicions, since Loucheur was not associated with any of the French industrial giants like Schneider-Creusot, Saint-Chamond, or La Marine and might have been proposing scarcely more than a scheme for his own profit.[6] Millerand asked around about Loucheur. Octave Homberg, a banking official just brought into the ministry of war, voiced the opinion that Loucheur was intelligent and audacious though perhaps a little unscrupulous as well, but he added that the situation justified including him in the munitions effort. In the end, the government decided to provide Loucheur with substantial funding to launch his manufacturing program.[7]

5. Geoffrey Fraser and Thadée Natanson, *Léon Blum: Man and Statesman* (Philadelphia, 1938), 138–39.

6. Giros, "Allocution prononcée," 57; Fraser and Natanson, *Léon Blum*, 138; Jean Noël Jeanneney, *François de Wendel en République: L'Argent et le Pouvoir, 1914–1940* (Paris, 1976), 40. In the course of the present book, the terms Schneider and Creusot will be employed both together and interchangeably in referring to the powerful metallurgical firm.

7. Octave Homberg, *Les Coulisses de l'histoire: Souvenirs, 1898–1928* (Paris, 1938), 149–50. Homberg's description of Loucheur in 1914 as "perhaps not very scrupulous" was probably only an impression but one that was reinforced after the war when the two men

Loucheur went directly to work with his customary energy. The speed with which he acted is evident in his creation of an important shell-producing operation in Lyon as part of his firm Eclairage Electrique. The company signed a contract with the government on November 26, 1914, for the delivery of 75-mm. shells. Loucheur and his assistants moved rapidly to achieve the goal of a daily production level of ten thousand shells. The plant, which had been an exhibition hall, was cleared of exhibits and readied for equipment. Orders went to America for the latest machinery, which was installed when it began arriving at the end of the year. The swift transformation of the structure allowed the factory to turn out its first shell on February 25. Some were skeptical that Loucheur could produce ten thousand shells daily, but he was very soon far beyond that. By the end of 1916, the Lyon complex was producing thirty thousand shells a day.[8]

Loucheur's success stemmed to a considerable degree from his methods. An essential step was establishing ambitious goals. In December, 1916, he told Aristide Briand, "First of all, one must begin by not having an insignificant program; one must set a large figure superior to need, do everything to attain it, and then one has a good chance of succeeding."[9] He also benefited from an assembly-line approach, since that enabled him to accelerate output and to tap a large pool of unskilled female labor. He employed certain principles of the Taylor system—a plant-management system devised by the American engineer F. W. Taylor that involved time and motion studies and bonuses for productivity. Combined with Loucheur's decisiveness, his genius for organization, and his selection of talented subordinates, such expe-

---

had what Homberg called a violent argument. Homberg, then serving as the president of the Commission des Changes, charged that industrialists from the Nord who were Loucheur's friends were so awash in government funding for reconstruction that they were investing much of their reserves in national defense bonds that paid high rates of interest. That is, he maintained that a favored few were making profits at the expense of the state at a time when the government was weighted by financial obligations. Homberg records that Loucheur, indignant at his allegation, used a ministerial meeting that Homberg attended to demand a retraction. Homberg did not waver, and the issue rested at that point. See *Les Coulisses*, 150–52.

8. Louis Jules Arrigon, *Industrial France and the War* (Paris, n.d.), 24–27; Loucheur, *Carnets secrets*, 21.

9. Loucheur, *Carnets secrets*, 21.

dients brought Loucheur into the top ranks of French munitions manufacturers. His preeminence was underscored when, through his Société de l'Eclairage Electrique, he became a munitions manufacturing group chief.[10]

One government official who took notice of Loucheur's accomplishments during the winter of 1914–1915 was Albert Thomas, a Socialist politician then working for the munitions service of the war ministry. In January, 1915, Thomas visited Loucheur's shell factory in Paris and reported to the war ministry that what Loucheur had done was remarkable:

> I visited the Paris facilities located in the old Gallia factory. I think I can say that in the course of my extended travels I have never seen a comparable effort. The contract agreed to by M. Loucheur dates from November 11, 1914. In the Gallia factory there had been absolutely nothing installed. . . . On December 26, production began. Loucheur hopes that next Saturday, the twenty-third, he will be able to produce about six hundred shells. From Monday on there will probably be an additional five hundred shells produced each day until the figure of five thousand [the number agreed to in Loucheur's contract] is reached. . . . He has assembled there the latest and most powerful equipment.[11]

Thomas was just as enthusiastic when he visited the facility of Eclairage Electrique in Lyon during March, noting that it was a "really marvelous effort."[12] Thus even before the first winter of the war had ended, Loucheur had gained the attention and respect of Thomas, who was to play a decisive role in his appointment to a government post in 1916.

Loucheur's supply of the military went beyond the fabrication of shells. He put gunpowder factories into operation in Lyon and Blancpignon and used a company called Le Chlore Liquide to produce asphyxiating gases. From his office in Paris, he oversaw war production plants

10. Pierre Hamp, "Louis Loucheur," *Revue hebdomadaire*, n.s., No. 22, May 28, 1921, p. 377; Loucheur, *Carnets secrets*, 18; Arrigon, *Industrial France and the War*, 28–29; Kuisel, *Capitalism and the State*, 28, 36; Mermeix [pseud.], *Au sein des commissions* (Paris, 1924), 301.

11. Thomas Report, January 21, 1915, in Series AP, Archives Privées, Subseries 94 AP, Albert Thomas Papers, Carton 176, AN.

12. Thomas Report, March 7–9, 1915, *ibid.*

in Paris, Lyon, Suresnes, Pont-de-Claix, Baux-Roux, Blancpignon, and Saint-Ouen.[13]

ALBERT THOMAS AND FRENCH ARMAMENTS PRODUCTION

While Loucheur was establishing a reputation in the field of munitions, Thomas was emerging as the member of the French government with the greatest responsibility for production in that area. In the fall of 1914, Thomas' friend Millerand had invited him to help the war ministry organize the country for industrial mobilization. The call to Thomas was in keeping with the spirit of the wartime *union sacrée*, or political truce, that brought Socialists to high government positions. The choice of Thomas seemed prudent not only because he was influential in socialist and labor circles but also because he was a loyal Frenchman who could be counted on to maintain labor peace in the factories. Thomas began his job by traveling throughout France in search of munitions workers and workshops for production. In May, 1915, his department assumed expanded responsibilities, and in July it became known as the undersecretariat of state for artillery and munitions. Though nominally accountable to the war minister, Thomas was largely independent of his superior for the day-to-day operations of his office. As undersecretary, Thomas was a major player in directing France's armaments production effort.[14]

He set up his offices at the Claridge Hotel in Paris, and he came with a staff of devoted friends, many of them fellow products of the Ecole Normale. One historian refers to Thomas' aides as a "brain trust." The undersecretariat, its mission growing, was transformed into a full-fledged ministry at the end of 1916. As an undersecretary, Thomas learned how to deploy and administer large numbers of individuals. He worked long hours, tried to maintain close contacts with the services and sections under his control, and frequently exhorted workers and in-

13. Giros, "Allocution prononcée," 57; Emmanuel Beau de Loménie, *Les Responsabilités des dynasties bourgeoises* (4 vols.; Paris, 1943–63), III, 66–67; Loucheur, *Carnets secrets*, 18.

14. Kuisel, *Capitalism and the State*, 35; Philippe Bernard, *La Fin d'un monde, 1914–1929* (Paris, 1975), 33; B. W. Schaper, *Albert Thomas: Trente Ans de réformisme social*, trans. Louis Dupont (Paris, 1957), 107; Hardach, "La Mobilisation industrielle," 89; Pierre Renouvin, *The Forms of War Government in France* (New Haven, 1927), 73–77.

dustrialists to intensify their efforts. Not all factions of his own party applauded the way he discharged his office, however; some members of the Socialist party's left wing jeered when they saw photos of him in a Schneider factory encouraging workers to produce to the point of risking their lives, to keep the military front supplied.[15]

Thomas' initiatives helped achieve some extremely impressive results in output. Between November, 1914, and January, 1917, for example, the number of 75-mm. shells produced monthly grew from 380,000 to more than 6 million. Thomas had organized and overseen a signal industrial success, and he had come to have a certain respect for French industrialists, finding them generally to be patriotic and cooperative.[16]

Nevertheless, despite the marked increase in output and the energy with which Thomas managed, deficiencies became manifest in the system, and they drew serious parliamentary attention. There were cases of profiteering, of industrialists failing to meet production pledges, of factories shipping defective munitions, of the bureaucracy floundering, and of fraud. Thomas and his subordinates tried to apply remedies—to curb profits and to impose more severe fines for defective goods—but they had little success.[17] It took a heavy-artillery crisis, however, before the government decided, in December, 1916, to bring Loucheur into what was to become a full-fledged ministry of armaments.

A CRISIS IN HEAVY ARTILLERY

When hostilities erupted in 1914, France was armed for a war of movement that emphasized light artillery and downplayed the more cumbersome heavy artillery.[18] The standby of France's arms was the 75-mm. gun, which was the best rapid-fire light piece available. Nonetheless, that gun was no match in either firing distance or destruction for what the Germans had. Heavy guns constituted one-third of the total German artillery force; the Germans had two thousand, to the three hundred of

15. Hardach, "La Mobilisation industrielle," 90; Schaper, *Albert Thomas*, 108; Kuisel, *Capitalism and the State*, 35. It is Hardach who uses the term *brain trust*.

16. Reboul, *Mobilisation industrielle*, I, 28; Kuisel, *Capitalism and the State*, 35–36.

17. John F. Godfrey, *Capitalism at War: Industrial Policy and Bureaucracy in France, 1914–1918* (Leamington Spa, Eng., 1987), 200–220; Kuisel, *Capitalism and the State*, 35.

18. Pascal Marie Henri Lucas, "L'Evolution du matériel militaire pendant la Grande Guerre (suite)," *Revue d'études militaires*, XXIII (April 1, 1935), 19.

the French. Some Germans even thought that France would not opt for war that summer, because of the inferior numbers of its heavy artillery. Moreover, the heavy guns that France did have were outdated: they had a short range and slow firepower, in contrast to the Germans' rapid fire and long firing range.[19]

The army stood by its preference for light artillery during the early months of the war, but others were concerned about France's disadvantage in heavy guns and worked to correct it. Deputies returning from the military front early in 1915—including Abel Ferry and André Tardieu—pointed out the need for improvement. Even more outspoken was Senator Charles Humbert, a member of the Senate's army commission who had for several years been warning about the military unpreparedness of France. In a speech before the Senate on July 13, 1914, he dwelled on Germany's palpable superiority over France in heavy guns and urged a rapid expansion of French heavy-artillery capabilities. Little heed was paid to the senator's counsel.[20]

During the winter of 1914–1915, attention focused on the production of 75-mm. shells and matériel. Only in the spring of 1915, after the manufacture of these had reached satisfactory levels, did concern turn to other things, like heavy artillery. The army started ordering heavy guns in February, 1915, and by the end of the spring was calling for intensified production. In August, responding to the offenses of 1915, which reaffirmed the importance of heavy artillery, the GQG asked for the production of more than five hundred heavy-artillery batteries. But satisfying the army's needs took time. Though Thomas tried to shift emphasis to heavy artillery, he encountered resistance among industrialists who were doing well financially with their existing product lines.[21] Further-

19. Ferro, *The Great War,* 93; Reboul, *Mobilisation industrielle,* I, 43–44; S. L. A. Marshall, *World War I* (1964; rpr. Boston, 1987), 45. Reboul states that the army asked for heavy artillery well before the war but did so without much conviction. The idea also encountered stiff resistance in parliament. France became concerned about Germany's strength in heavy guns in the years immediately prior to the war, but only in 1913 did the republic decide to move in the same direction as the Reich. Orders for one hundred ten 105-mm. guns were placed with Creusot, and an equal number were ordered from Bourges. Much smaller orders for two other calibers were made, too. None of the weapons had been delivered when war broke out in 1914. See *Mobilisation industrielle,* I, 40–41.

20. Bernard, *La Fin d'un monde,* 44–47; Mermeix, *Au sein des commissions,* 122–25, 150–84.

21. Reboul, *Mobilisation industrielle,* I, 46; Lucas, "L'Evolution du matériel militaire," 19–27; Hardach, "La Mobilisation industrielle," 95–96.

more, French bureaucrats, including Thomas, tended to maximize the production of what was easily manufactured, in order to impress parliamentary committees with rosy statistics. At least that was the view of the British leader David Lloyd George: "M. Albert Thomas, who knew his committee men well, gorged them with prodigious output figures. He made them multi-millionaires with field-gun ammunition, but the priesthood of the *soixante-quinze* would not give him the opportunity, of which he was the man to make the best use, to manufacture in sufficient numbers the heavy guns and howitzers which, whilst they would have the effect of reducing the number of the output, would have raised the French artillery to an equality in power with the Germans."[22] It is probable that even the GQG was not yet fully convinced that the situation demanded an all-out push for heavy artillery. In any case, production continued to languish.

Only in 1916 did the French begin to view the situation with a real sense of urgency, primarily owing to what happened at the battle of Verdun. The Germans launched a major attack toward the end of February near the old fortress of Verdun, with the intention of overrunning what the French considered to be an impregnable position in their lines. The Germans believed that if they succeeded, a French collapse might follow. After mounting a devastating artillery assault, the offensive forces made repeated attempts to break through the French front. The battle continued for several months with the French holding on tenaciously.[23] Although they eventually pushed the Germans back, France almost lost the battle. That hard truth reached the public through the newspaper *Le Matin* during May. An article that had escaped the censors jolted French public opinion, and in parliament there was a clamor for closed-door sessions of the two chambers to discuss Verdun. From June 16 to June 22, the Chamber of Deputies met in an unprecedented secret session. The Senate followed on July 9. Questions abounded concerning the competence of certain French commanders and the preparedness of the French military machine. During the debate, Thomas reported to the deputies on armaments manufacture and acknowledged the superiority German heavy artillery had over the French in number and quality. He attributed the imbalance in number that had been a factor in the early French setbacks at Verdun to the policy to move slowly

22. David Lloyd George, *War Memoirs* (6 vols.; Boston, 1933–37), IV, 343.
23. Ropp, *War in the Modern World*, 248.

in producing heavy artillery until the superior gun France sought was a reality. He assured his listeners, though, that in light of Verdun, he had ordered a significant increase in the production of models already in use. A massive supplying of France's troops would not wait for a successor to the 155-mm. Long, considered the best of the nation's heavy guns.[24]

Earlier in the furor over Verdun, the GQG had ordered modern versions of five models. It wanted 960 105-mm. guns, 1,440 155-mm. Long guns, 2,160 155-mm. Court (that is, Short) guns, 160 120-mm. guns, and 80 280-mm. guns.[25] The requisition, submitted on May 30, put Thomas in a panic, for it far exceeded output capacity. Thomas calculated how he could implement the mandate he had been given, particularly for the guns of top priority, the 155-mm. Court and the 155-mm. Long.[26] For the 155-mm. Court, he planned to turn to Creusot and Saint-Chamond, the two chief makers of France's heavy artillery, but he realized that a dramatic acceleration in production was needed to meet the order. He saw that it would be even more difficult to arrive at an adequate production level for the 155-mm. Long; brooding over the problem, he scribbled down such comments as, "A tremendous effort involved," and, "Faster, faster. All efforts toward that." He had no trouble settling on the principle for determining which current version of the gun to emphasize: "The speed of production."[27] But he was probably still unsure about how to obtain what he needed and about which variation of the 155-mm. Long to push, since the experts were uncertain about how quickly the

24. Abel Ferry, *Carnets secrets, 1914–1918* (Paris, 1957), 141; Edouard Bonnefous and Georges Bonnefous, *Histoire politique de la Troisième République* (2nd ed.; 7 vols. projected; Paris, 1965–), II, 130–39; Alistaire Horne, *The Price of Glory: Verdun, 1916* (New York, 1963), 41–44, 71–77.

25. Reboul, *Mobilisation industrielle*, I, 46.

26. The French demand for heavy artillery was hastened by a change in wartime tactics. In 1914, French military leaders believed that the role of artillery was as support for the infantry during an attack. But the devastating firepower of the machine gun in stopping advances and the introduction of barbed-wire barriers demonstrated the need for artillery bombardments before attacks were launched. Heavy artillery guns were therefore desired because of their greater firing distance and more powerful shells. The 155-mm. Court Schneider, Model 1917, could fire a ninety-five-pound projectile a maximum distance of 12,300 yards. This compared with the French 75-mm. field gun, which fired twelve-pound shells and had a maximum firing range of 9,350 yards. See Ferro, *The Great War*, 87–88, 93; Marshall, *World War I*, 45–46, 139–41, 235–39, 244–49; and U.S. War Office, *Handbook of Artillery, Including Mobile, Anti-Aircraft, and Trench Matériel* (1920), 80–93, 207–10.

27. Handwritten Notes of Thomas, not dated but probably June, 1916, in 94 AP, 86, AN.

guns could be produced. What Thomas did know was that the orders for approximately 1,100 of the 1,440 155-mm. Longs had not yet been assigned for manufacture. He asked industrialists what they could contribute to the effort.[28]

At a meeting with Thomas on June 19, Loucheur presented his production plan. He proposed the expansion of a finishing process Girolou had already performed as a Creusot subcontractor in the assembly of 155-mm. Long and 220-mm. Court guns. For that, he planned to raise fifteen million francs in cooperation with other industrialists. The outcome, a new industrial combination known as the Société en Participation pour l'Usinage d'Artillerie Lourde, came into being in September, with Girolou and Schneider-Creusot the dominant shareholders.[29] It is also likely that Loucheur told Thomas during their talk that his firm planned to undertake its own production of 155-mm. Longs and 220-mm. Courts. Their meeting marked the beginning of a dependence by Thomas on Loucheur for the production of heavy artillery, a dependence that continued for many months.

Other industrialists also met with Thomas, and on the basis of these discussions and other information, the undersecretary developed the heavy-artillery program of July 23 as a way to satisfy the requirements of the GQG. His plan included the establishment of output schedules and the organization of industrial groups, the most important of which was the Groupe Schneider, embracing not only Schneider-Creusot but also Girolou and another firm named Alsacienne. As the major producer of the group, Schneider was expected to turn out 390 155-mm. Court guns, a large number of 155-mm. Longs, and weapons of several other calibers by the end of June, 1917. It was also hoped that Girolou and Alsacienne would be able to manufacture 110 155-mm. Longs and 110 220-mm. Courts during the same period; their first guns were projected for January, 1917, with full-scale production by April, 1917. The group's key role was highlighted in the late summer of 1916 when Thomas, in some notes, affirmed that the Saint-Chamond 155-mm. Long was not functioning well: that left Schneider the only company providing a reliable 155-mm. Long. In September, Thomas was there-

28. Note of a Meeting at the War Ministry, June 7, 1916, *ibid.*
29. Contract, September 4, 1916, in Series B, Série générale, constituée par les documents de l'Administration Centrale, Carton 15617, MF; Handwritten Notes of Thomas Entitled "Loucheur," June 19, 1916, in 94 AP, 86, AN.

fore forced to scale back the objectives of the July program. But even the Groupe Schneider failed to come through on its July commission. Girolou and Alsacienne warned Thomas in the fall that they could not turn out any heavy guns before March, 1917, and he again, in November, adjusted the output schedule downward.[30] In spite of the discouragements, Thomas continued to look to the Groupe Schneider and Loucheur for what needed to be done.

Thomas' reliance upon Loucheur for assistance in intensifying production of the 155-mm. Long sheds light on Loucheur's appointment to a government post in December, 1916. It shows that Loucheur had the expertise, the willingness to move into a difficult situation, and the ability to produce results, that could serve Thomas, even if in launching his own production of the 155-mm. Long gun, his goals were initially too ambitious.

A RESHAPED GOVERNMENT

Parliamentary discontent with the condition of France's heavy artillery was again manifested in a report Tardieu presented to the Chamber of Deputies' army commission on September 27, 1916. Though it did not specifically lay blame with Thomas, it complained that efforts to create a strong, modern heavy artillery in France had been sluggish. What was needed, it maintained, was something to rouse those involved in the heavy-artillery programs.[31]

Thomas faced other problems as well in the fall of 1916. His administrative shortcomings—for instance, his inability to control industrial munitions profits—became more conspicuous as a transportation crisis that turned the delivery of raw materials to manufacturers haphazard gained in severity. The occurrence of raw-materials shortages, particularly in coal and steel, also caused delays in the manufacture of arma-

30. Albert Thomas to Louis Loucheur, January 28, 1917, in 94 AP, 63, AN; Fabrications d'artillerie lourde: Groupe Schneider, November 3, 1916, in 94 AP, 87, AN; Notes sur les fabrications de guerre, 1916, in 94 AP, 86, AN; Fabrications d'artillerie lourde: Groupe Schneider, November 3, 1916, in 94 AP, 87, AN; Thomas to Loucheur, January 28, 1917, in 94 AP, 63, AN.

31. Rapport sur l'artillerie lourde de campagne à tir rapide, by André Tardieu, Commission de l'Armée (Chambre), September 27, 1916, in 94 AP, 57, AN.

ments.[32] Such problems gave rise to even greater doubt within parliamentary and business circles about Thomas' ability to manage French munitions production.

Not only Thomas but the whole government headed by Briand after November, 1915, was under attack in the fall, largely because of its policies in the Balkans and because of discontent with the military leadership of Joseph Joffre, the French commander in chief. At the longest wartime closed-door session of the Chamber of Deputies, running from November 28 to December 7, 1916, Briand and his cabinet defended their policies and won a vote of confidence, but it was evident that the Chamber was ready to see some fresh, young faces in the government.[33] Briand understood what the Chamber wanted, and one of the newcomers to appear in his reshaped ministry was Loucheur.

When Loucheur began discussions about a post in Thomas' undersecretariat in early December, it was not for the first time. In November, he had been considered for the position of artillery service director when it was vacated by Albert Claveille, a prewar civil servant and technical expert who had left to take charge of the French transport system. But Thomas told Loucheur that because of the political climate, the naming of an industrialist as Claveille's successor would risk offending parliament. Instead he appointed Arthur Fontaine, who had previously worked with him. Fontaine went to the undersecretariat for munitions from the labor ministry.[34]

The political situation was fluid, though, and there were forces working behind the scenes in Loucheur's behalf. One of his admirers was Julien Rouland, a senator who later, in 1919, was to campaign for the modernization of France's industrial plants and equipment. He wrote to Loucheur on December 8,

Albert is going to take the war ministry. You must accept the undersecretariat for munitions.
This idea, which I have been pushing with all my power for the

32. Rapport sur l'artillerie lourde de campagne et l'artillerie à grande puissance, by André Tardieu, Commission de l'Armée (Chambre), March 17, 1917, in Series C, Procès-verbaux des Assemblées Nationales, Chambre des Députés, Carton 7503, AN.

33. Bonnefous and Bonnefous, Histoire politique, II, 170; Georges Suarez, Briand: Sa vie, son oeuvre (5 vols.; Paris, 1938–41), IV, 49–61.

34. Loucheur, Carnets secrets, 23; Newspaper Clippings from Le Matin, Le Journal, and Le Petit Journal, November 26, 1916, in 94 AP, 21, AN.

past fifteen days, even before the opening of the secret committee, with a small group of active and anonymous friends—in that way they are even more influential—has taken root and is going to succeed if you do not retreat.

Besides, you cannot give way. But whatever your patriotism, do not accept anything without getting absolute authority and liberty. Do not accept anything without getting complete independence vis-à-vis parliament, of which you are not a member and which you will have to ignore. It is on this condition that your entry into the controlling team of tomorrow can be a *measure* of salvation.[35]

Who constituted the small group of friends cannot be determined, but during December, Loucheur discussed with several members of parliament the state of his negotiations for a post. Among those he talked with were Joseph Noulens, of the Chamber of Deputies, and Henri Bérenger, of the Senate. Others encouraging him to accept were René Viviani and the minister of commerce, Etienne Clémentel. It is known that after consultation with Loucheur, a friend of his named Achille Fournier, who was a handyman for Schneider, went to seek out Senator Humbert's advice and to arrange an interview for Loucheur. Loucheur had dinner with Humbert, but only on December 15, after the negotiations for his entry into the government were complete.[36] Clearly, Loucheur had strong backing in influential places during the critical weeks of November and December. His awareness of that must have bolstered his resolve not to make concessions that would have reduced his power in office.

In discussions about joining the government, Loucheur insisted that he be given the post of undersecretary of state for munitions within what was to be the new ministry of armaments; furthermore, he stipulated that he be only nominally responsible to Thomas in his new capacity as armaments minister. Thomas, apparently assuming that Loucheur would submit to control, was taken aback by the contents of the letter spelling out the industrialist's demands. At what began as a tense meeting on the evening of December 10, the two men addressed the role Loucheur was to have in directing French munitions production.

35. Julien Rouland to Louis Loucheur, December 8, 1916, in Louis Loucheur Papers, II/R, HI.

36. Loucheur, *Carnets secrets*, 24–25, 28.

Abruptly, Thomas agreed to the conditions of a largely autonomous undersecretariat. After that, according to Loucheur, the ministerial appointee seemed to "breathe easier." Briand announced the composition of his realigned government to the press two days later. It was then that Loucheur, committed to moving toward a personal future that was in many ways different from his entrepreneurial past, set down in his diary the words "The die is cast."[37]

Loucheur and his champions considered his entry into the government a major success. Loucheur, somewhat disdainful of the administrative skills of politicians, was convinced that he could improve upon Thomas' work in munitions production, and he was anxious to begin by accelerating the manufacture of modern heavy artillery, where he had observed serious deficiencies in the preceding months. Loucheur's parliamentary supporters were all persuaded that the state of munitions production in France had become serious enough to warrant significant changes in Thomas' undersecretariat, and they believed that a dynamic technical expert like Loucheur was what the situation demanded. Even Thomas supported Loucheur's entry into his ministry, having admired the bold industrialist's effectiveness in increasing the munitions supply as early as the first winter of the war. The one thing everyone seemed to realize was that Loucheur's presence at the ministry of armaments would produce some important modifications in the organization and administration of France's munitions efforts.

37. Louis Loucheur to Albert Thomas, December 10, 1916, in Louis Loucheur Papers, 2/11; Loucheur, *Carnets secrets*, 21–26.

3

Baptism at the Ministry of Armaments, 1916–1917

When Loucheur became undersecretary of state, he had one major goal: all-out production. To that end, he surrounded himself with a group of like-minded men, revamped the heavy-artillery program, tried to maintain close cooperation with private industry, worked vigorously to assure steady supplies of raw materials—particularly coal and steel—and sought to make procedural changes regarding manpower. In his efforts, he demonstrated the same kind of dynamism he had shown in organizing munitions production as a private industrialist. But he often encountered government officials who had other priorities. As a result, essential elements of his plans were blocked, delayed, or reduced by several government ministries, including those of finance, supplies, and war. Occasionally even Thomas' end of the armaments ministry worked against him. In dealing with the GQG, Loucheur discovered that he could not always obtain all the manpower he sought. Nevertheless, he moved forward confident that he could create a munitions-producing system capable of meeting military needs.

Loucheur's responsibilities as undersecretary were defined in a decree in January, 1917. Placed under his control was the production of heavy artillery, explosives and gunpowder, and chemicals, as well as inspection of the production of the *service automobile*. He also had the right to take whatever action was needed for assuring munitions manufacturers of materials, to negotiate contracts in fulfilling his obligations, and to make recommendations to Thomas concerning salaries and working conditions, foreign purchases, matters of litigation, and various other questions, including the purchase and trade of buildings.[1] To

---

1. *Bulletin des usines de guerre*, January 8, 1917, in Series N 1872–1919, Subseries 10 N, Ministère de l'Armement, Carton 2, SHA.

meet the needs of the army as determined by Thomas, Loucheur had at his disposal the mobilized industrial strength of France, both public and private.

Loucheur brought in men who, in education and profession, stood in marked contrast to those close to Thomas. Several key members of Loucheur's staff were products of France's schools of engineering, and several had been associated with banking and private industry. Xavier Loisy, Loucheur's cabinet chief, was a graduate of the Ecole Polytechnique. Edmond Philippar, Loucheur's adjunct cabinet chief, and Paul Munich, his assistant cabinet chief, were also graduates of French engineering schools. Munich had been an engineer prior to the war, and Philippar had been a member of the board of directors at the Crédit Foncier d'Algérie et de Tunisie. Loisy had worked as a colonial inspector for the government. A few months later Albert Petsche joined Loucheur and played a large role with respect to coal; Petsche was an "X" who had cooperated with Loucheur in electrification projects prior to the war.[2] Thomas' principal assistants, on the other hand, were for the most part graduates of the Ecole Normale Supérieure and had teaching as their profession.[3] Thomas' adjunct cabinet chief, Mario Roques, was a Normalian who taught at the Sorbonne before the conflict. An exception to Thomas' practice of looking to the Ecole Normale Supérieure for aides was Arthur Fontaine, an "X" who worked in his manpower office.[4]

Loucheur and his colleagues brought to the armaments ministry a new spirit of organization, efficiency, and practicality. In day-to-day op-

2. Jean Michel Chevrier, "Le Rôle de Loucheur dans l'économie de guerre, 1914–1918" (Thèse de maîtrise, University of Paris X [Nanterre], 1972), 28, 31; "Service du cabinet du sous-secrétaire d'état—situation nominative du personnel au 1er mai 1917," in 94 AP, 51, AN; Mercier, *Albert Petsche*, 36–37.

3. The Ecole Normale Supérieure is the most prestigious school in France for the training of teachers in the humanities.

4. Chevrier, "Le Rôle de Loucheur," 27–30. Chevrier has performed a service by focusing on the men who worked closely with Loucheur as opposed to those who were Thomas' chief associates. One point of clarification needs to be made, though. Chevrier offers an evaluation of nine members of Loucheur's group and leaves the reader with the impression that it was already well in place while Thomas was armaments minister. The process was more gradual than that. Some of the associates whom Chevrier cites did not enter the government until later. Ernest Mercier, for example, joined Loucheur after he had become armaments minister in the fall of 1917. Philippe Girardet did not become part of Loucheur's ministry until the final days of the war. See Kuisel, *Ernest Mercier*, 6; and Girardet, *Ceux que j'ai connus*, 115.

erations, for example, Loucheur's subordinates were keen to make wider use of modern means of communication than members of the Thomas team believed necessary. In the spring of 1917, when Loucheur's staff decided to seek the installation of supplementary telephone lines, particularly between the undersecretariat headquarters and the Inspection des Forges, their request had to go through Thomas' end of the ministry, which concluded that members of Loucheur's undersecretariat were abusing the system by engaging in excessively long telephone conversations. The study it conducted cited calls of ten, twelve, and thirty minutes. The ministry denied the request.[5]

Loucheur's approach to problems is evident in the way he handled the production of heavy artillery, his highest priority in late 1916 and early 1917. He moved at once to mount an intensified program that took into account requests by the high command to accelerate the production of the 155-mm. Court gun. Already on December 18, he was meeting with aides to consider ways to increase output, and he went on to hold discussions with the ministry's artillery services and with Schneider.[6] By December 24, he could send a copy of the "new heavy-artillery program" for Thomas' approval. He insisted that a rapid decision be made to intensify the production of parts in state-run operations. Even more important, he asked that in the new order going to Schneider, with its emphasis on the 155-mm. Court, the government grant the same terms it had extended to the firm the previous summer, when implementation of the military requests of May 30 had begun. That meant state responsibility for the purchase and transport of the tooling machines that Schneider's subsidiary in the project, the Société d'Outillage Mécanique et d'Usinage d'Artillerie (SOMUA), required. It also meant the government's shouldering some of the construction costs for any new buildings. Loucheur explained that a speedy recall from the front of at least three thousand skilled and between eight and ten thousand unskilled laborers was necessary. He maintained that his program, despite the tests it would face, could succeed with a "little help from events."[7]

Thomas approved Loucheur's proposals on December 26 but reminded him, in light of his own experience, of certain possible impedi-

5. Chevrier, "Le Rôle de Loucheur," 32–33.

6. Albert Thomas to Louis Loucheur, January 28, 1917, in 94 AP, 63, AN; Loucheur, *Carnets secrets*, 29.

7. Louis Loucheur to Albert Thomas, December 24, 1916, in 94 AP, 87, AN.

ments in the execution of the program. He pointed out that, in general, the recall of workers took an average of twenty days. And he warned Loucheur to oversee production carefully to prevent the slowdowns and stoppages that had plagued the previous months. It was the voice of experience advising the optimistic newcomer.[8]

EARLY BUREAUCRATIC PROBLEMS

Thomas' words of caution took on a new meaning for Loucheur when he encountered resistance from the Thomas-controlled end of the armaments ministry and from the finance ministry. His early bureaucratic difficulties were a foreglimpse of conflicts Loucheur was to have within the government during the remainder of the war.

One of Loucheur's first problems was with the manpower service that members of Thomas' staff controlled. On January 3, Loucheur sent Thomas a memorandum in which he described some of the frustrations of industrialists dealing with the service. Loucheur complained about the delays resulting from the inquiries the service conducted when industrialists requested nominative recalls, that is, requested by name skilled personnel from the front lines. He also lamented the frequent failure of the service to meet fully the requests of industrialists after the investigations were completed.

On January 22, in pursuit of manpower for the heavy-artillery program, Loucheur sent to Thomas' service lists containing the names of workers employed in state armaments plants whom Schneider wanted transferred to their project. According to Schneider, the same lists had been submitted three times previously—in November, 1915, and in March and June, 1916—but nothing had happened. Loucheur called upon the service to act on the matter with dispatch. Here the dynamics of the tensions between the Thomas and the Loucheur teams become especially clear. Because all the contracts given to Giros et Loucheur for 155-mm. guns were signed under the name of Schneider, the most important firm in the heavy-artillery program, Loucheur's efforts to obtain manpower and launch new programs were vulnerable to attack: Loucheur could easily be accused of a kind of self-dealing. When Thomas' manpower service took Loucheur's request of January 22 to the armaments

8. Albert Thomas to Louis Loucheur, December 26, 1916, *ibid.*

minister, it argued that the state munitions plants had their own needs to reckon with and should not become a recruiting ground for private industry in general or for Schneider in particular.[9] The service saw itself as guarding the legitimate interests of the state against a threat from private industry, which had a new advantage in the assistance of Loucheur the businessman. Loucheur, on the other hand, was committed to his "intensive program for heavy guns," which he wanted "to realize at all costs."[10] He therefore did not flinch from importuning for what he believed necessary to achieve his goal.

On January 28, Thomas sent Loucheur a memorandum that contained not only his views on Loucheur's plea for several thousand workers but also his reactions to changes Loucheur had made in the heavy-artillery program of December 24 and reported to Thomas on January 11. Thomas remarked that though he had given his assent to Loucheur's program, which called for a significant increase in the production of 155-mm. Court guns, with minor compensatory adjustments for other models, he was extremely disturbed by Loucheur's new figures, which showed still further reductions for models other than the 155-mm. Court. The January production forecasts represented a significant reduction from the production schedule Thomas and the industrialists had agreed to the previous July 23, when the May request of the military was implemented. But Thomas seemed to contradict himself when, after criticizing Loucheur for not holding more closely to the totals approved on July 23 and asking him to explain why earlier production forecast figures needed to be lowered, he questioned the validity of Loucheur's requests for workers. Thomas directed that, pending the reaction of the French high command to Loucheur's ideas, the undersecretary should take the July agreement as a guide and should make every effort to raise the production levels of the various calibers of heavy artillery to meet the earlier projections.[11]

Thomas' response is interesting, for his criticisms on January 28 and the contradiction he incurred were surely an outward sign of his ambivalence toward Loucheur. Thomas' mixed feelings hung partly on the

9. Note pour M. le Ministre, January 24, 1917, in 94 AP, 63, AN; Contract to Participate in the Manufacture of Heavy Artillery Signed by MM. Schneider et Cie., MM. Giros et Loucheur, and Others, September 4, 1916, in B, 15617, MF.

10. Loucheur, *Carnets secrets*, 29.

11. Thomas to Loucheur, January 28, 1917, in 94 AP, 63, AN.

suspicions that were natural about a businessman who seemed more sympathetic to French industry than the minister's own men were. Thomas may also have harbored certain hostilities toward a new colleague who was in some ways a rival. But Thomas was well aware that he needed Loucheur's organizational talents to stimulate heavy-artillery production. If Loucheur failed to develop his program satisfactorily, Thomas knew that it was the armaments minister who would come under attack in parliament. That knowledge lay at the bottom of Thomas' predicament throughout his ministerial collaboration with Loucheur.

Two days after Thomas wrote his blunt memorandum, Loucheur again raised the question of manpower at a meeting with him and General Robert Nivelle, who had replaced Joseph Joffre as the commander on the northeastern front in December, 1916. Loucheur came away pleased, for Nivelle, who had previously expressed objections to nominative recalls, gave his consent to Loucheur's request.[12]

The ministry of finance, responsible for meeting war costs that far exceeded expectations, attacked Loucheur's munitions programs from another side. Alexandre Ribot, a seventy-four-year-old conservative republican who had become minister of finance in 1914, complained to Thomas in early January, 1917, that the envisioned sharp increase in foreign purchases of commodities like steel, copper, and zinc was overambitious, and beyond the limits of financial prudence. He contended that, after twenty-nine months of war, France had reached the point in its production programs where no dramatic increase in purchases abroad was necessary: "To want, in the future, to go beyond the programs painfully put into effect during the second half of 1916 would be an act of presumption and not of foresight. Parliament cannot adhere to such an adventurous policy." He recommended adjusting Loucheur's program to make it compatible with a purchase schedule more like the one in place and more in keeping with what was practicable.[13]

Faced with Ribot's opposition, Loucheur pared down his planned requisitions from other countries; nevertheless, he did so with a feeling of exasperation. Thomas evinced the same emotion when he wrote to Ribot after the cuts had been made. Thomas emphasized that the foreign purchases originally intended were part and parcel of the endeavor

12. Loucheur, *Carnets secrets*, 33.
13. Alexandre Ribot to Albert Thomas, January 6, 1917, in 94 AP, 63, AN.

to meet the army's munitions needs, and that that reality, as well as the arguments of the finance ministry, should count in any final determination.[14] But Thomas' plea was apparently to no avail, and the correspondence on the matter rested there.

Loucheur no doubt anticipated some resistance to his ideas within the government bureaucracy, but in view of the seriousness of France's munitions situation he was probably surprised that the finance ministry and Thomas' staff were not more understanding of his position. From his first days as undersecretary he was learning that success within a government system presupposed different strategies from those he had relied on as a private businessman. He soon proved that he had the ability to adjust.

CONTINUED CONFLICTS OVER MANPOWER

The tensions within the ministry of armaments concerning manpower continued during the spring and summer, but Loucheur's manpower problems originated not only in the ministry. He also had to defend himself against other ministries seeking workers, against a French high command reluctant to relinquish large numbers of soldiers for munitions production, and against a parliament whose legislative actions at times imposed manpower adjustments. Loucheur's task was difficult and at times extremely frustrating.

The farms needed workers to bring in the harvest, and the emphasis on agriculture during the summer months meant a reduced manpower pool for other services. Just when, by Loucheur's calculation, the steel mills were crying for twenty-six thousand hardy men, nine thousand workers were reassigned from munitions production to agriculture.[15] There was also legislation pending that would summon younger servicemen from behind the lines to combat units; a number of skilled munitions workers would be affected. Loucheur followed the progress of the legislation, finally known as the Loi Mourier, and in July he wrote to Thomas seeking an amendment to protect the workers his factories still

14. Louis Loucheur to Albert Thomas, February 7, 1917, *ibid.*; Albert Thomas to Alexandre Ribot, February 13, 1917, *ibid.*

15. Louis Loucheur to Acting Armaments Minister Paul Painlevé, June 11, 1917, in 94 AP, 133, AN.

had. What worried him was that the text of the law had already passed in the Senate and was scheduled for consideration in the Chamber of Deputies in the following days.[16] He apparently feared that the bill as it stood would cause trouble by moving the specialists to the military front, since the GQG would not be willing to send large numbers of replacement workers to the rear.

After Thomas' return from a trip to Russia in May and June, members of his staff prepared a report on the functioning of the ministry in his absence in which they complained of repeated encroachments by Loucheur into their areas of jurisdiction, including manpower. Loucheur, annoyed by what he viewed as weaknesses in the ministry's management of manpower, also prepared a memorandum for the returning minister, in which he objected that the number of workers at his disposal had diminished considerably during the preceding three months. Munitions production had lost six thousand skilled young workers, in addition to another forty thousand men who had been transferred to different occupations, such as mining and farming. He stressed the need to find several thousand workers for France's steel mills and to replace the skilled workers allocated to combat because of their age. Still, he tempered his insistence by suggesting that it might be possible to realize existing production aims with the retrenched work force if his undersecretariat assumed effective control over the placement and transfer of manpower. Loucheur demanded that his office be informed in advance of any personnel changes affecting his department's production areas; he proposed severe sanctions against officials who neglected their responsibility in that respect. In justification of his demands, he cited examples where Thomas' manpower service (*direction de la main d'oeuvre*) had been careless in placing and transferring workers.[17] Loucheur plainly felt that the best way to remedy the problem was to concentrate more authority in his hands.

The response of the manpower service to Loucheur's criticisms was a lengthy point-by-point rebuttal of the undersecretary's allegations and suggestions. The author argued that the service had already instructed inspectors not to make personnel changes in munitions plants without

16. Note pour M. Albert Thomas, October 24, 1917, in 94 AP, 121, AN; Louis Loucheur to Albert Thomas, July 19, 1917, in 94 AP, 133, AN.
17. Notes préparées pour le retour du ministre, June, 1917, in 94 AP, 176, AN; Louis Loucheur to Albert Thomas, June 26, 1917, in 94 AP, 133, AN.

first consulting Loucheur's department but that since the service's responsibilities for manpower needs encompassed more than Loucheur's areas of production, some personnel changes were bound to occur without prior consultation. The writer also stated that, after investigating Loucheur's examples of poor administration within the service, the only conclusion the service could reach was that Loucheur had been misinformed: the supposed difficulties had either never occurred or were the responsibility of other authorities. The memorandum even took Loucheur's suggestions for improvement to task, affirming that the result would be increased paperwork and possible injustice to those who carried out an order from the armaments minister for worker changes without the prior consent of Loucheur's *service technique*.[18] The essence of the response was that if the manpower service could be found wanting on minor matters, Loucheur was guilty of jumping to conclusions without proper information and making suggestions with little thought to the consequences. The intimation that Loucheur should tend to his own affairs and let the manpower service deal with its area of expertise, that is, manpower, was unmistakable.

The report Loucheur had put together for Thomas' return from Russia was stinging enough that the service did not stop there. It bolstered its case against his department by assembling some memorandums written by members of the service's staff. What bothered the manpower service was not only Loucheur's criticism but also his attempts to circumvent its bureaucracy when he went looking for workers. The memorandums that the director of the manpower service, Edouard Sevin, sent to Thomas on July 8 built the case that because of such attempts, the process of obtaining men for the munitions industry took much longer than if Loucheur had followed the proper procedures in the first place.[19] The complaints in the memorandums were, however, unintentionally, also a graphic presentation of the grounds Loucheur had for frequently feeling impatience with a slow, plodding bureaucracy that in his eyes prevented the undersecretariat from acting quickly to meet needs as they arose.

Loucheur's campaign to make the manpower system more responsive and efficient continued during the remainder of the summer. On

18. Note for Thomas from the Direction de la Main d'Oeuvre, July, 1917, in 94 AP, 362, AN.

19. Edouard Sevin to Albert Thomas, July 8, 1917, in 94 AP, 133, AN.

July 10, he suggested to Thomas that one representative from the minister's staff and one from his go to the chief of the personnel bureau of the GQG to work out ways for recruiting the workers he sought. He repeated his request on July 21 and underscored its urgency by appealing to Thomas to send the two representatives as early as the next day.[20]

Loucheur asserted the rights of his office when he felt that Thomas' subordinates were violating the initial agreement the men had reached on ministerial responsibilities. Loucheur wrote Sevin on August 13 to remind him that under no circumstances were manpower announcements and orders regarding worker transfers or withdrawals to be issued in factories over which the munitions department held authority before it gave approval. On that very day, he commented, he had ordered subordinates to ignore a certain number of bulletins issued by Commandant Jorré, a member of Thomas' staff, because they had not gone through his undersecretariat first.[21]

It is apparent that in struggling with Thomas' subordinates, Loucheur was not only relentless about obtaining compliance with procedures his undersecretariat had drawn up but was also determined to bring about changes in areas they controlled. Nor was he diffident about exceeding his defined responsibilities. The frustrations he experienced were the consequence of his technocratic orientation, which prized efficiency to a greater degree than Thomas' appointees were able to do.

The measure of Loucheur's success in galvanizing Thomas' aides to the kind of efficacy he desired is difficult to determine, but he clearly prevailed in some areas that mattered. On July 19, Loucheur told Thomas by letter that he was satisfied with Sevin's speed in implementing a proposal of his that made a single service responsible for assigning the steelworkers available in *dépôts de métallurgistes* to factories. Loucheur remarked, "We have been able to find a certain number of skilled workers and from this fact renew our hope of completing our heavy-artillery program within the prescribed time limit."[22] On August 19, he tasted another important victory when Thomas assured him that manpower inspectors would no longer make worker transfers without going through proper channels; the implicit pledge was that Loucheur's office would be consulted before any transfer touching his undersecretariat

20. Louis Loucheur to Albert Thomas, July 21, 1917, *ibid.*
21. Louis Loucheur to Edouard Sevin, August 13, 1917, *ibid.*
22. Loucheur to Thomas, July 19, 1917, *ibid.*

was made. Thomas thereby in effect conceded that manpower practices had not faithfully followed the agreement that he and Loucheur had reached the previous December. Thomas also guaranteed that workers obtained through the *dépôts de métallurgistes* would receive their assignments in strict accordance with the priorities Loucheur's department established.[23] These signs of Thomas' increased willingness to cooperate were an important step forward for Loucheur, but the undersecretary realized that much more was essential if he was to attain his production goals.

The intraministerial conflicts over manpower abated still further in September, when Loucheur replaced Thomas as minister of armaments. And though he continued to have difficulties in receiving all the workers he requested from the GQG for munitions production, those troubles were overshadowed by others during the remainder of the war.

THE DEVELOPMENT OF A RAW-MATERIALS CRISIS, 1914–1916

At the beginning of February, 1917, Thomas sounded the alarm about a shortage of raw materials for munitions production when he wrote to Loucheur, "I am very seriously concerned about the repercussions the slowdowns in industry caused by the lack of raw materials and coal we are currently experiencing may have for the inventory of stocks [of munitions]." He added that Nivelle needed to be apprised of just how serious the crisis might become.[24] The shortage came as no surprise to Loucheur, who had worked with it since entering the government. As the situation worsened, he found himself playing an increasingly large role in contending with it; the focus of his attention came to be steel and coal.

The problem went back to the very first weeks of the conflict, when the Germans in their drive across the northeastern corner of France deprived the French of an important part of their industrial base. By the time the battle lines stabilized, France had lost 64 percent of the production capacity it had had in pig iron in 1913, 58 percent of its capacity in steel, and 40 percent of its coal production. It was in a much reduced state that

23. Albert Thomas to Louis Loucheur, August 19, 1917, in 94 AP, 63, AN.
24. Albert Thomas to Louis Loucheur, February 2, 1917, *ibid.*

French industry began organizing itself for the war. When industrialists met in Bordeaux on September 20, 1914, Alexandre Millerand called on the Comité des Forges, a powerful federation of metallurgical industrialists led by Robert Pinot, to help organize metal production for the war. The Comité at once began reorganizing factories for the production of shell metal; it also entered into its warlong role as an important communications link between the government and the metallurgical industry. In addition to developing domestic resources, the French relied heavily on imports, especially from Great Britain. In the last months of 1914 and throughout 1915, imports from Britain came into France unencumbered by restrictions on either side of the Channel.[25]

As the war dragged on, the demand for pig iron, steel, and coal increased, and one by one these fell under the control of the British and French governments. The British inaugurated controls at the beginning of 1916 by regulating the export of pig iron, and then they insisted that France centralize its purchases. After negotiations between the two states, Thomas on March 6, 1916, granted the Comité des Forges centralized authority for hematite pig-iron purchases in Great Britain. At the urging of the British government, he extended the centralized purchasing system to all forms of pig iron in early May, again designating the Comité des Forges the sole buyer. The Comité moved quickly to allay the fears of those who distrusted its import monopoly but were obligated to work within it. It stressed that Thomas, as undersecretary for artillery and munitions, would superintend import distribution, taking into consideration the amount the British government allocated for export and the priority of need. In the succeeding months the Comité received additional responsibilities, and it played a key role in iron and steel up to the end of the war.[26]

The British began regulating the amount of steel delivered to France as well, and in this too they requested that France centralize its purchases. The government accordingly created, on May 11, 1916, an Interministerial Metals and Woods Commission (CIMB), which later became known as the Interministerial Metals and War Manufactures

25. Arthur Fontaine, *French Industry During the War* (New Haven, 1926), 270–71; Gerd Hardach, *The First World War, 1914–1918* (Berkeley and Los Angeles, 1977), 87–88; Pinot, *Le Comité des Forges*, 135, 177–89.

26. Gabriel Girault, *Le Comité des Forges de France* (Paris, 1922), 130–33; Pinot, *Le Comité des Forges*, 114–18; Hardach, "La Mobilisation industrielle," 100–101.

Commission (CIM). Placed under the supervision of Thomas' department and transferred to the newly created armaments ministry at the end of the year, it not only watched over purchases in Britain but also determined the needs of various government services and distributed the available steel according to priority.[27]

The French also established certain controls on coal in 1916, under the Bureau National des Charbons, which had been created on April 12, 1916. That bureau, operating within the ministry of public works, centralized orders for coal and issued import permits for it. The bureau transmitted orders to a French coal office in London, which distributed them for execution. By then the government had placed restrictions on whose orders could go to Britain.[28]

The controls on iron, steel, and coal, which had seemed adequate when introduced, proved inadequate by the end of 1916, when a raw-materials shortage developed, partly as a result of a transportation crisis in the fall. Increasingly effective, the German submarine force was sinking Allied shipping: the British merchant fleet was being dealt havoc by December. But the transportation problem was more complicated than that, for there were also breakdowns and delays in the French railroad system, making the delivery of materials haphazard and unreliable. Even in the best-equipped munitions factories, work stoppages occurred because of the erratic arrival of raw materials. But Thomas' office bore some responsibility for the crisis: the heavy dependence on imported steel and pig iron was because of Thomas' failure to develop domestic production early in the war. Not until 1916 did he make efforts to increase France's domestic steel potential by mounting a construction program that involved the country's best-known steel and iron makers. As the needs of exporting countries and France rose, and as the submarine campaign of Germany took its toll, France's position worsened. In December, 1916, it anticipated getting 180,000 tons of Martin steel from the United States and Britain but received only 85,000 tons. For the same month there was a deficit of more than 50 percent for deliveries of pig

27. Lyautey and Thomas Report to Poincaré, January 18, 1917, with Decree of January 18, 1917, in Subseries F 12, Archives du Ministère du Commerce et de l'Industrie, Carton 7664, AN; Girault, Le Comité des Forges, 130; Note sur la création d'un bureau central d'achats, n.d., in F 12, 7799, AN.

28. Georges Sardier, Le Ravitaillement en charbon pendant la guerre (Paris, 1920), 1–2; Maurice Olivier, La Politique du charbon, 1914–1921 (Paris, 1922), 122–23.

iron. By February 1, 1917, there were only about 75,000 tons of pig iron in stock and 72,000 tons of steel.[29]

The coal crisis was even more severe. With a three-million-ton stockpile of the fuel at the outset of the winter, the munitions plants reached the point of having practically no reserves by February, 1917. Production at some plants fluctuated according to the arrival of coal trains. In March, 1917, a report by the Chamber's army commission took Thomas to task for failing to see the need for greater participation by his department in coordinating coal supplies. His ministry assumed major responsibilities in that area only after Loucheur entered the government. Until then coal was under the ministry of public works, which had been anything but systematic about handling it. The industrial group of the Loire, for instance, which could have received supplies from nearby mines, was getting them from Britain, and so were plants located in southeastern France. On the other hand, certain factories close to the English Channel were sent coal from France's central basin. Government improvisation was apparent: rationing of private and public industries was instituted in order to meet a shortage in residential stocks. It was clearly a system without logic.[30]

It is no wonder that Thomas voiced grave concern about the raw-materials situation in February, 1917. In trying to meet the ministry's raw-materials needs, he and Loucheur came to work closely together.

STEEL

Loucheur, in his efforts to secure steel, took action in both the domestic and the international spheres. Envisioning that the domestic steel program would gradually reduce France's dependence on American steel, he in the meantime sought to augment shipments from abroad. Nonetheless, in late 1916 there was a significant drop in deliveries from the

29. Samuel Hurwitz, *State Intervention in Great Britain: A Study of Economic Control and Social Response, 1914–1919* (New York, 1949), 193–94; Rapport sur l'artillerie lourde de campagne et l'artillerie à grande puissance, by André Tardieu, Commission de l'Armée (Chambre), March 12, 1917, in C, 7503, AN; Hardach, "La Mobilisation industrielle," 101.

30. Rapport sur l'artillerie lourde de campagne et l'artillerie à grande puissance, by André Tardieu, Commission de l'Armée (Chambre), March 12, 1917, in C, 7503, AN.

United States, because of shipping problems.[31] What is more, plans for increased purchases abroad faced the unbending opposition of the finance ministry. Then, on January 31, 1917, the Germans announced unlimited submarine warfare, and the fear grew in France of being cut off from American sources.[32]

Steel from Britain continued vital to the French munitions effort. The manufacture of 75-mm. shells depended totally on steel from the British and the Americans, as did that of an appreciable portion of the shells of other calibers. It is understandable that the French worried about threats to their American and British supply lines.[33] The slowdown of steel imports from the United States in late 1916 helped Loucheur reach a decision to increase French production as rapidly as possible. He was in this continuing a policy set by Thomas some months before, but he acted on a much larger scale and with the same kind of boldness he had displayed in connection with heavy-artillery production. Beginning on December 20, he held meetings with French metallurgists about expanding steel output. Many producers shrank from committing themselves, out of fear of a peacetime glut on the market. Some metallurgists, however, whether or not because they were convinced by Loucheur's greater optimism, consented to expand their facilities, and within a few days the foreseeable domestic production had risen by thirty-five thousand tons a month. Even that was not enough to meet munitions demands, though, and Loucheur, conscious of the German submarine campaign, appealed for the construction of a large steel mill near Paris. A group of leading metallurgists consented to the project, which Loucheur saw as crowning the domestic steel network he was building, and within a week the Comité des Forges, acting on behalf of the industrialists, had raised the forty million francs required of the private sector, obtained options on land, and drafted plans for the mill. The state's financial participation in the undertaking was projected to be in the range of fifty to sixty million francs.[34]

31. Note en réponse aux conclusions du rapport de M. Gervais, sénateur, January 3, 1917, in 94 AP, 113, AN. Steel imports from the United States for armaments manufacture at the end of 1916 were 93,000 tons in September, 64,000 tons in October, 72,000 tons in November, and 58,000 tons in December.

32. Minutes, Commission de l' Armée (Chambre), August 3, 1917, in C, 7498, AN.

33. Note pour M. le Ministre, July 12, 1917, in 94 AP, 113, AN.

34. Note en réponse aux conclusions du rapport de M. Gervais, sénateur, January 3, 1917, ibid.; Minutes, Commission du Budget (Chambre), February 7, 1917, in C, 7559, AN.

Loucheur's need for government funding for new construction met resistance in the finance ministry. Loucheur and Thomas were endeavoring to change the whole way the French government financed industry. Up until then, the amortizing of new industrial construction was through price rises on industrial output. The state paid for greater steel-producing capacity by paying more for steel. That had worked so long as plant expansions were sufficiently modest for the industrialists to finance out of their own resources. But for the huge steel mill planned near Paris, the industrialists did not have the means to wait for their costs to be recovered through higher prices. Furthermore, as Thomas explained to the budget commission of the Chamber in February, the government had a manifest moral obligation to provide an immediate reimbursement, because it was pressure by the state—in the name of patriotism—that was forcing the industrialists to increase production.[35]

Loucheur conducted negotiations with the finance ministry, but he soon saw the hopelessness of winning it to his side. Aware that the ministry's support was essential for parliamentary approval of the funding he sought, he abandoned the project of the steel mill near Paris in April.[36]

An industrial manpower shortage became conspicuous in the early months of 1917 and was exacerbated the following summer, when a request for twenty-five thousand workers encountered resistance from the new commander in chief, General Philippe Pétain, largely because he was already committed to releasing a large contingent of soldiers to bring in the harvest. It is not known how many workers Loucheur finally obtained, but given the labor shortage, domestic steel production was no better in July than it had been at the beginning of the year.[37]

Loucheur had not despaired of an improvement in steel imports. At the beginning of January, 1917, he met with the British minister of munitions in London to discuss renewing the British shipments of steel that had been suspended because of unloading delays in French ports, partic-

35. Note en réponse aux conclusions du rapport de M. Gervais, sénateur, January 3, 1917, in 94 AP, 113, AN; Minutes, Commission du Budget (Chambre), February 7, 1917, in C, 7559, AN.
36. Minutes, Commission du Budget (Chambre), April 3, 1917, in C, 7559, AN; Pinot, *Le Comité des Forges*, 258–59.
37. Minutes, Commission de l'Armée (Chambre), August 3, 1917, in C, 7498, AN.

ularly at Nantes. In order to meet British conditions for restoring ship-ments, Loucheur, with Thomas' concurrence, sent a representative to Nantes from the ministry of armaments. The aide Loucheur assigned there reported to him daily, and within a matter of days had increased the daily tonnage of steel unloaded from about 250 to 600.[38]

Although Loucheur could in February tell Thomas of his achieve-ment at Nantes, he acknowledged in the same letter that few vessels were arriving at any French ports from Britain. In consequence, imports from across the Channel for armaments manufacture were down to twenty-eight thousand tons in January, from forty thousand the preced-ing month. Loucheur ordered Commandant Hausser of the French mis-sion in Britain to notify him daily about the shipping situation in Britain and to make urgent representations to the British admiralty for more shipping assistance. At the same time, Loucheur planned to exploit the information he received from Hausser to strengthen his case for more shipping capacity from the French maritime transport service.[39] Haus-ser and other French officials seem to have had little success with the British, for in the weeks that followed, the British admiralty reduced the tonnage capacity available for shipments to France.

Loucheur saw his efforts further threatened in April, when the French government decided to deploy part of the merchant fleet in ship-ping grain from the United States. He faced the distinct possibility that all American steel shipments would halt temporarily, since Washing-ton had itself settled on suspending steel deliveries to France in order to concentrate on wheat.[40]

Frightened by the ramifications of the focus upon cereals, Loucheur made his countermoves. For one thing, he wrote to Ribot, who in March had become the French premier. His letter asked the government to di-vide the available shipping capacity between grain and steel, and it im-plored Ribot to direct the French mission in London to designate more of the ships of its emergency fleet for steel deliveries. In another move, Loucheur requested that the French maritime transport service make a special appeal to the British admiralty for assistance and that it reduce

38. Note en réponse aux conclusions du rapport de M. Gervais, sénateur, January 3, 1917, in 94 AP, 113, AN; Louis Loucheur to Albert Thomas, February 3, 1917, in 94 AP, 63, AN.

39. Loucheur to Thomas, February 3, 1917, in 94 AP, 63, AN.

40. Paul Painlevé to Louis Loucheur, May 13, 1917, in 94 AP, 113, AN; Telegram from New York, signed Liebert, May 5, 1917, *ibid.*

coal imports by between thirty and forty thousand tons a month to free ships for steel.[41] He also went to French industrialists who had shipping tonnage, asking for their help. They promised to carry approximately seven thousand tons of steel per month.[42]

The minister of war, Paul Painlevé, who was doubling as armaments minister while Thomas was in Russia, wrote to Loucheur in mid-May that appeals by the maritime transport service to the British had failed and that there was little prospect of reassigning French vessels to the delivery of British steel. He also warned that, even in the event of extreme urgency, it was improbable that there would be imports of steel from the United States that month. He ventured that, under those conditions, Loucheur might want to consider adjusting production levels to conform to resources.[43]

Loucheur's response, handwritten on Painlevé's letter, was bitter and blunt: "I don't see what any program can consist in if there is neither steel nor coke. There is no other solution than what I indicated with respect to supplies from England, and I intend to examine it tomorrow with M. Viollette [the minister of supplies] in the presence of the premier, president of the council."[44] Loucheur's meeting with Ribot and with other ministers resulted in decisions favorable to his interests. Ribot agreed to provide some tonnage for steel from the United States, and just a few days later the maritime transport service ordered a number of ships that had previously been designated for coal deliveries from Britain to transport steel instead.[45]

Loucheur remarked in a letter to Painlevé on June 7 that the maritime transport service had yielded only after a month of his protests and proddings. Underlining the consequences of such slow, inefficient decision making, Loucheur concluded, "I hope [the maritime transport serv-

41. Louis Loucheur to Alexandre Ribot, n.d., attached to Louis Loucheur to Albert Thomas, May 3, 1917, *ibid.*; Louis Loucheur to Paul Painlevé, May 9, 1917, *ibid.* No document was found stating that it was Loucheur who insisted on the maritime transport service's appeal to the British admiralty for help, but several documents, taken together, indicate quite strongly that he told it to make the appeal.

42. Rapport fait à la Commission de l'Armée sur l'acier, by N. A. Gervais (Sénat), July 13, 1917, *ibid.*

43. Painlevé to Loucheur, May 13, 1917, *ibid.*

44. *Ibid.*

45. Louis Loucheur to Paul Painlevé, May 19, 1917, *ibid.*; Rapport fait à la Commission de l'Armée sur l'acier, by N. A. Gervais (Sénat), July 13, 1917, *ibid.*

ice's orders to Britain] are going to be carried out, but the fact that it did not take action there as early as the beginning of May deprives us permanently of a delivery of twenty-five thousand tons, representing three million 75-mm. shells."[46] His letter shows that he had finally been heard by other government officials, but only after the situation had worsened despite his unremitting pressure. It illustrates the obstacles he confronted not only in activating a government bureaucracy but also in working toward goals when the needs of more than a single ministry had to weigh in the balance.

Loucheur continued looking for ways to increase the shipping capacity for steel. In the ensuing weeks, he cooperated with others in implanting techniques that enabled a closer management and in centralizing the distribution of the tonnage available to France. In July, he proposed that the United States provide ships for delivering steel to France in return for artillery guns France was manufacturing for the American army.[47] To fill the void created by the curtailment of American deliveries, he turned to Britain, though he knew this afforded only a respite. Commandant Hausser warned the ministry of armaments in early July that although steel imports from Britain could be expected to surpass sixty thousand tons for the month, the British government wanted the figure reduced after that. And on July 27, he relayed Britain's insistence that the French revise their steel requisition for August and "not ask for a gram more than the quantity they absolutely cannot do without for immediate and rigorously indispensable use." Because of Britain's inflexibility, he recommended that Thomas come to London for discussions.[48]

Loucheur intended to prolong sizable shipments from Britain if he could. He wrote the undersecretary of state for maritime transport on July 31, emphasizing that France's shipping efforts of June and July had to be equaled in August and that sixty thousand tons of British steel needed to be imported. Loucheur's pressure produced results, at least during the first part of the month, when import levels were as high as he wanted. But there was great concern at that point, for the British had

---

46. Louis Loucheur to Paul Painlevé, June 7, 1917, *ibid.*

47. Rapport fait à la Commission de l'Armée sur l'acier, by N. A. Gervais (Sénat), July 13, 1917, *ibid.*; Note pour Loucheur, July 10, 1917, in 94 AP, 112, AN.

48. Note sur le tableau des prévisions d'importation des aciers, July 19, 1917, in 94 AP, 113, AN; Telegram Commandant Hausser to minister of armaments and war manufacture, Department of the General Organization of Production, July 27, 1917, *ibid.*

produced far less steel for France during the latter half of July than it required, and the effects of the shortfall were on the horizon. Loucheur told Thomas on August 11 that some kind of "energetic intervention" with the British was absolutely essential. He warned, "If we have no steel from this source either, we will have to close."[49]

Everything counseled accepting Hausser's suggestion of talks in London, and Loucheur, not Thomas, joined an economic negotiating team headed by the minister of commerce, Etienne Clémentel. Steel was not a separate item on the agenda of the formal meetings of August 16–27, but Loucheur seized the opportunity to discuss it with the British munitions minister, Winston Churchill, who agreed that the British should do their utmost to provide sufficient steel for the production of French 75-mm. shells during August and September. Loucheur committed himself to exploring the possibility of reducing his steel needs from Britain by increasing imports from the United States.[50]

In August, the British demanded that France centralize purchases in the hands of a single agent.[51] By an interministerial decision of August 31, 1917, involving Thomas and Clémentel, the Comptoir d'Exportation des Produits Métallurgiques became responsible for steel imports from Britain, under the jurisdiction of the CIMB.[52] The result was a much more tightly controlled system.[53]

Loucheur faced a new threat when the ministry of supplies informed him in late July that the tonnage to be allotted in the month ahead for steel imports would be far below what he was expecting. He immediately protested to the undersecretary of state for maritime transport, on the grounds that his agreement to significant reductions during June and July had been contingent on the minister of supply's formal assurances that in August and September the tonnage would return to its normal minimum. Loucheur also took his case to Thomas, warning of the risk to munitions production.[54]

49. Note pour M. le Chef du Service des Produits Métallurgiques, August 10, 1917, with note from Loucheur added, August 11, 1917, in 94 AP, 170, AN.

50. Etienne Clémentel, *La France et la Politique économique interalliée* (Paris, 1931), 156–65; Commandant Hausser to Albert Thomas, August 23, 1917, in 94 AP, 170, AN.

51. Pinot, *Le Comité des Forges*, 143–44.

52. On the CIMB, see above, pp. 34–35.

53. Comité des Forges de France, Circular No. 961, September 13, 1917, in 94 AP, 233, AN.

54. Louis Loucheur to undersecretary of state for maritime transport, July 27, 1917, in 94 AP, 87, AN; Louis Loucheur to Albert Thomas, July 28, 1917, *ibid*.

Thomas and Loucheur took their anxieties to an interministerial committee that a short time before had been set up to decide the allotment of shipping. Acknowledging that the transport of grain from the United States was absolutely essential, the two men appealed nonetheless for additional attention to France's desperate steel situation. To their argument that without more steel from the United States during August, war production in France might end in either September or October, the committee reacted by according them ships to transport an additional thirty-five thousand tons in August.[55] Once more Loucheur had demonstrated his skill and determination to defend his interests in difficult circumstances.

By August, he had long since given up the idea of moving France toward independence of the United States in steel. Partly because of his inability to obtain all the manpower he sought from the GQG, he had been unable to develop his domestic program as fully as he had anticipated. But he also pointed out to the army commission of the Chamber of Deputies on August 3 that in order to produce one ton of steel in France, it was necessary to import three tons of raw materials. It was far simpler to import the finished product, and after the United States entered the war and the serious U-boat threat to the sea-lanes between France and America abated somewhat, he must have decided to maintain import ties rather than to reduce them gradually. Even so, the drive for increased steel production at home continued, and on August 17, Thomas attended the lighting at Caen of the most powerful blast furnace French metallurgy had ever constructed. According to Thomas, another furnace was to be lighted in November.[56]

Despite the adversities, Loucheur and Thomas had impressive statistics for the Chamber's army commission in August. Not once after January, for example, had the number of 75-mm. shells in stock dropped below twenty million. Even though the production of these shells depended entirely on imported steel and even though a large number had been consumed during the spring offensive, the stock had risen to twenty-five million during July. The production of 155-mm. shells, partially dependent on steel imports, was also satisfactory. In March, the French had approximately five million of them on hand,

55. Minutes, Commission de l'Armée (Chambre), August 3, 1917, in C, 7498, AN.
56. Ibid.; Discours prononcé par M. Thomas, August 19, 1917, in 94 AP, 343, AN.

and although the inventory dropped to just above three million as a result of the spring offensive, the number on hand had again risen to five million.[57]

Thomas said that his ministry had "been forced to reduce the food for cannons in order to assure it for the population."[58] But the statistics seem to bear out that Loucheur kept the French army supplied with the materials it needed most. Working within the government was different from being a private businessman, and he could not always count on rapid decisions or undeviating support from a government bureaucracy. He learned that more than technical expertise was necessary to convince government officials and that even pressure tactics had a role to play.

COAL

When Loucheur entered the government in December, 1916, the ministry of armaments exercised no real authority over coal, even though war-related industries were the commodity's largest consumer in the last three months of 1916. Government responsibility for coal still rested in the hands of the ministry of public works, and its administration in the matter was poorly organized and weak.[59] By mid-July, 1917, Loucheur had become the "coal tsar" of France. Once more the government had called upon Loucheur the technical expert to find a solution to a problem.

First of all, France's problem was that it had been deficient in coal production even before the outbreak of hostilities. In 1913, it produced 41 million tons but consumed 59.5 million. Imports from Britain, Belgium, and Germany made up the difference. When war broke out, the imports

57. Minutes, Commission de l'Armée (Chambre), August 3, 1917, in C, 7498, AN.
58. *Ibid.*
59. Rapport sur l'artillerie lourde de campagne et l'artillerie à grande puissance, by André Tardieu, Commission de l'Armée (Chambre), March 12, 1917, in C, 7503, AN. According to Tardieu, the use of coal for the last months of 1916 was 3 million tons by war factories, 2.3 million tons by railroads, 1.55 million tons for gas and electricity, 275,000 tons for navigation, 900,000 tons by divers industries, and 2.7 million tons for home consumption.

from Belgium and Germany were lost. Compounding the difficulty was France's loss of a large number of mines in the war's first weeks. Domestic production dropped to 19.5 million tons in 1915.[60]

Even after the loss, shutdown, or slowdown of many industries, France continued to depend heavily upon coal imports, with the British left as the supplier. In 1916, consumption was approximately forty-four million tons, but domestic production was less than twenty-two million. To guarantee a steady supply at a reasonable price from Britain, the French in the spring of 1916 signed an agreement (the Runciman-Sembat accords) raising France's monthly total of British coal to two million tons.[61] In the fall, however, the British began reducing shipments to France, primarily because a portion of their shipping was going to the importation of desperately needed wheat. By December, only 1.4 million tons of coal a month were arriving in France from across the Channel.

Confronted with the deteriorating situation, Clémentel, the commerce minister, entered into negotiations with the British regarding shipping tonnage, freight rates, and export licenses. On December 3, an agreement between him and Walter Runciman, the president of the Board of Trade, centralized in London the chartering of neutral shipping, which carried large quantities of British coal to France. The Bureau Interallié des Affrètements Neutres was organized to allot this tonnage not only to France but also to Italy. By accepting the new allocation system, which contained appreciable cost benefits, France acceded, for the time being at least, to receiving less neutral tonnage than it absolutely needed.[62]

Such was the situation when Edouard Herriot joined the government in December as the new minister of public works responsible for coal. Facing the choice of either ignoring the agreement of December 3 and hiring neutral tonnage at whatever the cost or abiding by the con-

60. Ministère du Commerce, de l'Industrie, des Postes et Télégraphes, des Transports Maritimes et de la Marine Marchande, Direction des Etudes Techniques, *Rapport général sur l'industrie française, sa situation, son avenir* (3 vols.; Paris, 1919), I, 7–12. The consumption figure excludes coke. In addition, more than a million tons of the domestic production total were exported.

61. France, *Annales du Sénat: Débats parlementaires*, February 8, 1917, p. 140; Clémentel, *La France et la Politique économique*, 88–91.

62. Clémentel, *La France et la Politique économique*, 110–13, 327–30.

vention and receiving inadequate tonnage at rates agreed to by the Allies, he opted in the beginning for the former course. In authorizing the charter of several neutral ships at fees well above those of the December accords, he explained, "I prefer to be stolen from rather than killed." When the British denied the vessels permission to depart, Herriot decided to go to Britain for discussions. In the end, the British lifted their restrictions, but they also rejected Herriot's request for restoration of their commitment, as under the spring agreement, to send two million tons of coal to France monthly. They simply did not have the ships to make deliveries on that scale. Herriot backed off, though, from buying neutral shipping regardless of the cost. He decided to abide by the agreement of December 3 despite its provision of less tonnage than France required. His conclusion was that France would suffer financially by returning to a free market and would damage Allied solidarity as well.[63]

Toward the end of February, the French again requested a meeting with the British to discuss coal imports. Paul Cambon, the French ambassador in London, emphasized the gravity of the situation in a letter to the British Foreign Office on February 20: "Mr. Briand fears that if the present situation were to continue, production in the most important war establishments would be interrupted."[64] The French sent not only Herriot but also Loucheur, who was included partly because coal shortages were affecting war production but even more because he seemed to have a better command of the issues involved than Herriot. René Viviani, serving as minister of justice, told Loucheur just prior to the trip that Herriot was not equal to the challenge. The meetings produced little more than the hope that Parliament might approve import restrictions that would eventually release some tonnage capacity for shipping raw materials.[65]

Herriot left the public-works ministry not long thereafter, when the government of Briand collapsed. In the government of Ribot, which was its successor, the responsibility for coal was divided between the new minister of public works, Georges Desplas, and the head of a newly cre-

63. *Ibid.*, 138–40.

64. Paul Cambon to Foreign Office, February 20, 1917, in Foreign Office, General Correspondence, Contraband, FO 382, Vol. 1680, PRO.

65. Loucheur, *Carnets secrets*, 34; Minutes of the War Cabinet, March 1, 1917, Appendix III, in Cabinet Office, Records of the Cabinet, Minutes of Cabinet Meetings, Conferences of Ministers, CAB 23/2, PRO.

ated ministry of supplies, Maurice Viollette. Several weeks of uncertainty followed, and neither man emerged as the leader in defining coal policy.[66]

During March, Loucheur developed a geographically based coal distribution system. In his highly structured and comprehensive arrangement for all users, the state was to have the dominant role. First of all, France was to be divided into three primary regions: the first, located in the south of France, would depend on the coal produced in the mines of central and southern France; the second, encompassing Paris, the combat zones, and the eastern area of France, would have its needs filled by the functioning mines of the Pas-de-Calais and the Nord; and the third, including the coasts of France along the Atlantic and the English Channel, would rely completely on imports. Loucheur's zonal division aimed at systematizing and rationalizing the transport of coal in order to reduce slow or late deliveries. An allocation office at the ministry of supplies was to ensure that distribution was in keeping with established priorities. The plan presupposed a state monopoly in the sale of both domestically produced and imported coal, with standard prices set for each of several grades. The system of price equalization went by the name of *péréquation*, and was aimed at leveling out prices between expensive imported coal and the much cheaper domestically mined stock. *Péréquation* had first appeared in a government bill in 1915, but though the Chamber of Deputies had kept *péréquation* in the bill it passed, the Senate rejected the device in its disposition of the legislation in early 1916. Still, in the law that resulted, the government obtained some controls over coal prices.[67]

Loucheur's ideas, published in *Le Temps* on April 1, heightened an already intense public debate about the availability of coal. Opposition to *péréquation* and a state-controlled system of coal distribution was strong, and a Senate report issued at the time reflected the hostility many felt toward such arrangements. Some questioned as well whether the sources of coal that Loucheur's plan reserved for the Parisian zone were enough to meet demand and warned that a definitive zonal ar-

66. Olivier, *La Politique du charbon*, 140–41; Bonnefous and Bonnefous, *Histoire politique*, II, 450–51.
67. Réunion général des fabricants d'obus en acier et en fonte aciérée, March 3, 1917, in 10 N, 29, SHA; *L'Usine*, April 8, 1917, p. 3; Olivier, *La Politique du charbon*, 113–22, 126–27, 141–42.

rangement would need enough flexibility to meet the disruptions and uncertainties of war.[68]

The government moved to calm misgivings by announcing that it did not intend to assume the heavy burden of a sales monopoly for coal. The state was to be merely a distributor, supervising the apportionment of coal produced in and for France. Importers and mining firms were still to control their own sales. The ministry of supplies also issued a communiqué, stressing that it had accepted the responsibility for an allocations office in principle only. It added, "No solution will be adopted right now, however, and the question is merely under study."[69]

A short time later, Viollette took the lead in formulating coal policy. He introduced several measures with a view toward a better-organized, more tightly controlled structure for importing, allocating, and pricing the resource. One measure identified four categories of consumers according to their place in the war effort. Each category was to be divided into a number of coal groups responsible for distribution and *péréquation*. Industries engaged in the production of supplies for the war constituted one category, and Loucheur in May organized these into a system of regional collectivities. In operation just a few weeks later, the twenty regional associations he created were known as the Groupements Loucheur. Within each region, individual firms submitted statements of their coal needs to a centralizing agency, a group corporation, which went on to present the entire group's needs to Loucheur's office. Ultimate control over distribution consequently rested with Loucheur, although at the regional level, distribution was the responsibility of the group itself, as were coal purchases and the establishment of a standard price per ton (*péréquation*) for each grade of coal. No industrialist was allowed to procure coal outside the collaboration of his group.[70]

The Chamber of Deputies in general applauded Viollette's moves when he explained them to it at the end of May, but its support faded in June, when many of its members began to perceive his lack of forcefulness in presenting his schemes and theirs to the Senate. Expressions of disenchantment also appeared in the press, where one newspaper re-

68. *L'Usine*, April 8, 1917, pp. 3–4; Olivier, *La Politique du charbon*, 141–42.
69. *L'Usine*, April 8, 1917, pp. 3–4.
70. *Ibid.*, June 3, 1917, p. 1; *Groupement des industries de l'armement no. 10 pour l'approvisionnement du charbon* (N.p., 1917), 1–5.

marked, "If we do not have any coal, it is because we have a minister of supplies."[71] In response, the government, which was moving to consolidate control over coal in the hands of one man, transferred the responsibility of administering the import and supply of all combustibles to Loucheur on June 19. The consolidation was complete by July 3, when control of production in French mines shifted from the ministry of public works to Loucheur's undersecretariat. In effect, Loucheur became the minister of coal, for he had gained control of both its production and its distribution.[72]

Given not only the growing discontent with Viollette but also the French munitions effort's requirements for coal, the centralization of power is not surprising. André Tardieu had already hinted at the propriety of giving the armaments ministry control of the production and distribution of the fuel in March, when in his report he questioned the absence of a substantial role for the ministry, and Desplas, the minister of public works, had openly expressed his opinions in early July, when he commented that it was only logical that the ministry of armaments should control the entire matter.[73] Besides, Loucheur had been deeply involved in coal policy throughout the spring and had considerable knowledge of the subject. His experience, combined with his technical skills, made him a prime contender for a significant role in any government program. In any case, some politicians believed that Loucheur was ideally suited for ending the bitter debate in the press and parliament between those who opposed and those who favored government control of production, importation, distribution, and pricing. A deputy, Pierre Laval, made that point during a discussion in the Chamber on July 20: "Mr. Loucheur, I am delighted that someone thought of entrusting this service to you, for your name, your personality, your authority in the world of industry and in the world of commerce have at least had one result, which has been to silence the controversy and elicit praise from

71. L'Usine, June 10, 1917, p. 7.

72. Olivier, La Politique du charbon, 144–48; Bulletin des usines de guerre, June 25, 1917, in 10 N, 2, SHA; Comité des Forges de France, Circular No. 931, June 30, 1917, Circular No. 936, July 17, 1917, both in 94 AP, 275, AN.

73. Minutes, Commission des Mines (Chambre), July 6, 1917, in C, 7761, AN. After the creation of a separate ministry of supplies in March, 1917, the principal responsibilities for coal had been divided between that department and the ministry of public works. See Bonnefous and Bonnefous, Histoire politique, II, 450–51; and Olivier, La Politique du charbon, 140–41.

the very newspapers that yesterday criticized the same policy of [*péréquation* and government controls]."[74]

In the coal program that Loucheur implemented in mid-July, seven specific categories of users were the initial recipients of available coal, and one of those seven was the Groupements Loucheur. First priority belonged to private homes, for as Loucheur told a member of parliament, it was impossible to deal effectively with production in the factories unless there was peace in the home. He wanted, that is, to maintain the morale of the population and avoid unrest that might worsen the military situation.[75] A primary element in the distribution for private dwellings in Paris was to be the issuance of rationing cards. To improve the plan's chances of success at all levels, he established a system of communication and interaction between representatives of the ministry of armaments in Paris, the port cities, and the areas of the mines, and individuals and groups within the seven different categories. The Bureau National des Charbons oversaw the system, with the result that its role increased dramatically.

In reaction to a call by several deputies to reopen the question of coal management, Loucheur went before the Chamber on July 20 to deliver his maiden parliamentary speech. In a way that came to typify his approach, he explained his program by appealing to facts and figures. In addition to spelling out the actions he had already taken to enlarge supplies, he mentioned that he had met with Anatole de Monzie, the undersecretary for maritime transport, and another official, and that they had together developed a transportation plan for British coal which was based on the needs of the various departments located on the English Channel, as a replacement for the old illogical and inefficient delivery system.[76] Loucheur further remarked that although domestic output had risen to 2 million tons in April, he intended to raise it to 2.4 million and had already met with mine owners to explore ways of arriving at that goal.

In the address, Loucheur deplored the inequitable distribution system that had existed before and that allowed some industrial firms to

74. France, *Annales de la Chambre des Députés: Débats parlementaires*, July 20, 1917, p. 1932.

75. *Le Petit Journal* (Paris), July 18, 1917, p. 1.

76. Anatole de Monzie was appointed on July 4 to head an undersecretariat that combined two previously distinct jurisdictions, maritime transport and the merchant marine.

stockpile coal to the detriment of others; he lamented the rampant speculation inherent in the system, which had led to sales of coal for as much as three hundred or four hundred francs a ton, several times more than the average market price at that point. Loucheur made the case that it was largely to combat such injustices that a state-controlled distribution system had been created, and he even talked of introducing a government-sponsored bill to establish *péréquation* for the nation as a whole. His suggestion was obviously pleasing to the Chamber, which was supportive of the idea. The deputies also took satisfaction in Loucheur's position that private dwellings should receive first priority in the distribution process.

The Chamber reacted positively to what Loucheur said. All sides contributed to the ringing applause as he descended from the tribune; it was apparent that his program had strong support in the Chamber. Reactions in the press were also favorable, with *Le Figaro*, for example, expressing the conviction that he justly deserved the congratulations he received at the end of his speech.[77]

Taking advantage of the summer recess to avoid the less friendly Senate, Loucheur did what he had to to put his plan into operation by the early fall. One step consisted in shifting responsibility for *péréquation* from the coal groups to the Bureau National des Charbons, which used the state railway's financial office as its fiscal agent. In the system that developed, the state bought and sold coal at prices that taxed domestically produced coal and subsidized imports. By launching the program administratively rather than legislatively, Loucheur bypassed parliamentary hurdles. In the end, even the Senate did not pass harsh judgment on his way of proceeding. In late October, he could proudly tell the Chamber of Deputies that his plan was functioning well and that coal supplies were generally in line with what he had predicted three months earlier.[78]

What one sees in Loucheur is the government's willingness to turn to a technical expert when more politically oriented men had proved inadequate to a challenge. There was obviously a conviction among government leaders that Loucheur, as an efficiency-oriented businessman,

77. France, *Annales de la Chambre: Débats*, July 20, 1917, pp. 1939–43; *Le Figaro* (Paris), July 21, 1917, p. 2.

78. Olivier, *La Politique du charbon*, 152, 155, 161–62; Sardier, *Le Ravitaillement en charbon*, 160–61.

could reduce the difficult to the manageable quickly; in a sense they saw him as their "man of the hour" in dispatching economic problems.

LOUCHEUR'S RECORD

When Loucheur became an armaments ministry undersecretary, the most important area of production for him was heavy artillery, since it was that more than anything else that brought about his entry into the government. And even though production fell short of the output he had estimated for most heavy-artillery models during the first six months of 1917, production of the top-priority 155-mm. Court came close to reaching the number he had projected on January 11. Five hundred guns were turned out, whereas 540 had been expected.[79] It appears, furthermore, that by the beginning of the summer, production was running smoothly for this caliber and it was possible to anticipate, barring a catastrophe, continued manufacture close to the desired levels. A new complication arose when, on June 25, 1917, the GQG submitted a supplementary request to its original heavy-artillery requisition of May 30, 1916. It asked for a significant increase in the fabrication of 220-mm. Court and 280-mm. guns. It also wanted more in the area of aviation. At that point the armaments ministry had to acquaint Pétain with the realities of the moment: there were neither the raw materials nor the workers to build everything the commander in chief sought. Thomas therefore had the GQG rank priorities for artillery and aviation. Its choice was to put first the development of a new aviation program, second the manufacture of defense artillery (155-mm. Court and 220-mm. Court guns), and third the production of large-caliber heavy artillery (280-mm. guns).[80] It was not clear at the time how this would affect Loucheur's programs, but it was evident that there would be a change of emphasis reflecting the evolution of the war toward planes and big guns.

Loucheur's first months as an official amounted to an apprentice-

79. Prévisions d'entrée en service des matériels d'artillerie en 1917, January 11, 1917, in 94 AP, 87, AN. The projected production figures Loucheur sent Thomas for the 155-mm. Court on January 11 were close to if not the same as those he submitted on December 24, 1916. No table listing the exact output that Loucheur estimated for heavy artillery in December seems to exist.

80. Minutes, Commission de l'Armée (Chambre), August 3, 1917, in C, 7498, AN.

ship in the many dimensions of operating within a government. He quickly discovered that neither the support of influential political figures nor his technical expertise guaranteed cooperation from other officials. Because there were competing bureaucratic interests and priorities, he frequently had to do battle to preserve conditions that he considered essential for munitions production. In contrast to the independence he enjoyed in industry, he was suddenly faced with the constraint of priorities and ideas that challenged and subordinated his own. But notwithstanding his frequent conflicts with other factions in the bureaucracy, it seems that at the ministerial level there was a general respect for his organizational and administrative skills. The demonstration of that is in the increasing responsibilities assigned to his undersecretariat concerning coal. The ambivalence within government circles toward him had as its focus the technocratic principles, such as efficiency, practicality, and swiftness in action, that the bureaucracy found alien.

During these months, Loucheur's experiences nurtured his disdain for politicians and bureaucrats. But instead of being demoralized by the frustrations before him, he solidified his determination to persist in an approach to production that he was convinced would be decisive for winning the war.

4

A WINTER OF SHORTAGES AND CONTROVERSY
1917–1918

A scandal in which Jean Louis Malvy, the interior minister, faced charges of defeatism and even treason brought down the Ribot government in early September. Several days later the Republican-Socialist Paul Painlevé, who had served as a deputy from 1910 on, announced the formation of a new government, in which he, besides serving as premier, would retain the post of minister of war. But from the beginning, that government was weakened by the absence of Socialists. Nettled that Ribot had not let them participate in an international Socialist congress on war and peace, they withheld support from Painlevé for naming Ribot foreign minister.

A big winner in the new government was Loucheur, who replaced Thomas as minister of armaments.[1] Loucheur combined his responsibilities as undersecretary—a position that was abolished—with most of those Thomas had exercised.[2] As a result, he became increasingly vulnerable to attack from inside the government as well as from the public. But when he defended his actions against criticisms he had escaped while Thomas was in charge, he did so with skill and tenacity. His political stock was rising in the eyes of Georges Clemenceau, who by November was premier. In late 1917 and early 1918, Loucheur as minister of armaments broadened the ambit of his concerns from organization and

1. David Robin Watson, *Georges Clemenceau: A Political Biography* (New York, 1974), 258–65; Loucheur, *Carnets secrets*, 41–54; Thomas' Account of Cabinet Crisis of September, 1917, in 94 AP, 356, AN.

2. The undersecretariat for inventions was transferred from the ministry of armaments to the ministry of war.

production to close and effective inter-Allied cooperation more generally.

ORGANIZATIONAL CHANGES: AUTOMOBILE SERVICE AND ASSAULT ARTILLERY

Shortly after the new government was constituted, Painlevé attempted to reduce the armaments minister's authority. Resentment existed against the ministry of armaments at the GQG, which chafed at bureaucratic delays and the diminution of its influence over war production. Certain Chamber commissions blamed Loucheur for lags in factory output, and there was a feeling among some politicians that his ministry might better be an undersecretariat accountable to the minister of war. Ribot had suggested such an arrangement to Loucheur in early September in connection with his failed effort to constitute a new government.[3]

Painlevé proposed restoring to the war minister certain responsibilities for the automobile service that the armaments ministry had assumed when it was created in 1916. Painlevé and the ministry of war wanted to demarcate more precisely the production of an item from its use so that the use and maintenance of war-related materials might be managed by the war ministry, in their view the legitimate custodian. Painlevé wanted the personnel associated with the parts of the automobile service—which included assault artillery, or tanks—that were not involved in production to be transferred to the war ministry.[4] General Pétain, who actively supported him, held that the existing organizational structure for assault artillery was no longer warranted, since most preparatory measures related to the development of that unit had been settled.

Loucheur took issue with the distinction that had been turned against him: he believed manufacture, maintenance, and use too closely linked in the automobile service to separate them. He answered his opponents that this was particularly true for assault artillery, where important technical modifications were still occurring and would probably continue to occur, since some of the equipment in production had

3. Paul Painlevé to Louis Loucheur, September 15, 1917, in Subseries 6 N, Fonds Clemenceau, Carton 103, SHA; Loucheur, *Carnets secrets*, 41–43.
4. Painlevé to Loucheur, September 15, 1917, in 6 N, 103, SHA.

never been tested in combat.[5] He also believed that Painlevé's proposal threatened his power in other ways. His bitterness was highlighted in two statements he made on September 22 in a rebuttal letter. First, he contended that the decree Painlevé proposed would reduce his powers to what they were when he was undersecretary for war production. Second, at the end of the letter, he wrote, "I add that it would be very unkind—and I am certain that this argument will not fail to move you—to modify this [decree of December 31, 1916, which indicated the responsibilities of the armaments minister] shortly after the departure of . . . Albert Thomas, who while he was in charge of the armaments ministry did so many things that you are aware of and have publicly praised on several occasions."[6] Loucheur's account of what he would lose was probably exaggerated, but it reflects the deep uncertainty he felt. In the end, Painlevé had to postpone action on the matter, because Loucheur refused to sign the decree.[7]

Still, there was increasing sentiment within the army and parliament in late 1917 for an independent assault artillery service under the ministry of war. The British invented the tank early in the war and first employed it in battle during the Somme offensive of 1916. Before year's end, Joseph Joffre had placed an order for a thousand light models. Because of the novelty of the weapon, no assault artillery or tank service existed at the war ministry, and the responsibility for design and manufacture fell to Thomas. The top priority for both Thomas and Loucheur in early 1917, however, was heavy artillery. Consequently, progress had been slow when, in June, Pétain announced that the army wanted 3,500 light tanks. Thomas, in July, and Loucheur, in September, promised to deliver 450 tanks by the close of the year, and Loucheur went so far in October as to suggest that he would be able to provide 1,000 by early spring. Nevertheless, there was much concern over how slowly tank production was going.[8]

In the course of the debate over administrative reorganization, on November 13, Painlevé's shaky government collapsed, and the seventy-

5. Louis Loucheur to Paul Painlevé, September 22, 1917, *ibid.*
6. *Ibid.*
7. Note pour M. le Secrétaire Général de la Présidence du Conseil, September 30, 1917, in 6 N, 103, SHA.
8. B. H. Liddell Hart, *The Real War, 1914–1918* (Boston, 1964), 118, 205; Rapport de Monsieur Abel Ferry sur l'artillerie d'assaut, Commission du Budget (Chambre), May 10, 1918, in C, 7502, AN.

six-year-old Clemenceau became premier and minister of war. Clemenceau, a sharp voice against defeatism and the country's war leaders from early in the conflict, would not settle for less than a military victory. The president, Raymond Poincaré, who had felt the sting of Clemenceau's attacks, would not have asked the senator from Var to form a government if anything else had worked. But General Robert Nivelle's disastrous spring offensive, and the attendant French army mutinies, the domestic spy scandals, Italy's crushing setback at Caporetto, and the Bolshevik revolution in Russia all contributed to a rising sense of crisis that forced Poincaré's hand. With the support of the parliamentary Center and Right, Clemenceau promised to devote the government's efforts to "the war. Nothing but the war."[9]

When Clemenceau formed his cabinet, he was already familiar with Loucheur's work at the armaments ministry. Not only had Loucheur testified before the Senate's army commission, which Clemenceau chaired, but he had visited the senator's apartment to discuss the conflict. Appreciating Loucheur's technical expertise, Clemenceau wanted the industrialist in his government. At first he considered transferring Loucheur to a strengthened ministry of supplies, for like Ribot in September, he hoped to reduce the ministry of armaments to an undersecretariat responsible to the ministry of war. But, prevailing, Loucheur remained in charge of munitions production, and Clemenceau abandoned the idea of an armaments undersecretariat. The premier did not, however, drop the notion of creating a department for assault artillery, although he moved ahead carefully. The Chamber's army commission in December passed a resolution that called for the sort of office he had in mind.[10]

In early January, a government decree attached an assault artillery unit to the war ministry's artillery department. The decree guaranteed Loucheur exclusive control over tank production and stipulated that the GQG and the war ministry would embark on new tank programs only after securing the consent of the minister of armaments. Loucheur,

9. Watson, *Georges Clemenceau*, 249–72; Wright, *France in Modern Times*, 398–99.
10. Raymond Poincaré, *Au service de la France* (11 vols.; Paris, 1926–74), IX, 371–72, 374; Renouvin, *The Forms of War Government*, 73–77; Rapport de Monsieur Abel Ferry sur l'artillerie d'assaut, Commission du Budget (Chambre), May 10, 1918, in C, 7502, AN; Loucheur, *Carnets secrets*, 31–32, 35–36; Rapport sur l'organisation de l'artillerie d'assaut, Sous-Commission des Armements, Commission de l'Armée (Chambre), December 25, 1917, in C, 7503, AN.

who signed the decree, was apparently satisfied with the more limited scope and greater clarity of aims than Painlevé's proposal had had.[11]

Not long afterward, the two ministries took a final step in reorganizing what remained of the automobile service by dividing responsibility for it in the same way they had for assault artillery.[12] In both accords, Loucheur lost some of his authority to the minister of war. He emerged, though, with his administrative control over the production of tanks and other vehicles as firm as ever.

Loucheur, in appearances before the Chamber's army and budget commissions during January, 1918, had to reduce from a thousand to eight hundred his prediction of the number of light tanks that could be produced by early spring. He was thereupon assailed again in parliament. At the beginning of April, he wrote the army commission that he had put 117 light tanks at the disposal of the war ministry, but Clemenceau a short time later indicated that only 72 had arrived, and many of those functioned very poorly.[13] Loucheur remained confident, however, that his technical skills and energetic style of management could improve the output of tanks considerably over time. His optimism proved largely correct, for French tank production picked up rapidly in the spring and summer of 1918.[14]

AVIATION

Although the GQG, in reordering its requirements in the summer of 1917, made the production of aircraft a top priority, aircraft manufacture was plagued with difficulties. Loucheur believed nonetheless that he could weld together a reliable production system. When he assumed new responsibilities in that area in November, 1917, he described what he confronted: "The task that lies before me is the most difficult I have encountered in my life. That I can affirm very clearly. I do not know if I will succeed in dealing with it. I will do everything possible; you can

11. France, *Journal officiel de la République française: Lois et Décrets*, January 9, 1918, p. 372.

12. *Ibid.*, January 19, 1918, p. 746.

13. Rapport de Monsieur Abel Ferry sur l'artillerie d'assaut, Commission du Budget (Chambre), May 10, 1918, in C, 7502, AN.

14. Ropp, *War in the Modern World*, 268–69.

count on that. But I would not wish on anyone the job of sitting down here and assuming such a responsibility. It is terrible."[15]

The problems he faced were worse than they might have been, because at the beginning of the war the general assumption among the French was that the plane's usefulness would be primarily in tactical reconnaissance. Technological limitations made its use in strategic operations difficult. The common belief was that a large number of planes would be unnecessary and that a peacetime level of production would be enough. But as early as the fall of 1914, the French saw that production had to increase.

An inevitable problem was the decentralization of the aviation industry. In Paris alone, there were twenty-two firms participating in the construction of airplane engines in the summer of 1914. Orders went to all the aircraft firms, none of which was capable of mass production. To introduce some order to the industry, the government eventually selected only certain models for continued production, dividing their fabrication among all the manufacturers.[16] The lack of a central authority over the stages of airplane assembly was also damaging. In early 1917, the government established a special mission to study the feasibility of a unified, coordinated aviation arm, but the mission collapsed after a change of government in March. An undersecretariat of state for aviation came into being in the aftermath of the March ministerial crisis, but it failed to develop into the strong branch of government that many had anticipated. By the fall of 1917 there was still no authority to oversee all phases of the aviation program—conception, production, and allocation.[17]

Loucheur had a limited role in aviation production during the early fall of 1917, since the heaviest responsibility lay in the hands of the aviation undersecretariat. The ministry of armaments oversaw manpower and supplied raw materials. It filled aviation-related orders that came to it as well, but it did not always respond in the way desired. That led Jacques Louis Dumesnil, the undersecretary for aviation, to ask Loucheur to appoint a permanent aviation official at the armaments ministry.[18]

15. Minutes, Commission du Budget: Sous-Commission des Armements (Chambre), December 6, 1917, in C, 7560, AN.

16. Reboul, *Mobilisation industrielle*, I, 93–96.

17. Rapport sur l'aéronautique présenté à la Commission de l'Armée par M. d'Aubigny (Chambre), May 3, 1918, in C, 7502, AN.

18. Minutes, Commission de l'Armée (Chambre), October 12, 1917, in C, 7499, AN.

Loucheur accepted as useful Dumesnil's idea of having someone at the armaments ministry follow the execution of aviation orders to their completion, but the association between the two departments remained loose.

Loucheur also took part in discussions initiated by Dumesnil to establish a well-coordinated system of mass production throughout the aircraft industry. The two men met several times to discuss manpower, raw materials, and transportation. Dumesnil told the Chamber's army commission in October that after the selection of certain models and motors for increased production, he planned to reach an agreement with Loucheur on the means of production.[19]

A succession of programs concerning the number of planes to be constructed had been introduced after October, 1914. According to that of March, 1917, the objective was to have 2,665 planes on the northeastern front by the end of the year. In October, the figure rose to 2,870, with an expected completion date of late April, 1918. Even 2,870 planes seemed insufficient, however, for Dumesnil also announced in October an effort to make 4,000 planes the new official target.[20]

Loucheur decided that France's aviation needs dictated a more active role for him, especially after he learned that a plan for 4,000 aircraft was in the making, but only after Clemenceau took power in mid-November did he press for increased responsibilities. Working with General Henri Mordacq, a member of Clemenceau's personal staff overseeing military affairs, Loucheur convinced the new premier that an organizational change was imperative. Loucheur championed the "commonsense solution," concentrating the production of all war matériel—including planes—in the hands of one person in order to achieve a better assignment of hard-to-obtain raw supplies. In decrees issued on November 19 and 21, the government transferred the production responsibility for planes from Dumesnil to Loucheur, with Dumesnil becoming an adjunct member of Loucheur's staff in that area.[21]

The decrees brought protests from Philippe Pétain and members of

19. Minutes, Commission de l'Armée (Chambre), October 17, 1917, *ibid.*

20. Rapport sur l'aéronautique présenté à la Commission de l'Armée par M. d'Aubigny (Chambre), May 3, 1918, in C, 7502, AN; Minutes, Commission de l'Armée (Chambre), October 12, 1917, in C, 7499, AN.

21. Jean Jules Henri Mordacq, *Le Ministère Clemenceau: Journal d'un témoin* (4 vols.; Paris, 1930–31), I, 35–39; Rapport sur l'aéronautique présenté à la Commission de l'Armée par M. d'Aubigny (Chambre), May 3, 1918, in C, 7502, AN.

the Chamber of Deputies, particularly the army commission. They argued that the government decisions failed to concentrate power for efficiency. In their view, the decrees dispersed power by dividing responsibilities between the armaments ministry and an aviation undersecretariat that, despite being subject to Loucheur's jurisdiction in questions of production, remained accountable to the war ministry overall. Opponents also pointed out that the decree of November 19 failed to define exactly the roles of the two men and that there seemed to be no coordinating apparatus for the aviation program as a whole.[22]

Loucheur and Dumesnil appeared before the army commission on December 7 to explain the new arrangements. Subjected to intensive questioning, Loucheur conceded that the new role of the undersecretary of state was complex, but he added that for any question of production the final authority would be the armaments minister. He addressed the question of a coordinating apparatus for aviation by offering assurances that a small "air committee" consisting of representatives from the GQG, Dumesnil's undersecretariat, and his own ministry would be formed to meet daily, with the minister himself presiding at as many of its meetings as possible.[23]

Before the air committee came into being, however, Loucheur and Dumesnil recommended to Clemenceau that the organizational ties between their services be eliminated. But Clemenceau, under duress from Pétain and the army commission to give greater unity to the aeronautical effort, pressured the two officials into reversing themselves, and on December 19 they placed Colonel Paul Dhé, who already held a high post within Dumesnil's undersecretariat, in a concomitant post at Loucheur's ministry, thereby reconstituting the link between the two departments. Dhé's role was reinforced at the end of the month by the creation of the air committee Loucheur had promised. Apparently Loucheur was not pleased with having a representative of Dumesnil's in his ministry, for in February he tried to undermine Dhé's authority by giving a representative of the armaments ministry who worked through the colonel an administrative designation that made him independent

22. Rapport sur l'aéronautique présenté à la Commission de l'Armée par M. d'Aubigny (Chambre), May 3, 1918, in C, 7502, AN; Minutes, Commission de l'Armée (Chambre), December 7, 1917, in C, 7499, AN; Maurice Duval to Philippe Pétain, November 21, 1917, in Subseries 130 AP, Jacques Louis Dumesnil Papers, Carton 7, AN.

23. Minutes, Commission de l'Armée (Chambre), December 7, 1917, in C, 7499, AN.

of Dhé. Loucheur's action was nullified three days later, when he was told that he had gone beyond the limits of his authority.[24] He was thus forced to acquiesce in a compromise that he had to live with until the end of the war.

What Loucheur sought through the November decrees was the power to make significant changes in the process of producing aircraft, and once he had that, he went to work identifying weaknesses, determining needs, and rationalizing procedures. It is not always easy to determine which reforms were Loucheur's alone, but the pattern of what occurred makes it clear that he was the driving force behind much in the way of increased output and improved quality. Among other things, he emphasized planning for change in development, virtually eliminated subcontracting by airplane manufacturers, and corrected a number of weaknesses in the fabrication of the motors on French fighter planes.[25]

Not very optimistic when he assumed commanding control in November, he told a budget commission subcommittee of the Chamber shortly thereafter, "I don't want to make forecasts, promise you so many planes. My program is producing the maximum."[26] Loucheur was in no position to commit himself to any specific figures at that point, for he was still assessing the aviation production network and the implications of the program for four thousand planes, which was adopted officially in early December. But by January 9 he was ready to present the Chamber's budget commission with surprisingly cheerful figures: over three thousand planes would be in place for the army by April, he thought, and output could be increased rapidly to approach the ambi-

24. Rapport sur l'aéronautique présenté à la Commission de l'Armée par M. d'Aubigny (Chambre), May 3, 1918, in C, 7502, AN; Albert Etevé, *La Victoire des cocardes* (Paris, 1970), 240–41; Newspaper Article in *Le Petit Parisien*, December 31, 1917, p. 1, in F 12, 7681, AN; "Fonctionnement des Services et Bureaux de l'Aéronautique," from Louis Loucheur to Jacques Louis Dumesnil, December 14, 1917, in 130 AP, 12, AN; Note sur le fonctionnement des services de l'aéronautique, December 19, 1917, in 130 AP, 12, AN.

25. Minutes, Commission du Budget: Sous-Commission des Armements (Chambre), December 6, 1917, in C, 7560, AN; Minutes, Commission du Budget (Chambre), January 9, 1918, *ibid.*; *L'Usine*, March 10, 1918, p. 1; *La Journée industrielle* (Paris), March 22, 1918, p. 2.

26. Minutes, Commission du Budget: Sous-Commission des Armements (Chambre), December 6, 1917, in C, 7560, AN.

tious objective of four thousand aircraft.[27] The change in Loucheur's attitude caused Albert d'Aubigny, the chairman of the subcommittee on aeronautics of the Chamber's army commission, to request more details concerning the calculations behind "these reassuring promises." Loucheur sent d'Aubigny data on January 27, qualifying his promises—as he had done in his committee appearance on January 9—only to the extent of acknowledging that unforeseeable war-related conditions, transportation problems, or the weather might hamper output. He continued to express confidence that the production figures would be met.[28]

A report on French aviation issued by the Chamber's army commission at the beginning of May drew a comparison between the number of planes Loucheur had promised for the first three months of the year and the number the factories had produced. There had been a shortfall of 36 percent on the 3,407 aircraft promised even though there had been no obvious impediments outside of a brief shutdown at one plant. The report's conclusion was that the division of the aviation services and the assumption of new aeronautical responsibilities by Loucheur had done nothing to accelerate production, and that a single director had been needed from the start: "Errors in organization and in command, organizational vices—their root cause is one and it ceaselessly manifests itself in the sequence of facts we have just studied: *Aviation does not have a unified management.* The absence of an overarching authority with extensive powers, someone with absolute decision-making power in determining models and in organizing the production of them—such has been the primary cause of the crisis in which aviation has always floundered."[29] The report reflected the frustrations of members of parliament whose solution had been rejected. Convinced that a unified aviation authority should be established at the undersecretariat for aviation, the committee viewed Loucheur as an obstacle to achieving what was necessary. The time at which the report was issued also affected its contents.[30]

27. Rapport sur l'aéronautique présenté à la Commission de l'Armée par M. d'Aubigny (Chambre), May 3, 1918, in C, 7502, AN; Minutes, Commission du Budget (Chambre), January 9, 1918, in C, 7560, AN.

28. Rapport sur l'aéronautique présenté à la Commission de l'Armée par M. d'Aubigny (Chambre), May 3, 1918, in C, 7502, AN.

29. Rapport sur l'aéronautique présenté à la Commission de l'Armée par M. d'Aubigny (Chambre), May 3, 1918, in C, 7502, AN.

30. For more on this report and the significance of its timing, see below, pp. 107–108.

Loucheur's efforts failed to produce planes in the numbers anticipated, but it seems likely that without his decisiveness in early 1918, output would not have reached the level it did. Not only was quantity important to him but quality too: for at least one model, he ordered a temporary slowdown to allow quality to be improved.[31] But the army commission's May report focused on the problems. In contrast, General Mordacq, whose views probably represented those of Clemenceau, seemed to think that French air power by April, 1918, was not only impressive but growing steadily stronger month by month.[32] Loucheur could take comfort in knowing that his efforts were appreciated at least within Clemenceau's inner circle. He was generally prepared to handle production and organizational problems because of his business background and technical expertise. But he was much less experienced in another area that became his upon Thomas' departure in September, that of labor relations.

LABOR: A QUESTION MARK

The responsibilities Loucheur assumed in September, 1917, included controlling and administering the labor force classified as working for the national defense. Although he relinquished some of his authority in October by approving the assignment of the general task of civilian worker recruitment to the ministry of labor, he remained the government official at the center of determining and enforcing policies that affected the vast network of workers in defense-related jobs.[33]

He had two major concerns regarding labor through the fall and winter months. One was worker unrest in the aviation industry, beginning with a serious strike shortly after he became minister of armaments. Over the ensuing months, isolated disturbances took place, as well as an important convention of employee representatives. In response, Loucheur, who did not want to provoke serious disorders on the home front, developed a policy that combined conciliation and moderation with firmness and discipline. His second major concern was with the general

---

31. Minutes, Commission du Budget (Chambre), January 9, 1918, in C, 7560, AN.

32. Mordacq, Le Ministère Clemenceau, I, 39.

33. Le Temps, October 20, 1917, p. 3; William Oualid and Charles Picquenard, Salaires et Tarifs: Conventions collectives et grèves (Paris, 1928), 39–40.

conditions of workers' lives, which he sought to improve through such measures as wage increases and cost-of-living adjustments.

Forebodings of French labor unrest were considerable in late 1917, since the number of strikes had risen sharply in 1916 over the previous year and had continued to increase. Thomas devoted much time in 1917 to remedying the situation, beginning with two directives in January that dealt with wages and disputes. One of these attempted to gain some kind of wage uniformity in the armaments industry by setting minimum wage scales for various classifications of workers. Certain industrialists, however, temporized about implementing the salary schedules or ignored them altogether. Thomas, aware that what he had promulgated could engender conflicts, issued a sequel directive meant to circumscribe the ramifications of regulating pay industrywide. It called for the creation of regionally based arbitration commissions, composed of an equal number of representatives from management and labor, to encourage voluntary agreements in labor disputes and, failing that, to issue binding decisions, with penalties. A number of commissions were established, but only a few functioned with any effectiveness. The sole decision any arbitration commission issued in a critical dispute involved the aviation industry, in September, 1917, and ironically, it exacerbated the situation it was trying to calm.[34]

In early February, 1917, Thomas took another step to reduce labor-management tensions. Feeling that many conflicts could have been avoided by communication on a regular basis, he proposed that shop delegates—or shop stewards—be chosen from the ranks of labor to keep communication channels open. His idea was that each delegate would confer regularly with management on worker problems in the part of the plant the delegate came from. The option of implementing the proposal was left to individual factory owners, as were decisions on such matters as workers' voting eligibility. Thomas, who had not obtained parliamentary approval for his plan, had no legal right to make it compulsory. But one thing he tried to make clear from the beginning was that each shop delegate was to limit his activities to his own section of the factory. To go beyond that—with delegate committees, for example—would have run the risk of misunderstandings with orga-

34. Roger Picard, *Le Mouvement syndical durant la guerre* (Paris, 1927), 104–105, 118–20; Oualid and Picquenard, *Salaires et Tarifs*, 454.

nized unions, some of whose leadership had been chary of the idea of delegates from first hearing of it.[35]

Strikes continued, however, and in September, Loucheur faced a walkout of fifty thousand workers in the aviation industry. The strike developed out of the demand for raises that union leaders presented to the armaments minister in June, 1917. Although some manufacturers granted increases, these were much less than demanded. When an arbitration commission for the region of the Seine ruled on some of the issues in dispute, applying its decision to all national defense workers in the Paris region, it declined to pass judgment on the core questions of minimum wages and cost-of-living adjustments. Loucheur ratified the ruling, but the union leaders and the workers came away bitter. Not helping the cause of labor peace were revelations in the Chamber of Deputies of financial abuses and excessive profits by aviation manufacturers arising from their agreements with the government. The workers' resolve hardened to obtain what they considered satisfactory pay raises. Some workers had begun striking even before the arbitration commission's decision became public, but it was afterward that the strike advanced rapidly. The talk of strike spread to other unions, whose leaders endorsed a general sit-down action in the Paris metropolitan region.[36]

While strikers were wondering how the new minister of armaments would respond, Loucheur, uneasy about the workers' feelings toward him, told a group of laborers that he believed the strike was being directed against him personally.[37] He viewed the walkout as in part a protest not only against the departure of Thomas but also against a replacement whose background was in business. It was in any case clear that how he handled the crisis would have decisive consequences for his relationship with labor. He proceeded with his usual practical aplomb.

35. Picard, Le Mouvement syndical, 124; Gilbert Hatry, "Les Délégués d'atelier aux usines Renault," in 1914–1918: L'Autre Front, ed. Patrick Fridenson (Paris, 1977), 223; Bulletin des usines de guerre, September 10, 1917, in 10 N, 2, SHA; Report Dated September 11, 1917, in Series B A, Carton 1375, APP.

36. Oualid and Picquenard, Salaires et Tarifs, 396–97, 454; Report Dated September 11, 1917, in B A, 1375, APP; Yves Merlin, Les Conflits collectifs du travail pendant la guerre, 1914–1918 (Dunkerque, 1928), 15–16; "Situation dans les usines d'aviation," September 22, 1917, in B A, 1375, APP; Documents Relating to Strike Decisions and Discussions in the Aviation Industry, in Subseries F 7, Police Générale, Carton 13366, AN; "Dans les usines de guerre," September 24, 1917, in F 7, 13366, AN.

37. Report Dated September 27, 1917, in F 7, 13366, AN.

His approach was essentially a moderate one: he combined conciliation, understanding, and direct communication, on the one hand, with
firmness and intimidation, on the other. Skeptical union leaders were
pleasantly surprised when he was quick to send an invitation to union
secretaries to meet with him about the causes of the strike, rather than
relying solely on his own staff for data. In another conciliatory gesture,
he announced his commitment to the interior ministry's policy of not
stationing police at the fringes of union meetings.[38]

His invitation was accepted, and he met with both management and
labor on September 26. He assured the labor representatives that the
strikers' demands would get a fair hearing and that wages would be increased where there was justification, but he also warned that his assurances were contingent on the workers' returning to their jobs at once. If
they did not, he would move toward the requisitioning of both workers
and factories. Much to his relief, his conditions met with acceptance the
following day, and work at the strikebound plants resumed on September 28. Loucheur in gratitude decided not to take any reprisals against
the strikers whether they were classified as mobilized servicemen or
not.[39]

The issues of the strike remained, however, and Loucheur engaged
in some long, difficult negotiations with management and labor. The
starting point was a union-forged salary schedule that Alphonse Merrheim, the general secretary of the metallurgical union, gave to Loucheur
at the beginning of October. The industrial negotiators' first reaction
was to reject the workers' proposal and to make the counteroffer of a few
concessions where wages seemed especially low. Loucheur, taking both
sides into account, spelled out a possible wage compromise to the workers' delegates in early November, but they, under the leadership of Merrheim, found the offer insufficient. They questioned, too, the government's ability to break what they regarded as managerial intransigence.
Loucheur followed with another wage package, which included increases for all male and female workers, whether skilled or unskilled,
whose daily pay did not exceed fifteen francs. With this offer came the
admonition that the limit of what could be done had been reached. Both
sides accepted Loucheur's second package, and the crisis formally ended

38. R. Roche to M. Garin, September 26, 1917, *ibid.*
39. Oualid and Picquenard, *Salaires et Tarifs,* 454; Report Dated September 27, 1917,
in B A, 1375, APP; Report Dated September 27, 1917, in F 7, 13366, AN.

when the new wage scales were officially published on November 23, 1917.[40]

One of the paramount issues in the conflict had been cost-of-living adjustments, and Loucheur had shown his concern for those working in the munitions factories by recommending a system that added a fixed sum to daily wages, with the most poorly paid receiving the largest daily cost-of-living increase.[41] The question of the rising cost of living was to occupy him throughout the winter, and even before he concluded negotiations connected with the strike, he brought the issue before an interministerial conference on wage rates. Because he wanted flexibility in cost-of-living adjustments to obviate the need for constant revisions in basic wage rates, he recommended that cost-of-living increases be separate from regular pay scales. Since living expenses were expected to fall after the war, it is reasonable to assume that the cost-of-living bonuses were kept distinct to enable their elimination once economic conditions returned to normal. Loucheur employed this approach in the arbitration decision of November 23 to help the most poorly paid workers and to determine the cost-of-living compensation applicable for a set period of time, and he encouraged his regional manpower inspectors to apply the same principle in negotiations with workers and industrialists when there were legitimate claims for wage revisions because of higher living costs. In February, 1918, he expressed satisfaction with the negotiations there had been on the matter, and he announced that cost-of-living bonuses had been established for the most poorly paid munitions workers at the regional level. But he did not stop there, for in the same document, he requested monthly reports from his manpower inspectors on the existing prices of certain basic commodities, so that he could keep abreast of the relationship between the lowest wages and the cost of living.[42] Loucheur more than likely intended to use that information to make sure that any appreciable imbalance between the two could be adjusted before the outbreak of new labor unrest.

40. "Dans l'aviation," October 4, 1917, in F 7, 13366, AN; Report Dated October 19, 1917, in B A, 1375, APP; Report Dated October 26, 1917, in B A, 1375, APP; "Le Conflit de l'aviation et de l'armement," November 14, 1917, in B A, 1375, APP; Oualid and Picquenard, *Salaires et Tarifs*, 397; *Le Temps*, November 25, 1917, p. 3.

41. Ministry of Armaments Arbitration Decision, November 13, 1917, in F 7, 13366, AN.

42. *Bulletin des usines de guerre*, December 31, 1917, February 18, 1918, both in 10 N, 2, SHA.

The benefits workers received in war-related industries went beyond wages. In December, 1917, for example, Loucheur instituted annual seven-day leaves, with additional travel time, for mobilized workers assigned to locations away from their peacetime home. And the following September, he announced that the weeklong leaves would be granted with pay.[43] Loucheur also showed leniency in the disciplining of recalcitrant workers. Although the available evidence is not great, it tends to confirm that he was sensitive to workers' frustrations. In the spring of 1918, after stoppages occurred at a state construction plant in Bourges, the plant director recommended disciplinary measures, but Loucheur, arguing that workers in all war plants had proved their patriotism by their increased output, decided not to impose sanctions.[44] It appears that Loucheur, appreciating the strains and hardships that workers were enduring, believed that munitions production would fare better if he took a conciliatory, flexible approach to labor unrest rather than impose immediate severe penalties as an example.

Yet there were limits to his flexibility. He took a strong stand against the shop delegates in February, 1918, when he believed them to overstep their prerogatives. In early February, approximately a thousand delegates from the Paris area convened to discuss the war, and they passed a resolution calling for a peace without annexations.[45] On February 21, Loucheur circulated his repudiation of the convention's results and reaffirmed the proper role of the delegates: "Shop delegates were created in factories in order to facilitate the relations of workers in a *shop* or *a special function* with the management of an establishment. The functions of shop delegates can be exercised only within the walls of the factory, and the exchanges of view that take place at the factory between management and the delegates can have no echo whatsoever beyond."[46] Not only did he deem the delegates out of bounds in taking under consideration an issue that had nothing to do with operations in their factories but he held that they exceeded their mandate in joining together as a group to discuss any issues at all. Matters of a corporate order concerning workers were the legitimate domain of labor unions. Loucheur's remarks had the effect of

43. *Bulletin des usines de guerre*, December 17, 1917, September 23, 1918, both *ibid.*
44. General Gages to Louis Loucheur, March 26, 1918, Louis Loucheur to General Gages, April 1, 1918, both in 6 N, 149, SHA.
45. *L'Usine*, February 3, 1918, p. 1.
46. *Bulletin des usines de guerre*, March 4, 1918, in 10 N, 2, SHA.

underlining the shop delegates' role as merely practical agents for confronting small, local problems inside munitions plants before tensions reached more serious proportions.

The scheme of shop delegates had been controversial from its inception and segments of the business community, fearing the spread of bolshevism in the wake of Russia's November revolution, compared the meeting of delegates in Paris to that of a Russian workers' soviet.[47] The document Loucheur circulated on February 21 gave some reassurance to the industrialists, but the fear must have lingered about initiatives by the delegates.

The labor unions, too, had reservations about shop delegates. Some union officials, like Léon Jouhaux, the reform-minded general secretary of the Confédération Générale du Travail (CGT), endorsed Loucheur's effort to keep the delegate scheme functioning according to Thomas' original purpose. They held that the system posed no problem for labor as long as the delegates remained subordinate to the unions. But other labor leaders feared that some industrialists might try to supplant the unions with the delegates. They believed that the advantages of the delegate system were more than offset by the potential damage to worker solidarity and union power.[48] The fears and misunderstandings are not surprising, for the idea of shop delegates was conceived when tensions were high, and clarifications about their role were necessary on several occasions.[49] It seemed inevitable that the system would sooner or later come under concerted attack. That day arrived in the wake of a serious strike in May, 1918 (see below, pp. 89–91).

Loucheur's responsibilities regarding labor changed dramatically after Thomas' departure, for he suddenly had to control and administer a labor force of well over 1.5 million.[50] With labor, the challenge facing him was less that of taming a government bureaucracy, as was the case in munitions production and raw materials, than of getting a handle on a human problem with dimensions going far beyond forecasts, stopgap expedients, reliable solutions, and efficiency. On top of that, Loucheur had to take the place of a man whose solid reputation among the workers at first seemed to deepen labor's suspicions about his own business background. The way he comported himself was essentially pragmatic, but

47. L'Usine, February 3, 1918, p. 1.
48. Picard, Le Mouvement syndical, 129–30.
49. Hatry, "Les Délégués d'atelier aux usines Renault," 223.
50. Oualid and Picquenard, Salaires et Tarifs, 45.

with a humanitarian concern. Some of the steps he took during the conflict in the interest of human welfare prefigured measures he pushed after the war, such as the housing law of the 1920s known as the Loi Loucheur. But though a humanitarian spirit was present in him during the war, it was never predominant. His chief preoccupation was always to keep the factories producing without interruption.

COAL: A PROGRAM TESTED

After the structural reordering that put Loucheur in charge of assuring France's coal supplies, he had to operate, as in other areas, on a day-to-day basis. The French, remembering the previous winter's shortages and hardships, had little confidence in the government's capacity to do better in the months ahead. One of Loucheur's highest concerns was, of necessity, the French coal link with Britain. In late 1917 and early 1918, when Allied efforts to achieve closer cooperation were growing, Loucheur and other French officials were frustrated by Britain's determination to follow its own view on how best to allot its shipping capacity and its coal. Loucheur worked with Clemenceau and others to convince the British bureaucracy that an agreement satisfactory to all the Allies needed to be reached quickly. The British appeared to the French to be ignoring France's interests. The creation of a shipping pool is today the best-known instance of close Allied cooperation behind the front lines, but cooperation was sought as well in the more rational distribution of coal and other raw materials. Domestically, what was most pressing for Loucheur was the maintenance of adequate coal supplies to sustain the Allied military effort and to prevent a decline in public morale.

During the summer of 1917, Loucheur attempted to rationalize Allied coal shipments in order to make better use of available shipping tonnage. He proposed sending coal to Italy by rail from mines in southern France in exchange for an equivalent amount from Britain to France. The idea was introduced at the London conference of August, 1917, and a Franco-British agreement was reached, subject to further discussions with Italian representatives.[51]

51. Memorandum sur la situation de la France au point de vue du charbon, January 10, 1918, in FO 382/2078, File 1398, PRO; Clémentel, *La France et la Politique économique*, 335–36.

The French were in favor of a more comprehensive approach among the Allies in a variety of spheres. Etienne Clémentel, who spearheaded much of the drive toward Allied cooperation, complained that up to then only narrowly defined agreements of a temporary nature had been reached; he wanted to see a greater unification in the way the Allies shouldered their economic burdens. Loucheur, too, wanted to improve Allied cooperation. Thus, the tripartite coal plan was discussed again when the Allies met in Paris in late November and early December to lay the foundations for the Allied Maritime Transport Council, eventually the symbol of Allied economic unity and cooperation. The accord the Allies reached had France shipping between 150,000 and 200,000 tons of French coal from Marseille to Genoa in Italian vessels. The British were to replace what the French exported by making deliveries to Rouen and Bordeaux.[52]

The issue seemingly settled, Loucheur began shipments to Italy, but these were far from relieving the dire need there. Of the 700,000 tons a month that Italy judged the minimum it required, it was receiving only between 300,000 and 400,000 from all sources. Thus, the Italian government made a plea to the British for more, explaining that otherwise Italy would probably have to abandon its war effort.[53]

In view of the critical situation in Italy and the scarcity of Allied shipping capacity, the British felt exempted from providing coal to France equivalent to what France sent to Italy. In the agreement reached in Paris, Britain had committed itself to replacing the coal if the loss of it hurt France's ability to meet national allocations. But the British believed that the sharp increase in France's domestic production over the previous twelve months enabled French aid to the Italians without compensatory supplies from Britain.[54] They thought the French could send 150,000 tons of coal a month to Italy, and even increase that to 300,000 tons in the near term.

In January, 1918, in the middle of intense discussions between French and British officials abut this, Loucheur sent a memorandum to

52. Clémentel, *La France et la Politique économique,* 219–20, 228.
53. Note du Ministère des Affaires Etrangères à l'ambassade d'Angleterre, December 19, 1917, in F 12, 7785, AN; David Lloyd George to Georges Clemenceau, December 20, 1917, in FO 382/2078, File 1398, PRO.
54. Note du Ministère des Affaires Etrangères à l'ambassade d'Angleterre, December 19, 1917, in F 12, 7785, AN; Minutes of the War Cabinet, December 20, 1917, in CAB 23/4 (303), PRO.

the British Foreign Office on the conditions regarding coal in France. He characterized the situation as "extremely tense and precarious" and stressed that France had reached the limit of sacrifice. Should something alter the delicate balance in supplies, a catastrophe could occur, he said, with dire consequences for the Allies. He pointed out that although production had increased in France, the overall quality of the available coal had decreased because of the scarcity of the better grades from Britain. The situation of France's coal was not measurably better than in 1916, he maintained, and in the time since the beginning of that year France had failed to achieve a balance between supply and demand. Since the necessary British shipping capacity had been freed by France's deliveries to Italy, Loucheur urged Britain to begin making compensatory deliveries.[55]

Loucheur may have exaggerated to make his point, but the evidence supports the general assessment in his January memorandum. In the Chamber of Deputies, Antoine Drivet pointed out that the quality of some of the coal mined in France was so poor that the gross French production figures needed a downward revision of 10 to 15 percent; Loucheur agreed with his assessment. And Clémentel largely substantiated Loucheur's position when, in his book about France and the development of wartime Allied economic cooperation, he described the numerous problems the Allies faced during the winter of 1917–1918. He joined Loucheur in judging that there was an important gap between need and supply in France, estimating the supply shortfall to be between 500,000 and 600,000 tons a month.[56]

Because the description Loucheur gave the British Foreign Office contrasted significantly with what the population in France had been led to believe, he stressed the importance of confidentiality.[57] The British remained skeptical of French alarms, however, and the two countries continued for several weeks to quarrel over what it was appropriate for Britain to do respecting France's transport of coal to Italy. In early February, the British ambassador in Paris, reporting on his discussion of

55. Memorandum sur la situation de la France au point de vue du charbon, January 10, 1918, in FO 382/2078, File 1398, PRO.

56. Olivier, *La Politique du charbon*, 155–56; Clémentel, *La France et la Politique économique*, 235–38.

57. Aimé de Fleuriau to Foreign Office, January 19, 1918, in FO 382/2078, File 1398, PRO.

the question with Clemenceau that day, described the French premier as "despondent, preoccupied, and angered about coal."[58] When the British in mid-February proposed that the French supply a substantial amount of coal to Italy without compensatory deliveries, Clemenceau fumed that France was expected to "subsist with 3.5 million tons of coal a month, of which most is made up of mediocre quality, . . . while the current consumption in Great Britain surpasses 15 million tons of good quality."[59]

Wrangling persisted until mid-March, when the Allies convened in London for the first session of the Allied Maritime Transport Council. With Loucheur and Clémentel representing France, a provisional agreement was reached with Britain and Italy whereby the French would supply Italy with 350,000 tons of French coal between March 15 and April 15 while Britain would dispatch an equivalent amount to France between March 15 and April 30. The agreement was for only a brief period because of the Allied awareness of the situation's fluidity. The transport of coal to Italy after April was to be considered at another meeting of the council, scheduled for early April.[60] Loucheur's aspiration to reorganize Allied coal supply routes in the interest of efficiency had produced a tripartite coal agreement, and his prominent role in the process and his effectiveness as a negotiator were not lost on Clemenceau.

Loucheur was fortunate in having strong support in parliament and among the press for his coal policies as the winter of 1917–1918 approached. On the Left, for example, the Socialist newspaper *L'Humanité* congratulated him in November on overcoming the obstinate resistance of the Senate to a comprehensive coal plan without provoking hostile comment from the newspaper *Le Temps*. *L'Humanité* took satisfaction that the state-controlled system it had called for as early as the first winter of the war had finally come into being.[61]

L'Usine, which represented the interests of industrialists and commercial firms, was more cautious in its views. Keeping its readers informed of the coal situation on a weekly basis, the newspaper com-

58. Telegram Lord Bertie to Foreign Office, February 6, 1918, in FO 382/2079, File 1398, PRO.

59. Georges Clemenceau to Lord Robert Cecil, February 19, 1918, *ibid.*

60. Memorandum sur la question du charbon, n.d., with cover letter Aimé de Fleuriau to Lord Robert Cecil, March 18, 1918, in FO 382/2078, File 1398, PRO; Clémentel, *La France et la Politique économique*, 245–46.

61. *L'Humanité* (Paris), November 18, 1917, p. 2.

plained in the fall that reserves were inadequate and that there were flaws in the operation of Loucheur's system. *L'Usine* began to change its tone in January—the very month Loucheur was secretly telling the British that the crisis was more serious than the government was admitting publicly—and to present a more optimistic picture. The arrival of warm weather influenced it. At the end of January, it noted that the dramatic jump in temperature, from $-10°$ C to $+17°$ C, meant that less coal was needed for home heating, leaving more for industries unrelated to defense. *L'Usine* continued to report an improvement during February, and as the winter drew to a close, its enthusiasm for Loucheur's handling of the crisis waxed.[62] Toward the middle of February it wrote, "Well, Mr. Armaments Minister, you have proved yourself, and your distribution plan for combustibles—apart from a few criticisms that you know to be just—has produced better results than your critics expected. Intensify your efforts for the second year of its application, and we will applaud you with both hands."[63]

In dealing with French public opinion, Loucheur was careful not to present the total picture but to highlight that his program was working and there would be enough coal to get France through the winter.[64] He was trying to keep up public morale as France went through its fourth winter of the war, and his secrecy was not a sign of weakness or panic but a calculated response.

STEEL: A CONTINUING CRISIS

Shortly after Loucheur became armaments minister, a report on steel by the Chamber's army commission sharply criticized him for not keeping on schedule the domestic steel program that had been launched in January to augment production. The report also took him to task for what it considered an overreliance on foreign steel to meet France's needs. It concluded, "Whatever decisions are made, they cannot effectively remedy a situation created by nearly three years of inertia. At the very moment successive governments were proclaiming their determination to carry on the war 'to the very end,' they failed to

62. *L'Usine*, January 27, 1918, p. 9, February 24, 1918, p. 21.
63. *Ibid.*, February 10, 1918, p. 7.
64. France, *Annales de la Chambre: Débats*, October 29, 1917, pp. 2927–28.

make the decisions on which their affirmations of the 'certainty of victory' should have rested."[65] The commission's report, which showed little cognizance of the extent of Loucheur's problems during the first eight months of 1917, provoked an immediate response from the ministry of armaments. Loucheur's department attributed the problems in steel production to the unfavorable conditions besetting the nation. The greatest impairments were the shortage of manpower, the lack of coal, and the insufficiency of transportation. The very length of the rebuttal—sixteen pages—evinces Loucheur's sensitivity to criticism at a moment when, just having become minister of armaments, he was under attack from several quarters. When he appeared before the army commission in early December, he explained that the steel construction programs were completed but that production still lagged as a result of coal and manpower shortages.[66]

It was obvious to both Loucheur and the army commission that a continued dependence on Great Britain and the United States for steel was certain, and during the fall and winter, he took steps to ensure France an adequate supply from those two sources. In September, he met with Winston Churchill in Paris, following up their discussions in London the previous month. Churchill warned that the British would have to reduce the amount of shell steel they produced for France, but he eased French anxieties somewhat when he added that the British shipping controller would provide the capacity for delivering fifty thousand tons of shell steel to France from the United States in October and twice that in November. The two ministers met again in October to formalize and extend the September understanding. What Loucheur referred to as the Churchill Convention conceded as well the capacity for shipping to France fifty thousand tons of American shell steel in December and sixty thousand tons in January.[67]

While Loucheur tried to shore up France's steel supplies during the fall, his munitions programs came under increasing threat from an

65. Rapport sur l'acier présenté par M. Dalbiez, Commission de l'Armée (Chambre), n.d., with cover letter to Louis Loucheur dated September 19, 1917, in 10 N, 3, SHA.

66. Response of Loucheur to Dalbiez Report of September, 1917, n.d., *ibid.*; Minutes, Commission de l'Armée (Chambre), December 7, 1917, in C, 7499, AN.

67. Note faisant connaître les observations suggérées par les résolutions adoptées par la Commission du Budget de la Chambre des Députés le 31 décembre 1917, ministry of armaments to Georges Clemenceau, January 25, 1918, in 10 N, 37, SHA.

acute shortage of grain. The proportions of the deficiency were clearly laid out in a memorandum that Painlevé, the French premier, sent to David Lloyd George, the British prime minister, on October 9: "The grain situation of the Allies, and that of France in particular, is at present so critical that it risks putting in jeopardy the result of the war. For three months, France has lived from day to day and even from hour to hour upon what has come to it. The reserves for Paris and the large centers are enough for one day, those of the army for from one to three days. A number of localities have already had flour shortages, and such incidents are multiplying."[68] Loucheur was partly responsible for the magnitude of the crisis, for by insisting on ships for transporting steel during June and July, he had got a certain amount of tonnage reassigned from grain. To forestall a major catastrophe, he had to turn back to the ministry of supplies the shipping a French interministerial commission had allotted him for North Atlantic transport. The grain crisis also sheds light on why, during the last quarter of 1917, British deliveries of American shell steel fell far short of what the Churchill Convention specified.[69]

Loucheur could take comfort, however, in seeing how the food crisis prompted serious negotiations on pooling the shipping capacity of Britain, France, and Italy. Clémentel, who championed the principle of equal sacrifice as a means of helping France get through the winter, instigated the discussions. The most pressing matter was food, and Clémentel wanted the three European allies to pool their transport resources for the importation of such essential commodities as wheat. The talks that took place during October and early November resulted in the Agreement of November 3, 1917, which, though in many ways vague, enunciated the readiness of the three powers to provide tonnage for food "proportionally to the respective means of transport." In practice, this meant that the signatories would have to compute their combined shipping potential and then determine how much to allot for food imports. Such a procedure practically eliminated the distinction between foodstuffs and other imports, since the tonnage allotments were to be based on an assessment of the three nations' joint overall import

68. Clémentel, *La France et la Politique économique*, 172.
69. *Ibid.*, 170, 185; Note faisant connaître les observations suggérées par les résolutions adoptées par la Commission du Budget de la Chambre des Députés le 31 décembre 1917, ministry of armaments to Clemenceau, January 25, 1918, in 10 N, 37, SHA.

needs. The accord was therefore a significant acceptance of pooling in the employment of tonnage.[70]

The delegates from the Allied powers who met in Paris beginning on November 29 established an organizational mechanism that they charged with creating a nucleus of close Allied economic cooperation. The result was the Allied Maritime Transport Council, which formally met for the first time in March, 1918. It was in this system that Loucheur worked, even to the point of serving as a member of the council.[71]

Loucheur was facing short supplies of steel in part because Britain, lacking shipping tonnage, had prevailed on France to agree to a drastic reduction in what it expected from across the Channel in 1918. Ernest Mercier, representing Loucheur at a meeting of the Interministerial Metals and War Manufactures Commission (CIM), announced on February 27 that imports from Britain, expected to be about thirty-five thousand tons a month through March, would drop sharply thereafter and stand at approximately sixteen thousand tons a month beginning in June. In addition, he disclosed that Britain, an important source of shell steel in 1917, was discontinuing indefinitely the export of that grade to France; the French were going to have to rely on their own production of twenty thousand tons monthly and on what they could import from America. Arrivals of American shell steel had fallen because of the British failure to comply with the tonnage schedules of the Churchill Convention and because of the dearth of French shipping capacity.[72] By February, Loucheur was projecting an overall decrease of 30 percent in the availability of metallurgical products in general from a year earlier. That put anticipated resources 40 percent below the minimum anticipated requirements for the production programs of the various government ministries. Bringing the problem before the French Comité de Guerre, Loucheur recommended that a major reassessment of manufacturing programs using metallurgical products be conducted either with the direct involvement of Clemenceau or under an authority consti-

70. James Arthur Salter, *Allied Shipping Control: An Experiment in International Administration* (Oxford, 1921), 148–49.

71. *Ibid.*, 151–55; Clémentel, *La France et la Politique économique*, 243–44.

72. Commission Interministérielle des Métaux et des Fabrications de Guerre, February 27, 1918, in Subseries F 30, Administration Centrale du Ministère des Finances, Carton 1501, MF.

tuted by the Comité de Guerre. In early April, the Comité began to carry out the reassessment itself.[73]

Meanwhile, Loucheur had high hopes for obtaining increasing amounts of steel from the United States. His hopes stemmed in part from an agreement made the previous summer, whereby the French agreed to provide artillery to American forces arriving in Europe in exchange for raw materials. The effects of the agreement were evident in February, 1918, when 82,000 tons of steel arrived from the United States, well above the amount of previous months. In March, the quantity rose to 122,000 tons.[74]

Loucheur became embroiled in a domestic controversy over the role of the Comité des Forges and the Comptoir d'Exportation des Produits Métallurgiques as the government's agents for securing and distributing iron and steel products. At the beginning of the fall of 1917, the government was using the Comité des Forges as the sole purchaser and distributor of British pig-iron products and as its distributing agent for state-purchased American and French pig iron. By a decision of August 31, 1917, the government made the Comptoir d'Exportation the sole French representative in the purchase of British steel products. Ties between the two agencies were close, since the Comptoir's primary function before the war had been to promote the export of metallurgical products from firms largely affiliated with the Comité. Criticism, especially from users of such products, had already been leveled against state intervention and the government's reliance upon the Comité des Forges, but the decision of August 31 incited a new assault on the system.[75]

The leader of the campaign for decontrol and against the Comité des

73. Minutes, Comité de Guerre, April 6, 1918, in Subseries 3 N, Comité de Guerre, Carton 2, SHA. The Comité de Guerre, comprising the ministers of war, finance, marine, armaments, and foreign affairs, was created by Briand at the end of 1916. Many, especially in parliament, hoped that it would oversee the general conduct of the war in the same fashion as the British War Cabinet, but, in contrast to its cross-Channel counterpart, it never developed into a powerful decision-making body. Most questions it dealt with were submitted to the French Council of Ministers for approval. See Renouvin, *The Forms of War Government*, 92–94.

74. Minutes, Commission de l'Armée (Chambre), April 5, 1918, in C, 7500, AN; Minutes, Commission du Budget: Sous-Commission des Armements (Chambre), September 6, 1918, in 94 AP, 57, AN; Edward M. Coffman, *The War to End All Wars: The American Military Experience in World War I* (New York, 1968), 40.

75. Pinot, *Le Comité des Forges*, 115–18, 122, 143–44, 298–303, 15–18; Jeanneney, *François de Wendel*, 70–71.

Forges was Jules Niclausse, president of the Syndicat des Mécaniciens, Chaudronniers et Fondeurs, an employers' association. Niclausse was concerned about the injury that iron and steel shortages were inflicting upon private industries that were not defense-related. At a meeting with Clémentel on September 3, he pointed out that unemployment in the industries his association represented had grown alarmingly and that, absent concessions, the association's members stood to be at a disadvantage against foreign competition after the war. Blaming the ministry of armaments for their plight, Niclausse sought the restoration of the right to import raw materials without passing through a central authority. He contended that the outcome would be lower prices and greater quantities of imported iron and steel.[76]

Niclausse' campaign caused the Chamber of Deputies' tariff commission to hold hearings during the winter. Witnesses included Robert Pinot and Loucheur, both of whom defended the government's control measures. Loucheur, testifying in late January, 1918, argued that in view of the intensification of German submarine warfare in 1917, restrictions and centralization for steel products coming from Britain were in order; thus the Comptoir d'Exportation was called upon to serve as the government's centralizing agent for British steel. Challenging Niclausse' optimism about the free market, he suggested that if members of the Syndicat des Mécaniciens, Chaudronniers et Fondeurs could find a few tons of steel in Britain on their own, it would be at double the price then being charged by the British, who were in accord with the French wish to avoid the inflation that competition among the Allies would ignite. Loucheur asserted that the Comité des Forges had been extremely useful in organizing French industry in the initial stages of the conflict. But at the same time that he disclaimed any grounds for personal dissatisfaction with the Comité's having responsibility concerning British metallurgical products, he acknowledged the difficulties involved in requiring competitors of the Comité to use its services when obtaining British iron. Admitting that the ideal entity for centralizing purchases was the state itself, in virtue of its impartiality, he added that that channel did not exist.[77]

Nevertheless, Loucheur had for a while been considering whether a

76. Jules Niclausse to Etienne Clémentel, November 8, 1917, in F 12, 7673, AN.
77. Minutes, Commission des Douanes (Chambre), December 28, 1917, January 24, 1918, both in 94 AP, 233, AN.

state agency might replace the Comité des Forges in purchasing and distributing foreign metallurgical products. He thought that the CIM could take on the job, but he also realized that for it to be able to, a financial mechanism would be needed to accept consumer payments and forward them to the foreign seller. Loucheur discussed the idea in a letter to the finance minister in December and proposed that the financial transactions be handled through a special treasury account. The finance minister was agreeable to Loucheur's initiative but reminded him that a law was necessary to create such an account.[78]

Loucheur had already directed Mercier to investigate a state-controlled and operated system, and in early January, Mercier's report went to the ministry of commerce. The date shows that Mercier was in contact with Loucheur in the latter part of December to give him the results of his study. Although Mercier concentrated on the Comptoir d'Exportation, he presented his impressions on the overall system of metallurgical purchases and distribution, including the Comité des Forges. Aware that Loucheur wished the state to assume directly the authority it had granted the Comptoir d'Exportation to import steel, Mercier nonetheless rehearsed the merits of the established system and the problems connected with a transfer of responsibilities. In the Comptoir's favor were its experience, the backing it had from the Comité des Forges, and the widespread business relationships in which it was a participant. Moreover, it allowed far more flexibility in finances and payments than any state-run apparatus would, even with the creation of a special treasury account. Mercier's recommendation was that the organization and functions of the Comptoir be maintained, especially under certain modifications that he felt critics would accept.[79]

Informed of what Mercier's recommendations would be and facing an extremely difficult metallurgical situation, Loucheur wrote to Pinot on December 31, 1917. He declared his intention to make the state the sole buyer of domestically produced pig iron and expressed his wish to use the Comité des Forges to distribute it subject to the control of his ministry. His plan was for the Comité to play the same part regarding all pig iron that it then played regarding some, namely, that imported from

78. Louis Lucien Klotz to Louis Loucheur, December 21, 1917, in F 30, 1500, MF.

79. Note au sujet de la centralisation des commandes de produits métallurgiques, n.d., with attached note Ernest Mercier to Monsieur le Capitaine Guillet, January 3, 1917 [sic; the year was 1918], in F 12, 7673, AN.

Britain and the United States and that manufactured in France and purchased by the state. Loucheur believed that this would enable industrialists to know more certainly how much pig iron they could expect each month. He also made clear in his letter that he expected to use his instrumentalities to arrive at contracts with producers that would aim at uniform consumer prices for each grade of iron made in America, Britain, and France. He set March 31 as the effective date for the new policy, and he asked Pinot to relay the contents of his letter to iron consumers.[80]

Not unexpectedly, Niclausse sharply attacked Loucheur's plan. He questioned the wisdom of passing even more power into the hands of the Comité des Forges and complained that industrialists who had managed to avoid working with the Comité until then faced the prospect of having to participate in the system however much that went against their will.[81] It was obvious that Loucheur's letter of December 31 had done much to keep alive the controversy regarding the wartime role of the Comité des Forges.

The strong opposition from Niclausse and his allies deterred Loucheur from pushing ahead. In February, however, he was still writing of his preference for letting the Comité des Forges have a role, because it was already in place and did what it was appointed to do.[82] After the uproar subsided, he renewed his effort to implement the plan he had outlined to Pinot. But it did not go into effect on March 31; he was forced to accept a postponement.

SUCCESS OUT OF TURMOIL

In spite of all Loucheur's problems, the minister had a positive report to make to the Chamber's budget commission in early December, 1917, regarding production between September 1 and December 1. In September, responding to Pétain's expanded request for artillery, Loucheur had devised a new production strategy that projected completing Pétain's requisition by April 1. Loucheur told the commission that, apart from two models, the 145-mm. and 155-mm. modèle 76, his production schedules had been approached or surpassed. Especially important was the output

80. Pinot, Le Comité des Forges, 281–83.
81. Jules Niclausse to Etienne Clémentel, January 28, 1918, in F 12, 7673, AN.
82. Louis Loucheur to Etienne Clémentel, February 20, 1918, ibid.

of the 155-mm. Court, emphasized by the army; this had gone well over Loucheur's prediction of 472, with 547 produced. He could gloat that since artillery-shell production was more than adequate to meet the demand for certain calibers, he was going to be able to reduce output in order to conserve steel.[83]

Loucheur's statistics confirm that his artillery and shell programs were generally on schedule. Brought into the government in part to intensify heavy-artillery production, Loucheur was meeting the expectations of those who had placed their confidence in him. Even an outsider like Winston Churchill appreciated what Loucheur had done, commenting in the fall of 1917 that the French heavy-artillery program had come into its own and that by April, 1918, the French would have nine thousand modern guns and the assurance of receiving large monthly deliveries. He added, "Our comparable figure in the field in France will be approaching 8,000, which is the maximum establishment that our army has at present arranged for. Our infantry will not therefore be quite so well supported with artillery as the French."[84]

In the light of the numerous problems Loucheur confronted, his performance during the fall and winter of 1917–1918 was impressive. He assumed responsibilities in the aviation industry with a view toward improving product quantity and quality, he continued turning out heavy-artillery guns and shells in numbers that approached or surpassed program projections, and he began to give more attention to tanks. He kept France supplied with enough coal to meet minimum needs, he established an acceptable rapport with labor, and he played a key role in developing the Allied economic unity that Clémentel and he concurred was essential to victory in the war. As for his political career, these months were a turning point, for his accomplishments and personal qualities won him not only the respect of many political professionals and an important segment of public opinion but also the esteem and friendship of the man who was to be a prime force behind his rise as a full-fledged politician in 1919—Georges Clemenceau.

83. Minutes, Commission du Budget: Sous-Commission des Armements (Chambre), December 6, 1917, in C, 7560, AN.
84. Winston Churchill, The World Crisis, 1916–1918 (2 vols.; New York, 1927), II, 29.

5

THE FINAL MONTHS OF WAR, 1918

At 4:40 A.M. on March 21, 1918, a calm on the western front was shattered when the Germans launched an intensive artillery barrage at the point where the British defense lines joined the French. The bombardment lasted five hours and was succeeded by an infantry thrust that quickly drove a wedge between the British and French forces. On March 22, the heavy bombing of the French military headquarters at Compiègne forced the staff there to turn its attention to its own safe relocation and away from the rapidly changing battle scene. And on March 23 the German extra-long guns called Big Berthas began shelling Paris every fifteen minutes. Many Parisians fled the city rather than expose themselves to the rapidly increasing threat from the east. Even within the French government, preparations were made to flee at a moment's notice and to resettle in Tours. In the March drive the Germans sought to divide the French and British forces permanently and to make them capitulate in open fighting before they could benefit from the arrival of American troops.[1]

The Allied military situation remained unstable through the ensuing weeks, and Loucheur found himself confronted with a new crisis, for as the Germans advanced, the Allies shifted transportation priorities to troops and military supplies, thereby disrupting the delivery network for coal and other materials. What is more, with Paris once again threatened, he had to make plans to relocate critical industries to other parts of France. He was faced as well with serious labor unrest during May. As the overall situation of the Allies seemed to deteriorate during the

---

1. Cyril Falls, *The Great War* (New York, 1961), 331–32; Geoffrey Bruun, *Clemenceau* (Hamden, Conn., 1962), 148; Ferro, *The Great War*, 215.

spring, Loucheur suffered a new round of attacks within the government. Although some of his problems receded during the summer, when the Allies began pushing the Germans back, he remained under pressure to keep munitions production at a high level, especially since the general expectation was that the war would extend into 1919. Coal, steel, labor, and munitions production, in their linkage, continued to be at the center of Loucheur's preoccupations during the last months of the war. Shortly after the Germans began their March offensive, however, the French and British, galvanized by the military crisis, decided on a unified military high command for the two powers. It was Loucheur's role in connection with this that exhibits the close relationship he had by then achieved with Clemenceau.[2]

LOUCHEUR, CLEMENCEAU, AND A UNIFIED HIGH COMMAND

Loucheur gained Clemenceau's respect and friendship in the months following the ministerial crisis of November, 1917. As armaments minister, Loucheur had almost daily meetings with Clemenceau. That gave him an important advantage, since outside of Stephen Pichon, the foreign minister, he was the only cabinet member to have personal contact of that frequency with the premier. At the outset of their working relationship, however, Clemenceau had less than complete confidence in Loucheur, in part because of rumors about his being a war profiteer who, as minister of armaments, would hand out lucrative contracts to others.[3] Clemenceau's reservations faded as he came to appreciate the armaments minister's optimistic views, political skills, production expertise, and energetic spirit in undertaking assignments. There was a natural affinity between the two, since they were both preeminently men of action rather than words. Loucheur's qualities, joined with his ability to make his own worth known, gained him the full confidence and friendship of Clemenceau, to the point where the premier used the French term of affection *mon petit* when talking to him.[4]

Loucheur was already acquainted with the idea of an Allied unified

2. Poincaré, *Au service de la France*, IX, 371.

3. For a discussion of war profiteering, see below, pp. 200–201.

4. Lloyd George, *War Memoirs*, V, 197; Mermeix [pseud.], *Le Combat des trois: Notes et Documents sur la conférence de paix* (Paris, 1922), 133–35.

high command. At a meeting of the Comité de Guerre, in October, his enthusiastic endorsement had helped Premier Painlevé win consent for establishing an inter-Allied war committee, as a first step toward the creation of a unified high command.[5] Loucheur later wrote that he provided the key support for a unified approach to military operations at the October meeting and immediately thereafter: "[Painlevé] followed me at first, and then (as was quite natural, since he was the head of the government) he preceded me."[6] Loucheur's enthusiasm for the proposal, which was under discussion in several quarters during September and early October, was related to his interest in seeing close Allied cooperation in other spheres: he was working for greater Allied economic unity at the same time. Loucheur went to London in October as part of a delegation led by Painlevé to discuss closer military cooperation with the British, but the key negotiations were handled on the French side by Painlevé and Henry Franklin-Bouillon, appointed shortly before as a minister of state.[7]

Loucheur was one of the leading figures in the drive that led to the formation of a Supreme War Council in early November. Given the task of coordinating the military operations of the war, the council proved less effective than a unified high command would have been, but it was the best mechanism that could be devised in the circumstances. Its weakness was apparent at the time of Germany's March offensive, when neither Philippe Pétain nor Field Marshal Sir Douglas Haig, the commander of the British Expeditionary Force in France, was willing to turn over to the council the reserve forces it demanded.[8] When the Germans struck, an effective unified authority over the movements of the Allied forces was still missing.

In the following days, Loucheur's close ties to Clemenceau and his interest in a unified high command made him a participant in events that culminated in a historic meeting of French and British representatives at Doullens on March 26. On March 24, Clemenceau sent him to review the military situation with Pétain, who expressed doubts to him about the

5. Typewritten Account About the Unified High Command, by Paul Painlevé, 1928 or 1929, in Subseries 313 AP, Paul Painlevé Papers, Carton 104, AN.

6. Louis Loucheur to Comtesse de Courville, August 14, 1922, in Louis Loucheur Papers 10/C, HI.

7. *Ibid.*; Lloyd George, *War Memoirs*, IV, 549–50.

8. Loucheur to Comtesse de Courville, August 14, 1922, in Louis Loucheur Papers 10/C; Falls, *The Great War*, 310, 334.

Allies' chances of holding back the Germans. During the talk, Loucheur stressed the importance of maintaining contact with the British forces. Unable to reach Clemenceau that evening after his return to Paris, Loucheur discussed Pétain's assessment with Ferdinand Foch, then serving as the French army chief of staff. Foch, pacing back and forth in Loucheur's office "like a lion in a cage," professed confidence in the Allied forces. But he was critical of Pétain, holding that the commander in chief, though skilled at executing campaigns, was ungifted in strategy. He also mentioned an earlier conversation that day with Clemenceau in which he had impressed on the premier the need for a unified high command.[9]

The next morning, Loucheur related his conversations to Clemenceau on their way to see President Poincaré at the Elysée palace. At that meeting, the three men agreed on the absolute necessity of closing the breach between the British and French forces as quickly as possible. Loucheur was sent to Pétain's headquarters to learn what preparations he had made in that regard and to help arrange an afternoon meeting with Lord Milner, the British secretary of state for war.[10]

When Loucheur met with Pétain in the early afternoon of the same day, he still found the French commander gloomy:

> [Pétain] reflects on what would happen if the French and English armies are separated: the English army will fall back on Calais and defend its bases. The French army could remain in its present trenches between Soissons and Alsace with one diversionary line descending from Soissons south as far as it could. That means a quasi surrender of all of France and the almost complete cutoff of provisions. I point out to him that it is necessary to do everything possible to keep from arriving at such a stage; in order to do so, we must move as many troops from the east of France as necessary. He tells me he has already done that. He tells me that the severity of the Oise battle has made him very anxious and that Clemenceau should be pressured to ask for peace.[11]

At the late-afternoon meeting with Milner, however, Pétain, who was present with Poincaré, Clemenceau, Loucheur, and Foch, sounded more

9. Loucheur, *Carnets secrets*, 52–53, 178; Guy Pedroncini, *Pétain: Général en chef, 1917–1918* (Paris, 1974), 331.

10. Loucheur, *Carnets secrets*, 53–54; Richard Griffiths, *Marshal Pétain* (London, 1970), 70.

11. Loucheur, *Carnets secrets*, 179.

optimistic, describing how he was in the process of shifting several French divisions to help the beleaguered British forces. When the French asked Milner what the British intended to do to ensure the complete cooperation of the two countries' armies, he made no commitment but spoke of his need to confer with Haig and General Henry Wilson, the chief of the Imperial general staff.[12]

As agreed, the two sides met the next morning at Doullens—Haig, Wilson, Milner, and Sir Herbert Lawrence, Haig's chief of staff, for the British; and Clemenceau, Poincaré, Loucheur, Foch, and Pétain for the French. The formula they arrived at on the basis of suggestions from Milner and Haig in support of Foch, empowered Foch to coordinate the efforts of both armies.[13] Loucheur's personal contribution that day was to make two copies of the original text at the request of Clemenceau. As the meeting ended, Poincaré declared, "I believe, gentlemen, that we have taken an important step toward victory."[14] Foch soon moved reinforcements to the battle zone, and the breach between the French and British forces was closed. On April 5, the Germans shut down their offensive and began looking elsewhere to attack.[15]

Loucheur's role in the events that led to the decisive meeting at Doullens was more substantial than his contribution at the meeting itself. He had worked in behalf of Foch in 1917, championing him for an important post in Allied decision making during the Anglo-French meetings of October in London. In view of Loucheur's optimistic nature and his sustained support for Foch, it seems likely, too, that in March, 1918, he spoke more highly of his old squadron chief than of Pétain. Nevertheless, Clemenceau did not come down decisively on the side of Foch's ideas until March 26.[16]

Loucheur's presence at Doullens was symbolically significant, for it reflected both the closeness of his relationship with Clemenceau and the political esteem he enjoyed within the government. Outside of Cle-

12. *Ibid.*, 55–56, 179–80; Falls, *The Great War*, 334–35.

13. Falls, *The Great War*, 335; Pedroncini, *Pétain*, 332–35; Griffiths, *Marshal Pétain*, 70–72.

14. Loucheur, *Carnets secrets*, 59–60. In 1928, Loucheur marked the occasion's tenth anniversary by publishing an account of what occurred between March 24 and March 26. See Louis Loucheur, *Le Commandement unique: Comment il fut réalisé à Doullens, le 25 mars 1918* (Lille, 1928).

15. Falls, *The Great War*, 336.

16. Loucheur to Comtesse de Courville, August 14, 1922, in Louis Loucheur Papers 10/C; Pedroncini, *Pétain*, 331.

menceau and Poincaré, he was the only French government official present. And Clemenceau's affection for him was evident when, in asking Loucheur to make two copies of the Doullens agreement, he laughed and said, "As compensation, I'll give you the rough draft."[17]

UNREST ON THE LABOR FRONT

The Germans launched another attack in April, this time against the Anglo-Portuguese lines at the extreme northern end of the Allied front. Known as the Lys offensive, it too showed initial success but was considered over before the month ended. Although the Allies had halted German advances on two occasions, they still feared final defeat, and tensions on the military front remained high in May.

There was also uneasiness on the domestic front. When the Germans launched their March attack, Clemenceau, watchful for revolutionary outbreaks among the workers, kept four cavalry divisions in the interior as a precaution. Nothing untoward happened then, but serious labor unrest erupted during May.[18] The most widespread unrest was in Paris and touched Loucheur directly, since the disruptions affected armaments production. On May 11, about a hundred shop delegates (see above, pp. 65–66, 69–70) from Renault gathered at the Restaurant de la Victoire, in Billancourt, and ratified the idea of an immediate general strike. Their design was endorsed the following day at a meeting of six hundred war-factory delegates, and on the morning of May 13 more than twenty thousand Renault workers went on strike. The strike quickly spread to other war-production firms in the Paris region, and at its height it is estimated to have included as many as 200,000 workers. The strikers were clamoring for the government to declare its conditions for peace, but they were also protesting the call-up to military units of young conscripts working in munitions factories. The rumor spread that Americans would replace the workers the army removed.[19]

17. Loucheur, *Carnets secrets*, 60.

18. Falls, *The Great War*, 337–42; "L'Etat de l'opinion en France d'après le contrôle de la correspondance du 15 mai au 15 juin 1918," in 6 N, 147, SHA. There were also strikes by metallurgical workers in Bourges and St. Etienne.

19. Reports on Workers' Activities at the Renault Factory on May 11, 1918, dated May 12, 1918, in F 7, 13367, AN; Report on Strikes in the War Factories of the Paris Region, May 13, 1918, *ibid*.; Hatry, "Les Délégués d'atelier aux usines Renault," 232; Report on Strikes in the

As labor turmoil spread, Loucheur's ministry began taking steps to deal with it. On the morning of May 13, Colonel Weil, a spokesman for the armaments ministry, warned delegates of Renault that mobilized workers who went on strike risked being returned to the front and that strike leaders would be subject to penalties. Loucheur more than likely approached Thomas for help. The Socialist parliamentary group decided to send a delegation, including Thomas, to talk with Loucheur and Clemenceau on the afternoon of May 14. Obviously in touch with the strikers, they complained about the way the Loi Mourier was applied to young workers, and they emphasized the emotional damage that the rumor of American workers was having in the factories. Loucheur's rejoinder was that the government was recalling mobilized factory personnel exactly as the Loi Mourier prescribed. He assured the delegation, however, that no substitution of American for French workers was planned.[20] It can be assumed that Thomas and the Socialists passed the information they got from him on to the strikers and that, in view of the major impending German offensive, they appealed to the workers' patriotism to end the walkout.

Loucheur, convinced that the disruptions were largely traceable to the shop delegates, began imposing penalties on certain of them. Alphonse Merrheim, whose Fédération des Métaux took control of the strike movement on May 16, protested that some of the government measures were repressive, and he bid the working class not to tolerate them. He even appealed to the Socialist parliamentary delegation to call upon the government to give an account of itself. But the government continued to act against the strikers by recalling those with military deferments to their military reporting stations; a substantial number called up were shop delegates.[21] Although the government relented to a degree after the end of the strike and placed a significant portion of those

---

War Factories of the Paris Region, May 13, 1918, in F 7, 13367, AN; Report on a Meeting of the Personnel of the Maison Hanriot on May 13, 1918, dated May 14, 1918, in F 7, 13367, AN; Newspaper Clipping from *Le Journal du peuple*, May 15, 1918, in F 12, 8023, AN.

20. Report on a Meeting of the Personnel of the Maison Hanriot on May 13, 1918, dated May 14, 1918, in F 7, 13367, AN; "Dans les usines de guerre," May 15, 1918, *ibid.*

21. Report on Meeting of *délégués d'atelier* from War Factories in the Paris Region on May 15, 1918, dated May 16, 1918, *ibid.*; Hatry, "Les Délégués d'atelier," 232–33; Report on Meeting of *délégués d'atelier* from War Factories in the Paris Region on May 15, 1918, dated May 16, 1918, in F 7, 13367, AN.

recalled in other factories, the damage done to the institution of the shop delegate was severe. One observer noted at the end of July, "In many shops, it appears impossible or almost impossible to replace the delegates who departed or resigned, and where candidacies might be advanced, there has been no attempt at having elections. In these conditions, it seems unlikely that a movement might develop that would involve the mass of workers in the war plants."[22]

The Fédération des Métaux was reluctant to prosecute the strike, given the anticipated German offensive. It discussed its options with the Socialist parliamentary delegation, Loucheur, and Clemenceau, and on May 18 union representatives called upon the workers to return to their jobs. The strike's end was tantamount to a worker surrender, for the government made no concessions.[23]

Loucheur's attitude toward the strike was influenced by two particulars. One was his conviction that the shop delegates were the chief cause of the strike. It was not the first time that they had engaged in controversial activities, and Loucheur had put them on notice in his directive of February 21, which strictly limited their functions. Yet less than three months after that warning, the delegates appeared to be the fomenters of labor trouble. Loucheur, seeing them that way, believed that a firm hand was necessary to avert disruptions elsewhere and to diminish their influence in the war factories. He must have had grave reservations about the usefulness of the shop delegates from this point on, if he had not had them before, and he was certainly undisturbed to see the delegates weakened as an institution in the final months of the war.

The other influence upon Loucheur's attitude was the pending German offensive, which did not allow the luxury of domestic distractions. Even a pacifist like Merrheim was unwilling to risk the adverse military and social consequences that might result from a prolonged strike at that juncture.[24] A combination of patriotism and fear of the German military machine seems to be what carried the day in reestablishing order in the factories. Certainly no one associated with the labor move-

22. Report on Worker Spirit in the War Factories of the Paris Region, July 31, 1918, in F 7, 13367, AN.

23. Hatry, "Les Délégués d'atelier," 232.

24. Nicholas Papayanis, "Collaboration and Pacifism in France During World War I," *Francia*, V (1977), 425.

ment wanted to see the working class taxed with weakening the Allied military effort at that crucial point.

The offensive came on May 27, in an attack against the French on the Chemin des Dames. Originally intending it as a diversion that would allow a renewal of operations against the British, the Germans were astonished at how rapidly their army advanced in the first days, and they abandoned their original plan and concentrated their efforts against the French. The Allied forces finally dug in, and the offensive was broken off on June 11. Nevertheless, the Germans had achieved a success whose repercussions went beyond the battlefields. In Paris, the result was an emotionally charged atmosphere in which Clemenceau was forced to defend his military policies before the Chamber of Deputies.[25] Loucheur's course was affected, too, as will become apparent.

The Germans made a final push in mid-July but were quickly forced into a general retreat after their defeat at the second battle of the Marne. With the Allies having the upper hand, it was only a question of months until the conflict ended.[26] But during the summer and early fall the Allies were unaware of how close the war was to being over, and Loucheur continued to focus on war production into the final days of fighting.

COAL

If the German spring offensives contributed to the creation of an Allied unified military command and the decision of the Fédération des Métaux to abandon its strike, they also tested the effectiveness of Allied cooperation as embodied in the coal accord of mid-March. The March attack in particular shook not only the supply system between Britain, France, and Italy but also the delicate balance Loucheur had maintained at home during the winter.

The most critical developments concerned transport from the mines of the Pas-de-Calais to Paris and the east of France. Before the German attack in March, the mines of that region turned out 900,000 of the estimated 2.1 million tons of coal the French produced monthly. The principal rail line for deliveries from the area passed through Amiens, the fate of which was in doubt for several days, though the Germans in

25. Ferro, *The Great War*, 216.
26. *Ibid.*, 216–17.

the end failed to take the city. Nevertheless, priority on the railroads went to the carriage of troops and military supplies, so that shipments of coal out of the Pas-de-Calais region dropped drastically. Loucheur told the Chamber's army commission on April 15 that the French had managed to ship only a third of the coal normally conveyed by rail to other parts of France. But by then he was availing himself of other expedients, including different routings by rail and a reliance on coastal shipping between Dunkerque and Rouen. Loucheur feared that the Germans might overrun the area of the mines; he secured the word of Foch that there would be special consideration given to protecting the mines from attack.[27]

To replace the undelivered coal, Loucheur and the French turned to the British. Loucheur told the Allied Maritime Transport Council, which held its second session between April 23 and April 25, that apart from 300,000 tons available to the department of the Nord and the British army, shipments of coal from the Pas-de-Calais were not reliable. He appealed to the British to fill the void, suggesting a delivery figure of 400,000 to 450,000 tons a month.[28]

The British had decided several days before the conference to assist the French in the wake of the German thrust. The British government had sent word to Lord Bertie, its ambassador in Paris, that it was in favor of the export of 150,000 to 200,000 tons of coal to help offset France's interrupted supplies. The delegation of British officials sent to France to work out a delivery program arrived at a satisfactory arrangement at the April session of the Allied Maritime Transport Council. A program of 1.74 million tons of British coal for France per month was the basis of the accord.[29]

British anxiety at this point concerned shipping and manpower. There was a general understanding in London that although obligations to deliver coal to neutral nations had to be kept, ships for France would be given priority, albeit "as unostentatiously as possible."[30] Sir Joseph

27. Minutes, Commission de l'Armée (Chambre), April 5, 1918, in C, 7500, AN.

28. Clémentel, *La France et la Politique économique,* 255.

29. Foreign Office to Lord Bertie, April 20, 1918, in FO 382/2079, File 1398, PRO; Richard A. S. Redmayne, *The British Coal-Mining Industry During the War* (Oxford, 1923), 192; Salter, *Allied Shipping Control,* 213. At the end of 1917, British coal deliveries to France averaged 1.5 million tons a month.

30. Memorandum of a Meeting at the Ministry of Shipping, April 22, 1918, in FO 382/2079, File 1398, PRO.

Maclay, the shipping controller, came up with so many vessels to carry coal that in early May he was complaining that he had to send a significant number away in ballast because of insufficient cargo.[31] The greater problem was with manpower, for early in the year the British government had decided to conscript fifty thousand men working in the mines, and after the Germans launched their spring attacks the figure was raised by another twenty-five thousand. Although the government attempted to replace some of the withdrawn workers with miners already in the army who had low medical classifications, the replacement moved ahead slowly, and coal production lagged. Exacerbating the manpower shortage in May and June were labor unrest and the outbreak of an influenza epidemic.[32]

French rail deliveries of coal to Italy were disrupted by the transfer of Allied troops from the Italian front to the area threatened by the German March offensive. Loucheur for a time thought of discontinuing deliveries and letting Britain assume the burden alone. In ensuing negotiations, which likely focused on the increased supply of coal from Britain to France, the French retreated and committed themselves to dispatching coal to the Italians at a reduced level. Anticipating such a move, the Maritime Council executive diverted to Italy sizable shipments originally destined for Gibraltar and the Mediterranean. In the months that followed, the amount of coal the British shipped to Italy by the long sea route increased substantially.[33]

As France's domestic coal supply became more tenuous during the spring and France leaned more heavily on Britain, panic and speculation spread. On June 15, Loucheur issued an administrative order imposing government controls meant to curb excessive prices. Since he wanted a uniform cost for imported coal to simplify the government's administration of prices, one thing the order did was set up a system of *péréquation* for freight rates on coal from Britain. Until then rates had varied according to the type of vessel used. Loucheur's order also established a maximum price for each of the components in the price consumers paid

31. Supply of Coal for Export, Ministry of Shipping, May 8, 1918, in Ministry of Transport, MT 25, Ministry of Shipping, 20/52422/1918, PRO.

32. Redmayne, *The British Coal-Mining Industry*, 188, 192–94; Lord Robert Cecil to Louis Loucheur, May 31, 1918, in FO 382/2079, File 1398, PRO.

33. Minutes, Commission de l'Armée (Chambre), April 5, 1918, in C, 7500, AN; Salter, *Allied Shipping Control*, 165, 190.

for French and British coal. Consumers were called upon to verify stated component prices against the government-fixed rates and not to pay more than the official ceiling. Loucheur was convinced that France would see a significant drop in coal prices and would have an effective deterrent against speculation.[34]

While Loucheur was attempting to stabilize the price of domestic coal, the British announced a general price increase for theirs. Loucheur reacted mildly to the announcement, writing to Pichon on June 24 that in light of the increased expense of mining British coal, it would be inappropriate to object to the new rates, especially since the higher prices applied within Britain as well as to exports. Loucheur felt, though, that the French should use the occasion to request that the two countries take up the issue of postwar prices for coal and freight. Loucheur's suggestion represented the beginning of a French effort to secure a postwar extension of the British policy, begun in mid-1916, of selling coal to the French and Italians below prices charged other countries. His idea received the endorsement of other ministers, and the British agreed to continue the preferential policy after the war, although they did not fix a specific period for that.[35]

By August, the military position of the Allies had improved enough that Loucheur could begin increasing coal shipments from the mines in the Pas-de-Calais. He told the Chamber's army commission on August 3 that the number of trains leaving the mines had risen in the previous days and that, with the imminent completion of a new rail line, coal shipments would rapidly improve.[36] He knew that domestic production was still well below minimum needs, however, and he continued to hope that the British would augment their shipments. Joining with other French officials to obtain satisfaction from the British, he in mid-August used the forum of the Interallied Armaments and Munitions Council—created as an offshoot of the Allied Maritime Transport Council—to impress on Churchill the urgency of the situation and to encourage British action. At the same time, the French delegates to the Allied Maritime Transport Council, joined by the United States and

34. Sardier, *Le Ravitaillement en charbon*, 91–94.

35. Louis Loucheur to Stephen Pichon, June 24, 1918, in Series Z, Europe, 1918–1929, Grande-Bretagne, Vol. 94, MAE; Etienne Clémentel to Stephen Pichon, July 26, 1918, *ibid.*; Olivier, *La Politique du charbon*, 55.

36. Minutes, Commission de l'Armée (Chambre), August 3, 1918, in C, 7500, AN.

Italy, sent a message to Lloyd George about how desperate conditions had become. They pointed out that although France's minimum domestic production was considered to be 2.2 million tons a month, output in the aftermath of the March offensive had fallen to 1.5 million tons. They lamented that though the British had been expected to help compensate for the domestic shortages, what they shipped to France after April fell more than a million tons under expectations. For the week ending August 17, practically all British tonnage for carrying coal to France had been immobilized because of the unavailability of coal.[37]

The British were well aware of the dimensions of the coal emergency not only on the continent but at home, and they responded with a campaign to increase production. Lloyd George opened this on August 10 with a speech to a group of Welsh miners in which, referring to the enemy, he encouraged the miners, "Sling coal at them! Hurl it in wagon loads! Every extra wagon load means winning victories which represent liberty, justice, and peace throughout the world."[38] Several days later Sir Guy Calthrop, the British coal controller, read messages to delegates to a British Miners' Federation conference from Clemenceau, Haig, and Foch, all of whom called upon the miners to raise their output. The government also, as part of its campaign, directed the return of miners from military service as rapidly as possible.[39]

At the same time, the British reminded the French that they too bore responsibility for lower than expected coal deliveries from Britain. In early August, Lord Robert Cecil, British assistant secretary of state, mentioned to Loucheur that much of the problem lay in the inability of French ports to absorb the coal when it arrived. It appeared unlikely to him that conditions in the ports would improve markedly any time soon, but he acknowledged that even if they did, Britain would probably not be in a position to satisfy French coal requirements, because of the withdrawal of miners for the army. He suggested that the French try to bring the Bruay mines, located in the Pas-de-Calais, into full production.[40]

Loucheur's response tried to exculpate France. His position was

---

37. Conseil Interallié de l'Armement et des Munitions, August 14–15, 1918, in F 12, 7799, AN; Captain Pilliard to Louis Loucheur, August 18, 1918, in F 12, 7683, AN.

38. Redmayne, *The British Coal-Mining Industry*, 190.

39. *Ibid.*, 189–91.

40. Lord Robert Cecil to Lord Bertie, August 8, 1918, in FO 382/2079, File 1398, PRO.

that, despite appearances, the ports were ready to receive the coal France sought: if Britain shipped the coal, the French would handle it in their ports. Loucheur went so far as to venture that Britain might part with some of the coal reserved for its own people, by adding 300,000 tons a month to what it sent France. He assured Cecil that everything possible was being done to increase production at the Bruay mines and that a significant improvement in output could be expected there in the second half of August.[41]

When Loucheur sent his message to Cecil on August 13, he probably knew that transportation facilities were inadequate for taking coal from the ports to other parts of France and that shippers repeatedly encountered hindrances when they tried to unload their coal. Loucheur not only wanted to keep pressure on the British, he was genuinely confident about rectifying conditions in the ports. His optimism stemmed partly from measures the government had taken in July that addressed the transportation crisis, among them that of employing Loucheur's ministry in the repair of locomotives and rail cars.[42] Anyway, he had resolved a similar crisis in the French ports in early 1917.

Despite Loucheur's efforts at home, with the British, and within the Allied Maritime Transport Council, where the issue was discussed at its last two wartime meetings, on August 29 and August 30 and between September 30 and October 2, coal imports from Britain remained well below the April program level of 1.74 million tons monthly. In September, 1,244,174 tons arrived, and in October, 1,251,073 tons. The output of the British mines was insufficient, but delaying the removal of coal from the ports also continued to plague the French during the fall. Loucheur could not get the French railroads to perform at the level he in August had boldly assured the British they would, primarily because of continued military demands.[43]

Notwithstanding Loucheur's best efforts, France at the end of the war was on the threshold of another winter with nonexistent stockpiles, grave disarray in transportation, reduced domestic production, and in-

41. Louis Loucheur to Lord Robert Cecil, August 13, 1918, *ibid.*

42. Sir Joseph Maclay to Lord Robert Cecil, August 19, 1918, *ibid.*; Minutes, Comité de Guerre, July 15, 1918, in 3 N, 3, SHA.

43. Salter, *Allied Shipping Control*, 197, 201, 213; Draft Letter Lord Robert Cecil to Louis Loucheur, August 15, 1918, in FO 382/2079, File 1398, PRO; *L'Usine*, October 24, 1918, p. 17; Louis Loucheur to Captain Pilliard, November 3, 1918, in F 12, 7785, AN.

adequate shipments from Britain. In Paris, arrivals of coal were far below anticipated levels, and in Lyon deliveries for the months from August through November were dramatically less than in the comparable period for 1917.[44]

The last eight months of the war show that the balance in coal supplies that Loucheur had managed to achieve during the winter of 1917–1918 was exceedingly fragile; it was easily upset during the Germans' March offensive. Although Loucheur attempted to regain mastery in the following months, he was beset by much beyond his control: labor problems in Britain, a transportation crisis at home, and the German destruction of French mines in the last weeks of the war. He did benefit during these months from Allied cooperation. The Allied Maritime Transport Council provided much assistance in coordinating the coal programs of Britain, France, and Italy. Moreover, he was able to use the council as a forum in which to appeal for more coal.

METALLURGY

The March offensive led to similar difficulties in the areas of iron and steel, including serious shortages, a transportation crisis, and speculation. France had a history of relying heavily on Britain for both metals, but as their availability from that source decreased in 1918, Loucheur had to try to locate new sellers. Though shortages of iron and steel touched the general public less directly than those in coal did, the metals were crucial to the French war effort. Loucheur was also under the obligation of providing munitions to the American forces as they arrived in France, and he had to find suppliers capable of meeting France's nonferrous metallurgical needs. His approach was to introduce measures aimed at stabilizing prices and further centralizing the ordering and distribution process. Although he applied his remedies in connection with several metals, he gave special attention to pig iron, with the supply of which he had grappled before. Pig iron became increasingly important during the last months of the war.

The French were anticipating tangible reductions in the steel and pig

44. Henri Marcesche, *Le Charbon: Elément de réparations et de négotiations dans le traité de Versailles et les accords qui l'ont suivi* (Lorient, 1933), 17; *L'Usine*, October 17, 1918, p. 19; François Dutacq, *La Ville de Lyon et la Guerre* (Paris, 1924), 106.

iron arriving from Britain, but for steel at least, they hoped to forestall as long as possible British action on a decision made during the winter to cut deliveries sharply. On the other hand, records from a meeting of the CIM in February suggest that France was resigned to accepting an immediate cut in British shipments of hematite pig iron from twenty thousand tons a month to ten thousand. At that meeting it was proposed that the quantity of British steel projected for all French programs during the remainder of the year—not more than 250,000 tons—should be apportioned so that the largest consignments might be received at the outset, 35,450 tons monthly, with gradual reductions as the year progressed. Loucheur was likely behind this strategy, since it was in line with his wartime method of meeting the demands of the moment and postponing delivery reductions for as long as he could. But the hopes of February about deliveries from Britain were soon frustrated, for in May the French estimated monthly British shipments for their programs at about 24,000 tons, or 5,500 tons under the 29,500 tons they had projected in February for May. Though the Comité de Guerre, in making its quarterly revisions for metallurgical products on July 15, increased the monthly figure to 40,000 tons for the period from July through September, it appears that deliveries continued to fall well short of French needs.[45]

Nor was an increase in domestic production the answer, for the coal shortages and transportation crisis resulting from the German attacks left the French unable to maintain steel and pig-iron production even at earlier levels. In 1918, total steel production reached but 59 percent of capacity, while output of pig iron was at 56 percent; this compared with output levels of 94 percent of capacity for steel and 100 percent for pig iron in 1916.[46] Production capacity levels were higher in 1918 than in 1916, owing to the construction program Loucheur did so much to develop in 1917, but the low employment of capacity in 1918 is still an index of how serious production binds were in that year.

Loucheur decided to rely heavily upon the United States for steel. Because of France's arrangement with America involving raw materials for artillery and the Churchill Convention guaranteeing ships for the de-

---

45. Commission Interministérielle des Métaux et Fabrications de Guerre, February 27, 1918, in F 30, 1501, MF; Minutes, Commission du Budget: Sous-Commission des Armements (Chambre), September 6, 1918, in 94 AP, 57, AN; Minutes, Comité de Guerre, July 15, 1918, in 3 N, 2, SHA.

46. Fontaine, *French Industry During the War,* 274.

livery of American steel products, Loucheur was able to obtain a rise in American steel imports for armaments production from 82,000 tons in February to 122,000 tons in March. But imports from the United States fell after the German attack in March, dipping to 59,000 tons in July.[47]

Steel shortages became so critical in the first months of 1918 that in April Pétain wrote to Clemenceau that the French should insist not only on an increase in the monthly steel allotment from Britain but also on full British compliance with the Churchill Convention. Clemenceau passed the letter on to Clémentel, who reckoned Loucheur the man to raise the issues with the British. How Loucheur reacted on other occasions leaves little doubt that he maintained close contact with the British on steel, although the evidence is scant regarding his specific actions. The major known fact is that he and Churchill discussed steel generally at a conference of one of the subcouncils of the Allied Maritime Transport Council in August. Although the result of what they said is not known, Loucheur's overall efforts must have had some effect, for the French, in determining their steel estimates for the last quarter of 1918, calculated that the monthly British deliveries would amount to about 44,000 tons, which was 4,000 tons above the projection for the third quarter of the year.[48] Meanwhile, Clémentel reminded the British at the end of July that because of the British failure with respect to the provisions of the Churchill Convention, American steel destined for France remained held up in ports and factories in the United States.[49] Since the British lacked the capacity to fulfill their commitments, Loucheur turned to the United States. He sent telegrams and worked through French representatives in America to apply pressure, only to be told, most likely in June or July, that more steel would be in transit as soon as the French removed what was already in their ports.

To reduce the delays at French ports, Loucheur joined with Albert Claveille, the minister of transport, in instituting a system of shuttle trains. First developed for the large state arsenal at Roanne, the system had trains leave the ports fully loaded and return to the port as soon as

47. Minutes, Commission de l'Armée (Chambre), April 5, 1918, in C, 7500, AN; Minutes, Commission du Budget: Sous-Commission des Armements (Chambre), September 6, 1918, in 94 AP, 57, AN.

48. Etienne Clémentel to Georges Clemenceau, May 2, 1918, in F 12, 7785, AN; Conseil Interallié de l'Armement et des Munitions, August 14–15, 1918, ibid.; Minutes, Comité de Guerre, October 3, 1918, in 3 N, 3, SHA.

49. Clémentel, La France et la Politique économique, 275.

they were unloaded at their inland destination. With expansion to other steel consumption centers, the French achieved a 30-percent increase in the steel they could remove from the ports to the interior each month. To ensure efficient operations, Loucheur appointed a permanent liaison agent at the transport ministry.[50]

Once the ports were cleared, American supplies increased, and French government officials were optimistic enough when the Comité de Guerre made its steel estimates for the last quarter of the year to anticipate an average monthly arrival of more than 125,000 tons of steel from the United States for Loucheur's ministry. As a result, the total steel consumption the French projected for the final three months of the year was well above that for July through September.[51] The figures indicate that Loucheur and other government officials could believe that the worst of the steel crisis was over and that conditions would continue improving.

Loucheur at the end of the winter of 1917–1918 was still working on a comprehensive pricing and distribution system for pig iron. He had written to Robert Pinot at the end of 1917 to ask that the Comité des Forges serve as distributor in the system, but he hesitated to implement his plan in the wake of strong criticism (see above, pp. 81–82). Once the criticism quieted, he decided to move ahead, mentioning on March 18, in a letter to Pinot, an effective date of June 1. The Germans launched their great offensive three days later, however, and Loucheur postponed the implementation until July 1.[52]

Until July, 1918, then, there was no control for most pig iron produced in France. The only controls, created in 1916–1917, placed the Comité des Forges in charge of the purchase and distribution of pig iron coming from Britain as well as the distribution of pig iron the government purchased in the United States and France. The amount of French pig iron covered was not large. Since most domestically produced pig iron escaped controls, there were inconsistencies and abuses, such as wide variations in price and distribution procedures.

Loucheur's purpose was to assure all users a steady supply of pig iron at equitable prices regardless of the supply's origin. According to the

50. Minutes, Commission du Budget: Sous-Commission des Armements (Chambre), September 6, 1918, in 94 AP, 57, AN.

51. Minutes, Comité de Guerre, July 15, 1918, October 13, 1918, both in 3 N, 3, SHA.

52. Pinot, Le Comité des Forges, 286–89.

structure he set up, the CIM determined the pig-iron allotments for government ministries and public services. At a lower level, the metallurgical products service at Loucheur's ministry set the allocation amounts for individual users. The final participant in distribution was the Comité des Forges, which under the control of the armaments ministry carried out the allocation of actual lots of pig iron to consumers at fixed prices. Loucheur set up a *chambre de compensation* to maintain price equity among consumers and processing firms. The system of intervention that he turned to in order to check injustices, hoarding, and speculation remained intact until after the termination of hostilities in November.[53]

For steel, too, government price controls existed, but there they were far more limited in scope. The controls appear to have originated with the naming on September 1, 1917, of the Comptoir d'Exportation des Produits Métallurgiques as the single purchaser of British steel. Loucheur, acting on recommendations from the CIM, established base prices for this steel. The French were also helped in September, when the United States instituted a price-control program covering pig iron and steel and applied the fixed prices to sales abroad as well as at home. No specific controls seem to have been implemented in 1917, however, for steel produced in France, although transactions concerning the metal were subject to scrutiny by the CIM so far as it was responsible for the distribution of all steel products. Loucheur and Clémentel tightened up the system in March, 1918, when they issued a joint decision prohibiting sellers of products of either steel or iron from charging more than 3 percent above the price they had paid at the mill. But the French never established the same kind of pricing program for steel that they arranged for coal and pig iron. The government's unwillingness may have been related to the power and influence of the country's steel interests, though a more likely explanation is that the system would have proved too difficult to control—especially if it had embodied a producer's-cost-plus-profit approach, which had been considered in the United States, where it was rejected as unmanageable.[54]

Although the tendency toward centralization in metallurgy was evident prior to March, 1918, the Germans' spring attacks gave a new sense of

53. *Ibid.*, 122–27; Girault, *Le Comité des Forges*, 135–38.

54. Comité des Forges de France, Circular No. 961, September 13, 1917, in 94 AP, 233, AN; Bernard Baruch, *American Industry in the War* (New York, 1941), 122–26; *L'Usine*, March 28, 1918, p. 7.

urgency to the expansion of government controls over raw materials. In early May, Loucheur and Clémentel presented a legislative bill that would have put under government authority many raw materials up to then exempt from control. It was just one of several attempts Loucheur was involved in during the spring to create a more centralized war economy.[55]

Loucheur continued to press for more centralization through the final weeks of the war. In September, he broached to Clémentel the idea of a single purchasing agent for all iron products from the United States. Clémentel balked, though, probably because of the negative reception he anticipated in business circles. Instead, he suggested that users of American iron centralize their purchases through their own business associations or, failing that, through the Comptoir d'Exportation des Produits Métallurgiques, or the Consortium des Marchands de Fer, which represented nondefense metallurgical consumers. Loucheur accepted Clémentel's preference, but the mechanics of organizing such an arrangement make it likely that the interministerial decision was not carried out before the war ended, when the need was over. Nevertheless, the episode constitutes evidence that the government's centralizing tendencies did not wane in the last weeks of the conflict. Loucheur's way of dealing with metallurgy was to the end the one he had had on first entering the government. Throughout his war tenure, his primary preoccupation was meeting the needs of the moment to prevent any serious cutbacks in the manufacture of munitions.

ARMAMENTS PRODUCTION

During the war's last months, armaments production took on a new importance because of the determination of both sides to achieve a decisive victory. Loucheur was under pressure from military and government officials to maintain stocks of weapons and shells at a high level, and to increase the production of certain equipment, such as tanks and planes. Moreover, he was under obligation to furnish certain military equipment to the arriving American forces. It is evident from the crises in coal and raw materials that his task was not easy, and his problems were compounded by the threat of German bombardments and the dis-

55. An assortment of documents in F 12, 7662, 7673, 7786, AN.

ruption of France's transport system. He was constantly forced to make adjustments, even to the point of launching a program of relocation for the production of some vital war materials. During April and May, he came under attack in parliament and elsewhere. Throughout these months, however, he maintained the unswerving support of Clemenceau and tackled his problems with the same boldness and zest he had demonstrated from the outset of the conflict.

With the German offensive in March came long-distance bombing attacks on Paris. The bombardments made it clear that French munitions production, the better part of which was located in the region of the capital, was no longer safe from enemy guns. But even before then, Loucheur had worried about the heavy concentration of armaments factories in the area, since he believed it was damaging to the morale of Frenchmen elsewhere in the country. He had consequently begun making provision earlier in the year to have certain aviation equipment, for example, manufactured in other parts of France. The German bombings dictated a prompt movement of key industries from Paris to other areas, and at the beginning of April, Loucheur shifted some production to locations like Lyon and Bordeaux.[56]

The site figuring largest in his relocation plans was the gigantic state arsenal at Roanne, built on the orders of Thomas in anticipation of a long war. The questionable financial procedures Thomas had resorted to in initiating the project and the poor planning associated with it had created a controversy within parliament. Loucheur, aware that the arsenal had not been in full use prior to the spring offensives, decided that it was an excellent spot to concentrate the production of 75-mm. shells. To make the modifications necessary for the high-level production he projected, he called at the beginning of June upon André Citroën, a strong advocate of efficiency and productivity who, he was convinced, was well qualified to organize the facilities for a work force of fifteen to sixteen thousand. Citroën had already turned out a remarkable number of artillery shells at his own firm and had been responsible for innovative improvements in working conditions. At Roanne, Citroën was to oversee the construction of barracks sufficient to house several thousand workers, he was to bring an adequate water supply from Roanne to the

56. Minutes, Commission de l'Armée (Chambre), April 5, 1918, in C, 7500, AN; Minutes, Commission du Budget: Sous-Commission des Armements (Chambre), June 7, 1918, in C, 7557, AN.

arsenal grounds, and he was to coordinate preparations for the assembly end of the production operation.[57]

Loucheur's selection of Citroën for the job was not universally applauded. There were suspicions within parliament during the summer about Citroën's intentions at Roanne, and Loucheur had to defend his appointment before the Chamber's army commission in August. The question came up on that occasion whether the arsenal would remain the property of the state. The fear was that the arsenal might be turned over to an industrial group, with Citroën playing a self-serving role in the transfer. Some deputies saw Citroën's purchase of property adjacent to the arsenal as foreshadowing the eventual takeover of the facility by private interests. Loucheur pledged that the arsenal would remain the state's property and explained that if Citroën purchased land, he was acting at the instance of the minister under whom he worked.[58] In defense of the appointment, Loucheur stressed that since Citroën had been in Roanne, there had been significant achievements in the production of shells, with steady improvements still expected. Loucheur also made clear that Citroën's assignment was not long-term but would be completed in six weeks.[59]

Loucheur's confidence in Citroën had proved well founded. When Citroën arrived at the arsenal in June, output consisted of 1,000 75-mm. shell casings per day and a total of 1,170 75-mm. finished shells in the time the arsenal had been open. Three months later a day's production reached 40,000 shell casings and 8,000 finished shells. In addition, Citroën succeeded in erecting barracks and in providing enough other basic necessities to allow for a sharp increase in the number of employees. At one point the count of workers reached 10,400.[60]

Loucheur kept an adequate supply of artillery shells ready for the Allies throughout the final campaign. When the Germans began their attacks in the spring, more than 34 million shells were in stock for Allied use. Despite the large number consumed during the spring and summer,

---

57. Godfrey, *Capitalism at War*, 257–88; *L'Usine*, November 6, 1919, p. 6; Minutes, Commission du Budget: Sous-Commission des Armements (Chambre), in C, 7557, AN; Chevrier, "Le Rôle de Loucheur," 75–78.

58. Loucheur told the commission that he had a written undertaking from Citroën to sell the property to the state for less than the state would have paid to purchase the property directly from the original owner.

59. Minutes, Commission de l'Armée (Chambre), August 3, 1918, in C, 7500, AN.

60. *L'Usine*, March 6, 1919, p. 11.

22.5 million shells were still available for the French and American forces as of August 10, and there was the expectation of rebuilding the supplies during the winter. By September, 1918, Loucheur had developed a shell program for 1919 with an average daily production of 350,000 shells, since an average daily consumption of 450,000 shells was anticipated for the months of greatest fighting, March through October 31. The projected consumption rate amounted to a sharp rise over 1918, but it was in line with the pattern by which shell consumption had moved steadily upward after the beginning of the war, reaching an average of 250,000 shells a day for the period between March 21 and August 1, 1918, in contrast to 175,000 shells a day between March 1 and October 31 of the preceding year.[61]

Loucheur's program for heavy artillery was also a success. In the first six months of 1918, 1,915 heavy-artillery guns were produced, and 1,090 were made in the final months of the war. That contrasts with heavy-artillery production of 345 guns for the second six months of 1916. The salutary effects of Loucheur's program were manifest in the war's last battles, as a French army officer brought out: "In March and in June, 1918, at the time of the German offensives, we had succeeded in providing our armies with large numbers of heavy artillery, which proved to be of the utmost value to us. Although technically inferior to the German heavy artillery, ours almost always dominated because of number. In any case, ours always prevented theirs from giving their infantry the support that it so earnestly wished to receive."[62]

For tanks, whose military value only slowly became evident, large-scale production did not get under way until the first part of 1918. The French, in compliance with an agreement worked out with the British and Americans at the end of 1917, concentrated on the light tank, and by the end of August, 1918, there had been 2,139 delivered—still, however, far from the total of 3,800 that Pétain wanted. On September 6, Loucheur could report to a budget commission subcommittee of the Chamber that production of light tanks had reached more than six hundred in July and that he looked toward exceeding that number in the months ahead.[63]

61. Minutes, Commission du Budget: Sous-Commission des Armements (Chambre), September 6, 1918, 94 AP, 57, AN.

62. Reboul, *Mobilisation industrielle,* I, 49–50.

63. Conférence des tanks réunie au Ministère de l'Armement et des Fabrications de Guerre, December 3, 1917, in Series Guerre, 1914–1918, Grande Bretagne, Vol. 551, MAE; Minutes, Commission du Budget: Sous-Commission des Armements (Chambre), September 6, 1918, in 94 AP, 57, AN.

In aviation, Loucheur's influence had become decisive only after the issuance of decrees on November 19 and November 21, 1917, by which he assumed full authority for the production of planes (see above, p. 60). In the months that followed the reorganization in November, the output of airplanes began to surge, as did the army's demand for them. Daily production doubled by the end of the war, and the number of deliveries in the last ten months of the war far surpassed that of any previous full year. At the same time, the building and testing of approximately sixty prototypes were going on when the armistice was signed. Loucheur's exact role in the developmental work is uncertain, but he was surely involved even if his contribution was less than for aircraft production. At the end of the war, France had well over 3,200 planes ready, far more than in 1940.[64]

Despite Loucheur's performance in the final months of the war, he still drew sharp criticism, much of it from within government agencies. In the difficult days following the March offensive, even some in Clemenceau's immediate circle judged the armaments minister unduly ambitious and inordinately attentive to personal business interests. But Clemenceau was prepared to disregard the attacks because of Loucheur's devotion to maximum production and military victory.[65] In May, the Chamber's army and budget commissions issued confidential reports critical of much in the areas of aviation and assault artillery. Loucheur was a prime target in both reports, which questioned his motives and credibility in the two areas.

The army commission's report came out in favor of organizational unity for aviation. According to the commission, Loucheur's grip on aircraft production merely complicated an effort already burdened by bureaucratic rivalries, confusion, and delays: "At the present time, at the very moment when military events have ended up showing the necessity of a unified high command, aviation has three heads and even four." Conceding that for the first quarter of 1918 airplane production in France was 62 percent higher than for the same period in 1917, the commission observed that British production during the first two months of 1918 was 223 percent above the corresponding months of 1917. It concluded that

64. Etevé, *La Victoire des cocardes*, 252–53, 260–61, 290, 293; Ferro, *The Great War*, 95. Ferro claims that the number of planes ready for action was 3,437; one can assume that the figure was probably somewhere between 3,200 and 3,450.

65. Mordacq, *Le Ministère Clemenceau*, I, 280–81.

such figures showed "once again the insufficiency of the results obtained" in France.[66]

The budget commission's report addressed Loucheur's management of assault-artillery production. The report commended Loucheur for his "prodigious activity, his unique training, and his gift for decision." But it criticized the government for giving him too many heavy responsibilities, since the result for specific areas, like assault artillery, was "jolts, delays, unfulfilled promises, and eventually, on the part of the very ones who have the most faith in him, intense debate in committee. It is not in the public interest to entrust so many and such diverse tasks even to the current minister of armaments." The report cited several instances where Loucheur failed to acquit himself satisfactorily. It noted the minister's failure to produce the eight hundred light tanks he had made a formal commitment to build during the first quarter of 1918. It asked why his ministry took two months to grant permission for the opening of an inter-Allied plant at Châteauroux to assemble heavy tanks.[67] And it attributed a six-week delay in the placement of an order for French-produced tanks to the "poor organization of the assault-artillery services at the armaments ministry."[68]

Issued at a time of extreme difficulty for the Allied armies, the reports stressed the growing importance of aircraft and assault tanks in the war and called for increased production of both and a consideration of administrative realignments. It is clear that Loucheur's production networks for aircraft and assault artillery were far from perfect. The reports demonstrate that Loucheur suffered from a credibility gap because of his failure to meet overly optimistic projections in the early months of 1918. But optimistic and even unrealistic projections were an integral part of his production methods. Although they held the danger of not being realized, they also, in Loucheur's judgment, stimulated greater output. Loucheur made adjustments in early 1918 to promote airplane output, and at the very moment the reports were issued, improvements

66. Rapport sur l'aéronautique présenté à la Commission de l'Armée par M. d'Aubigny (Chambre), May 3, 1918, in C, 7502, AN. For further discussion of the report's contents, see above, p. 63.

67. An Anglo-American request was formally made on December 21, 1917; Loucheur's ministry gave its authorization on February 18, 1918.

68. Rapport de Monsieur Abel Ferry sur l'artillerie d'assaut, Commission du Budget (Chambre), May 10, 1918, in C, 7502, AN.

in tank production were occurring.[69] Still, he had much to do, and if nothing else, the reports were a way of impressing that message upon him.

The army commission continued its battle with the government over aviation in another report it issued shortly after the armistice, in November, 1918. It expressed bitter disappointment that its recommendation of a unified authority over aviation had not been followed. The report was particularly caustic in dealing with Jacques Louis Dumesnil and with Loucheur, because they had flouted the findings of the commission. Besides relating two examples of their administrative ineptness in a footnote, the report speculated that they left the fortunes of aircraft manufacture in the care of the "lucky star under which they had been born to ministerial life [which they hoped] would know how to guide them triumphant through the maze of their agencies." It went on to complain that neither a program for the production of 6,000 planes, first announced by Dumesnil in April, 1918, nor a program for 4,000 developed the previous autumn, with completion promised for July 1, 1918, had started and that an even earlier program for 2,870 planes had not been concluded, at least as of October 1. It deplored the failure of the French to develop a respectable number of bombers, in spite of repeated commission urgings.

In the eyes of the commission, all the deficiencies it discovered stemmed ultimately from the government's indisposition to heed the call for a unified authority over aviation. The commission again paid little attention, however, to the degree to which production had improved after the organizational changes of the previous November, nor did its report take into account causes of disruptions and slowdowns like coal and raw-material shortages.[70] Furthermore, it appears that by the end of the war a part of the program for four thousand planes had been not only launched but completed, although the program for bombers was indeed far from finished.[71]

For Loucheur, the last months of the war were filled with uncertainties and tensions. Although he undertook no onerous new assignments

---

69. Some of the changes Loucheur introduced in airplane production are mentioned above, on p. 62.

70. Rapport sur l'aéronautique présenté à la Commission de l'Armée par M. d'Aubigny (Chambre), November 19, 1918, in C, 7502, AN.

71. Etevé, *La Victoire des cocardes*, 294–95.

during the period, he went from crisis to crisis. Not least vexing was the persistence of parliamentary reservations about him. With the end of the war, his place in the government as a wartime technical expert was over, but there was still a task for him in the dismantling of the massive industrial complex that had grown so rapidly. Clemenceau looked to him as France began the transition from war to peace. The question now was how long Loucheur would remain in public service. Would he eventually return to business or opt for a full-fledged political career? In November, 1918, the answer was still unclear.

As a student at the Ecole Polytechnique, in 1890. Loucheur attended the Ecole Polytechnique from 1890 to 1892.

Archives de l'Ecole Polytechnique

On a visit to the aviation camp of Villacoublay on June 25, 1918. Loucheur (center foreground), Jacques Louis Dumesnil, undersecretary for aviation (to Loucheur's left), and President Raymond Poincaré (in front of Dumesnil) observe the flight of a French airplane.

Musée d'Histoire Contemporaine—BDIC

As depicted by Etienne Clémentel. Having a strong interest in art, Clémentel, the minister of commerce, occasionally did drawings of cabinet officials during meetings.

Inspecting a Big Bertha in August, 1918. Premier Georges Clemenceau (third from left) and Loucheur (to Clemenceau's right) inspect the platform of a captured German 420-mm. gun—a Big Bertha—in the Bois du Châtelet (Aisne). The Germans had fired the gun on Paris earlier.

Musée d'Histoire Contemporaine—BDIC

At the promotion ceremony for Ferdinand Foch, on August 6, 1918. Georges Leygues, minister of marine (left foreground), Loucheur, Premier Clemenceau, and President Poincaré honor Ferdinand Foch (back to photographer) on Foch's promotion to marshal of France. *Frank D. Coleman Collection, Hoover Institution Archives, Stanford University*

At the Paris peace conference, in 1919. Loucheur (left) is with Winston Churchill (standing), Prime Minister David Lloyd George, of Great Britain, and Bernard Baruch, a member of the American peace delegation.

Brown Brothers

As a member of Aristide Briand's seventh government. Cabinet members of the govern-
ment that Briand formed in January, 1921, pose for an official photo: seated, left to right,
André Maginot, Paul Doumer, Laurent Bonnevay, Briand, Pierre Marraud, Louis Barthou,
Léon Bérard; standing, Lucien Dior, Yves Le Trocquer, Daniel Vincent, Georges Leredu,
Gabriel Guist'hau, Albert Sarraut, Loucheur, Edmond Lefébvre du Prey.

L'Illustration

At the Wiesbaden talks, on October 6, 1921. Loucheur (left) and Walther Rathenau, of Germany, relax after signing an accord on payments in kind.
L'Illustration

In a political caricature. The left-wing cartoonist Marcel Arnac did this in collaboration with Victor Méric, a well-known journalist of the Left. Loucheur was on a number of occasions the target of left- and right-wing cartoonists after World War I.
Roger-Viollet

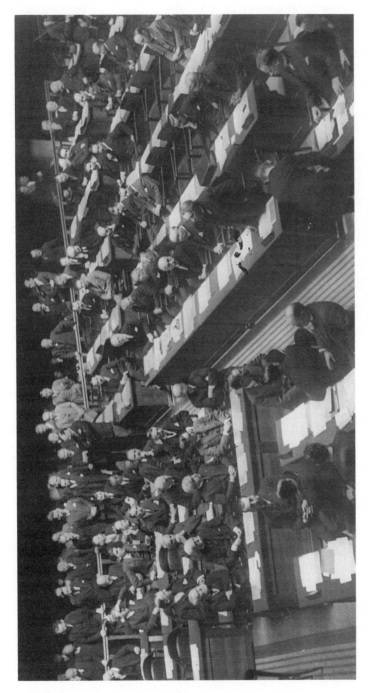

At the League of Nations' debate over Germany's application for membership, in March, 1926. Foreign Minister Briand (standing) makes a point during the debate. Loucheur is seated to Briand's right. The League's vote was postponed until September, 1926; Germany was admitted.

L'Illustration

At a meeting of the Second Committee of the League of Nations on September 21, 1928. Léon Jouhaux, the general secretary of the Confédération Générale du Travail, speaks in behalf of an economic program intended to appeal to workers. Loucheur, the committee's *rapporteur*, sits at Jouhaux' right.

L'Illustration

As a member of Poincaré's fourth government, on September 1, 1928. Those present for the government's second-anniversary celebration at Poincaré's home in Sampigny were, seated, left to right, Sarraut, Barthou, Poincaré's wife, Poincaré, Briand; standing, Leygues, Alfred Oberkirch, Loucheur, André Tardieu, Henri Queuille, Edouard Herriot, Maurice Bokanowski. Bokanowski died in an airplane crash the day after the photo was taken.

L'Illustration

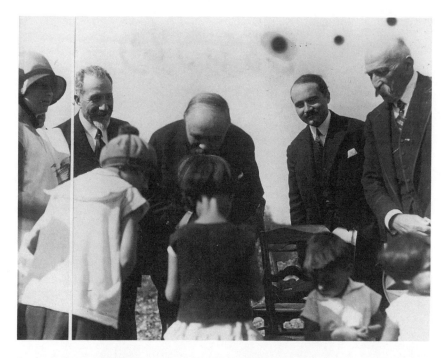

At the inauguration of a low-cost public-housing project in September, 1928. Loucheur (leaning over) and Leygues (right), whose wife founded the Ligue contre le Taudis, receive some words of welcome from children at the workers' *cité* in Villeneuve-sur-Lot.

L'Illustration

At the inauguration of a children's medical clinic. Loucheur, as minister of labor and health, represents the government at the opening of a facility in Paris.

Keystone

On board for a conference at The Hague in August, 1929. Foreign Minister Briand, with Henry Chéron, the finance minister (to his right) and Loucheur (leaning from the next window), leaves Paris to discuss questions related to reparations.
L'Illustration

Conversing prior to a session at the conference of The Hague. Briand (left) and Loucheur (right), on the terrace of their hotel in Scheveningen, the Netherlands, make preparations for the meeting.

Keystone

Toward the end of his life. This portrait shows a confident man whose eyes reflect the warmth and passion of his character.

Courtesy of Jacques de Launay

6

The Postwar Transition, 1918–1919

On November 11, 1918, an armistice was signed with Germany. The Allies cheered a triumph for democracy, and throughout France there was celebration. In Paris, representatives from more than two dozen nations participated in the spectacular festivities, including a victory parade of Allied troops down the Champs Elysées, where forty-seven years before Prussian troops had marched after defeating the French in the Franco-Prussian War. The people of France were grateful that victory and peace had been achieved.

But with peace came problems. France had geared itself to a wartime economy involving the production of large amounts of war matériel, the operation of greatly expanded war munitions plants, and the consumption of great quantities of raw materials. With unexpected suddenness, Germany had laid down its arms, and France was facing the priorities of peace. One necessity was to transform the French economy from its wartime to a peacetime footing as rapidly as circumstances allowed. Loucheur had a hand in this, first at the armaments ministry and later in its successor organization, the ministry of industrial reconstruction.

Loucheur's ministry of industrial reconstruction grew out of a recommendation by the department of commerce in early 1918 that a new ministry oversee industrial development and demobilization after the war. The proposal was for the relevant parts of the ministries of armaments and of commerce to be assimilated into the new ministry, which could also direct industrial reconstruction in the devastated regions of France. Shortly after hostilities ended, Clemenceau acted on the idea, giving Loucheur the ministerial responsibilities entailed, among them those regarding raw materials and import policy. At the same time, the premier considerably reduced the influence of Clémentel, whose department had been prominent in determining French economic policy during the war. All this prepared the way for Loucheur's emergence as Clemenceau's chief economic adviser in early 1919.[1]

The two men most closely associated with the development of postwar economic policy in late 1918 were Loucheur and Clémentel. Although they agreed on the need for industrial modernization, they differed on how to achieve that goal. Clémentel, whose staff drew up postwar economic plans during the conflict, fashioned a grand design incorporating producers' ententes (or cartels), regional economic bodies, the promotion of modern industrial ideas, and a partnership between government, labor, and management. A strong ministry of national economy was envisaged to supervise the dynamics of the economic network and to guide economic activity when private efforts proved inadequate. Clémentel's design included international cooperation: in September, 1918, in a memorandum that served as the basis for France's economic policy in peace talks with the Allies, he included among his proposals an extension into peacetime of the Allies' pooling of scarce raw materials at fair prices. The French business community strongly opposed an economic scheme that conceded the state a determining role, however, and Clémentel's idea met resistance from the United States (see below, p. 152).[2]

Loucheur had no detailed plan for economic renewal to present at war's end, primarily because he had been focusing his energies on munitions production and had believed right up to the last weeks of the struggle that the conflict would continue into 1919. Furthermore, he almost certainly had worked with the expectation that his services to the state would conclude once the wartime emergency was over. Nevertheless, he voiced certain opinions about the French postwar economy to the Chamber's commission on economic reorganization in 1917, and they helped mold his general approach once he began to concentrate on peacetime economic policy after the armistice.[3]

In late 1918, Loucheur was far more interested than Clémentel in reducing the state's intrusions into the economy and in returning to commercial liberty as rapidly as possible. He thought that much in the way

1. Kuisel, *Capitalism and the State,* 50.

2. *Ibid.,* 44–48, 53.

3. Minutes, Commission de Réorganisation Economique (Chambre), October 18, 1917, in C, 7771, AN.

of economic recovery could be through private initiative. Yet he also believed that some state involvement was unavoidable, and his pragmatic nature allowed him to advocate government participation where he deemed it necessary. He joined with Clémentel in calling for a system of Allied resource pooling, but he proved adaptable when it became apparent the scheme did not hold broad appeal.

During the months of transition, Loucheur wanted to lay the foundations for a strong, efficient, competitive, and modernized French economy. He criticized what he felt were weaknesses in prewar French economic life: small, inefficient businesses, economic individualism and jealousy, high tariffs, an insufficient interest in exports, and an overdependence on other countries for manufactured goods and raw materials.[4] He hoped to make France a major exporting power capable of competing with Germany, Britain, and the United States. From the start, he spoke in favor of strong industrial associations and lent his support to attempts to create powerful producers' ententes for the iron and steel industries. He encouraged mass production, with a number of specialized factories contributing to the manufacture of a product. And to combat the excessive reliance on other countries for manufactured goods, he thought of temporarily transforming state munitions factories to manufacture products undeveloped or weakly developed in France, such as sewing machines, typewriters, and fertilizers.

Loucheur was anxious to see France's position strengthened in regard to raw materials and energy. He saw that, because coal was the backbone of French industrial life, the cost of other goods and materials would depend on its price. That is why he fought fervently to establish coal prices low enough for the nation to remain economically competitive with the rest of the industrialized world; it also helps account for his keen interest in Allied resource pooling at equitable prices. To satisfy France's energy needs, Loucheur promoted production at home, sought sources abroad, and recommended the development of untapped forms of energy, especially hydroelectric power.

Loucheur wanted to bring to economic liberalism a modernizing thrust based on strong government encouragement and some state involvement. He underscored the need for a new kind of French economic spirit in a speech to the Chamber of Deputies on February 14, 1919: "[French industrialists] must be audacious, but we must also have con-

4. *Ibid.*

fidence in them. . . . It is this policy of audacity and confidence we must pursue today, and I declare in descending from this rostrum that on the lips of all Frenchmen there must be but a single hymn, the hymn to production."[5] Carrying out his plans and ideas proved far more difficult than articulating them, however. He repeatedly ran into resistance from interest groups. Industrial pressure, a press campaign, and attacks against certain steel interests in the Chamber of Deputies forced him to reconsider his plans for powerful industrial associations in the metallurgical industry. And many workers were not as interested in production as they were in a shorter work week. Securing coal at a competitive price became the most formidable problem of all, since it depended so greatly on circumstances Loucheur could not control.

EARLY ACTIONS AFFECTING INDUSTRY

Pervasive state involvement in the economic life of France, or *étatisme*, had reached unprecedented levels at the end of the conflict. As soon as the war was over, the private sector appealed for a return to commercial freedom. Loucheur agreed in principle about the desirability of relaxing state intervention in the economy, but he was also conscious that the economy could not return to a peacetime footing without a period of adjustment and that the state's role would be pivotal during that time.

Accordingly, he devised measures to stimulate peacetime production by private industry. He also had to decide what to do with the state-owned and state-operated munitions plants that had employed large numbers during the war. Here he was caught between those who wanted to see the state undertake permanently the manufacture of certain products that were not war related and those who resented any kind of state-run peacetime production. He saw a vital role for the French metallurgical industry, and while reducing wartime controls in the period following the armistice, he attempted to use the government's influence toward the formation of powerful industrial ententes. Since coal was in extremely short supply, it could not be completely deregulated without creating chaos. Loucheur had to decide how the wartime sys-

5. France, *Annales de le Chambre: Débats*, February 14, 1919, p. 567.

tem should be modified to suit the peacetime situation. He had to determine how to maintain coal supplies at adequate levels during the winter of 1918–1919.

The demobilization before him was awesome, for there were twelve thousand factories under the control of his ministry at war's end. For the vast majority of them, his concern was to convert war-related production into peacetime manufacture with minimum disruption. He placed a high priority on avoiding unemployment. Thus, he phased out the making of some war-related materials progressively, letting military needs and the availability of workers decide the pace. He met with industrialists to help smooth the shift to peacetime goods in ways that preserved jobs.[6] Creusot employed sixty-five thousand workers at the end of the war, directly and in its subsidiaries. To keep the company's employment up, Loucheur decided to place an order for between four hundred and five hundred locomotives, and he told the Chamber's army commission on November 15, "Creusot, after resisting a little, was wonder-struck to learn that with its workshops, where construction demands a tremendous effort . . . , instead of manufacturing two hundred locomotives in two years, it could, by the way I suggest, manufacture five hundred and even six hundred. All it need do is enlist some help and have certain pieces mass-produced in a uniform way in other workshops." It is evident that Loucheur intended a close oversight for large industries such as Creusot, partly because of the large numbers of workers involved but also because he believed the French economic recovery had to be based on heavy industry. He also planned to encourage the linking of less efficient firms with larger companies so that the principle of mass production would continue.[7]

At the same time that he was attempting to stimulate peacetime production, the government was under attack for not lifting controls. A number of industrial associations and newspapers were vocal against *étatiste* policies right after the armistice. Feeling ran high enough to spawn industrial leagues whose primary purpose was the battle against

6. Loucheur to inspectors of private firms in war work and regional manpower inspectors, November 13, 1918, in F 12, 8023, AN; Loucheur's Circular, November 13, 1918, in 94 AP, 370, AN; Minutes, Commission de l'Armée (Chambre), November 15, 1918, in C, 7501, AN; Commission Interministérielle des Métaux et des Fabrications de Guerre, November 8, 1918, in F 12, 7666, AN.

7. Minutes, Commission de l'Armée (Chambre), November 15, 1918, in C, 7501, AN.

étatisme in every form.[8] The government's stand on imports was particularly deplored. Loucheur, responsible for imports after the creation of the ministry of industrial reconstruction, refused to yield, however, in spite of his own bias toward commercial liberty. He explained to the Chamber of Deputies on February 14 that two paramount considerations lay behind the government's stance on imports. One was the financial stability of the French franc, threatened because of a large balance-of-payments deficit. The other was the need to give French industry time to recuperate from the wartime crisis before exposing it to a buffeting from outside. He acknowledged, though, the care required to keep the system from reinforcing high prices. The *robinet de l'importation* (importation faucet) had to be modulated, Loucheur explained. He cited one instance where British steel products had been allowed into France in order to force domestic producers to reduce their prices.[9] The explanations failed to satisfy the opponents, and their protests lasted into the spring.

Loucheur did move rapidly to abolish another wartime instrument of state control, namely, consortiums. Comprising manufacturers and merchants dependent on a commodity like cotton or jute, consortiums had been formed to centralize foreign purchases of staples. The consortiums were closed corporations, so that industrialists or merchants who refused to join were excluded from foreign purchases. Controlled by government committees that coordinated transportation and regulated prices, they had been largely under the administration of the ministry of commerce during the war but came under Loucheur's supervision when he was appointed minister of industrial reconstruction. Business circles that tolerated the consortiums in wartime demanded their dissolution with the restoration of peace. Loucheur, of a like mind, acted swiftly to dismantle them. He was able to tell the Chamber of Deputies in February that only three remained, one of which was scheduled to disband at the end of March.[10] For opponents of *étatisme*, Loucheur's action was a

8. *La Journée industrielle*, January 10, 1919, p. 1, January 11, 1919, p. 2; *Le Temps*, December 26, 1918, p. 3, February 16, 1919, p. 1, February 23, 1919, p. 1; *L'Europe nouvelle*, February 22, 1919, pp. 346, 348, March 1, 1919, pp. 425–27; Résolution votée le 25 janvier 1919 par l'assemblée plénière des groupements agricoles, commerciaux et industriels de Lyon et de la région, in 6 N, 152, SHA.

9. France, *Annales de la Chambre: Débats*, February 14, 1919, p. 559.

10. Godfrey, *Capitalism at War*, 106–27; Frank Arnold Haight, *A History of French Commercial Policies* (New York, 1941), 84–86, 101–102; Kuisel, *Capitalism and the State*, 50; France, *Annales de la Chambre: Débats*, February 14, 1919, pp. 559–60.

welcome sign, but for Clémentel, who had seen continued utility in the consortiums, it amounted to a major defeat.

STATE-OWNED INDUSTRIES

Munitions production programs, operating on a large scale at the beginning of November, were cut back sharply with the signing of the armistice. A problem then was what to do with the greatly expanded state-owned munitions plants. Loucheur wanted to keep them in a quasi state of readiness in case the armistice did not hold until the peace treaty. But he also had to look toward transferring most munitions personnel to other forms of work. Refitting segments of the state plants for the production of peacetime goods, especially items for which France was highly dependent upon imports before the war or for which there was a general public need, such as locomotives, box cars, telephone equipment, and spare parts for rail equipment, seemed part of the solution.

Loucheur evinced some of his thinking about the state-owned war plants when he appeared before the Chamber's army commission on November 15. He believed that the state-run chemical factories should be converted to fertilizers. Though proclaiming himself a strong defender of private industry, he remarked that these factories might even assist in the regulation of fertilizer prices, since the safety valve they provided could prevent the reemergence of a powerful cartel, the Cartel des Carbures. He suggested that state participation in the production of fertilizers would be favorable to the development of a strong agricultural sector. He also left the impression that the state might become involved in making other goods, telephone equipment being his example. His statements that day heartened Albert Thomas, who commented, "It was a good, solid, although moderate doctrine of *étatisme*."[11]

But opposition was powerful. Newspapers challenged the concept of state-run plants in a number of articles and published protests from industrial and commercial associations. The newspaper *Les Débats* recalled the debacle of the experiment of national workshops in 1848. Strong resistance arose in parliament, where Raphaël Milliès-Lacroix,

11. Minutes, Commission de l'Armée (Chambre), November 15, 1919, in C, 7501, AN; *Proposition de loi* Presented by Albert Thomas, Chambre des Députés, 1919 Session, in 94 AP, 367, AN.

the *rapporteur* of the Senate's finance commission, was among the most outspoken.[12]

Loucheur's toning-down of his initial zeal for state-run factories was evident in mid-December, when he declared before the Chamber's budget commission that portions of plants should be reserved for peacetime purposes only in a very limited way. He mentioned Roanne, where, instead of keeping thousands of workers, he planned to retain only a skeleton crew of one or two thousand to produce railway equipment. He justified operation of the state plants by warning, "We must not, if one day the misfortune of war comes again, find ourselves in the same trap as in 1914."[13]

On December 30, appearing before the Senate, he clarified his point of view to a degree in answering Milliès-Lacroix' questions. He agreed with the senator that the state plants should not become tributaries of private industry. He also more emphatically avowed his determination to reduce the number of workers in the state factories to prewar levels, and he began speaking of using state plants for peacetime production only temporarily. That his ideas were unsettled was altogether plain when he requested more time to frame a rational program.[14]

Loucheur was still talking about the question on February 14, when he went before the Chamber of Deputies. He reported that some of the emptied space in state plants was to go for the repair of rolling stock at a monthly rate of 1,500 railway cars by the end of April and 2,500 by the end of June. He also related that eight hundred workers were engaged in making iron fittings at Roanne, where an assembly line for the production of new railway cars was envisioned too. Other plants would manufacture tobacco products and telephone and telegraph equipment. Loucheur pointed out that the state-run chemical plants built during the war were producing fertilizers for agriculture, but he no longer talked about using them to hold down prices. Loucheur did his best to reassure those fearful of state intrusions, but he left many questions unanswered, and his presentation drew criticism from both the Left and the Right.[15]

12. Newspaper clipping from *Les Débats,* November 27, 1918, in F 7, 13367, AN; *Le Temps,* December 1, 1918, p. 2; *Proposition de loi* Presented by Albert Thomas, Chambre des Députés, 1919 Session, in 94 AP, 367, AN.

13. Minutes, Commission du Budget (Chambre), December 12, 1918, in C, 7561, AN.

14. Collection of Declarations by Loucheur Between November 15, 1918, and March 30, 1919, Regarding State Industries, in 94 AP, 367, AN.

15. France, *Annales de la Chambre: Débats,* February 14, 1919, pp. 557–58, February 21, 1919, pp. 692–703.

In the ensuing weeks, he showed that his commitment to state-owned peacetime factories was even less than his February speech had led the deputies to think. At the end of March, he told the Chamber that he had scaled back his projection for the repair of railroad cars to 1,500 a month by June, and he was no longer mentioning the production of cars at Roanne. He emphasized that the manufacture of agricultural implements at several plants was only provisional. And he reverted to his earlier idea that state factories might appropriately produce goods France had been a heavy importer of prior to the war, like typewriters and sewing machines. Three days later he stressed in the Senate that the cardinal purpose of operating state plants was to have facilities for producing arms should the need arise. It was increasingly apparent that making peacetime goods there was of receding interest to him. In early April he again revised the figure for railway-car repairs, this time to six hundred a month by June. Thomas sarcastically surmised that by June the number would be down to zero.[16]

Loucheur also continued to reduce the output of the state arsenals to levels he felt compatible with peacetime needs. At St. Etienne, for instance, 12,000 workers had been employed at the peak, but by May, 1919, the force was down to 3,800, and Loucheur's goal was to whittle the number to 2,500, with the remaining personnel turning out the telephone and telegraph equipment, typewriters, sewing machines, and rolling stock that bulked so large in his thinking.[17] But Thomas complained that neither Loucheur's principles nor his plans were clear: "He vacillates a little between the *étatisme* of the Left of the Chamber and, if we dare say it, the *privatisme* of the Senate. The worst thing in our view is that there is still no definite program for the [state] concerns in general, [for] no industrialist owning the impressive complex that our state concerns make up would lack that."[18]

Partly to placate the Left, Loucheur on February 24 established a special committee to study the state munitions plants and their possible peacetime role. The committee, when it made its report on May 20, was receptive to redirecting the factories toward civilian ends. It recom-

16. *Proposition de loi* Presented by Albert Thomas, Chambre des Députés, 1919 Session, in 94 AP, 367; *La Journée industrielle*, April 16, 1919, p. 2.

17. *L'Usine*, June 5, 1919, p. 17.

18. *Proposition de loi* Presented by Albert Thomas, Chambre des Députés, 1919 Session, in 94 AP, 367, AN.

mended reforms aimed at greater efficiency, fuller accountability, and a participation by all personnel in the profits. The committee's conclusions, however, were a dead letter.[19] Loucheur was more intent on other matters, and the need to keep the factories in a state of semireadiness for war seemed less pressing as the peacemaking process neared a successful outcome. Anyway, many of the munitions workers had found other jobs. Loucheur apparently decided that it was best simply to avoid discussing the report unless he was forced to do so.

In March, 1920, the leftist newspaper *L'Information ouvrière et sociale* tried to energize a discussion by complaining that nothing had resulted from the report though almost a year had elapsed.[20] But it was obvious by then that a network of state-run factories was no longer a live option. For Loucheur, economic and political considerations did not allow it, and the emergency that had made the idea alluring had long since passed.

METALLURGY

Loucheur was particularly concerned that France approach metallurgy from a new angle, since he realized that, with Lorraine recovered, France would experience a dramatic increase in production. What he sought was a system of strong producers' ententes that would foster efficiency, productivity, and exportation.

Before the war, most of France's steel and iron output had been for domestic consumption, and the manufacturers had demonstrated little interest in exporting. The government had abetted an inward focus through protective tariffs that enabled high profit margins at home. For the industry as a whole, exports were a kind of safety valve; producers turned to the export market—where they realized a very low profit— only to protect the prices they wanted for domestic sales. The belief grew that France's metallurgical industry had not developed as rapidly in the prewar years as it might have had it been more aggressive in international markets or been forced to compete against imports at home. Robert Pinot attempted in *Le Comité des Forges de France au service de*

19. Newspaper article from *L'Information ouvrière et sociale,* March 28, 1920, p. 1, *ibid.*

20. *Ibid.*

la nation to defend the industry by showing that France had surpassed most of the other main producing nations in growth, stated in percentages, for both steel and iron between 1903 and 1913. But the percentages did not impress Loucheur; he looked at the actual number of tons produced, and for both metals, France lagged far behind the United States, Germany, and Britain in 1913.[21]

During the war Loucheur and Clémentel had concluded that an effective way of organizing the French metallurgical industry afterward would be to create an industrywide *comptoir général de vente*, an entente of producers capable of coordinating production, prices, and France's efforts on the international plane.[22] The government had endorsed such a *comptoir* at the beginning of 1917, and Loucheur later established a permanent liaison with the Comité des Forges on the question. The report of the commission the Comité had charged with conducting a feasibility study came out in early 1918, and it laid down the general organizational lines of the *comptoir*. A later, more detailed study revealed that a broadly based *comptoir* was unrealistic because of the great diversity of products within the industry. The government and the producers decided that it was preferable to proceed by stages, creating *comptoirs* for specific areas of production first and joining them together later.[23]

Parallel to participating in discussions concerning *comptoirs*, Loucheur was trying to stimulate a quick, large-scale renewal of peacetime production in metallurgical products. He told the Chamber's army commission on November 15 that production would not resume with any kind of vigor unless the price of both coal and steel fell, and he affirmed his determination to secure price reductions as soon as possible. He knew he could count on the backing of the Comité des Forges, which shared his conviction. The Comité collaborated with him closely on the matter in the weeks after the armistice.[24]

21. M. Brelet, *La Crise de la métallurgie: La Politique économique et sociale du Comité des Forges* (Paris, 1923), 27; Pinot, *Le Comité des Forges*, 44–47; France, *Annales de la Chambre: Débats*, February 14, 1919, pp. 566–67.

22. *Comptoirs*, or producers' ententes, had existed before the war, but their power and scope were much more limited than what Loucheur and Clémentel hoped for the postwar era.

23. Henri Flu, *Les Comptoirs métallurgiques d'après-guerre* (Lyon, 1924), 47, 51–53.

24. Minutes, Commission de l'Armée (Chambre), November 15, 1918, in C, 7501, AN; Pinot, *Le Comité des Forges*, 220–21, 328–29.

Before the end of the month, Loucheur had announced steps to reduce the price of British and French coal by 30 to 40 percent in the domestic market. On December 13, he told a delegation from the Comité des Forges that a price cut of approximately 33 percent for metallurgical products was planned. All the new prices, including those for coal and coke, were to be retroactive to November 11. The government also pledged to maintain import restrictions, control the flow of products from Lorraine and the left bank of the Rhine, and absorb 80 percent of any losses the new prices caused for stocks produced before November 11.[25]

A condition accompanied the state's generosity, however. In order to qualify for financial assistance, metallurgical manufacturers had to participate in a *comptoir*. Loucheur set this condition since he believed that the groups would assure France's competitive position internationally and that fixed domestic prices would head off speculation.

On December 18, the government announced the new prices as well as the end of state-imposed formalities and restrictions for ordering steel products. But Loucheur's lifting of state controls came only after the country's principal steelmakers had signed a provisional agreement establishing the Comptoir Sidérurgique de France. Instead of dealing with a state-directed apparatus, producers would pass through the *comptoir* in filling consumer orders.[26] A system of centralization remained for steel products, but with the government playing a much less visible role than during the war.

At the beginning of 1919, Loucheur strengthened the Comptoir Sidérurgique by giving it a monopoly on the steel products sequestered in Lorraine. The profits from its sale of these went to the state, which applied the money to its 80-percent share of producer losses resulting from the retroactive price reductions.[27]

Because the formation of an iron comptoir moved more slowly, Loucheur did not lift controls on pig iron in his December 18 announcement. Iron producers, desiring the benefits contingent upon joining a *comptoir*, gathered on December 24 and decided that the differences in their production methods and the wide geographic distribution of their fac-

25. *Bulletin des usines de guerre*, December 2, 1918, in 10 N, 2, SHA; Pinot, *Le Comité des Forges*, 330–33.

26. Flu, *Les Comptoirs métallurgiques*, 53.

27. Pinot, *Le Comité des Forges*, 225, 330–35.

tories favored the organization of two *comptoirs,* one for hematite pig iron and the other for phosphorous pig iron. For hematite pig iron, a new body would be constituted, but for phosphorous pig iron the prewar Comptoir de Longwy would be the centralizer.

With one iron *comptoir* reconstituted and another in the process of formation, Loucheur announced on December 31 the cessation of state centralization and price equalization for pig iron. Until the new group was operational, the Comité des Forges would centralize orders for hematite pig iron. To enlarge the two *comptoirs'* influence, Loucheur gave them a joint monopoly on the sale of iron products coming from factories in Lorraine. He also made participation in one of the iron *comptoirs* virtually unavoidable, by stipulating that the coke that producers received from the state, which still controlled its distribution, would depend in part on the amount of iron they turned over to a *comptoir* for sale.[28]

Loucheur's optimism regarding the postwar role of *comptoirs* continued into January. He began discussing similar bodies for other metallurgical products, as well as incentives by which the state could ensure participation in them. He was pleased when on January 10 a commission assigned to frame statutes for the *comptoir* in hematite pig iron completed its work and sent out draft contracts. On January 15 he made another strong bid for *comptoirs* at a meeting with industrialists.[29]

Opposition soon developed, however, among small producers fearful of losing state benefits if they did not join a *comptoir* and of being overpowered by large firms if they did—especially since Loucheur clearly preferred large, efficient enterprises to small ones. The small manufacturers worked behind the scenes to mount a virulent press campaign against *comptoirs.*[30] Parliamentary opponents of the government widened the debate to include the conduct of the metallurgical industry during the war. The most outspoken critic was Edouard Barthe, a Socialist deputy, who in a speech to the Chamber in late January ques-

28. Flu, *Les Comptoirs métallurgiques,* 53–56.

29. *Ibid.,* 56–57.

30. *Ibid.,* 57–58. It is also possible that Jules Niclausse, the influential industrialist who favored lower tariff rates on steel and who was an opponent of the Comité des Forges, was involved in fomenting the controversy that centered on the metallurgical industry; it has been asserted that he provided important information used in attacks made in parliament. There is certainly evidence to support such claims, although it is not conclusive. See Jeanneney, *François de Wendel,* 71–72.

tioned the wartime role of the Comité des Forges, the government's attitude toward it, and wartime decisions affecting the metallurgical industry generally.[31] Loucheur, because of his wartime relations with the Comité, entered the debate and repeatedly contested Barthe's interpretations. On February 14, he responded to the criticisms of Barthe and others in an economic policy speech. Aware of the suspicions the attacks had aroused in the public, he tried to distance himself to some extent from the metallurgical industry, and he never once mentioned the *comptoirs* he had been so instrumental in developing. He instead gave much attention to the position of privilege the industry had enjoyed before the war, arguing that the prewar arrangements could not continue if France wished to maintain a commercial balance, especially when the nation was on the threshold of becoming a significant exporter of metallurgical products as a result of France's absorption of Lorraine. He talked about an *oreiller de paresse*, that is, high protective tariffs, as encouraging inefficiency and unrealistic prices.[32]

Although the attacks and criticisms came from only a vocal minority, Loucheur decided to suspend his drive for powerful *comptoirs*. He had become the target of a press campaign that the extreme right-wing journalist Léon Daudet launched during January accusing him of designs to create a newspaper trust. The campaign was vehement enough that the British ambassador in Paris referred to it in a report to the British Foreign Office.[33] Loucheur had to take care not to jeopardize his political position by continuing to push the controversial idea of *comptoirs* and on February 12 he announced a suspension of efforts to the iron producers he had convened. No longer would financial assistance depend upon a firm's membership in a *comptoir*; instead a special arm within his ministry would handle such matters. The government, moreover, planned to terminate its controls on iron products at the end of March.

Loucheur never really resumed his efforts in behalf of *comptoirs* after the attacks of January and February. In the weeks following his speech of February 14 the *comptoir* movement endured more setbacks.

31. France, *Annales de la Chambre: Débats*, January 24, 1919, pp. 176–80, January 31, 1919, pp. 288–302.
32. *Ibid.*, February 14, 1919, pp. 566–67.
33. Lord Derby to Lord Curzon, January 20, 1919, in Foreign Office, General Correspondence, Political, FO 371, Vol. 3751, PRO.

In early March, the industrialists associated with the *comptoir* for hematite pig iron were reimbursed for their membership fees; the organization had failed to develop. The Comptoir de Longwy, too, had its state appointment as a centralizer withdrawn, and it returned to its prewar function as an agent for the sale of French-produced phosphorous pig iron. Later in the month, the Comptoir Sidérurgique lost its monopoly over steel products sequestered in Lorraine to an association of producers from the areas ravaged by the war.[34]

The opprobrium surrounding the metallurgical industry faded during the spring, however, as a parliamentary commission investigating its wartime practices and decisions concluded that the charges against it were unfounded. New efforts to organize *comptoirs* became possible, but this time without government assistance. A *comptoir* for hematite pig iron was created in May with statutes only slightly different from the original group, and *comptoirs* were organized for other metallurgical products. But since the anti-*comptoir*, antimetallurgy campaign left the government unable to pressure reluctant producers into joining or to concede monopolistic powers, the drive for reorganization of the metallurgical industry waned.[35]

At least on this occasion, when faced with vocal opposition and an uncomfortable political situation, Loucheur chose to retreat rather than risk damaging his reputation as a minister. That may have been politically shrewd, but it may also have been compelled by objective limits. From that point on, Loucheur appears to have let the metallurgists carry on without his active assistance.

COAL

Loucheur recognized that coal was even more critical than iron and steel for a strong peacetime economy. At the end of the war, he faced a coal crisis precipitated by the retreating Germans' destruction of mines in northeastern France, by a transportation crisis, and by a slowdown in coal mining in Britain. The demobilization exacerbated the situation. France's long-term needs also concerned him. With the restoration of

34. Flu, *Les Comptoirs métallurgiques*, 58, 99.
35. *Ibid.*, 58–59; Charles S. Maier, *Recasting Bourgeois Europe: Stabilization in France, Germany, and Italy in the Decade After World War I* (Princeton, 1975), 74–76.

Alsace-Lorraine, these were going to be considerably greater than the 59.5 million tons France consumed in 1913.[36] Loucheur at first hoped for generous supplies from Britain and Belgium and looked to the peace settlement to secure coal as a form of reparation from Germany. At home, the coal emergency meant an extension of government controls into peacetime, so that one of Loucheur's tasks at war's end was to adapt his wartime controls sufficiently to satisfy critics without compromising their effectiveness.

Shortly after the armistice, Loucheur told the Chamber's army commission of his plans to stimulate a rapid return to full-scale industrial production through sharp reductions in the price of coal. He had available a *péréquation* fund of approximately 250 million francs to help make the plan work. Toward the end of November, he circulated an announcement of a reduction of the average price for a ton of coal to sixty-five francs, thirty to forty francs beneath what it had been.[37] For that, bureaucratic machinery of some sort was necessary, and Loucheur tried simply to keep the Bureau National des Charbons in operation. But opposition to continuing the wartime system was strong. Large firms, especially those associated with steel, opposed *péréquation*, which favored smaller consumers lacking the might to negotiate favorable coal prices. And though many French industrialists saw a need for some government controls, they preferred a transitional scheme that gave private interests predominance. What they suggested was an *office central des charbons*, a private organ functioning under state control to oversee the Bureau National des Charbons, which they wanted to become merely an instrument for execution.[38]

Loucheur, sensitive to criticisms against the existing system, established a study committee at the beginning of January but made it clear that the critical situation required keeping an administrative institution in place to oversee distribution and *péréquation*.[39] Loucheur had no intention of abandoning devices, including *péréquation*, that he con-

36. Ministère du Commerce, *Rapport général sur l'industrie française*, I, 7–8. This figure excludes coke consumption.

37. Minutes, Commission de l'Armée (Chambre), November 15, 1918, in C, 7501, AN; *Bulletin des usines de guerre*, December 2, 1918, in 10 N, 2, SHA.

38. Walter A. McDougall, *France's Rhineland Diplomacy, 1914–1924: The Last Bid for a Balance of Power in Europe* (Princeton, 1978), 105; *L'Usine*, February 6, 1919, p. 21; *La Journée industrielle*, February 16–17, 1919, p. 2.

39. *L'Usine*, January 23, 1919, p. 21.

sidered crucial to the peacetime transition. The committee made its report in May, and Loucheur endorsed its recommendations, implementing a new structure that took effect on July 1. To some surprise and disappointment, no private executive office was part of the plan. Instead, the Bureau National des Charbons retained control over distribution. With minor modifications, categories of consumers that Loucheur's system of 1917 had established were also kept. The primary innovation was in the way individual consumers procured their coal. Previously, members of groups bought through the groups to which they belonged, but the new system let them obtain whatever coal their groups had allotted them through channels of their own choice.[40] That was not a drastic move toward commercial freedom, but it was a cautious first step and about as large a one as was safe at that point.

Loucheur warned that domestic coal mining would not reach prewar levels for several years because of the considerable destruction in northeastern France: almost twenty million tons a year were out of production.[41] But he failed to foresee the extent to which the yield of mines operating during the war would drop after the armistice. The demobilization of workers and the return to an eight-hour day in March contributed to the fall in output. In the Loire region, between 1918 and 1919, the coal produced in February fell from 388,191 to 366,698 tons, in March from 441,620 to 341,759 tons, and in April from 435,284 to 281,299 tons.[42]

The British had failed to meet their obligations to the French in the conflict's last months and had experienced a slowdown in their mines right after the armistice. But they did continue their wartime policy of providing coal to the French and Italians on a priority basis at prices below what they charged neutrals, and in January, Britain also concluded separate agreements with France and Italy guaranteeing them shipping capacity up to a determined maximum—that which France and Italy had in service at the end of October, 1918—at a fixed maximum rate. The arrangement with the French made them responsible for assuring any additional tonnage they needed for their import services, including those for coal. The agreements of January, which were transitional between the wartime pooling of Allied shipping capacity and full market

40. Sardier, *Le Ravitaillement en charbon*, 174; *L'Usine*, May 29, 1919, pp. 21, 23.

41. France, *Annales de la Chambre: Débats*, February 14, 1919, p. 560; H. Bonin, *La Reconstitution des houillères du Nord de la France* (Paris, 1926), 45.

42. Acting consul in Lyon to Lord Curzon, June 26, 1919, in FO 382/2484, PRO.

freedom, provided Loucheur with some relief. He had told the interministerial coal commission in September, 1918, that tremendous difficulties could be expected in the early postwar period because of demands for shipping capacity from countries trying to renew their peacetime operations.[43]

Although British coal production improved with the demobilization of miners, demand far outstripped supply. As a result, British exports to France remained low. During the first quarter of 1919, an average of 1.19 million tons arrived monthly, well below the figure of 1.74 million agreed to the previous spring and the 2 million that had been delivered earlier in the war. The 1919 figure was also below the average for British coal deliveries in the war's last months.[44] For Loucheur, the statistics were indeed grim.

In March, Loucheur declared that French coal deliveries to Italy would have to terminate, since French supplies were then running a million tons a month short of French needs. Because of the meager supplies, the Italians in early April went before the Supreme Economic Council (SEC), which had replaced the Allied Maritime Transport Council as the chief Allied organization for economic matters. Loucheur was unresponsive to pleas to help Italy, articulated with particular force by the Americans, but as the gravity of the country's plight became evident, he changed his mind. At the meeting of the SEC on April 22 he assured the Italians of five thousand tons of French coal daily. An SEC coal committee recommended that 800,000 tons go to Italy every month from nations participating in the council, but in view of Britain's and France's own problems that kind of goal was unattainable. The five thousand tons a day that France sent for a brief time in April fell to two thousand by early May. Toward mid-May, when a French coal strike appeared possible, deliveries to Italy were halted.[45] The burden after that fell primarily to the British.

Toward the end of May, though, the British announced an end to reduced coal prices for France and Italy. That was just as the French were

43. Captain Pilliard to Louis Loucheur, November 30, 1918, in F 12, 7785, AN; Salter, *Allied Shipping Control*, 222–23, 226–27, 332–35; Commission Interministérielle des Charbons, September 10, 1918, in F 12, 7683, AN.

44. Olivier, *La Politique du charbon*, 51, 55–57; Salter, *Allied Shipping Control*, 360.

45. Minutes of the Brussels Conference, March 17, 1919, in Series Y, Internationale, 1918–1940, Vol. 151, MAE; Minutes of the Supreme Economic Council, April 7, 1919, April 11, 1919, April 22, 1919, all in Y, 152, MAE; Memorandum of the Comité des Charbons, April 25,

experiencing rapidly increasing labor tensions in domestic mining. It was particularly galling to the French that while Britain imposed higher prices on France and Italy, it kept the domestic price artificially low. Britain's dual pricing system dealt a setback not only to Loucheur's domestic coal program but also to his hopes that French industry could compete in world markets.[46]

Belgian coal had been unavailable to France beginning in 1914, but at the start of 1919 an agreement was struck committing Belgium to send 350,000 tons monthly. The French transportation system was badly in need of repair, however, and incapable of hauling large quantities from Belgian mines. For March, the total from Belgium was only fifteen thousand tons. Improvement occurred thereafter, but deliveries remained far below the agreed level. In July, Belgian industrialists, aware of insufficiencies at home, launched a movement to restrict shipments abroad.[47] In mid-1919, it seemed clear to Loucheur that Belgium would continue an uncertain provider.

The French started receiving coal from the Saar, in Germany, as early as December, 1918, and the Luxembourg Protocol, of December, 1918, mandated an uninterrupted delivery of German coal to Alsace-Lorraine. But no coal beyond that came from Germany before September, 1919.[48] A primary prewar source remained essentially closed to France for much of the energy-straitened year. In consequence, Loucheur's determination solidified to reinforce the links he had with Britain and Belgium.

By mid-1919, Loucheur had been unable to find a satisfactory solution, but he had demonstrated flexibility by introducing a transitional coal distribution system that allowed more individual freedom than his wartime structure did. He appeared ready to return to commercial freedom as soon as conditions were favorable. When that might be he did not know, for the energy shortfall was European in scope. His hope in

1919, in Records of the American Commission to Negotiate Peace, 1918–1931, Microfilm 135, HHPL; Coal Committee Report on Coal for Italy, May 16, 1919, in Supreme Economic Council Documents, Bound Typescript, Vol. 3, Document 146, HHPL.

46. Paul Cambon to French foreign ministry, May 30, 1919, in Z, Grande Bretagne, 96, MAE; Louis Loucheur to Etienne Clémentel, June 23, 1919, in F 12, 8075, AN.

47. Olivier, *La Politique du charbon*, 178–79; *L'Usine*, July 24, 1919, p. 21.

48. Note sur la situation charbonnière de la France depuis l'armistice, September 12, 1921, in Y, 191, MAE.

early 1919 lay to a large degree in negotiating substantial German coal deliveries into the reparations section of the peace treaty.

THE LIBERATED REGIONS

One of the responsibilities of the ministry of industrial reconstruction was administering programs of industrial recovery in the liberated regions, which held the greater number of the twenty thousand factories and workshops destroyed in France during the conflict. Complicating the job was the damage that vital portions of France's transportation system had undergone: more than five thousand kilometers of railroad track, a thousand kilometers of canals, and five thousand bridges needed repair or replacement.[49] In February, 1919, Loucheur told the Senate that restoring the devastated areas was a "formidable task unlike any that man has faced in the history of the world."[50] Born and reared in the war-torn department of the Nord, he was shaken indeed by the devastation he had seen there.

The core administrative agency in Loucheur's assignment was the Office of Industrial Reconstruction (ORI) which until its incorporation into Loucheur's ministry had been a part of the ministry of blockade and the liberated regions. The office purchased, either directly or through other agencies, supplies, tools, and materials essential for industrial revival and sought to assure that they were distributed equitably. A ministry of the liberated regions remained, but it focused on tasks other than industrial reconstruction.[51]

The state's role in rehabilitating the liberated regions proved to be large, and documents of the immediate postwar period contain numerous references to the territory's primacy in France's efforts toward economic recuperation. The government had committed itself to the principle of state responsibility for individual war damages in legislation proposed in 1915, although it planned to recoup its expenses from the Germans.[52]

As early as 1915, industries from the devastated regions organized an

49. Claude Fohlen, *La France de l'entre-deux-guerres, 1917–1939* (2nd ed.; Paris, 1972), 32–33.

50. *L'Usine*, February 20, 1919, pp. 7, 9.

51. William MacDonald, *Reconstruction in France* (London, 1922), 53–54, 123–24.

52. The government did so in the presentation of a legislative proposal to the Chamber of Deputies on May 11, 1915. See MacDonald, *Reconstruction in France*, 63–64.

association, eventually consisting of about a thousand different firms in four groups: mines and metallurgy; textiles; electrical and machinery construction; and agriculture and other industries. It laid its own groundwork for reconstruction by creating regional and technical committees to order rebuilding priorities and to propose possible clauses for the peace treaty. It also compiled dossiers on what the enemy had taken and what the resumption of production required. Its most far-reaching action during the war was to establish a private corporation, the Comptoir Central d'Achats, as the sole purchaser of materials needed for industrial reconstruction in the liberated regions.[53]

In December, 1918, Loucheur, following his wartime pattern of meeting with industrialists monthly to hear grievances and discuss government efforts to aid them, went to the department of the Nord, where 60 percent of the wartime damage to French industry had occurred.[54] He developed a close partnership between the government, as represented by the Office of Industrial Reconstruction, and industry, working through the Comptoir d'Achats. A strong proponent of the Comptoir, he saw it as getting industrialists what they needed at prices generally below what they could secure on their own. Loucheur's support for the Comptoir, whose functions circumscribed the role of the state, remained intact even when some industrialists criticized how the corporation operated. When industrialists went directly to the state for help, Loucheur saw to it that the Comptoir became involved, despite the authority the law gave the state to make purchases on behalf of an industrialist: "People will protest, 'The state is becoming the buyer and the provider!' Not at all. It does not buy directly. All commercial transactions are carried out by the Comptoir d'Achats, that is to say, in the final analysis, by the war-ravaged industrialists [*sinistrés industriels*] themselves. . . . The state advances the funds, that is all."[55]

But Loucheur's interest in centralizing industrial reconstruction went beyond the Comptoir d'Achats, and during the spring he was instrumental in uniting war-affected industrialists into *groupements sinistrés*. The *groupements*, which represented such products as steel, iron, cement, and glass, were given privileges and monopolies by the state that allowed them to obtain from the Germans the products they normally

53. *Ibid.*, 127; *Le Progrès du Nord*, March 4, 1919, p. 1.
54. Loucheur, *Carnets secrets*, 105; *L'Usine*, February 20, 1919, pp. 7, 9.
55. *Le Progrès du Nord*, March 4, 1919, p. 1.

manufactured. The *groupement* for iron and steel, for example, had the right to purchase material for use and resale from German territories occupied by the Allied armies. Loucheur's ministry set the prices the *groupements* paid and, on the recommendations of the *groupements*, made the final decisions on the resale prices.[56] Loucheur plainly wished for the state to protect the interests of the war-ravaged industrialists in a way that required the Germans to bear a palpable share of the burden.

Loucheur and the industrialists of the liberated regions took a keen interest in legislation regarding payments for war damages. In early January, he complained that the bill under consideration contained such cumbrous procedures that the most elementary claims would encounter delays of five years. In contending for a law that could be swiftly implemented and administered, he addressed the Senate on February 15, imploring the body to reduce the formalities for victims to an absolute minimum.[57] The legislation on damage payments passed in parliament and became law on April 17, 1919. Close to four years had passed from when the legislation was first proposed, with numerous debates in both chambers. The law made holders of war-damaged real or personal property in France and Algeria eligible for indemnities as determined by cantonal damage commissions. The ratified version, despite warnings by Loucheur and others, was bureaucratically intricate.[58]

In early 1919, Loucheur focused as well on the recovery and replacement of machinery the Germans had taken from the French during the war. In January, he told industrialists that he was skeptical about how much could be recovered, and he cautioned that replacement in kind was not necessarily the best way to obtain satisfaction, for it could result in the loss of orders for French industry. A special office took charge of machinery losses to German appropriators, and Loucheur asked French manufacturers to state the whereabouts of stolen machinery if they knew it. In his speech to the Senate on February 15, he could refer to a hundred thousand filed claims. Estimating that the figure

---

56. Convention entre l'Etat et le Groupement des Commerçants en Fer et Industriels Producteurs Sidérurgiques Sinistrés, n.d., in Subseries AJ 24, Office de Reconstitution Industrielle des Départements Victimes de l'Invasion, Carton 128, AN; Loucheur to general commissioner of the republic, Department of Commerce, Industry, and Mines, at Strasbourg, and to inspector general of Administration of the Rhineland, head office of the economic department, at Paris, June 6, 1919, *ibid.*

57. *L'Usine,* January 9–16, 1919, p. 3, February 20, 1919, p. 7.

58. MacDonald, *Reconstruction in France,* 70–73, 89.

would probably reach 200,000, he asserted that the administrative machinery for handling the situation was in full operation.[59]

In spite of the problems, progress was made in reconstructing the industrial plant of the liberated regions in the first months of peace. In mid-May, Loucheur and Albert Lebrun, the minister of the liberated regions, presided over the first relighting of a blast furnace there since the end of the war. Loucheur spoke on the occasion about the importance of production, and he encouraged the workers to redouble their efforts so that, despite a new eight-hour work law, production could increase.[60] For production to be one of his themes was certainly in line with the role he envisioned for the liberated regions, for he knew that the devastated areas, with their large industrial base, would be the keystone of any strong French economy.

By the end of the spring, much of the organizational structure for industrial reconstruction was in place. Loucheur was true to his past in centralizing vital functions of the system—in this case, through industrial associations and the Comptoir d'Achats. As in metallurgy and coal, he wanted to preserve as much initiative as possible for private enterprise without undermining the effectiveness of his structure, which also allotted a role to the state. He recognized, though, that negotiations with other states—especially Germany—were needed to move forward on matters like the restitution of materials, reparations in kind, and the organization of a German reconstruction labor force. In order to make progress, Loucheur availed himself of not only the Paris peace conference but also bilateral talks with the Germans (see Chapters 7 and 8).

A speech Loucheur made to the Chamber of Deputies on February 14, 1919, makes clear that what he sought for France was an economy based on the technocratic principles of production and efficiency. His approach proved to be more moderate than the "grand design" the ministry of commerce had devised during the war, not only because of his confidence in private initiative but also because of his awareness of what private enterprise was prepared to tolerate in the way of government intervention. In spite of Loucheur's efforts, one thing already seemed certain by the end of the spring: France's peacetime economy would be something less than the highly efficient, output-oriented system he was so interested in seeing develop.

59. *L'Usine*, January 9–16, 1919, p. 5, February 20, 1919, p. 7.
60. *La Journée industrielle*, May 18–19, 1919, p. 1; *Le Temps*, May 18, 1919, p. 2.

7

Peacemaking, 1919

On January 18, 1919, the Paris peace conference opened officially with a plenary session of the Allies at the French foreign ministry. The meeting, essentially ceremonial, was one of only six plenary sessions held before Germany signed the Treaty of Versailles in June, even though in theory all conference decisions were to be approved by a full session of the conference. The real task of drafting the peace treaty took place elsewhere and was dominated by France, Britain, and the United States, whose delegations were led by their national leaders—Georges Clemenceau, David Lloyd George, and Woodrow Wilson—who became known collectively as the Big Three.[1]

The chief economic representative in the French delegation was Louis Lucien Klotz, the finance minister, but he was not highly regarded by Clemenceau, who commented at one point that he "was the only Jew he ever met who knew nothing of finance."[2] Loucheur does not appear to have had much esteem for Klotz either, referring to him on more than one occasion as "dead wood."[3] Loucheur's rise to preeminence on economic questions for the French was thus that much easier, though his presence at the peace conference was as a technical expert and he was only one of several from the French delegation to have that status. But he quickly detached himself from the other French technical experts and became Clemenceau's leading economic adviser there, partly out of the confidence and respect he had already won from the French premier

1. Raymond J. Sontag, *A Broken World, 1919–1939* (New York, 1972), 1–2.
2. Philip Burnett, ed., *Reparation at the Paris Peace Conference from the Standpoint of the American Delegation* (2 vols.; 1940; rpr. New York, 1965), I, 24.
3. Simone Loucheur, Interview, June 17, 1977.

during the war.[4] Loucheur had proved himself an able negotiator during the conflict, and Lloyd George commented years after the peace conference: "[Loucheur] was indeed one of the shrewdest men I ever met amongst the political figures with whom I had to deal at these International Conferences."[5] His decisiveness and flexibility, and his skill at formulating precise, workable solutions for difficult financial problems, also gained him both influence and respect.

LOUCHEUR'S APPROACH TO PEACE IN 1919

Although Loucheur appeared primarily at technical meetings and was not conspicuous in determining policy in its broadest sense, he had a consistent vision of Europe's reconstruction and the continent's economic and political future. The conceptions he later articulated in speeches and articles guided his activities at the peace conference more than is often recognized.

For him, harmony and peace in Europe centered on economic questions, particularly on the creation of international producers' ententes that, he argued, would lead to the reduction of tariffs. What he advocated foreshadowed in some ways the European Economic Community, and he did not recoil from the prospect of economic cooperation's leading to a European political union.[6]

Loucheur recognized even in 1919, before his thinking had fully ramified, that economic stability was vital for avoiding crises in Europe. He feared that the devastation of French industry and the dynamic industrial potential of Germany put France in danger of inhabiting a permanent state of economic inferiority. In behalf of France and the other war-damaged countries, like Italy and Belgium, he called not for the economic annihilation of Germany but for equality of opportunity for all European nations. In his view, the continuation of Allied war controls,

4. Mermeix, *Le Combat des trois,* 132, 124–26; Marc Trachtenberg, *Reparation in World Politics: France and European Economic Diplomacy, 1916–1923* (New York, 1980), 40.

5. David Lloyd George, *The Truth About Reparations and War-Debts* (London, 1932), 14.

6. Louis Loucheur, "La Conférence économique de Genève," *Revue économique internationale,* II (April, 1927), 37; Jacques de Launay, *Major Controversies of Contemporary History,* trans. J. J. Buckingham (Oxford, 1965), 124–30; *L'Europe nouvelle,* November 28, 1931, pp. 1487–88.

especially in the area of raw materials, would be a step toward that. Although much has been written about Etienne Clémentel's plans for a "new" world economy based on close economic cooperation and an extension into peacetime of the Allies' system of resource pooling,[7] his views were but one expression of the kind of spirit the French government took with it to the peace conference. Another was Clemenceau's willingness to lean on the talents of young men, like Loucheur and André Tardieu, who were open to new modes of international cooperation and were well experienced in war economics.[8]

Loucheur joined with Clémentel in seeking both to extend Allied controls into peacetime and to preserve the channel of Allied credits to France. Their efforts met resistance in late 1918, however, as the United States developed a policy of dismantling the wartime inter-Allied economic structure and limiting financial assistance for the reconstruction of Europe. The French persisted in trying to salvage as much of the wartime structure of economic cooperation as possible, but it became increasingly apparent that any hope of obtaining the kind of Allied cooperation they sought was unrealistic.

The French assumption that the United States could be maneuvered into a receptivity to cooperation and credits for reconstruction drove it to claim high reparations from Germany. The large sum was meant as a bargaining card: the French expected the Allies to give them the credits they needed in return for accepting a smaller settlement from Germany. They also desired to placate domestic public opinion, which was crying for Germany to pay dearly. Although Loucheur's attitude toward Germany was demanding at the outset of the conference, he softened his views as time went by.[9] On other economic questions, too, he showed a willingness to compromise with Britain and the United States, but he never lost sight of French postwar security. He came to be regarded as the most reasonable of the French negotiators at the conference, but in late 1918 and early 1919 he had little to say publicly about French expectations. He was apparently following the lead of Clemenceau, who when

7. See, for example, Trachtenberg, *Reparation in World Politics*, 1–27; and Denise Artaud, *La Question des dettes interalliées et la Reconstruction de l'Europe, 1917–1929* (2 vols.; Lille, 1978), I, 78.

8. Walter A. McDougall, "Political Economy Versus National Sovereignty: French Structures for German Integration After Versailles," *Journal of Modern History*, LI (1979), 9.

9. Trachtenberg, *Reparation in World Politics*, Chapters 1, 2.

he spoke about peacemaking to the Chamber of Deputies on December 29, 1918, refused to spell out precise demands in order to retain flexibility at the conference. Loucheur was specific, however, about the coal he believed France should receive from Germany. On December 4, he told the Chamber that the Germans had systematically destroyed enough French mines to reduce domestic output by twenty million tons a year, and he argued that Germany should provide France with that amount.[10] In a major economic policy speech before the Chamber on February 14, 1919, he declared that France wanted an additional eight million tons, the amount of its prewar imports from that country. Of the twenty-eight-million-ton total, he said, "It is on this, obviously, where we will have the most important bargaining, [which] will decide, from an economic standpoint for many years to come, whether, yes or no, our country will be able to maintain the industrial place in the world to which it has a right."[11] In late 1918, Loucheur seemed to think that Germany could make substantial deliveries without serious disruptions to its own economic life.[12]

Loucheur's objectives also became plain in the report of a committee he chaired on the disarmament of Germany. Issued at the beginning of February, 1919, the Loucheur Report argued—on the premise that modern war has an economic base—that the disarmament of Germany should include control of its armaments factories. The report contained a secondary proposal for the "absolute control by military occupation of . . . Essen and the principal Krupp establishments, the greater part of the Rhenish-Westphalian coal fields and the metal industries which depend upon these." The recommendations shocked Wilson, who referred to the report as a "panic programme." The program never came to anything, because of criticism from the Americans and British.[13] Loucheur probably knew that the economic controls he recommended would be rejected; nevertheless, his report was a way of reminding Allied leaders to consider economic factors thoroughly as they laid new foundations for European security.

10. Ray Stannard Baker, *Woodrow Wilson and the World Settlement* (3 vols.; Garden City, N.Y., 1922), II, 348; Burnett, ed., *Reparation at the Paris Peace Conference*, I, 47; Trachtenberg, *Reparation in World Politics*, 29–30; France, *Annales de la Chambre: Débats*, December 4, 1918, p. 2892.

11. France, *Annales de la Chambre: Débats*, February 14, 1919, p. 560.

12. Minutes, Commission de l'Armée (Chambre), November 15, 1918, in C, 7501, AN.

13. Baker, *Woodrow Wilson*, I, 361–62.

REPARATIONS

It was apparent to the Allied negotiators that a number of forums smaller than the plenary session were needed. To provide one such forum, the Commission on the Reparation of Damage (CRD) convened for the first time on February 3. Consisting of twenty-nine members, the commission was itself too large to deal effectively with some problems, so it created three subcommittees: one to evaluate the damages done; a second to determine the financial capacity of Germany to pay, as well as the means of payment; and a third to recommend measures of control and guarantees. Klotz was on the first subcommittee, Loucheur on the second.[14]

France and Great Britain agreed in favoring the inclusion of war costs in the reparations bill, but the United States vehemently opposed that. The French, however, insisted on a priority for the reparation of material damages, whereas the British, aware that Germany's capacity to pay was limited, feared that what they collected under such a plan would be inadequate since the British Empire had incurred little physical damage. The strategy of the French appears to have been to place large claims in the hope that the United States would move in to share the part of the financial burden beyond Germany's capacity to pay. The principal voice for France's exorbitant demands was Klotz. His efforts to bring about American acceptance of the idea of pooling war costs, however, ended in total failure in early March.[15]

In the face of American firmness, Loucheur seems to have joined with other French officials in recommending a more conciliatory stance. Apparently, they hoped that by acceding to the American proposal of writing into the treaty a moderate fixed sum, they would see the immediate "mobilization" of the reparation debt through the sale of German bonds in the United States. They expected most of the proceeds to go to France to pay for reconstruction. This became the French approach in late February, at least in the behind-the-scenes activities of Loucheur. With that shift in tactics, France gave up demanding to be indemnified for war costs.[16]

Loucheur worked with Lord Cunliffe, of Britain, and Thomas La-

14. Burnett, ed., *Reparation at the Paris Peace Conference*, I, 17–19, 47, II, 280–81.
15. Trachtenberg, *Reparation in World Politics*, 53–56.
16. *Ibid.*, 40–41, 55–56.

mont, of the United States, on the second subcommittee of the CRD. Cunliffe, the chairman, was a hard-liner on reparations. A member of a London banking family, he had served as the governor of the Bank of England during much of the war, until he was forced to step down in 1917 for defying the government's authority. Nevertheless, he continued to have a good personal relationship with the prime minister, Lloyd George. Lamont had been named a partner in the Wall Street banking firm of J. P. Morgan and Company in 1911, and in that capacity had participated in arrangements to finance the governments of France and Britain during the war. On February 22, these three men were constituted a special committee to draft a subcommittee report, and they met privately to set an acceptable total figure for the German war debt. Cunliffe wanted to demand 190 billion gold marks, Lamont suggested 120 billion, and Loucheur recommended 160 billion.[17] Loucheur told Lamont confidentially, however, that "the French would be glad to abide by any figure which, in behalf of the American delegation, [Lamont] felt was feasible."[18] Negotiations between the three men collapsed during the first week of March, when Cunliffe refused to reduce the sum Britain demanded.

On March 10, the three major Allied powers renewed their effort to arrive at a figure acceptable to all. On the committee of three that they appointed, Loucheur was the only member who had served in the earlier group, and his position regarding the fixed sum became even more flexible. Representing the United States was Norman Davis, who had spent many years in Cuba as president of its first trust company; he defended the continued American position of moderation. The big change was on the British side. Edwin Montagu, the secretary of state for India, was known primarily for his efforts at constitutional reform there, but he was also recognized by American financial experts at the peace conference as the skilled banker who had come to them during the war to arrange Allied purchases. Montagu proved to be much less unbending than Cunliffe. Davis got Loucheur to acknowledge that Germany could not pay more than forty billion marks, although Loucheur warned that if he was quoted, he would deny having conceded that. The three experts

17. *Ibid.*, 57; Burnett, ed., *Reparation at the Paris Peace Conference*, I, 47nn1, 3, pp. 49–50; Stephen A. Schuker, *The End of French Predominance in Europe: The Financial Crisis of 1924 and the Adoption of the Dawes Plan* (Chapel Hill, N.C., 1976), 11n.

18. Thomas W. Lamont, *Across World Frontiers* (New York, 1951), 131.

finally agreed on 120 billion gold marks and even began working out the percentages to be granted France and Britain.[19]

When the committee presented a requested progress report to their heads of government on March 14, Lloyd George remonstrated against the low sum, objecting that Klotz and Cunliffe had repeatedly made higher demands, but Davis later asserted that he persuaded the prime minister to accept the special committee's figure. Davis left the meeting believing that "the tacit understanding was that [the three Allies] would proceed to work out a solution on a sane, constructive basis along the line proposed by the experts."[20] Loucheur noted in his diary that Lloyd George protested, but made no reference to the British leader's acceptance.[21]

If Lloyd George did accept the committee's recommendation, he almost at once began to back away. Four days later, on March 18, he denied that there was any agreement on a reparations total. He also replaced Montagu, who had been called back to Britain because of the death of his mother, with Lord Sumner, a highly placed lawcourt judge with a masterly command of the English language. Sumner's inclination was to be much more exacting about reparations than Montagu was; his attitudes were largely in tune with Cunliffe's. The reparations sum of 220 billion marks that he recommended to the committee of three was entirely disproportionate with what Loucheur and Davis were suggesting. Loucheur had in mind a minimum of 124 billion and a maximum of 188 billion, and Davis a minimum of 100 billion and a maximum of 140 billion.[22] The chances of the Allies' reaching an agreement looked bleak.

On the morning of March 26, Loucheur appeared before a newly formed council of four—consisting of Wilson, Clemenceau, Lloyd George, and Vittorio Orlando, the prime minister of Italy—and Lloyd George questioned him about Germany's capacity to meet the Allies' financial demands. Lloyd George seemed to have changed his mind and was cautioning that an unreasonable assessment against Germany could prove costly to the Allies and could impel the defeated nation toward bolshevism. He spoke as if unaware that his representative to the

---

19. Burnett, ed., *Reparation at the Paris Peace Conference*, I, 53–55.
20. *Ibid.*, 55–56. See also Trachtenberg, *Reparation in World Politics*, 60–61.
21. Loucheur, *Carnets secrets*, 71.
22. Trachtenberg, *Reparation in World Politics*, 61–63.

special committee of three was the greatest obstacle to agreement on a moderate reparations figure. When the British prime minister took issue with Loucheur's optimism about the level of disbursements Germany could sustain, Clemenceau assured his colleagues that Loucheur, "as an experienced businessman, would be very careful to do nothing that could kill the hen that laid the golden eggs." Both Clemenceau and Loucheur suggested that the setting of a reparations figure could, if necessary, be broached directly to Germany.[23]

Discussion continued during the afternoon of March 26, with Loucheur sitting in for Clemenceau while the premier was at the Chamber of Deputies. Loucheur was again drawn into debate with Lloyd George, this time over the cost of the physical damages within France. Even though Loucheur's estimate—eighty billion gold francs, or sixty-four billion gold marks—was significantly below those arrived at earlier by Klotz and Albert Lebrun, the minister of the liberated regions, Lloyd George deemed it excessive and unrealistic. He was unwilling to jeopardize Britain's claims to a significant portion of the reparations funds collected. Only the day before, he had proposed that the split between France and Britain be 50 percent to 30 percent—not an especially generous suggestion from an empire whose home territories had not experienced physical damage in the war.[24]

The exchange between Loucheur and Lloyd George ended only when Davis recommended that the remainder of the meeting address the apportioning of German reparations among the Allies. Loucheur advanced the argument that France's willingness to engage in any negotiation at all on this question entailed a great sacrifice, for it meant abandoning its claim to absolute priority for the devastated regions. He recalled that he had originally defended a percentage split of 72 percent for France and 18 percent for Britain, but had later in a conversation with Montagu allowed that the figure might be 58 percent to 25 percent. He said that, even though he had no authorization from Clemenceau, he was ready to endorse a division at 55 percent to 25 percent. Sumner still championed Lloyd George's idea of 50 percent to 30 percent but finally consented to an American compromise at 56 percent to 28 percent. But

23. Paul Mantoux, *Les Délibérations du conseil des quatre, 24 mars–28 juin 1919* (2 vols.; Paris, 1955), I, 24–31.

24. *Ibid.*, 33–35; Loucheur, *Carnets secrets*, 74; Trachtenberg, *Reparation in World Politics*, 62.

Loucheur would not accept the American proposal, believing it was unjust to France.[25] To Loucheur, justice required an absolute minimum ratio of 2.2:1 in the distribution between France and Britain.

In view of the impasse, the council of four decided before the end of the month not to specify a fixed sum for reparations in the treaty, and the split between France and Britain was left open. The French, working to a great extent through Loucheur, had shown a willingness to compromise on the two issues but found their major European partner less flexible in substantive negotiations. The responsibility for calculating the damages eventually fell to a reparation commission.[26]

Though a fixed sum was not agreed upon, the French pushed a bond proposal during April in the interest of mobilizing at once a portion of the debt. Tardieu, as a delegate to the conference, came up with the plan, which he outlined in a memorandum to Clemenceau, Klotz, and Loucheur on April 5. Lord Sumner, who had independently arrived at the same idea, joined in recommending acceptance, and the plan was unanimously approved in principle when it was brought before the council of four on April 7. A number of technical questions relating to the bonds remained, including the amount of the bond issue. Loucheur's role in these negotiations was minimal: he intervened primarily to clarify and expedite the debate. But he was obviously in favor of a bond scheme, since it would yield promptly at least some of the funds industrial reconstruction in France required. The eventual decision was to float an immediate German bond issue of sixty billion gold marks and to follow that with supplementary issues as the proposed reparation commission determined them to be within Germany's ability to pay. The French could view the inclusion of the bond issue in the treaty as at least a partial victory. What is more, the American credits they had sought beginning in 1918 were to become a reality, since most of the bonds would be purchased in the United States.[27]

In late March and early April, the Allies had to decide between the American position limiting German reparations payments to a thirty-

25. Mantoux, Les Délibérations, I, 35–40.

26. Burnett, ed., Reparation at the Paris Peace Conference, I, 60, 75.

27. André Tardieu, The Truth About the Treaty (Indianapolis, 1921), 309–16; Burnett, ed., Reparation at the Paris Peace Conference, I, 81–83, 898–903; Council of Four Meeting with Financial Experts, April 10, 1919, in Louis Loucheur Papers, 12/26, HI; Trachtenberg, Reparation in World Politics, 84–85.

year period at Germany's "utmost capacity" to pay and the French position rejecting a time limit and insisting on full restitution by the Germans "at whatever cost to themselves." Loucheur reasoned that the suffering of France would last much longer than thirty years, but the British sided with the American position, at least at the start.[28]

When the French were unable to prevail at lower levels, they brought the subject before the council of four. As with some other sessions of the council of four, the morning meeting of April 5 was stormy. Both Klotz and Loucheur challenged the Anglo-American preference for a formula mentioning Germany's capacity to pay over thirty years, since they worried about what would happen if Germany failed to fulfill its obligations by the end of the three decades. Loucheur also underscored the British delegation's stand in lower-level meetings that the time limit would not be adjustable. When Lloyd George and Sumner countered that, on their understanding, the deadline could be extended as necessary, Loucheur commented, "If you [the British] had expressed yourselves that clearly at the technical meetings, our discussion today would not have had to take place."[29] The British shift in position—and that is what it was—broke the deadlock. Loucheur noted in his diary, "Lloyd George abandons his advisers; he goes with our point of view. House accepts in principle."[30] Clemenceau at the afternoon session on the same day summarized the position that the council of four was to go on to adopt. Germany would have to pay the total debt the Allies imposed regardless of the length of time required. He conceded, however, that if later governments saw fit to reduce the amount imposed, they certainly had the right to. Thus, Article 233 of the Treaty of Versailles was to direct the Reparation Commission to use a thirty-year time frame in computing Germany's schedule of payments, but it was also to state that the time frame was not binding and could be enlarged if necessary.[31]

On April 7, a draft of the general clauses of the reparations section of

28. Trachtenberg, *Reparation in World Politics*, 71; Burnett, ed., *Reparation at the Paris Peace Conference*, I, 71–72, 788–800.

29. Mantoux, *Les Délibérations*, I, 151–58.

30. Loucheur, *Carnets secrets*, 74. For several years, Colonel Edward House was President Wilson's closest adviser, and he was an influential member of the American delegation at the peace conference.

31. Mantoux, *Les Délibérations*, I, 160–61; Burnett, ed., *Reparation at the Paris Peace Conference*, II, 216–17.

the peace treaty went before the council of four for discussion and approval. Much to the consternation of Colonel House, who headed the American delegation that day, the French, particularly Klotz but also Loucheur, began recommending minor changes in the text that had supposedly already been accepted by all the parties. House commented in his diary, "We wasted the entire afternoon, accomplishing nothing, for the text when finished was practically what it was when we went into the meeting."[32] The session was a fitting close to the main reparations negotiations of the Allies: given the often exasperating and tension-riddled transactions that had already occurred, it was probably to be expected that at a session where House and others considered the consensus "absolute," complications would arise.

METHODS OF PAYMENT

Working out the ways Germany could make payments to the Allies was initially the responsibility of the CRD's second subcommittee, but in early April the council of four appointed two specialized committees to take on part of the task. Loucheur was a member of all three groups.

When the second subcommittee discussed imposing taxes on Germany in order to collect payment, Loucheur argued that the Allies had no business interfering in the way other countries taxed themselves; a defeated power had to manage that by itself. At the subcommittee meeting of March 24, the idea of giving the Allies taxing prerogatives over Germany was dropped. Restitution by equivalent was a possibility Loucheur hedged at, fearing that the Germans might merely turn over only their junk to the French. Nevertheless, he saw some promise in the option if it was handled adroitly.[33] But he saw even more in payments in kind—in works of art, German labor, physical restoration, ships, and coal. Loucheur was understandably interested in coal, especially since German deliveries of it would pose no competitive threat to the French. On February 18, he told the second subcommittee that the Allies could demand sixty million tons of German coal, of which thirty million

32. Burnett, ed., *Reparation at the Paris Peace Conference*, I, 856–57.
33. Trachtenberg, *Reparation in World Politics*, 76–77.

would properly go to France.[34] Loucheur was to stress payment in German coal throughout the conference.

Although he approved of some categories of payments in kind, he did not approve of all. Except for certain sorts of machinery that the liberated regions needed, he argued against importing finished German products, for he feared a negative impact on French industry. Even when he supported bringing German machinery into northeastern France, he had reservations. The German foothold would oblige the French to turn to the defeated nation for spare parts and equipment replacements. Loucheur also anticipated that when plants equipped with German machinery expanded their installations, the orders would again go to the Germans.[35]

The two specialized subcommittees that the council of four established for methods of payment on April 7 were for dealing with treaty annexes about payments in kind. One committee was concerned with German labor, the other with coal. The committee that addressed German labor soon found its topic inseparable from the more general question of the physical restoration of the devastated areas. On April 7, Loucheur proposed placing the Germans under the obligation to provide on demand and by priority industrial and agricultural products to the powers affected—which largely meant France.[36] Aware of Allied sensitivity to any system of national priority, he explained that he was not seeking a form of direct preference for France, and he accepted a provision in the treaty's text to guard against such an interpretation. On apportionment, the treaty read that "the value of property transferred and services rendered by Germany . . . shall be reckoned in the same manner as cash payments effected in that year." A time limit for laying claims upon the Germans for materials needed in reconstruction was also included, as was a clause to protect the "general interests" of the Allies.[37] Nevertheless, Loucheur had secured a victory. Whether France intended to exercise this option on a large scale was doubtful, however, for as Loucheur said when the plan was first discussed by the appropriate technical committee in April, "Frankly, I hesitate to urge this plan,

34. Burnett, ed., *Reparation at the Paris Peace Conference*, II, 598–99.
35. John Foster Dulles, "The Reparation Problem," *New Republic*, XXVI (March 30, 1921), 133–35.
36. Burnett, ed., *Reparation at the Paris Peace Conference*, I, 863–65.
37. *Ibid.*, 120–21.

because it will mean that Germany will at once be put to work at full capacity. We had hoped to place our orders in France and with our Allies. We still hope to do so as far as possible, and that is the reason why France is unwilling to definitely bind herself to take reparation in this form."[38]

Loucheur's proposal of April 7 contained a section on bringing a German labor force to France. This was discussed by the same advisory committee. The work force Loucheur envisioned was not to exceed 400,000 and was to be under the supervision of the French architects and engineers in charge of rebuilding the devastated areas. But the sessions of the CRD's second subcommittee had already heard reservations expressed about such a force, and the council of four abandoned the idea completely at its meeting of April 23, because it smacked of slavery.[39]

Coal was what was at the front of Loucheur's mind, though, and as a member of the special coal committee that the council of four appointed on April 7, he recommended that France be granted the option of receiving twenty-seven million tons as payment in kind from Germany annually. That was a drop of three million tons from the request he had made to the second subcommittee of the CRD in February. But Loucheur by April believed Germany's annual export capability to be only thirty-nine million tons, with the coal of Silesia included, and thirty million tons without, rather than the sixty million tons he had supposed in February. Kenneth Lee, the British adviser on coal, argued that even the new projections were inflated and that twenty million tons were the most that Germany could export. Loucheur obviously recognized that France could not obtain all the German coal he felt it deserved, especially since Italy and Belgium—and conditionally, Luxembourg—also had claims.[40] Nevertheless, he wanted to provide France with a theoretical maximum whatever the practicalities, for obtaining a substantial supply of coal from Germany had been the only matter on which his public pronouncements had been specific prior to the peace conference.

The technical committee accepted Loucheur's proposal: Germany would be required to deliver seven million tons of coal to France annu-

---

38. *Ibid.*, 873.

39. *Ibid.*, 113, 864–65; John Foster Dulles, "The Reparation Problem," 133–35.

40. Burnett, ed., *Reparation at the Paris Peace Conference*, I, 122–23. Burnett in his index expresses some uncertainty about Lee's first name by setting a question mark against Kenneth.

ally for a ten-year period; for five years it would be obliged to deliver up to twenty million tons annually to compensate for the difference between what the French mines produced before the war and what they could produce afterward. During the next five years, the German obligation arising from the disabled mines would not exceed eight million tons annually.[41]

Loucheur argued that the price paid for this coal should be no higher than the cost to produce coal in the Pas-de-Calais mines. Because the British, however, feared the effect of cheap German coal on their own competitive position, France compromised and accepted the price charged to German nationals, for coal delivered by land, and either the German or British export price—whichever was less—for coal delivered by sea.[42]

<h2 style="text-align:center">BELGIUM</h2>

Belgian claims to reparations created some tense moments for the discussions between the major Allied powers. During the war the Allies had repeatedly promised that Germany would be expected to pay for the damages it had done in Belgium, and President Wilson in the seventh of his Fourteen Points presented the German restoration of Belgium's loss as a device for preserving respect for international law. At no time, however, had the Allies formally committed themselves to the principle of Belgian priority. But in late February, the Americans suggested in Paris that Belgium be given priority to two billion gold marks. Much more controversial was the effort by Belgium to include its war costs in its total claim against the Germans. The British were particularly opposed to this, arguing that it would necessitate applying the same principle to all the Allied powers.[43]

The Belgians campaigned for both priority and war costs by applying pressure, including an appearance by King Albert before the council of four on April 4. The lobbying had some effect, for at the April 5 session of the council of four the United States came out in favor of an Allied recog-

41. *Ibid.*, 123, 983–84.

42. *Ibid.*, 123.

43. *Ibid.*, 3–4, 126–28, 697; Sally Marks, *Innocent Abroad: Belgium at the Paris Peace Conference of 1919* (Chapel Hill, N.C., 1981), 55–56, 181–86.

nition of Belgium's claim to war costs. The British opposition persisted, however, and two days later Lloyd George and Clemenceau aligned themselves in the insistence that France and Belgium be treated equally. Lloyd George added that "the proper course was when all the clauses had been provided to let Belgium see them and state her case."[44] The British prime minister's advice seems to have been followed, for the special committees of financial experts created by the council of four continued their work in isolation from the small Allied powers for most of April. Without giving details, Tardieu says in his account of the peace conference that Loucheur attempted but failed during this time to break down British resistance to making concessions to Belgium.[45]

The questions came to a head in late April and early May. On April 23, Loucheur, representing the major powers, reported the contents of the reparations section of the treaty to representatives of several smaller Allied countries. The following day, Paul Hymans, the Belgian foreign minister, modified his country's position to the extent of no longer asking full priority but asking only priority to 2.5 billion gold francs (2 billion gold marks). On April 25, Loucheur, as go-between, presented the claims of the small states to the council of four but also suggested that the council hear the case of Belgium separately. It was not until April 28 that the Big Three acceded to the suggestion and scheduled a meeting for the next day. Aware that the Belgians resented their exclusion from certain phases of the reparations negotiations—most notably those bearing on the apportionment among beneficiaries—Loucheur gave them sympathetic assurances but warned that he could not support their claims in every particular.[46] That was tantamount to advising them to moderate their demands.

The showdown came on April 29. Ignoring Loucheur's signals, the Belgians held firm to the claims they enunciated on April 24. And Lloyd George, though evincing a willingness to concede to the Belgians a priority to 2.5 billion francs, continued vehement against the reimbursement of war costs. Even Clemenceau, who had supported the Belgians in their quest for priority, was exasperated by their intransigence. Lloyd George

44. Burnett, ed., *Reparation at the Paris Peace Conference*, I, 126–28.

45. Tardieu, *The Truth*, 225.

46. Paul Hymans, *Mémoires*, ed. Frans van Kalken and John Bartier (2 vols.; Brussels, 1958), I, 428, 434, 401–402; Tardieu, *The Truth*, 225; Mantoux, *Les Délibérations*, I, 368; Sally Marks, *Innocent Abroad*, 190–91.

requested that Loucheur and Lamont retire from the meeting for a time in order to devise a formula regarding war costs which was acceptable to all and defensible in the House of Commons. Lamont describes what happened next:

> Loucheur and I retired and before so very long returned with our for-
> mula which was far more the work of Loucheur's agile brain than my
> solution. We recommended that Germany was to be obligated espe-
> cially "to reimburse Belgium for all the sums borrowed from the Allies
> as a necessary consequence of the violation of the Treaty of 1839," in
> which Germany had joined Britain and France in pledging the neutral-
> ity of Belgium. Inasmuch as all sums borrowed by Belgium were used
> for the prosecution of the war, this phrase was simply an euphemism
> for granting Belgium the war costs that she had demanded.[47]

The Belgians accepted the wording only after Wilson, with the support of Clemenceau and Lloyd George, threatened to let them make a sepa-rate peace with Germany. By May 3, details for the Belgian settlement were complete, with all parties agreeing that Belgium had priority to 2.5 billion francs and that Germany was liable for Allied loans made to Bel-gium prior to the armistice.[48]

One other aspect of Loucheur's springtime activities involving Belgium—though on the periphery of the peace negotiations—casts light on his approach to peace and economic questions in the 1920s. Anx-ious for closer economic cooperation with Belgium, Loucheur was par-ticularly interested in the establishment of a metallurgical cartel en-compassing France, Belgium, and Luxembourg, and eventually Britain and Germany. He discussed that at a meeting with Clémentel and Bel-gian officials on May 31 in Paris, portraying it as a counterweight to America's productive power. Although Loucheur did not say so, he probably saw it as a way of controlling the economic potential of Ger-many as well. The proposal, with its suggestion of British and German participation, had the effect of assuaging the Belgians' apprehensions about French domination, and they accepted it, but talks between the two countries ultimately broke down over other issues.[49] This was just

47. Lamont, *Across World Frontiers*, 135–36. See also Loucheur, *Carnets secrets*, 76.
48. Burnett, ed., *Reparation at the Paris Peace Conference*, I, 128.
49. Marks, *Innocent Abroad*, 237–39.

the beginning of Loucheur's efforts to arrange international producers' cartels, however.

THE SAAR

Since Loucheur considered the coal of the Saar vital to the economic well-being of postwar France, he became active in the difficult negotiations between Britain, France, and America over that area in late March and early April. The chief French expert on the Saar was Tardieu, and both men worked closely together, and with Clemenceau, to coordinate French policy in the face of a strong American position of a contrary stamp.

The French based their initial list of demands on a memorandum by Tardieu. On the economic side, they wanted ownership of the Saar mines to be turned over to France not only to compensate through their output for the damages Germany had inflicted but also to provide coal for Alsace and Lorraine. Politically, France wanted to recover that part of the Saar left to it by treaty in 1814 but taken after the battle of Waterloo in 1815. They proposed that the remainder of the Saar basin be placed under a special political regime that would protect the economic unity of the area.[50]

The first extended discussion of the French proposals by the council of four occurred on the morning of March 28. After Tardieu and Loucheur presented the French case and departed, the debate grew heated. On this occasion, Lloyd George took the middle ground, favoring French ownership of the mines and governance of the territory by an autonomous regime, but opposing French territorial annexation of any part of the basin. Wilson set himself against all the French proposals, bending only so far as to agree that France might be given the use of the Saar mines for an undetermined period of time.[51] The ensuing clash between Wilson and Clemenceau, at a time when tensions were already high, was emotional and explosive; it ended with Clemenceau calling Wilson pro-German and stalking from the room.[52]

After that dramatic session, Loucheur joined with Clemenceau and

---

50. Tardieu, *The Truth*, 251–61.
51. Mantoux, *Les Délibérations*, I, 63–75.
52. Ferdinand Czernin, *Versailles, 1919* (New York, 1964), 258–59.

Tardieu in revising the French position. The three men decided to press their case for ownership of the mines. They also agreed to argue in favor of a special political authority under the supervision of the League of Nations to assure the French of their mining rights in the area, and a plebiscite of residents to determine the region's political fate at the end of a fifteen-year period. But they gave up asking for territorial concessions.[53]

During difficult negotiations over the next few days, Wilson, the chief obstacle to an agreement, slowly began to yield, first by accepting French ownership of the mines. He still balked at the idea of an independent political administration for the area, however, because he perceived it to be in violation of his Fourteen Points. On April 8, he relented so far as to recommend that an arbitration commission deal with problems between the German government and the French-owned mines, but Clemenceau rejected the suggestion. It appeared to some that the peace conference might collapse. On the evening of April 8, Loucheur attended another crucial meeting with Tardieu and Clemenceau. They decided not to acquiesce to Wilson but instead to send a statement to the heads of government justifying their position on a political authority. The wisdom of their resoluteness was confirmed the next day, when Wilson transformed the arbitration commission he was championing into an administrative commission and agreed that it entailed a suspension of German sovereignty over the territory. With Wilson's concession, the French had essentially what they wanted in the Saar basin, and the issue ceased to be a serious point of contention among the Allies.[54]

Loucheur's participation in the question of the Saar was less than Tardieu's, but he was present with Tardieu and Clemenceau not only to defend the original French position before the council of four on March 28 but, even more significant, to decide with them privately what French policy should be.

GERMAN REACTION AND ALLIED SECOND THOUGHTS

On May 7, the Allies presented the treaty to the Germans. During the next three weeks an exchange of notes occurred in which the Germans

53. Tardieu, *The Truth*, 265–66; Etienne Weill-Raynal, *Les Réparations allemandes et la France* (3 vols.; Paris, 1947), I, 81.
54. Tardieu, *The Truth*, 271–77.

took issue with a number of the treaty's articles.[55] Ray Stannard Baker, chief of the United States press service, noted in his diary on May 28, "Everyone is now asking: 'Will the Germans sign?' Up to noon every day I think they will; after luncheon I am not sure; and just before going to bed I am persuaded they will not. On the whole I think they will—with fingers crossed."[56] On May 29, the Germans sent the Allies a definitive set of "counterproposals," and of the forty thousand words their document contained, approximately eight thousand dealt with reparations, the issue that most concerned Loucheur.[57] Count Brockdorff-Rantzau, the leader of the German peace team, expressed the dismay the German delegation felt over the reparations section in his letter to Clemenceau accompanying the German observations: the German people, he said, would find themselves "condemned to a perpetual slavery" if the provisions were implemented.[58]

Lloyd George, fearful that the Germans might not sign and sensitive to growing opposition to the treaty at home, had second thoughts and ventured that it might be justified to grant concessions to the Germans in several areas, including reparations. He presented alternative proposals to the council of four on June 2: the first, which he preferred, was for Germany to contract to restore the devastated areas, with no fixed sum attached, but to agree to a figure based on estimates for other categories of restitution, like pensions; the second was for the Germans to present a sum of their own within three months, provided they signed the treaty in its existing form. Lloyd George's opposition to the Allies' setting a fixed sum in the treaty was unaltered.[59]

At that point the Americans saw an opportunity to reopen the question of a fixed sum in a way that they thought could gain the support of the French. When the American delegation met with the president at a special meeting on June 3, Lamont was convinced that difficulties with Germany on the reparations question "would fade away" if the Big Three instructed their technical experts to come up with a fixed sum immediately instead of postponing the calculation for two years. He also believed from what had been said in a meeting with Tardieu that

55. Burnett, ed., *Reparation at the Paris Peace Conference*, I, 131.
56. Baker, *Woodrow Wilson*, II, 111.
57. Burnett, ed., *Reparation at the Paris Peace Conference*, I, 131.
58. *Ibid.*, II, 53.
59. *Ibid.*, I, 135–37.

morning that the French would be open to the idea of a fixed sum. Members of the delegation voiced their skepticism about the feasibility of Lloyd George's plan for a contract of restoration, and Lamont went so far as to impute to the British prime minister a reluctance to face the public reaction of his countrymen to a fixed sum.[60] Wilson, bolstered by his experts, renewed the American effort for a fixed sum at the council of four, but even though Lamont and Bernard Baruch, another member of the American delegation, added pressure by talking to the British prime minister in private, Lloyd George refused to budge.[61]

If the British and Americans had reservations about the reparations section of the treaty, though for different reasons, so did Loucheur. He confessed to Baruch on May 20 that the economic clauses had been an error and that political considerations in France had lain behind his acceptance of them. He inclined toward a meeting of Allied technical experts and Germans to discuss Germany's economic needs, but he was unable to convince Clemenceau that such a session was desirable.[62]

Although Loucheur was amenable to adjustments in the reparations clauses, both he and Clemenceau had by the beginning of June shifted away from their willingness to fix a reparations figure in the treaty. Loucheur explained why in a plan he presented on June 5: "Mr. Clemenceau wants to get over the crisis of public opinion until the Peace Treaty has been actually signed and the summer has gone. Then he will let his people into any figures that may be necessary in the early autumn."[63] The French also were loath to do anything that could be interpreted as showing Allied weakness in the face of German protests.[64]

Loucheur's plan, besides being tailored to French public opinion, was sensitive to the American push for a fixed sum and to Lloyd George's second proposal. Loucheur proposed that the claims of the small powers be reduced to an absolute minimum so that Germany's total bill would be about 120 billion gold marks; his figure was the same as what the American delegates suggested in a report three days later. But instead of stating a sum in the treaty, Loucheur recommended reaching, in line with the second proposal Lloyd George made on June 2,

60. *Ibid.*, II, 109–18.
61. *Ibid.*, I, 137.
62. Trachtenberg, *Reparation in World Politics*, 94.
63. Burnett, ed., *Reparation at the Paris Peace Conference*, II, 124.
64. Trachtenberg, *Reparation in World Politics*, 95.

a special agreement with Germany allowing it to assess the damage and to propose within ninety days a sum that it believed the Allies could accept—presumably near 120 billion gold marks.[65] Though there would be no fixed sum in the treaty, all parties concerned, aware of the approximate amount involved, could have assumed that the issue would be settled by early autumn.

Loucheur's proposal of June 5 was a brilliant attempt at compromise, but the British were unwilling to agree to such a moderate reparations bill at the peace conference. The Americans continued to insist on the inclusion of a fixed sum for a while but abandoned the effort in the face of stiff resistance from both the French and British. All that was salvaged of Loucheur's plan was the idea that Germany should be given a chance to offer a reparations sum of its own within a certain time period, which was extended from three to four months. That concession was incorporated into the Allied reply of June 16 to the German observations about the treaty.[66]

All the major Allies saw the need for modifications regarding reparations, but it was apparent that reaching agreement on changes of a substantive nature was virtually impossible. In the end, the treaty remained as it was, although the Allies, in replying to the German observations, seemed to be saying that the reparations clauses would be interpreted in a moderate way. What would have enabled success was a sense of mutual trust, but in view of the suspicions on both sides at the time, that was probably out of the question.[67]

Loucheur's activities at the conference marked a new stage in his political career, since it was there that he emerged as a top level negotiator on international economic questions. This standing was confirmed toward the end of the year when Clemenceau used him as a diplomatic emissary in sensitive negotiations with the British.

Through serving as minister of armaments, Loucheur seems to have grasped more thoroughly than others that the military strength of a nation depends to a significant extent on its economic base. Therefore, one of his main aims after the war was to give France the economic means to ward off aggressors. He tried throughout the peace conference to obtain

65. Burnett, ed., *Reparation at the Paris Peace Conference*, II, 124–25.
66. Trachtenberg, *Reparation in World Politics*, 96; Burnett, ed., *Reparation at the Paris Peace Conference*, I, 138–39.
67. Trachtenberg, *Reparation in World Politics*, 96–97.

concessions that, without jeopardizing Germany's ability to recover economically, would allow France to rebuild its devastated regions and move toward an economy based on production. Yet he realized that the Germans would eventually outstrip the French economically, regardless of the measures taken at the conference.[68] Accordingly, he also sought other ways of assuring French economic security, as in his attempts to create a metallurgical cartel with neighboring countries and to maintain Allied economic controls. His international outlook continued during the 1920s, when he became one of the chief partisans of a brand of European economic cooperation that made Germany an essential part of the system.

68. Arno Mayer, *The Politics and Diplomacy of Peacemaking: Containment and Counterrevolution at Versailles, 1918–1919* (New York, 1967), 647.

8

FROM ECONOMICS TO POLITICS, 1919–1920

A deep sense of uncertainty and uneasiness gripped France in mid–1919. The peace treaty had been signed with Germany, but the specter of German domination continued to haunt many of the French who were dissatisfied with the treaty's security arrangements and with what they saw as inadequate guarantees for the payment of reparations. There was also uncertainty about the French economy. Persistent coal shortages were worsened by the outbreak of a miners' strike in June. There were bitter complaints about the government's stand on import controls and about other aspects of its economic policy. Misgivings about economic policies, expressed in the press and parliament, forced the government to defend its actions in the Chamber of Deputies during July, and though Clemenceau obtained a vote of confidence, the challenge symbolized the frustrations the French felt over their situation and their country's.[1]

In this atmosphere, Loucheur began his last months as a close political associate of Clemenceau's. He remained involved with the question of reparations, as a defender of the pertinent section of the Treaty of Versailles and as a negotiator in its implementation. But his role as a negotiator went beyond reparations to attempts at establishing economic links with Germany and discussions with Britain on a wide range of economic issues. During May, June, and July, he participated in formulating government policy on import and export controls; he also sought to deal with industrial problems in the liberated regions and to meet France's extremely urgent coal demands. Politically he reached a crossroads: he had to decide whether to present himself for the Chamber of

1. Trachtenberg, *Reparation in World Politics*, 99; France, *Annales de la Chambre: Débats*, July 22, 1919, pp. 3266–82.

Deputies or return to his career as a private businessman. He was at another of the turning points of his life.

THE TREATY: DEFENSE AT HOME AND NEGOTIATIONS ABROAD

During the debate on the Treaty of Versailles in the Chamber of Deputies, several Socialists questioned the clauses on reparations, and the tenor of their criticisms was caught by Vincent Auriol before the Chamber on September 10: "Guarantees of payment . . . , of justice . . . , of solidarity? Where are they? You say: guarantees. I say: uncertainties! Uncertainties on the amount of reparations, on the delays of payment . . . , on the distribution of expenses. . . . All the problems are exposed, none are solved. You have made proclamations of principle; you have left unsettled all the difficulties."[2] He questioned Louis Lucien Klotz's contention that Germany could make annual reparation payments of eighteen billion gold francs, and he pointed out that there was no provision for granting priority to the devastated regions in the allocation of the payments received.

On the Right in the Chamber, one of the most outspoken deputies was Louis Marin, who shared the Socialists' concern about the absence of adequate guarantees. In contrast to the Socialists, however, he believed that Germany could easily meet the reparations demands the government seemed to favor.[3]

Loucheur and Klotz defended the reparations clauses on behalf of the government. Loucheur participated periodically throughout the Chamber debate, but his main presentation was on September 11. Like Klotz, he tried to skirt the question of guarantees by emphasizing the size of the sums France would receive from Germany. He endorsed Klotz's figure of 300 billion gold marks—or 18 billion gold francs annually—as what Germany could be expected to pay; he was apparently trying to divert attention from what France would actually obtain and when. He contended that German exports of coal, as extrapolated from prewar trends, would rapidly rise to eighty million tons a year, allowing the defeated nation to meet its treaty obligations not only to France (twenty-seven million tons annually) but to other Allied nations as well (another seventeen million

2. Weill-Raynal, *Les Réparations allemandes*, I, 129–30.
3. *Ibid.*, 130–33.

tons). But his rosy predictions stood in sharp contrast to the assessments he had made at the peace conference. His speech, often based on weak arguments, was intended to mislead the Chamber.[4]

While trying to mask the treaty's critical problems, the government was also appealing to French public opinion as the country reached the threshold of a national election campaign. To project themselves as firmer on reparations than they had been, Loucheur and Clemenceau depicted France as having thwarted attempts to include a fixed sum in the treaty since the figure proposed had been below what France supposed reasonable. During the negotiations, France had in reality argued for a fixed sum well below the amounts Klotz and Loucheur cited during the debate as what to expect.[5]

Though the treaty was accepted in a vote of the Chamber at the beginning of October, a unanimous resolution called upon the government to pursue negotiations with France's allies in order to obtain reparation priority for the devastated regions, a satisfactory system of Allied guarantees for payment from Germany, and an Allied agreement for an equitable distribution of war costs. That the principle of priority was included in the resolution shows how little cognizance the Chamber had of the course the peace negotiations took, for the government had along the way abandoned the pursuit of priority. Nevertheless, the government still refused to own up; it was only in 1921, after Tardieu pub-

4. France, *Annales de la Chambre: Débats*, September 11, 1919, pp. 3849–55; Trachtenberg, *Reparation in World Politics*, 105. That the government was deeply concerned about parliament's reaction and therefore ready to distort the negotiating position it had taken at the peace conference is evident in a statement Loucheur made after a Chamber session on reparations: "I could not tell the truth; they would have killed me." Alfred Sauvy quotes Loucheur but does not tell exactly when Loucheur made his statement. More than likely, however, the comment is from 1919. See Sauvy and Anita Hirsch, *Histoire économique de la France entre les deux guerres* (3 vols.; Paris, 1984), III, 42.

5. Trachtenberg, *Reparation in World Politics*, 106. Loucheur also told the Senate's commission on foreign affairs on August 13 that France had rejected the inclusion of a fixed sum in the treaty. On this occasion he stated the minimum and maximum annual payment figures proposed by France at the conference and pointed out that the French proposal of a maximum reparation payment of 235 billion gold francs was unacceptable to the Americans. At no time during his appearance, however, did he mention that the British had been much more demanding than the French in the discussions. Loucheur also argued that Germany would be able to make annual payments of eighteen billion gold francs at the end of the first five years of peace. See Minutes, Commission des Affaires Etrangères (Sénat), August 13, 1919, Procès-verbaux, AS.

lished his account of the peace conference, that the Chamber learned what had happened.[6]

Although parliamentary approval of the treaty was completed with the Senate's vote of October 11, the Chamber's resolution made it clear that the Allies still had vexing matters to address.[7] In compliance with the resolution, Clemenceau and Loucheur went to London in mid-December to discuss priority for the devastated regions. They sought to settle at the same time the percentage split of reparations revenues between Britain and France once payments began. Loucheur, presenting the French case, argued in favor of a division of 55 percent to 25 percent in favor of France. In effect, he picked up where he had left off at the peace conference, for those were the same figures he had suggested as the final French concession when negotiations abruptly came to an end in March. Loucheur pointed out that the split he was proposing represented a considerable loss for the French, since reconstruction costs had continued to mount. If an exact calculation of the expense of rebuilding determined the percentages, Loucheur contended, the distribution would be more like 60 percent to 20 percent.[8]

In support of priority for the devastated areas, Clemenceau argued that France had suffered much more than any other country from the German invasion and had seen ten of its richest provinces severely damaged. Loucheur, offering the reinforcement of technical details, shocked Lloyd George by maintaining that reconstruction costs in the affected areas had risen to 125 billion francs, 47 percent above an estimate he had announced in October.[9]

The British accepted only one of France's two appeals. Although lamenting the sacrifice the French plan meant for Britain, Lloyd George announced his country's acceptance of the split Loucheur had proposed, as a way of upholding Franco-British solidarity. But he rejected France's claim to priority for its devastated regions, arguing that acceptance would entail similar consideration for Belgium and would negate Britain's chances of collecting anything significant for many years.[10] The French, in ex-

6. Weill-Raynal, *Les Réparations allemandes,* I, 135–36.

7. *Ibid.,* 136.

8. Secretary's Draft Notes of an Anglo-French Conference, December 12, 1919, in Series Papiers d'Agents, André Tardieu Papers, Vol. 42, MAE.

9. Weill-Raynal, *Les Réparations allemandes,* I, 138–39.

10. Tardieu, *The Truth,* 349–50.

change for British acceptance of their proposal on revenue division, agreed to abandon attempts to achieve priority. The British position must have come as no surprise, since during the peace conference Britain had opposed granting Belgium priority, even with its significantly smaller claims. Raising the question along with that of percentage shares may, however, have helped France obtain the ratio it had been seeking.[11]

At the beginning of December, Loucheur made another trip to London for discussions. When, on November 19, the United States Senate failed to ratify the Treaty of Versailles, the chance of American involvement in assuring peace and stability in Europe faded and close cooperation and agreement between France and Britain appeared all the more vital. At a session with Lloyd George on December 3, Loucheur touched on the opposition forces to the bolsheviks in Russia and on Anglo-French cooperation in the Allied peace settlement with Turkey, but his overriding concern was with improved relations directly between the two conferring nations. Loucheur made that clear from the outset of the conversation, when he emphasized the importance of the two countries' arriving at a "complete understanding" on foreign-policy matters, since if they could reach agreement on general and economic policy, the United States might be willing to join them. The suggestion of American participation was probably nothing more than wishful thinking, but it underscores the importance Loucheur attached to cooperation among the Allies, including the United States.[12]

No policy decisions were reached at Loucheur's meeting with the British leader, but Lloyd George and Clemenceau talked about the same issues in a private conversation in London on December 11. That session served to clear up some diplomatic misunderstandings between the two countries. In addition, Clemenceau told the prime minister that he was going to name Loucheur to replace Klotz as finance minister and that he had that morning wired Loucheur to come to London for discussions with

11. The proportion 11:5 was put in the minutes of the meeting to allay fears of countries that were not represented at the conference although they were entitled to reparations. The 55:25 scale nevertheless remained the basis for distributing reparations between the French and British, with the remaining 20 percent to be allotted to the other countries eligible for payments. At the Spa Conference, in mid-1920, however, France's final total was reduced to 52 percent and Britain's to 22 percent. See Tardieu, *The Truth*, 350–51; and Weill-Raynal, *Les Réparations allemandes*, III, 819.

12. Note of a Conversation Between the Prime Minister and M. Loucheur, December 3, 1919, in CAB 23/25, PRO.

Britain's chancellor of the exchequer, Austen Chamberlain. Loucheur seemed on the verge of a new plateau in his political career, since he had previously headed temporary ministries devised to meet emergency situations. But when Clemenceau offered him the ministry of finance, he declined it, apparently preferring for the time being to maintain his considerable influence on economic matters without a ministerial shake-up. In any case, Loucheur's talks with Chamberlain, which concerned France's sagging franc, produced no solution for that problem.[13] Because of the complexity of the issues and the conflict of national interests, the two sides failed in December to achieve the solidarity they were seeking.

Loucheur also negotiated with the Germans during the summer and fall of 1919 on issues related to the peace treaty and Franco-German economic cooperation. Because of his orientation to concrete results and realities, he showed a certain flexibility in the negotiations he conducted both as French representative to and as president of the temporary Committee for the Organization of the Reparation Commission (CORC).

During the summer, the coal crisis was aggravated by strikes in the French mines. In late June, Loucheur suggested discussions with the Germans to the Supreme Economic Council on a number of treaty-related matters, including coal. But his difficulties went deeper than the immediate coal shortages, for France was extremely vulnerable in its supplies of coke, only a small portion of the coal mined in France and the Saar being suitable for coking. With the accession of Lorraine and its tremendous smelting capacity, the need for coking coal became greater than ever. But Lorraine was vulnerable in another way too, for it was geared primarily to the production of semifinished materials, while the industrial means of transforming them into finished products were in Germany. Though the French could count provisionally on a potential market in Germany for their semiproducts, since the Treaty of Versailles guaranteed access to the German market for five years, there was still the uncertainty of what the Germans would do once they regained their sovereignty over tariffs.[14]

13. Secretary's Notes of a Conference Held at 10, Downing Street, December 11, 1919, in CAB 23/25, PRO; Loucheur, *Carnets secrets*, 113–14; Secretary's Draft Notes of an Anglo-French Conference Held at 10, Downing Street, December 13, 1919, in André Tardieu Papers, 42.

14. Supreme Economic Council Meeting, June 30, 1919, in Y, 154, MAE; Schuker, *The End of French Predominance*, 222–23.

Knowing the magnitude of France's needs in coal and the hazards of trying to force treaty compliance upon the Germans, Loucheur decided that accommodation might produce better results than intransigence and coercion. He knew that France was negotiating from political strength, and he was convinced, like other government officials, that France held a strong card in its iron ore.[15] On August 1, joined by representatives of his wartime business ally, Schneider-Creusot, he proposed to the German treaty delegation at Versailles a steel cartel including Belgium and Luxembourg as well—the same idea he had discussed with Belgium two months earlier.[16] A German delegate at Versailles named Ernst Schmitt, acting on behalf of his government, approached officials of Krupp, suggesting further talks. But the industrialists of Germany resisted cooperating that way with France. The negotiations made little headway and were dropped in November.[17]

In the discussions Loucheur had with Germany on coal, he took the position that a minimum delivery to France of twenty million tons annually would eventually be necessary but that for the time being a monthly transfer of a million tons was acceptable. His flexibility extended beyond amounts, for he also seemed willing to discuss ways of helping the Germans increase their coal production. Impressed by Loucheur's "initiative" and "broad conceptions" in the general negotiations, the Germans were also anxious to arrive at a modus vivendi. On August 24, their delegation warned the German foreign office that temporizing on coal would taint the negotiating atmosphere in Versailles and impede the discussion of other topics vital to Germany. On the same day, the delegates confided to Loucheur that they had recommended to their government that deliveries begin at once.[18]

The urgency of the German delegation's report apparently persuaded Berlin to accept the arrangements Loucheur and the other Allied representatives were offering, and the two sides signed a protocol on Au-

15. Trachtenberg, *Reparation in World Politics,* 111–13.

16. Regarding Loucheur's proposal to Belgium, see above, pp. 165–66.

17. Georges Soutou, "Der Einfluss der Schwerindustrie auf die Gestaltung der Frankreichspolitik Deutschlands, 1919–1921," in *Industrielles System und politische Entwicklung in der Weimarer Republik,* ed. Hans Mommsen *et al.* (Dusseldorf, 1974), 544–45.

18. German delegation in Versailles to Berlin, August 3, 1919, in Louis Loucheur Papers, 12/2, HI; Report from Emile Haguenin, August 16, 1919, *ibid.*; German delegation in Versailles to Berlin, August 24, 1919, *ibid.*

gust 29. Under the agreement, the Reich was immediately to begin shipping 1.66 million tons to the Allies monthly and was to increase that amount after the full implementation of the Treaty of Versailles in January, 1920.[19] Loucheur expected German deliveries to France during the remainder of 1919 to be at least a million tons a month.[20]

His hopes for additional understandings with the Germans were heightened by the success concerning coal, and in September he expanded the discussions to include cooperation in exploiting the hydro-electric potential of the Rhine between Strasbourg and Constance. The German delegation in Versailles shared Loucheur's enthusiasm on economic cooperation. The attempts at greater collaboration were to be blocked not so much by the German government as by German industrialists. The German negotiator Schmitt wrote in a memorandum in October that efforts to cooperate with France were being frustrated by heavy industry, which, confident in its potential economic superiority, had virtually no interest in an economic partnership with France.[21]

The industrialists were opposed to their government's fulfilling commitments to make reparations to France in coal, for they had needs of their own and were not eager to extend an advantage to their French rivals. In the first years after the war, the German coal mines came increasingly under the direct control of iron and steel producers, who naturally wished to meet their own requirements first.[22] They felt that if the French wanted German coal, they should pay premium prices for it instead of the bargain rates—the same price that German nationals paid—provided by the peace treaty. The industrialists also tenaciously resisted delivering coke to France, since they wanted to develop their own iron-producing capacities, which the loss of Lorraine had greatly reduced.

The confidence the French had in their leverage to obtain coke as a result of the long-standing German dependence upon Lorraine for iron ore turned out to be excessive. The war had disrupted the exchange of iron ore and coke between the Ruhr and Lorraine, so that by the end of

19. By the Treaty of Versailles, the Allies were entitled to requisition as much as 3.5 million tons of coal a month.

20. Bordereau d'envoi à Monsieur Laroche, September 12, 1921, in Y, 191, MAE; Weill-Raynal, *Les Réparations allemandes*, I, 427–29.

21. German delegation in Versailles to Berlin, September 25, 1919, in Louis Loucheur Papers, 12/2; Trachtenberg, *Reparation in World Politics*, 113–14.

22. Weill-Raynal, *Les Réparations allemandes*, I, 419–22.

the conflict the Germans depended less on low-grade ore from Lorraine than on high-grade ore from Sweden. The Germans had, besides, begun using scrap metal to help meet their needs, and that source grew in the postwar years. German industrialists could afford a defiance, because they were much less vulnerable to economic retribution from France than French manufacturers were to the actions of Germany. The attitude of German industrialists about the ore of Lorraine was that, as one of their number later put it, the French could "choke on it."[23]

Faced with resistance from the industrial community, transportation problems, and widespread shortages at home, Germany found itself unable to ship to France the million tons of coal a month that Loucheur had expected; its delivery levels to the Allied recipients combined ranged from 350,000 to 650,000 tons. In late October, Loucheur began insisting that the German government force its coal producers to fulfill their contracts, warning that France might otherwise adopt a less conciliatory tone in negotiations. At the beginning of December the Germans promised to provide a million tons during the month, but they did not. And in January, 1920, the first month in which the protocol of August 29 took full effect, their coal deliveries to the Allies appear to have been a mere 300,000 tons. Even though the negotiators on both sides were interested in achieving closer cooperation through voluntary settlements, realizing their hopes proved exceedingly difficult, and an endless series of wrangles began over Germany's coal obligations as stipulated in the Treaty of Versailles.[24]

The negotiations at Versailles during the summer and fall also included a number of discussions about a German labor force to help rebuild areas of France damaged during the war. Although the concept had been dropped by the council of four at the peace conference, both the French—particularly Loucheur—and the Germans remained interested, and they began exploring the possibility together in early July.[25] The German government's commitment to the idea was underscored by

23. Maier, *Recasting Bourgeois Europe*, 198–99; the citation is from Schuker's *The End of French Predominance*, 227.

24. Maier, *Recasting Bourgeois Europe*, 200; Kurt von Lersner to Berlin, November 4, 1919, in Louis Loucheur Papers, 12/2; William F. Ogburn and William Jaffe, *The Economic Development of Post-War France: A Survey of Production* (New York, 1929), 231.

25. Weill-Raynal, *Les Réparations allemandes*, I, 442.

its wanting to name Walther Rathenau to the post of "high commissioner charged with the direction of restoration work in the devastated regions."[26] In September, Berlin secretly informed the Quai d'Orsay that, with France's consent, it planned to assign the great wartime organizer of Germany's economic power to the position. Rathenau had contended, in meeting with the German foreign minister in early July, that the reconstruction of northeastern France would be the crux in getting German relations with the Allies in order. Besides having an interest in the project and brilliant organizational skills, he was a powerful industrialist who stood more of a chance of obtaining the support of his peers for cooperation with France than a civil servant or a politician would have had. Yet when word reached Loucheur of Germany's choice, he rejected it on the grounds that Rathenau's part had been too great in the systematic destruction of French industry in the devastated regions during the war.[27] Loucheur wanted someone whose name was less emotionally charged.

The work-force talks continued into December, and an agreement seemed well within reach when the French decided provisionally to halt them. On December 21, Loucheur wrote in the margin of a letter from Tardieu dealing with the negotiations that the decision had been reached because of "political difficulties." He did not give any particulars, but French opinion in the devastated areas was so hostile to a German work force that he and the Germans had agreed that it would work in isolation from the local population. The hostility of French labor unions was a factor as well. Loucheur later accused them of undermining the plan, and though labor leaders denied being "xenophobic," there is evidence, for example, that the leadership of the building trades union took a negative position, which was even stronger at the local level.[28]

26. Beaumont to foreign ministry, September 13, 1919, in Series A, Paix, 1914–1920, Vol. 90, MAE.

27. David Felix, *Walther Rathenau and the Weimar Republic: The Politics of Reparations* (Baltimore, 1971), 68; Louis Loucheur to Stephen Pichon, September 22, 1919, in A, 90, MAE; Stephen Pichon to Emile Haguenin, September 22, 1919, in A, 90, MAE. Given the positive discussions that took place between Loucheur and Rathenau at Wiesbaden in 1921, one can assume that Rathenau would have cooperated with Loucheur in 1919, although Loucheur's decision to reject Rathenau's name in 1919 was correct in view of the hostile state of French public opinion.

28. Trachtenberg, *Reparation in World Politics*, 116–17.

Had the Clemenceau government not fallen in January, 1920, Loucheur might have resumed negotiations on the use of German workers, but with his departure the issue appeared closed. Even within Germany there was a feeling that without Loucheur behind it, the work force had little chance. The suspension of the negotiations marked a turning point, not because the French abandoned the aim of cooperating with Germany regarding reparations but because their policy lost its drive. Apart from coal, the French did not energetically pursue any specific forms of payment in 1920. Their policy that year was largely passive, even though the Treaty of Versailles took effect in January, providing a legal basis from which they might have operated.[29] Loucheur's absence from the government had its effect.

THE LIBERATED REGIONS

The *groupements sinistrés* that Loucheur had organized as a way of assisting industrialists who had suffered war damage were given monopolies in the purchase of certain German products from Alsace-Lorraine, the Saar, and some of the occupied areas of Germany (see above, pp. 147–48). Loucheur expected them to provide French consumers—especially in the liberated regions—with badly needed raw materials. But he also believed they would help reestablish an economic balance in France, since the participating industrialists could renew contacts with clients immediately instead of having to wait until their factories resumed operations.[30]

The *groupements* did not function smoothly, however, at least in iron and steel. Inflation dealt a blow to the government's price control system for the purchase and sale of German products by the Groupement des Sinistrés du Nord et de l'Est. Labor unrest raised manufacturing costs as both Lorraine and the Saar were hit by periodic strikes that caused slowdowns. Transportation breakdowns created scarcities that also exerted an upward pressure on costs.

Higher expenses made producers anxious to renegotiate prices for

29. Emile Haguenin to foreign ministry, February 16, 1920, in A, 91–92, MAE; Trachtenberg, *Reparation in World Politics*, 118.

30. Thomas W. Grabau, *Industrial Reconstruction in France After World War I* (New York, 1991), 72–75.

their products, but buyers wanted to hold to the prices stated in contracts. Between the makers and the buyers was the *groupement*, which went to the ministry of industrial reconstruction for a solution. But Loucheur's ministry was not very sympathetic. In the Saar, where the *groupement* suggested in September that the ministry create the kind of stability in raw materials needed for German firms to fill the association's orders, the government turned a deaf ear, since it was planning to terminate the *groupement*'s monopoly in the region in any case.[31] In March, 1920, government officials informed the *groupement* that for unfilled metallurgical orders in the Saar (83,000 tons), its clients had the choice of canceling or accepting long delays and appreciably higher prices. In Lorraine, too, the government acted against the wishes of the *groupement*. In September, Loucheur endorsed price increases that were retroactive to June in sequestered factories, and when the *groupement* tried to get outstanding orders filled at the original contract prices after the installation of French managements, the Office of Industrial Reconstruction ruled that buyers had to pay the new prices or cancel their orders. In most cases in both Lorraine and the Saar, the customers elected to cancel their orders.[32] Even in reintegrating war-ravaged industrial concerns into the French economy, the *groupement* appears to have been less effective than Loucheur had hoped, for the firms could not deal adequately with their prewar clients when their suppliers failed to fill so many of their orders.

In contrast to the system of *groupements*, the Office of Industrial Reconstruction (ORI) had increasing success in rehabilitating industry in the devastated areas. But it too experienced some problems in 1919. From its original purpose as coordinator and centralizer in procuring essential materials and machinery, its tasks began to expand in the spring of 1919, and eventually its control over industrial reconstruction became almost total. The ORI worked closely with private industry, as represented by the Association Centrale pour la Reprise de l'Activité dans les Régions Envahies and its subordinate organizations, one of which was the Comptoir Central d'Achats. The ORI and the Comptoir Central d'Achats collaborated to obtain means of production for firms lacking them. The beneficiaries had to submit to government control, including procedures that they sometimes found exasperating in view of the un-

31. The group's monopoly was terminated in November, 1919.
32. Grabau, *Industrial Reconstruction*, 102–11.

certainties and crises of 1919 and the bureaucratic mix-ups attendant upon the dramatic speed with which the network grew to handle arriving orders.[33]

The ORI also assisted in implementing the electrification program the ministry of public works had established for northeastern France. It did not build the coal-burning power plants or the high-tension lines, but it became the chief promoter of electrification in the region. Because of its influence with industrialists, it was often able to break down resistance to the transformations that electrification meant for factories. Power companies consequently became less hesitant about making large capital investments.[34]

The programs the ORI helped launch in 1919 began producing conspicuous results in 1920, and it came to be cited as a model of efficiency and competence.[35]

IMPORT CONTROLS

Restrictions prohibiting all foreign imports except those exempted by the government were extended into the postwar period not only to protect the French franc but also to allow French industry to readjust and rebuild without foreign competition. The policy of import restriction, however, kept out of France equipment and raw materials that the nation needed for reconstruction. There was also the argument that it fed inflation and that freer trade would promote economic stability. As early as February, 1919, a bill in the Chamber of Deputies would have removed import prohibitions from raw materials used to manufacture exports of equal or greater value. And on April 10, a proposition of resolution was introduced calling for the free movement into France of agricultural machinery, raw materials, and manufactured goods essential to France's export industries. The same proposition would have

33. *Ibid.*, 118–19, 133–35. Grabau indicates that the Comptoir Central d'Achats, for example, had sixty-four persons manning its central offices in October, 1918, but by January, 1920, the staff had grown to a thousand.

34. *Ibid.*, 139–41.

35. *Ibid.*, 132, 141.

directed France to return to a policy of commercial liberty as quickly as possible.[36]

With public and parliamentary pressure mounting, Loucheur brought the issue of controls before his ministerial colleagues for discussion.[37] In the debate that erupted, the ministerial division of opinion was set out clearly in the positions that Clémentel and Loucheur took at a meeting on May 1. Clémentel argued that, to alleviate industrial problems without jeopardizing the franc or French industry, there should be an importation of raw materials but restrictions should remain against the entry of foreign manufactured products. He opposed any lifting of controls on the export of raw materials, holding that the result would be shortages and price increases. Loucheur, on the other hand, felt that Clémentel was offering "insufficient palliatives" and that France's economic health hung upon a return to total commercial liberty for imports and exports whether raw materials or manufactured goods. He conceded, though, that several French industries whose competitiveness had been compromised by the war and the sharp rise in the price of coal should be given the protection of increased customs duties.[38]

The government's decisions generally followed Loucheur's thinking. Toward the middle of May a government decree virtually eliminated restrictions on exports, and on June 13 a decree lifted controls over the importation of most items. But another decree placed an ad valorem surtax on a number of imports, since the fixed duties on these items were still what they had been before the war, when prices were much lower. The arrangement was expected to be in place a short time, pending a complete revision of the rates. It proved unworkable, though, when customs officials were unable on short notice to set up the complicated machinery for import valuations. In July, the government adopted instead a system of coefficients: if something had undergone a twofold price increase since 1913, the fixed duty was multiplied by the coefficient of 2 to determine the new tariff. In an apparent effort to keep duties from rising alarmingly in a single increment, a maximum coefficient of 3 was established. Two further decrees took effect

---

36. *Ibid.*, 88; Haight, *A History of French Commercial Policies*, 103–104; Minutes, Conseil Economique, May 1, 1919, in F 12, 7657, AN.

37. *La Journée industrielle*, May 14, 1919, p. 1.

38. Minutes, Conseil Economique, May 1, 1919, in F 12, 7657, AN.

in July: one virtually completed the elimination of government restrictions on imports, and the other restored export prohibitions to a
number of foodstuffs in the interest of moderating domestic prices.[39]
The substance of the decrees suggests that Loucheur's views were decisive in their formulation. His receptivity to protectionism came just a
few months after he had criticized France's prewar system of high
tariffs.

Both press and parliament were riled. Many of the advocates of a
return to commercial liberty felt outrage at the elevation of customs
duties. Le Temps warned that reprisals by other countries were a distinct possibility and complained that the special tariff commission, responsible for periodic adjustments, would engender the instability of
constant fluctuations in duties. The Chamber of Deputies heard members argue that the new system would weaken the country, favor speculation, and boost the cost of living.[40]

The government defended itself in the Chamber during the latter
part of the month. Loucheur maintained that "economic policy, contrary to what some think, ought to adapt itself at any hour, at any moment, to the new problems that are placed before us. And it would be
pure nonsense to attach oneself to an inflexible theory, whatever it
was, which could be the cause of the worst kinds of mistakes."[41] By
eliminating almost all import prohibitions and falling back on customs duties for protection, the government, in key respects, had set
France on the road back to the tariff regime that existed before the
war.[42]

Although the government survived in the Chamber of Deputies,
its tariff decisions remained unpopular with an important segment of
public opinion. Many of the French were growing impatient with what
they viewed as a generally ineffective economic approach, and the
economy became a focal point for Clemenceau's opponents in the final
months of 1919.

39. Haight, A History of French Commercial Policies, 109–10; Le Temps, July 14, 1919,
p. 1, July 13, 1919, p. 1.

40. Le Temps, July 14, 1919, p. 1, July 20, 1919, p. 1.

41. France, Annales de la Chambre: Débats, July 22, 1919, p. 3273.

42. Haight, A History of French Commercial Policies, 102–20. France was not alone
in relying on trade barriers after the war. Other trading countries turned to protectionism
during the early 1920s, after an economic recession ended a postwar boom in 1920. See Dan
Silverman, Reconstructing Europe After the Great War (Cambridge, Mass., 1982), 237–41.

COAL

After Britain's decision to end its wartime pricing concessions for France and Italy, the French coal crisis intensified for Loucheur, beginning with a strike in the mines. But the crisis was continental in scope. Even in Great Britain, France's chief foreign supplier, production was off enough to raise doubts about the possibility of any sizable exports.

Although Loucheur collaborated with the labor minister, Pierre Colliard, throughout the strike, he appears to have had the decisive voice in determining the government's response. Two groups of miners went on strike. The first were in the Nord and the Pas-de-Calais, in unions grouped around certain members of the Chamber from their region. A few days later the second group, members of the Fédération Nationale des Travailleurs du Sous-Sol in other regions of France, joined them. Coal production came to a virtual standstill.

According to the 1913 statute that set an eight-hour workday for miners, neither the time coming out of the mine nor the half-hour lunch break counted as part of the eight hours. Among the demands the Fédération issued at the beginning of May, 1919, was that a miner's descent, lunch break, and ascent be made part of his eight-hour shift. The Radical-Socialist deputy Antoine Durafour introduced a proposal in the Chamber, with the backing of its mines commission, whereby each shift would begin upon the descent of the first miner, end with the arrival of the last miner out of the mine, and include a half hour for lunch. The Fédération, at its national congress in Marseille in late May endorsed Durafour's formula and threatened to strike on June 16 if parliament did not enact it by June 12.[43]

In the Nord and the Pas-de-Calais, where negotiations were already taking place on a redefined eight-hour day and increased pay, miners walked out of the mines at the beginning of June. But talks continued between the union representatives and mine owners, with a tentative settlement reached on both questions on June 6. The two sides agreed, pending parliamentary action, to accept the government's position, namely, that a miner's time would be calculated from "the last miner down to the last miner up, including a half hour of rest down below."[44] The pact was overwhelmingly rejected in a vote of the miners, who then

43. Olivier, *La Politique du charbon*, 169–72.
44. *Le Temps*, June 7, 1919, p. 4.

dispatched a delegation to Loucheur to request that the mine owners be allowed to raise coal prices enough to permit the wage increases the workers sought. Loucheur, citing economic problems, rejected the request but proposed government arbitration of the dispute. Both the miners and owners accepted. Working with Colliard, Loucheur announced new wage schedules on June 18, but the miners, insisting that the government also accept Durafour's proposal, remained on strike.[45]

When Durafour's proposal went before the Chamber of Deputies, the government, with Loucheur in the fore, protested that the twenty minutes of daily output from each worker that Durafour's bill would lose but that the government's plan would not was more than the country could afford. On June 16, five days after the Chamber voted for the government's formula, the Fédération ordered its miners out on strike, and since it refused to negotiate a settlement unless the government yielded on descent time, Loucheur was forced to capitulate. Deploring the "misunderstanding" on the question between the miners, the Chamber's mines commission, and the government, he announced that the government was prepared to accept Durafour's bill. Reintroduced in the Chamber of Deputies, it passed on June 20; four days later Loucheur defended the government's acquiescence to it in the Senate, and there, too, it was accepted without modification.[46]

At that point the Fédération resumed negotiations, but talks with the mine owners soon reached an impasse. When Colliard suggested government arbitration and the two sides accepted, the labor minister joined Loucheur to work out a decision, which was announced on July 9. Two days later the strike by the Fédération was over and its miners were once again producing coal. By then, too, the miners' walkout in the Nord and Pas-de-Calais had ended, since Durafour's formula had become law.[47]

Loucheur had probably hoped that once the Fédération was presented with a fait accompli, it would not carry out its threat to strike, especially since union representatives in the Nord and the Pas-de-Calais had accepted the government's way of calculating the eight-hour workday in their agreement with mine owners on June 6. Furthermore, he

45. Olivier, *La Politique du charbon*, 171–75; *Le Temps*, June 20, 1919, p. 3.

46. *Le Progrès du Nord*, June 22, 1919, p. 1; *La Bataille* (Paris), June 25, 1919, p. 1.

47. *La Bataille*, July 4, 1919, p. 1; *Le Petit Journal*, July 10, 1919, p. 1; Olivier, *La Politique du charbon*, 175–76.

must have seen the government's proposal as generous and significantly more favorable to the miners than the eight-hour day they had obtained in 1913. When the miners, who knew the gravity of France's coal crisis, surprised him by refusing to compromise, he was realistic and flexible. At that point his focus had to be productivity, regardless of concessions. Of course, more than one deputy pointed out during the session of the Chamber of Deputies on June 20 that the strike could have been avoided and that the government was responsible for it.[48]

The strike was costly for France. The production figures tell much of the story: May, 1,534,524 tons; June, 622,773 tons; July, 1,354,892 tons. Only many months later did France fully recover. But the price of coal had jumped by a minimum of twenty francs a ton.[49] There was, too, the daily loss of twenty minutes' production from each miner, amounting to a 4.4 percent increase in unit labor costs. Loucheur could only hope that other sources would offset the shortages that came from the mining dispute, on top of France's normal shortfall.

Britain continued to be France's chief source of foreign coal, and Loucheur did his best to keep deliveries high and to dissuade the British from their dual pricing system, which charged more for exported coal than for that on the domestic market. Loucheur understood that the British wanted to protect themselves from inflated world prices and maximize revenues from the international sale of their coal. Toward the end of June, he mentioned to Clémentel that the best way for France to combat the new dual pricing would be by reducing imports from the country that had instituted it, but he recognized that that was not feasible. Instead, he recommended that France take the issue before the Supreme Economic Council (SEC).[50] Agreeing, Clémentel suggested that France capitalize on its moves toward complete economic liberty by presenting the SEC with a resolution that prescribed "the suppression of all restrictions between Allies, and the reestablishment of equal treatment for all."[51]

The memorandum the French submitted at the end of June accordingly contrasted France's measures in behalf of economic liberty against the mechanisms of other Allies. The memorandum cited British coal

48. France, *Annales de la Chambre: Débats*, June 20, 1919, pp. 2477–79.
49. Olivier, *La Politique du charbon*, 175–76.
50. Louis Loucheur to Etienne Clémentel, June 23, 1919, in F 12, 8075, AN.
51. Etienne Clémentel to Louis Loucheur, June 27, 1919, *ibid.*

pricing as a particularly egregious violation of the Allies' professed preference for free commerce. It asked the Allies mutually to guarantee equal terms for the purchase of all products and materials. Where state controls were deemed necessary, it argued, the country imposing them should take precautions that its allies were not adversely affected.[52]

The British remained committed to their dual pricing system. Much to their consternation, though, the French proved just as committed against it. On July 22, Loucheur decried to the Chamber of Deputies how Britain, in the middle of a worldwide coal crisis, had placed its limited quantities of export coal on the open market so that the French ended up paying much more than British consumers. He left no doubt that France did not accept the British decision, had protested against it diplomatically, and would continue its protest.[53] Four days later, when he was in London to discuss the system, coal deliveries, and related matters with officials, the British were markedly cool toward him. Not surprisingly, they refused to budge.[54]

When, at the beginning of August, the French again brought the coal pricing methods before the SEC, the British agreed to review the matter, warning, however, that in view of projected annual production of 185 million tons, which was insufficient for even domestic needs, discussions were probably useless.[55] The study the British Board of Trade office completed in September merely endorsed Britain's policy of sell-

52. Annex A to the Extrait du Procès-verbal, Supreme Economic Council, June 30, 1919, in Y, 154, MAE.

53. France, *Annales de la Chambre: Débats*, July 22, 1919, p. 3273.

54. To Captain Codrington (Foreign Office), August 7, 1919, in FO 382/2484, PRO; Note from Paul Cambon, July 19, 1919, in Foreign Office, FO 368, General Correspondence, Commercial, Vol. 2114, PRO.

55. Supreme Economic Council Meetings, August 1–2, 1919, in Y, 191, MAE; Telegram Aimé de Fleuriau to foreign ministry, August 4, 1919, *ibid.* Loucheur was undoubtedly dismayed at the failure of the British to respond more positively, but he must have been pleased by an action the Supreme Economic Council took in the first days of August. Herbert Hoover, the director of the American Relief Administration, spoke to the SEC on August 1 about the seriousness of the coal crisis and recommended that a coal council be established in Europe to stimulate production and assure an equitable distribution among the European states. The recommendation was accepted by the SEC, and organization of the commission began, with Loucheur selected to represent France. He was active in converting the idea into reality. Instead of focusing on the shortages of all European powers, however, the commission, which did not have the powers needed to enforce its recommendations, devoted most of its time to finding coal for Austria. See Hoover Memoran-

ing export coal on the open market, but Sir Auckland Geddes, its president, disclosed to Loucheur that a previous increase in British production would permit the coal licensed for export to France in the last quarter of the year to be raised from 2.25 million to 3 million tons.[56]

In early November, Loucheur learned that Britain intended to end its system of export licensing entirely. Through the issuance of licenses, the British government controlled how much coal was shipped to other countries, and from the system's wartime inception, it had been skewed in France's favor. France was still receiving approximately half the coal Britain shipped abroad in 1919, but dismantling the system could be expected to thrust French importers into fierce competition with other nations on the open market, and the price was almost certain to go up. What is more, the export licensing system was the instrument the Bureau National des Charbons (BNC) employed to assure an equitable distribution of British coal in France.[57] France was going to have to make major adjustments in its levers of allocation.

The French worked to salvage a priority guarantee for Britain's export coal. Clemenceau and Loucheur wanted France to have priority to 1.5 million tons monthly. At first they tried to get a fixed price set for the coal as well, but Loucheur abandoned that aim when he met with British officials during the London conference in mid-December. At the conference, the British were deaf to pleas for a minimum monthly French allotment, but before December was over, Loucheur had secured their agreement for delivery of the 1.5 million tons a month that Clemenceau and he had sought. The British also agreed to postpone the end of export licensing by several days in order to review the question. That delay gave Loucheur and the BNC some time for reorganizing French controls on the apportioning of British coal. When the licensing system ended, on New Year's Day, 1920, the BNC was ready. For Loucheur, the gain was that he could anticipate a steady supply from a critical source,

dum, August 1, 1919, in Y, 191, MAE; Résolution du Conseil Suprême, August 5, 1919, *ibid.*; *Le Petit Journal*, August 6, 1919, p. 1; and Derek H. Aldcroft, *From Versailles to Wall Street, 1919–1929* (Berkeley and Los Angeles, 1977), 60.

56. Sir Auckland Geddes to Louis Loucheur, September 19, 1919, in Louis Loucheur Papers, 11/Miscellaneous.

57. Secretary's Draft Notes of an Anglo-French Conference, December 12, 1919, in André Tardieu Papers, 42; Jacques Seydoux to foreign ministry, November 5, 1919, in Z, Grande Bretagne, 96, MAE.

even if the suspension of export licensing resulted for a while in a bidding war among French importers.[58]

During the last months of 1919, coal delivered from Britain never fell below a million tons a month, and in four of the last six months, the import levels were either above or close to 1.4 million tons.[59] Given Britain's limited quantities for export, these were impressive amounts, if well below France's needs. Loucheur's greatest setback concerned pricing. His numerous attempts to dissuade Britain from its dual pricing system were unsuccessful, and the price the French paid rose sharply toward the end of the year.

Loucheur sought fulfillment of the commitment Belgium had made in early 1919 to send 350,000 tons of coal to France monthly, but he was dogged by the growing opposition of Belgian industrialists to selling any coal abroad when Belgium had its own shortages (see above, p. 145). After shipments from Belgium to France peaked in July, 1919, at 333,000 tons, they deteriorated as the Belgians tried to revise the amount they were obliged to send. The first indication of their less compliant attitude came in September, when, to pressure the French into authorizing the delivery of German coke to Belgium, they declared a cutback in their monthly coal consignment to France. After Loucheur and other French officials protested the move's baselessness at a time that coal production in Belgium was on the rise, the Belgians reversed themselves, fearing reprisals in a vulnerable area like iron ore. Nonetheless, coal shipments still failed to improve: in October and November the Belgians managed to deliver only 193,169 tons and 92,406 tons respectively.[60] Disturbed, Loucheur first sent a special representative to negotiate with the Belgian government. When that failed, he suspended shipments of French iron ore. In reaction, the Belgian government sent its economics minister, Henri Jaspar, to Paris to meet with Loucheur, and Jaspar left with an acceptance by France of a new monthly quota of only a hundred thousand tons. Loucheur must have concluded that it was the best he could hope for just then, since the Belgians had sent less than fifty thou-

58. Philippe Berthelot to Paul Cambon, November 19, 1919, in Z, Grande Bretagne, 96, MAE; Secretary's Draft Notes of an Anglo-French Conference, December 12, 1919, in André Tardieu Papers, 42; *L'Usine*, January 8, 1920, p. 21, January 1, 1920, p. 21, January 15, 1920, pp. 19, 21; Olivier, *La Politique du charbon*, 214–16.

59. Olivier, *La Politique du charbon*, 188.

60. *L'Usine*, September 4, 1919, p. 25; Olivier, *La Politique du charbon*, 178–80, 188.

sand tons during December.[61] Unfortunately for him, the decline in imports came in the fall and winter, when it was most acutely felt. Public dissatisfaction with his handling of the shortages expanded as 1919 drew to a close. When he left his ministerial post in January, 1920, the possibility of France's finding relief through Belgian coal seemed much slighter than he had thought it in the summer of 1919.

Loucheur also turned his attention to the United States. America was a last resort: in the prewar years, France had not imported any coal from the Western Hemisphere, largely because of the costs involved.[62] By 1919, however, the war had resulted in much higher prices for European coal, so that American sources were more competitive. A fundamental impediment, though, was the scarcity of shipping capacity from the United States. Loucheur knew that in shipping tonnage France's position was unenviable. He commented to Clémentel in June, 1919, that the British government was unlikely to grant the licenses its nationals needed to haul coal from the United States to France and that American shipping companies were preoccupied with capturing coal markets from the British in South America. Loucheur was also woefully aware of how weak the French merchant marine was; in July he complained to the Chamber of Deputies that France's economic strength was being sapped because of its heavy dependence upon other countries' shipping resources.[63]

Loucheur came up with an idea that held promise over the long term. He envisioned creating, with American cooperation, a special Franco-American shipping route manned by large oil-driven cargo vessels capable of carrying twenty to thirty thousand tons of coal and equipped with automated machinery to expedite unloading. He planned on one or more specially equipped ports to handle the ships. He sent his suggestion to Clémentel for consideration in late June.[64] At the same time, he was taking concrete steps toward the improvement of the French merchant ma-

61. Olivier, La Politique du charbon, 188, 234–35; Le Progrès du Nord, January 14, 1920, p. 1; L'Usine, January 22, 1920, p. 23; Philippe Berthelot to French ambassador in Brussels, January 7, 1920, in Series Z, Europe, 1918–1929, Belgique, Vol. 124, MAE.

62. Olivier, La Politique du charbon, 236–37.

63. Loucheur to Clémentel, June 23, 1919, in F 12, 8075, AN; France, Annales de la Chambre: Débats, July 22, 1919, p. 3274.

64. Loucheur to Clémentel, June 23, 1919, in F 12, 8075, AN. Clémentel, in responding to Loucheur, focused on France's problems with Great Britain over coal. He did not even mention Loucheur's concept of a special Franco-American shipping route. See Clémentel to Loucheur, June 27, 1919, in F 12, 8075, AN.

rine. Under the terms of an agreement he signed with two associations of steel producers on July 30, the steelmakers were to provide steel at preferential prices for the construction of the French merchant fleet and were in return to receive the coal they required at the price then anticipated for German coal—a price significantly below that of French coal at the time. Loucheur hoped that German coal deliveries would carry the program, but when they did not, he had to scramble for other sources. Since the non-German coal was more expensive, the *caisse de péréquation* had to offset the difference. The cost charged to it was significant, but Loucheur saw that as unavoidable for building the kind of merchant fleet that could ship a large volume of coal over long distances.[65]

But Loucheur had to seek more immediate solutions as well. At the end of June, 1919, he informed the Chamber of Deputies that France was negotiating for a fleet of ships to transport seven to eight million tons of coal across the Atlantic to France. His announcement, just three months after he had begun exploring American coal purchases, was mostly to bolster French morale during the miners' strike; he neglected to mention what he had told Clémentel only a few days before: that France's chance of finding the shipping it needed was slight. Again on July 22 he spoke to the Chamber of the possibility of obtaining American coal, and again mostly as a way of inspiring hope.[66] Yet his references to important quantities of American coal were not just a psychological ploy, for he sincerely believed that such coal would eventually become significant for France.

Others presented a less optimistic picture of America's potential as a supplier. The newspaper *L'Usine* wondered whether France could fill the ships carrying coal to France for their return to the United States, since French exports to America consisted mainly in luxury items. And in August, 1919, Herbert Hoover warned the European states that their collective monthly shortfall of twenty million tons was a void that the United States could not be counted upon to fill: even if adequate shipping became available, the United States had at most only one or two million tons for export.[67]

65. Brelet, *La Crise de la métallurgie*, 137–38. The amount charged to the *caisse* appears to have approached twenty-six million francs.

66. *Le Petit Journal*, July 2, 1919, p. 2; Loucheur to Clémentel, June 23, 1919, in F 12, 8075, AN; France, *Annales de la Chambre: Débats*, July 22, 1919, p. 3273.

67. *L'Usine*, July 10, 1919, p. 9, August 21, 1919, p. 21.

Nevertheless, France received shipments from the United States in the last months of 1919. The first deliveries, contracted by large users of coal such as the Groupement Charbonnier des Industriels Parisiens, began arriving in August. The amount that month was merely 31,750 tons, but the monthly figure rose above 130,000 tons in October and November, before falling precipitously in December and January because of a strike in American mines.[68] Still, Loucheur remained optimistic about American coal. On a visit to the liberated regions in January, he encouraged industrialists there to begin using it to build stockpiles. Even though the price stayed high through late 1919 and early 1920, Loucheur's confidence proved well placed, for as 1920 advanced, not only did freight costs drop to levels that made American coal more affordable but France's imports of it increased dramatically, reaching 826,134 tons in November.[69]

Although the initiatives that Loucheur helped develop for American coal began to produce notable results only after his departure as minister of industrial reconstruction, his understanding that conditions and patterns had changed from what they were before the war and that the United States could become a vital fuel source for France proved invaluable for his nation.

On August 29, Loucheur had signed a protocol with the Germans for the delivery of German coal to France prior to implementation of the peace treaty (see above, pp. 178–79), but the quantities sent in late 1919 fell far short of expectations. Even in the Saar, Loucheur's plans were thwarted. Strikes during the spring of 1919 hampered production there, and France also had monthly quotas for exports to Italy. In late June, Loucheur told Clémentel that the Saar was not yet capable of contributing much toward solving France's coal crisis. The situation did not change significantly for the rest of the year.[70]

At home, Loucheur experienced strong criticism because of severe shortages. The Parisian press took him and his coal network to task

68. Olivier, *La Politique du charbon*, 238–39, 242; Susan Armitage, *The Politics of Decontrol of Industry: Britain and the United States* (London, 1969), 131–35. The strike of American miners began on November 1 and affected 72 percent of the nation's mines. The walkout lasted for over a month.

69. *Le Progrès du Nord*, January 14, 1920, p. 1; Olivier, *La Politique du charbon*, 238–39.

70. Olivier, *La Politique du charbon*, 181, 188; Loucheur to Clémentel, June 23, 1919, in F 12, 8075, AN.

throughout the fall. Protests also came from industrialists in Paris who, because of interruptions in electrical service stemming from the insufficiency of coal, were forced in early November to begin a biweekly alternation between day and night shifts in order to conserve power during peak hours. Many industrialists believed that Loucheur was at least partly to blame for the bind they were in and for the increased costs their compliance incurred. In Paris, frustrations reached a pitch that found consumers ransacking a coal storage area.[71]

Shortages existed in other parts of France as well. In one area of the Ardennes, for example, monthly coal deliveries in November and December were anticipated at 30,000 tons, but only about 3,500 tons were received in each of the two months. And in Lorraine, blast furnaces had to be shut down. Loucheur admitted that industry in general was obtaining barely one-third of the coal it needed.[72]

Such were the conditions when Loucheur's responsibilities for coal ended upon the fall of the Clemenceau government in the latter part of January, 1920. For many consumers it was a moment of relief and hope: relief that Loucheur was no longer administering coal, and hope that improvement would result from a government decision to combine coal provisioning and transportation in the same ministry. Still, Loucheur had increased France's coal imports in 1919 by almost four million tons over the preceding year. Disappointingly, that was offset by an almost equal drop in France's domestic production, though output at the close of the year was higher than it had been in many months. In the end, Loucheur's departure did nothing to abate the crisis, which lingered on for several months.[73]

Also related to Loucheur's coal activities, since increased coal output was an anticipated outcome, was a Loucheur-sponsored mining bill that became law in September, 1919. The need had long been recognized to reform the state's way of granting mining concessions to private firms. The only statute that dealt seriously with the question was an 1810 law by which the government granted concessions in perpetuity to private companies to control and exploit the mines they opened and to retain all the profits they derived from the coal and other mineral resources they extracted. Many in France considered the law unjust inso-

71. Olivier, *La Politique du charbon*, 257–58; *L'Usine*, January 15, 1920, p. 19.

72. *L'Usine*, January 8, 1920, pp. 19, 21; Olivier, *La Politique du charbon*, 259.

73. *L'Usine*, January 29, 1920, p. 1; Olivier, *La Politique du charbon*, 265–66, 288–89.

far as the state waived its claim to any share of the profits. Parliamentary criticism became strong enough before the war that the ministry of public works for a time suspended issuing concessions altogether. When it began granting them again in 1912, it did so on a very small scale. In September, 1917, the assignment of developing new mining legislation to deal with concessions went from the ministry of public works to Loucheur's ministry of armaments.[74] The transfer of responsibility reflected government confidence in his ability to produce results quickly and efficiently, but his selection may also have had a political motivation, since he was a businessman and some of the strongest objections to modification of the existing arrangements came from industrialists.

What Loucheur proposed was a *régie intéressée*, that is, a system in which the state would join with private concerns in owning and controlling the mines. Before the Chamber of Deputies on October 29, 1917, he explained that the two points of greatest revision in his scheme were a limitation on the length of time concessions endured, and government participation in profits. He reminded the Chamber, however, that the state, as a stockholder, would share in losses as well. Loucheur rejected the Socialists' demand for nationalizing France's mining industries, but he also took a more moderate position than the industrialist and conservative deputy François de Wendel, who resisted any time limit on concessions.[75]

Loucheur saw the advantage of quick legislative action in increased production of raw materials, which for him was the "great economic weapon for our battle of tomorrow."[76] On November 9, 1917, he created a Comité Consultatif des Mines, which drafted a bill that was presented to the Chamber of Deputies on January 8, 1918. The proposal, in part the government's response to France's wartime need for critical mineral resources, placed a ninety-nine-year limit on concessions and provided for state participation in mining profits on a graduated scale.[77] This bill was referred to the Chamber's mines commission for study, and only in De-

74. *L'Usine*, February 17, 1918, p. 9; *L'Europe nouvelle*, January 12, 1918, pp. 25–27, January 26, 1918, pp. 79–80.

75. *La Journée industrielle*, June 16–17, 1918, p. 1; France, *Annales de la Chambre: Débats*, October 29, 1917, pp. 2920–41.

76. France, *Annales de la Chambre: Débats*, October 29, 1917, p. 2931.

77. Projet de loi (Chambre), January 8, 1918, in C, 7761, AN.

cember, 1918, did the Chamber pass a modified version of it. The Chamber's text then had to be reconciled with a bill the Senate had passed the previous June, so that the new mining law did not become a reality until September, 1919. The basic principles the government proposed were retained, however, and with final passage, Loucheur was able to grant concessions that had been held up pending the bill's enactment.[78]

It took Loucheur almost two years to achieve what he sought for the mines, but his success helped end the semiparalysis regarding new mining concessions. It also meant that the state had a new source of revenue; indeed, that was the chief concern of most people. Although Loucheur was unable to benefit much from the law during the time he continued as minister, it facilitated the expansion of coal production later.

POLITICS

At the same time that Loucheur worked on economic questions in 1919, he appears to have been preparing the way for a continued career in politics, notwithstanding his protestations of wanting to return to private business. The strongest evidence is the enthusiasm he developed in late 1918 for purchasing shares in French newspapers. He acquired part interest in the influential Parisian newspaper Le Petit Journal at the end of the year and later was a party to the purchase of several provincial newspapers, including Le Progrès du Nord, in Lille. The historian Carlton J. H. Hayes once wrote that there were far better financial investments than a newspaper, and when a wealthy businessman became interested in one, it was usually less for financial gain than for indirect benefits, in the form of increased exposure for the political views of the owner. Indications in 1930 were that Le Petit Journal, over which Loucheur gained total control in 1920–1921, was at the financial break-even point or losing money but was nonetheless an asset for Loucheur's political career.[79] What was a political asset then was no less one in 1919.

78. Minutes, Commission des Mines (Chambre), June 14, 1918, ibid.; France, Annales de la Chambre: Débats, December 13, 1918, pp. 2984–96; Projet de loi (Chambre), July 4, 1919, in C, 7761, AN; L'Usine, September 25, 1919, p. 21.

79. La Journée industrielle, March 11, 1919, p. 2; Loucheur, Carnets secrets, 148; Carlton J. H. Hayes, France: A Nation of Patriots (New York, 1930), 150, 447.

Immediately after the war, many looked upon Loucheur as interested in being more than a *ministre d'occasion*. Lord Derby, the British ambassador to France, reported in January, 1919, that some thought of him as a future premier. Others predicted that he would seek election to the Chamber of Deputies.[80] The circumstantial evidence is that Loucheur's wartime service as a minister persuaded him to consider a career in politics and to begin planning for one in case he ultimately decided to move in that direction.

Loucheur indicated his political intentions officially in the fall of 1919. Spurred by encouragement from Clemenceau, by a desire to continue assisting in the French economic recovery, and by the deep personal satisfaction he found in government service, he let it be known in October that he was going to stand for the Chamber of Deputies in the national elections on November 16. His candidacy became official on October 21, when he agreed to campaign as a member of a group of candidates in the Nord called the Fédération Républicaine du Nord.[81]

The press's reaction was mixed. Some newspapers frowned upon Loucheur's decision. The leftist *La Bataille* and the conservative *L'Usine* contended that his electoral campaign distracted him from more important objectives, like securing coal for France.[82] On the other hand, the business newspaper *La Journée industrielle* supported his decision, arguing that the government should not be left "to political professionals, whose most serious shortcoming is perhaps their incompetence." Encouraging the idea of an "industrial party," it stressed that parliament needed "many courageous industrialists, energetic realists, fully aware of the difficulties of their task and determined to make of our country a great nation organized for production and guided toward expansion." The newspaper's endorsement of Loucheur as representative of a potential brand of parliamentary members was strong enough that *Le Progrès du Nord*, which enthusiastically supported his candidacy, reprinted the commentary.[83]

Loucheur conducted a short but vigorous campaign, mainly on economic issues. On October 27, he told the congress of the Fédération Républicaine du Nord that he intended to campaign with a special focus upon

---

80. Lord Derby to Lord Curzon, January 20, 1919, in FO 371/3751, PRO; *L'Europe nouvelle*, December 28, 1918, p. 2243.

81. Simone Loucheur, Interview, June 17, 1977; *Le Petit Journal*, October 22, 1919, p. 3.

82. *La Bataille*, October 23, 1919, p. 1.

83. *Le Progrès du Nord*, October 25, 1919, p. 1.

France's transportation system and financial predicament.[84] That was savvy, given the relevance of the topics for voters in the Nord. Loucheur assured his audiences that Germany would be expected to pay large reparations sums and fulfill the treaty to the letter. He also vowed to ensure that businesses not be overburdened with taxes as the state reestablished financial order.[85] He stressed the importance of modernizing and expanding the transportation system to meet the needs of the postwar era. Describing the nation's railroads as nothing more than "children's playthings," he pointed out that they were inadequate to meet the peculiar requirements of the Nord arising out of wartime damage and destruction. He told the voters that it was necessary to "think big" in rebuilding the transportation network. That meant electrification of the rail lines, larger train stations, and the laying of more track. It meant a canal system capable of handling coal barges with a capacity of not merely three hundred tons, as until then, but of a thousand tons.[86] Even in normal peacetime circumstances, the Nord, which depended heavily on canals and railroads, would have responded positively to Loucheur's expansive scenario.

During the campaign, he showed particular sensitivity to the accusation that he had been a war profiteer. His most outspoken critic on the question, the neoroyalist journalist Léon Daudet, who was renowned for his invective against government officials, had attacked him in the royalist daily *L'Action française* on several occasions during 1919. According to Daudet, Loucheur made immense sums during the war as a munitions manufacturer—enough to begin building a newspaper trust.[87] Daudet bitingly nicknamed him "Loucheur—tout en or" ("Loucheur—all gold"), but Loucheur eventually avenged the aspersion by referring to the journalist as "Daudet—tout en ordure" ("Daudet—all scum").[88] Daudet's political group, headed by the journalist himself, went on flogging the issue during the election campaign, depicting Loucheur as France's most notorious war profiteer.[89] When a heckler reiter-

84. Several articles on Loucheur's campaign speeches appeared in *Le Progrès du Nord* between October 28 and November 16, 1919.

85. *Le Progrès du Nord*, November 12, 1919, p. 1.

86. *Ibid.*, October 31, 1919, p. 1, November 12, 1919, p. 1, October 31, 1919, p. 2.

87. *L'Action française* (Paris), January 13, 1919, p. 1, January 15, 1919, p. 1, January 16, 1919, p. 1, January 19, 1919, p. 1, March 3, 1919, p. 1, March 11, 1919, p. 1.

88. Simone Loucheur, Interview, June 17, 1977.

89. Flyer of the Liste d'Action Française et d'Union Nationale, 1919 election campaign, in 313 AP, 171, AN.

ated the accusation on November 9 in Dunkerque, Loucheur was obviously waiting for the occasion. He explained that on entering the government in December, 1916, he established a special committee, presided over by a member of the French Legion of Honor, to handle profits due him from war-related contracts; the committee was to turn the profits over to the government.[90] As a government minister, he added, he had lived on other income, and because of his scrupulous renunciation of potentially lucrative profits, successive premiers had told him, "Loucheur, you are an honest man."[91]

Loucheur remained silent both then and later, though, on Giros et Loucheur's wartime profits prior to December, 1916. Those were considerable, far more than the two million francs the renamed A. Giros et Cie. earned in 1917 and 1919 and then left to the public treasury. (The firm had no profit in 1918.) The net profits of Girolou from August 1, 1914, to the end of 1915 were slightly more than six million francs, compared with a peacetime profit of 717,000 francs that the firm's average annual earnings in the three years preceding the war would have projected for the period. But extraordinary profits among French munitions manufacturers were not uncommon. The government imposed a war profits tax in 1916, although the amounts collected were but a fraction of the profits made.[92]

The accusation of profiteering appears to have made no dent in Loucheur's candidacy. Yet his desire to speak out confirms that he considered the charge serious. To his dismay, his antagonists kept the issue alive for years, and in 1925 he went before a court of honor and proved the falsity of a number of the reckless charges against him. Nevertheless, the epithet "profiteur de guerre" haunted him to the end of his life.[93]

He was elected to the Chamber of Deputies on November 16, receiv-

90. The committee he referred to did forward his profits for the years in question to the government in March, 1920, waiting to do so until Loucheur was no longer a government minister. See J. Faure, J. Petsche, and S. Derville to minister of finance, March 10, 1920, in B, 15617, MF.

91. *Le Progrès du Nord*, November 10, 1919, p. 1.

92. Giros et Loucheur War Profits Tax Declaration for the Period from August 1, 1914, to December 31, 1915, in B, 15617, MF; Hardach, "La Mobilisation industrielle," 102.

93. Louis Loucheur to Gabriel Castagnet, December 10, 1925, in Louis Loucheur Papers, 1/2; Loucheur's List of Rumors Regarding His Fortune and Possible Responses, 1925, *ibid.*; Louis Launay, *M. Loucheur* (St. Cloud, France, 1925), 11–16; Loucheur, *Carnets secrets*, 106–107.

ing more votes than anyone else on the Fédération Républicaine's list. *Le Progrès du Nord* reported that a colleague in the Fédération expressed delight over this: "Our great joy is the election of M. Loucheur."[94] For Loucheur it was gratifying that members of parliament could no longer consider him an outsider. Since he had Clemenceau's backing, he could anticipate a continued role in guiding economic affairs, and not long thereafter Clemenceau offered him the post of minister of finance. Although Loucheur declined, the offer shows the extent to which Loucheur enjoyed Clemenceau's confidence in economic policy.[95]

The Clemenceau government ended on January 18, 1920, after the premier's failure to be elected president of the republic in a parliamentary vote the preceding day. The setback was a humiliating and bitter experience for the Tiger, but it reflected the mood of the country at the beginning of 1920. Many believed that the raison d'être of the Clemenceau government had ended with the return of peace; they were anxious to dismantle the wartime dictatorship he had enjoyed and to reaffirm parliamentary control over the executive. With the election of a more conservative Chamber of Deputies in November, 1919, it was only a question of time until the change occurred, though the manner of its occurrence, in the rejection of Clemenceau for a largely honorific post, was surprising.[96]

Disenchantment on the Right with what was regarded as too lenient a peace with Germany was one reason behind Clemenceau's fall. But widespread dissatisfaction with the government's economic policies also played a part.[97] There the chief culprit was Loucheur. When he left office in January, the French economy, though expanding, was dominated by an attempt to reestablish prewar patterns. Many of Loucheur's initiatives toward economic renovation had gone unfulfilled. Nevertheless, he did play a critical role in the last months of 1919 by encouraging such things as a modern French merchant fleet and the large-scale electrification of French industry.

When the Clemenceau government resigned, France also lost Loucheur's voice of moderation in dealings with Germany. Loucheur had proved to be a realist with an awareness that economic cooperation and

94. *Le Progrès du Nord,* November 20, 1919, p. 1.
95. Loucheur, *Carnets secrets,* 113–14.
96. Wright, *France in Modern Times,* 334–35; Bruun, *Clemenceau,* 199.
97. Bruun, *Clemenceau,* 199.

negotiation would in the long run yield better results than coercion could in implementing the economic clauses of the peace treaty. Although he was prudent about exposing that knowledge before French public opinion, it was evident in the flexibility he brought to his talks with the Germans during the fall of 1919. It was unfortunate that someone so involved in the authorship of the reparations section of the peace treaty was thrust from the peace process. The assignment went to a group whose understanding of the reparations clauses came from reading, not from being present when that section of the treaty, with its many subtleties, was drafted.[98]

The resignation of the Clemenceau government marked the end of the most significant phase of Loucheur's public service career. Notwithstanding his service as a government minister in 1921 and later, he was never again as influential in the economic affairs of France as in the pivotal year of 1919.

98. Weill-Raynal, *Les Réparations allemandes*, I, 142.

9

RECONSTRUCTION, 1920–1922

The desire of many French citizens to return to the conditions they had known before the war was reflected in the character of the Chamber of Deputies after the elections of November, 1919. Dominated by moderate and conservative groups that went under the name of the Bloc National, the Chamber seemed set on removing the state as far as practicable from French economic life. But not all the French wished to return to the old way of doing things. Leftist groups were pushing for a more active state role in the economy, and in the winter and spring of 1920 the labor movement pressed for nationalizing the railroads by threatening, and resorting to, strikes. The labor agitation came to a head in May, when the railway workers and other unions joined in a general strike. Although that was quickly broken, the union movement's commitment to nationalization remained strong.[1] The Left was thus a constant reminder that the state was not completely free to deregulate the economy. The government also found its aspirations toward decontrol restricted by the realization that certain of the country's economic objectives, such as the reconstruction of the liberated regions, dictated some state involvement.

Reparations remained at the fore of discussions among European diplomats and politicians. By the beginning of 1920 it had become clear that Germany was not only dismayed by the Versailles settlement generally but was particularly offended by a set of reparations clauses whose justification rested on the defeated powers' responsibility for the outbreak of World War I. Aware of German feelings, the French kept

---

1. Kuisel, *Capitalism and the State*, 62–71, 77–80; Adrian Jones, "The French Railway Strikes of January–May, 1920: New Syndicalist Ideas and Emergent Communism," *French Historical Studies*, XII (1982), 517–38.

close watch on the German fulfillment of reparations commitments which was already under way. A special concern, which Loucheur expressed in December, 1919, was that the Germans were not in compliance with coal delivery obligations agreed to late the previous summer.[2]

In this atmosphere of international uncertainty and domestic tension, Loucheur took up his tenure as a deputy from the Nord. He affiliated with the Républicains de Gauche, a parliamentary group that included André Tardieu, as well as Yves Le Trocquer, the minister of public works in 1920. Though without a ministerial post after Clemenceau's government collapsed, Loucheur immediately became a leader of an influential interparliamentary association of senators and deputies from the liberated regions, and he was named to the powerful finance commission of the Chamber of Deputies.[3] In January, 1921, he accepted a call from Aristide Briand to serve as minister of the liberated regions in a newly formed cabinet. Far from falling into political obscurity, Loucheur in 1920, 1921, and early 1922 remained a powerful voice on economic questions, particularly those related to reconstruction; he also became a leading spokesman on inexpensive housing.

Throughout this period, Loucheur approached problems through methods he had employed as a minister during and immediately after the war. He stressed the technocratic principles of efficiency, production, and organization. Though still favoring decontrol in principle, he was pragmatic enough to see the need for a degree of state involvement in some areas of the economy and society.

LEGISLATIVE ACTIONS IN 1920: RAILS AND INEXPENSIVE HOUSING

The preponderant share of the rail network was in private hands after the war, operating on an agreement the railroad companies and the government had reached in 1883. Its terms, considered by many to be overgenerous toward the rail companies, enabled the system to function by and large satisfactorily prior to World War I. But under the demands of the war, the network was beginning to break down by late 1916, although it did not become critically deficient until 1918. At the armistice,

2. Trachtenberg, *Reparation in World Politics*, 122–23.

3. Frederick Wurzburg, "The Politics of the Bloc National" (Ph.D. dissertation, Columbia University, 1961), 58–59; *Le Temps*, January 31, 1920, p. 2.

France's railroads were in a deplorable state, and the rail companies were in no position to rebuild on their own. Some form of government action seemed imperative.[4]

Albert Thomas introduced a nationalization bill in the Chamber of Deputies in April, 1919, by the terms of which the government was to exercise a repurchase option contained in the original franchises it had granted to the five privately owned rail systems in the mid–nineteenth century. The state was to pay an indemnity to the owners computed on the average net earnings of their systems during the five best years of the preceding seven. The rail companies, however, objected that the reference period was atypical and would be unfair to them. They further contended that the proposal was illegal, for it rescinded the state's commitments under the agreement of 1883. When they suggested that the government not only purchase all rolling stock but also assume the sizable indebtedness the companies had incurred, they strangled Thomas' bill completely. Such a large state undertaking was at that point well beyond the capacity of the treasury, and the bill was sent to committee and left there to die.

The Left attempted railroad nationalization again in 1920, when the Socialist Léon Blum presented to the Chamber of Deputies a plan originated by the Confédération Générale du Travail that would have formed a unified autonomous rail network with its personnel, the public, and the government all represented in its management. The government was to expropriate the companies' fixed properties and rolling stock with fair reimbursement. Immediately attacked, Blum's proposal, which came on the heels of the 1920 railroad strikes, was overwhelmingly defeated.[5]

Two other rail reorganization bills received attention in 1920: a government plan that Le Trocquer, the minister of public works, introduced and a measure that Loucheur sponsored. Le Trocquer's proposal, presented in mid-May, envisioned a "common fund" among the five private rail companies; money in the joint account was to derive from net profits and cover deficits. Two new boards were to coordinate and over-

---

4. Jean Vandel, *Les Chemins de fer français depuis la guerre, 1919–1924* (Paris, 1925), 8–30; Marcel Peschaud, *Les Chemins de fer pendant et depuis la guerre, 1914–1920* (Paris, n.d.), 58–64.

5. Kimon A. Doukas, *The French Railroads and the State* (New York, 1945), 25–32, 121–23.

see the general operations of the five carriers: a superior railroad council and a joint management committee. The bill provided for government absorption of the companies' huge debts and a state guarantee of railroad securities. It was a modified form of this bill that became law in 1921.[6]

Loucheur's bill, in late May, based railroad reorganization on the pattern of the *régie intéressée,* a structure he had already had success with in the mining industry.[7] The bill empowered the government to repurchase the rail lines in accordance with current franchises, with company owners receiving full indemnity for all acquired properties and creditors being paid at par value. Both owners and creditors were to be compensated through annuities that budget appropriations would enable. Loucheur made sure that the state, in buying back the rail lines, would not become responsible for their profitable operation. Running the railroads and drawing profits from them would become the right of a corporation whose shares were to be owned by several groups, including the rail workers. For that right, the corporation would pay the government an annual rent.[8]

Loucheur took care over the bill's provisions for workers. The issuance of 250,000 labor shares was to let a labor cooperative be part owner of the operating corporation. Loucheur explained, "These shares would not be distributed to employees but handed over to a labor cooperative. This innovation contains nothing revolutionary. It constitutes a system of accession to property which has more merit than the simplistic formula of participation in profits. But this formula must have as a corollary the participation in losses. The system consists of transforming labor shares into capital shares that would support the risks of the enterprise and would attach the worker to them morally."[9] Loucheur's motive seems to have been to include rail workers in ownership in a way that would allow them representation on the board of directors. Loucheur believed that a better spirit of cooperation between labor and management would result, in line with his stated goal of replacing class confrontation in France with class cooperation.[10]

6. *Le Temps,* May 19, 1920, p. 2; Doukas, *The French Railroads,* 127–30; Kuisel, *Capitalism and the State,* 69.

7. For a definition of *régie intéressée,* see above, p. 197.

8. *Le Progrès du Nord,* May 31, 1920, p. 1; Doukas, *The French Railroads,* 126–27; Vandel, *Les Chemins de fer français,* 108–10.

9. Vandel, *Les Chemins de fer français,* 108–109.

10. *Le Temps,* December 16, 1920, p. 2; *Le Progrès du Nord,* December 16, 1920, p. 1.

Loucheur's proposal, which had the backing of a small group of centrist deputies, was an attempt to find a middle ground between the nationalization schemes of the Left and the milder proposals of the government, but it failed to attract enough support in the Chamber to make headway. One opponent called the labor clauses an attempt to erect an "entity of socialistic metaphysics."[11] A report of the Chamber's public-works commission expressed fears that the plan would entail tremendous government outlays in repurchasing the rail lines and that it would lure the government into taking control of the system. The government's takeover and operation of the Western Railroad beginning in 1909 illustrated the pitfalls of direct government control, it cautioned. Loucheur withdrew his bill in December, 1920, when it was evident that sentiment in the Chamber was clearly behind the proposals of Le Trocquer.[12] Although Loucheur's bill was rejected, it was a technocrat's response to a serious economic problem and to the need for modernization. Because of the complexity of the solution it proffered, however, it was considered unworkable.

Loucheur was not quite finished, however. In early December, he introduced a resolution to transform the Western Railroad from a state-owned operation into a *régie intéressée*. The resolution also called for exchanges of rail lines with nearby rail companies to allow for a more logical and effective organization of the rail networks in the region. A revised form of the resolution that made no mention of a *régie intéressée* received Chamber approval on December 18.[13]

Another domestic issue that commanded Loucheur's attention in 1920 was a serious shortage of inexpensive housing. Alexandre Ribot, author of a public-housing law of 1908, voiced the sentiment of many of the French when, in March, 1920, he told the French Senate, "No question is of greater national interest than that of low-income housing. So far, efforts have been inadequate."[14] Although a housing crisis, which included slums in places like Paris, existed before 1914, the war exacerbated the situation by dramatically reducing construction and by bring-

11. *Le Progrès du Nord*, May 31, 1920, p. 1; Doukas, *The French Railroads*, 127.

12. *Le Temps*, November 4, 1920, pp. 1, 2, December 16, 1920, p. 2.

13. France, *Journal officiel de la République française: Chambre des Députés, documents parlementaires* (1920), Annex No. 1755, Proposition de résolution, December 7, 1920, pp. 398–99; *Le Progrès du Nord*, December 10, 1920, p. 1; France, *Annales de la Chambre: Débats*, December 18, 1920, pp. 527–28; *Le Temps*, December 20, 1920, p. 1.

14. *Le Temps*, March 14, 1920, p. 2.

ing damage and destruction to some 740,000 homes in the devastated regions.[15] Nevertheless, there was little enthusiasm in the private sector for residential construction after the war. The high cost of labor and materials, as well as a capital shortage, were restraints: interest rates were 8.25 percent in 1921, as against 4.85 percent in 1914. The government's rent controls were also a deterrent. Shortly after the outbreak of hostilities, the government began a series of moratoriums on the rent payments of mobilized soldiers and mandated extensions of the soldiers' existing leases. In 1918, government legislation provided for the partial or complete cancellation of wartime rents for several categories of householders, including mobilized soldiers. The law also gave renters with leases dating back before August 1, 1914, the right to extend them, without modification, for two years after the end of the war; that meant a continuation of 1914 rents. An expansion of rent controls in 1919 added protection for most leases signed during the war. As a result, 90 to 95 percent of lessees were under rent control by the end of 1919. Since new construction was expensive and parliament was unprepared to end the artificially low rents, there was little incentive to build.[16]

When the minister of health and social provision, Jules Breton, appointed a committee in early 1920 to make recommendations about the country's housing problems, Loucheur was named chairman.[17] The committee, which included several members of parliament with housing expertise, such as Ribot, Jules Siegfried, and Paul Strauss, put its findings in a report that Loucheur wrote, and the report provided the basis for a housing bill that Loucheur and Laurent Bonnevay submitted to the Chamber of Deputies in July, 1920.[18] Their bold proposal called for constructing 500,000 low-cost homes over a ten-year period, at an annual expenditure of 750 million francs. The financial commitment they were suggesting was considerably more than the state then had avail-

15. "Rapport sur le problème du logement," by Conseil National Economique, n.d., in F 12, 8801, AN; Norma Evenson, *Paris: A Century of Change, 1878–1978* (New Haven, 1979), 212–16.

16. Bureau International du Travail, *Les Problèmes du logement en Europe depuis la guerre* (Geneva, 1924), 127–33, 140–46; Sauvy and Hirsch, *Histoire économique*, II, 262–67; Bonnefous and Bonnefous, *Histoire politique*, II, 113–19, 271–72, 432–34.

17. The government created a separate ministry of health and social provision in January, 1920. That ministry was combined with the ministry of labor in March, 1924.

18. "France" (document on housing), 1922, in Housing, Carton W 8/4/1/22, BIT; Jean Lévêque and J. H. Ricard, *Une Politique du logement* (Paris, 1928), 79–80.

able for such construction. Bonds were to be issued annually to finance the project, with the government assuming responsibility for payment of one-half of the interest and amortization expenses. After the Chamber of Deputies made a number of changes, the most notable of which was to limit the government's financial commitment to 750 million francs, that is, to the completion of the program's first stage, it passed the bill in November, 1921. But it languished for several years after that because of Senate inaction.[19]

Other recommendations in the committee's report bore Loucheur's imprint. There was the advocacy of construction priorities for the liberated regions, with precedence for structures needing repair but not total reconstruction. There was the suggestion of an interministerial committee with responsibility for the monthly distribution of available construction materials to all parts of France, and of a *comptoir d'achat* to procure construction materials at the lowest prices possible. There were admonitions to use standardized materials and modern methods of construction. To coordinate the undertaking, the committee recommended establishing an *office national du logement salubre et économique*.[20] The committee's plan was not enacted, but it was strong testimony to Loucheur's concern about improving living conditions on humanitarian grounds and to his awareness that from a technocratic standpoint improved living conditions could raise worker morale.

MINISTER OF THE LIBERATED REGIONS: INTRODUCTION

On January 12, 1921, the government of Georges Leygues, formed the preceding September, fell. Alexandre Millerand, president of the republic, sent out the call to Briand after his first choice failed to constitute a cabinet. Briand, who had begun a slow shift leftward late in the war, was still closely enough identified with the Right, because of his association with France's prewar nationalist revival and the country's war party in 1914, to be acceptable to the Bloc National. Millerand, despite knowing that Briand's position toward Germany was more pliable than his own, decided that having Briand lead the government was better than having

19. "France" (document on housing), 1922, in W 8/4/1/22, BIT; Lévêque and Ricard, *Une Politique du logement,* 80.
20. Loucheur's Report on Housing, 1920, in B, 39895, MF.

him oppose it. It was clear during the ensuing negotiations that Briand wished to make Loucheur his finance minister. But strong pressure within the Chamber obliged him to turn to Paul Doumer, an austere senator whose experience with government finance dated from the early 1890s and whose attitude toward Germany the Chamber expected to be more forceful than Loucheur's. Briand appointed Loucheur minister of the liberated regions.[21]

Loucheur's agreement to serve came at a price to him. Clemenceau, a bitter political enemy of Briand, felt betrayed and ended his friendship with his former minister. Also undermined was the close relationship Loucheur had developed with Tardieu, a Clemenciste committed to the strict application of the Treaty of Versailles. It was the end of Loucheur's association with the small group of Clemencistes sitting in parliament; his flexibility regarding foreign policy was in the final analysis incompatible with the group's "firm line."[22]

Loucheur was certainly well versed on the liberated regions. As a government minister, he had worked there in 1919 on industrial reconstruction, and he continued to follow the subject in 1920. Because of his knowledge, his organizational talents, and his penchant for bold initiatives, he quickly emerged as the leading light in Briand's government.

The ministry into which Loucheur moved had much greater control over the reconstruction of the liberated regions than it had had earlier. At the end of 1918, responsibilities for the devastated areas were divided among several ministries, although the ministries of industrial reconstruction and of the liberated regions had the largest roles. After the enactment of the Law of April 17, 1919, the ministry of the liberated regions became the key agency in the overall reconstruction of northeastern France, and at the beginning of 1920 its authority over reconstruction became even greater. The Office of Industrial Reconstruction, which had been a major force in redeveloping the industrial sector of the overrun departments, moved at that time from the dismantled ministry of reconstruction to the ministry of the liberated regions.[23] In addition,

21. Bonnefous and Bonnefous, *Histoire politique,* III, 207–12; Leslie Derfler, *President and Parliament: A Short History of the French Presidency* (Boca Raton, Fla., 1983), 96–97, 113.

22. Rudolph Binion, *Defeated Leaders: The Political Fate of Caillaux, Jouvenel, and Tardieu* (New York, 1960), 284–85; Simone Loucheur, "Histoire familiale," in Simone Loucheur Papers, in family possession, Paris.

23. MacDonald, *Reconstruction in France,* 78–83.

the ministry for the first time included an undersecretary of state to act as a liaison between it and other ministries connected with reconstruction.

At the time of the changes, Loucheur, believing that conditions demanded a more radical ministerial realignment than what the government offered, proposed creating positions at the ministry of the liberated regions for several secretaries of state who would not only work as liaisons with other ministries but also exercise ministerial powers over government staff in the devastated areas. Loucheur's idea was reminiscent of the arrangement at the war ministry when several undersecretaries of state handled a combination of war-related activities. His goal was a highly centralized ministerial apparatus in Paris complemented by decentralization at the regional level.[24] The interparliamentary group from the liberated regions endorsed Loucheur's concept of a "superministry," but the government never acted on it.[25]

After taking charge of reconstruction in 1921, Loucheur devoted much energy to the work of the agencies for damage evaluation that were known as cantonal commissions and to reconstruction finance. He also participated in negotiations with Germany regarding reparations payments in kind and held some discussions with Britain in late 1921 on reparations and war debts between the Allies.

CANTONAL COMMISSIONS

The cornerstone of reconstruction was the Law of April 17, 1919, which, known as the Charte des Sinistrés, guaranteed to those who had suffered property damage during the war (sinistrés) the right to full indemnity (see above, p. 148). Sinistrés who restored damaged real property received the property's value on the eve of the war plus a coefficient,

24. Le Progrès du Nord, May 16, 1920, p. 1.

25. Senator Léon Chênebenoit referred to it in a newspaper article as the grand ministère for the period of reconstruction, drawing a comparison between it and the grand ministère of the war, namely, the war ministry. See Le Temps, April 29, 1920, p. 1. Loucheur's idea was brought up at the meeting of the Chamber's commission on the liberated regions on February 13, although the commission refrained from giving its support, contending that decisions on that should come from the government. See Minutes, Commission des Régions Libérées (Chambre), February 13, 1920, in XIIe Législature, Carton A-66, Commission des Régions Libérées, Procès-verbaux, AANV.

which represented the sum needed, beyond the value in 1914 of the damaged property, to complete reconstruction after the war. *Sinistrés* who chose not to apply their indemnities to restoration received only the value of the damaged property in 1914.[26]

The Charte des Sinistrés provided for the establishment of cantonal commissions to fix indemnity sums in particular cases, providing satisfaction to both the state—represented at commission hearings by administrative agents—and the property owners. When disputes arose, appeals were possible to a tribunal of war damages. Technical committees assisted the cantonal commissions by establishing price lists for real property.[27]

Numerous problems soon arose. Organizing the commissions and instructing them on procedural matters took much time, as did the elaborate process for evaluating claims. The commissions were overwhelmed by the sheer number of claims, with their welter of supporting documents. Some commissions failed to grasp the urgency of their assignment, convening only one or two times a week or for only a few hours. Moreover, the different cantonal commissions did not handle claims uniformly. There were even questions heard about the competence of commission members.[28] Most of the problems still plagued the system in January, 1921, and when Loucheur became the minister of the liberated regions, his program of action gave their correction a high priority. Boldly, he declared that the cantonal commissions would complete by the end of the year their appraisals of the value damaged property had in 1914. As of January 1, the cantonal commissions had made final decisions in only 621,312 of 2,765,317 claims submitted; that was merely 22.5 percent of the total. But Loucheur had in the past set seemingly unattainable targets and often reached them, so his announcement of this ostensibly impossible completion date was in keeping with his production-oriented style of management. He also let it be known that he would repair the legal inconsistencies arising from poor communication between cantonal commissions. And he designated the ministerial undersecretary of state, Georges Lugol, to work with the

26. Grabau, *Industrial Reconstruction*, 50.

27. *Ibid.*, 52–53.

28. *Ibid.*, 63; MacDonald, *Reconstruction in France*, 89–90; Georges Leredu to prefects, Circular No. 658, December 9, 1920, in AJ 24, 135, AN; Minutes, Commission des Régions Libérées (Chambre), November 17, 1920, in XIIe Législature, A-66, AANV.

commissions in ironing out their problems.[29] Lugol, a deputy representing Seine-et-Marne, had served on several parliamentary committees, including that for the liberated regions.

Even before taking office, however, Loucheur had attempted to improve the commissions' effectiveness. One of the several recommendations he made in April, 1920, as the head of a subcommittee of the interparliamentary group from the liberated regions was for there to be an undersecretary of state with authority derived from both the ministry of justice and the ministry of the liberated regions to supervise the cantonal commissions. Loucheur did not specify to which ministry the undersecretary was to be attached, but in view of his plan for a "superministry" it is reasonable to assume that it was the ministry of the liberated regions. Loucheur saw that as a way of transferring to the minister of the liberated regions some of the sway the ministry of justice had over the cantonal commissions. Loucheur also favored organizing a small group of inspectors to monitor the commissions' activities, thereby improving output and correcting errors in decision making. The interparliamentary group accepted his proposals, hoping to pressure the government into taking action.[30]

Others, too, saw the need for changes in the operations of the cantonal commissions. Emile Ogier, in career service with the government, and minister of the liberated regions from January, 1920, until Loucheur's appointment, admitted when he was nominated that the cantonal commissions' work would "not be finished for several years" without "needed changes" in their "composition and procedures."[31] Ogier modified procedures and increased personnel to expedite the work of the commissions. But in spite of intensive lobbying by members of the interparliamentary group from the liberated regions, Ogier was slow to act toward restructuring ministerial control over the cantonal commissions. Not until July did he come forward with a proposal about that. His recommendation, which he incorporated into a bill dealing with several aspects of reconstruction, was for completely concentrating authority over the commis-

29. *Le Temps,* January 20, 1921, p. 4; Grabau, *Industrial Reconstruction,* 144–46.

30. Rapport présenté au nom de la sous-commission nommée par le Groupe Interparlementaire des Régions Libérées, sur les mesures à prendre en vue de régler au plus tôt l'évaluation des dommages de guerre dans les régions dévastées, signed by Loucheur, April 1, 1920, in Series BB, Ministère de la Justice, Subseries BB 30, Versements disparates de 1904 à 1961, Carton 1582, AN.

31. *Le Temps,* January 30, 1920, p. 4.

sions in the ministry of the liberated regions, which he thought should even appoint their presidents. He also recommended enlarging the pool from which the presidents were drawn, to make it easier to increase the number of commissions. As another means of accelerating progress, he suggested that prefects be granted the prerogative of dividing cantonal commissions into sections with the same powers as the plenary groups.[32]

The bill was referred to the Chamber's commission on the liberated regions, whose members debated the degree of control the minister of the liberated regions should have over the cantonal commissions. The commission's members were leery of Ogier's idea, because they believed that the cantonal commissions needed some independence to safeguard impartiality in making awards. Concluding that appointment of cantonal commission presidents by the justice minister helped ensure independence, the commission, despite supporting authority for the ministry of the liberated regions over the operations of the cantonal commissions, did not recommend that its authority include choosing their presidents.[33]

The result was an impasse and a parliamentary delay of many months in reforming the cantonal commissions. Ogier tenaciously held to his position, and the most far-reaching improvement the government undertook during this time was in the productivity bonuses it decided in December to grant cantonal commission presidents who held a minimum of two days of hearings a week.[34]

After Loucheur moved into the offices of the ministry, he revived the issue of control over the cantonal commissions by asking Bonnevay, the minister of justice, to consent to a decree delegating to Loucheur's undersecretary of state all his own power over the cantonal commissions. Bonnevay was unamenable, but Loucheur's initiative marked the beginning of discussions that eventually included not just the two men's ministries but also the Chamber's commission on the liberated

32. Emile Ogier to prefects of the liberated regions, Circular No. 280, May 11, 1920, Circular No. 305, May 22, 1920, both in AJ 24, 135, AN; Le Temps, April 4, 1920, p. 2, April 17, 1920, p. 3, April 24, 1920, p. 2; Projet de loi No. 1203 (Chambre), July 2, 1920, in BB 30, 1582, AN; Rapport fait au nom de la Commission des Régions Libérées par M. Charles Desjardins, Chambre des Députés, July 7, 1920, in BB 30, 1582, AN; Extrait des renseignements fournis par M. le Ministre des Régions Libérées par lettre du 2 octobre 1920, in C, 7769, AN.

33. Rapport fait au nom de la Commission des Régions Libérées par M. Charles Desjardins, Chambre des Députés, July 7, 1920, in BB 30, 1582, AN.

34. Alfred Morain (préfet), La Reconstitution du Nord dévasté au 1er septembre 1923: Exposé présenté au Conseil Général (Lille, 1923), 151, in ADN.

regions. The compromise the three parties reached in early April delegated control over the cantonal commissions from the ministry of justice to the undersecretariat of state for the liberated regions but kept the right to appoint commission presidents in the hands of the justice ministry. It was thus very similar to what the Chamber's commission on the liberated regions had favored the preceding July. Permission for the change was incorporated into the Finance Law of May 31, 1921, and a decree issued on June 14 completed the transfer.[35]

Loucheur expressed his sentiments on the partial nature of the solution the compromise afforded when, in the latter part of April, he told the Chamber of Deputies that the government proposal would reduce but not eliminate an "anomaly" in the area of authority.[36] Greater efficiency and output appear at the heart of his wish for an even greater role for his ministry, but others believed that a concentration of power in one ministry could erode the justice of the cantonal commissions' decisions and awards, and it was they who prevailed.

The Law of May 31, 1921, did enlarge the pool from which presidents of cantonal commissions could be drawn. It also created inspection units in each devastated department to review the cantonal commissions' activities; though the inspectors were technically subordinate to the justice minister, they were in practice under the control of Lugol as a part of his delegated responsibility from the minister of justice.[37]

In February, 1921, Loucheur directed the regional branches of the Office of Industrial Reconstruction to conduct preliminary evaluations of industrial claims for war damages. In the department of the Nord alone, these came close to eighteen thousand, and Loucheur's action eliminated the cantonal commissions' need to undertake their own investigations when deciding the amount of industrial *sinistrés'* indemnities. Even though the bureaucratic mechanisms of the pro-

35. Louis Loucheur to Laurent Bonnevay, January 22, 1921, in BB 30, 1582, AN; director of civil affairs at the ministry of justice to Georges Lugol, January 28, 1921, *ibid.*; Projet de loi No. 2236 (Chambre), February 28, 1921, *ibid.*; Minutes, Commission des Régions Libérées (Chambre), March 9, 1921, March 22, 1921, April 12, 1921, April 15, 1921, in XIIe Législature, A-66, AANV; Ministère des Régions Libérées, *Bulletin des régions libérées*, June 25, 1921, p. 224.

36. Ministère des Régions Libérées, *Bulletin des régions libérées*, May 7, 1921, p. 156. Loucheur made his comments to the Chamber on April 19, 1921.

37. *Ibid.*, May 7, 1921, p. 156, July 9, 1921, pp. 226–27. Implementation came from the Decree of June 29, 1921.

gram failed to operate as smoothly as Loucheur had anticipated, they eased the workload of the commissions. In May, Loucheur set up committees of *préconciliation* to hold preliminary hearings on claims that exceeded 500,000 francs.[38] The purpose was to bring the *sinistré* and the state to an agreement on an indemnity sum before the case reached a cantonal commission, so that the commission could merely give its approval to the agreed-upon amount. Loucheur foresaw in the preliminary hearings not only an acceleration of the cantonal commissions' progress but also a greater consistency in the determination of large indemnities.[39]

Even so, Loucheur fell short of his goal of completing the cantonal commissions' basic evaluation work by the end of the year. In late May, when he conceded in a speech to the Senate that the goal could not be reached, he added, "This date [the end of December, 1921] I continue to regard as valid even though persuaded I will not attain it, but I am persuaded too that at the end of the year we will have already reached between 1.5 million and 1.6 million decisions out of the 2.8 million to decide—or more than half, around 60 percent. Continuing thereafter, I hope, at a rate of 100,000 per month, we will have ended in 1922 the work of the cantonal commissions."[40] The number of decisions rendered by January 1, 1922, exceeded Loucheur's prediction in May: the cantonal commissions had made final decisions on 1,645,983 claims out of 2,905,414 submitted, representing 56.6 percent of the total. But it was not until the end of 1923 that their task was essentially finished.[41] On balance, Loucheur's methods, which included pressuring colleagues, setting goals, and emphasizing output and efficiency, were effective in producing results.[42] But problems about the processing of claims remained

38. Committees of *préconciliation* were established at two levels. Departmental committees dealt with claims by *sinistrés* that ranged between 500,000 and a million francs. For amounts in excess of a million francs, a central committee of *préconciliation* was set up in Paris.

39. Morain, *La Reconstitution du Nord*, 150–51, 158–64, ADN.

40. France, *Annales du Sénat: Débats*, May 31, 1921, p. 1451.

41. Grabau, *Industrial Reconstruction*, 145–46. As of January 1, 1924, the cantonal commissions had made 2,931,591 decisions concerning 3,013,705 dossiers submitted; that was 97.7 percent of the total.

42. Loucheur's undersecretary of state, Georges Lugol, contributed to the results achieved by the cantonal commissions in 1921, although Loucheur set the tone and was the driving force behind what was accomplished.

after Loucheur's departure, as is evident from the continued flow of circulars from Loucheur's successor, Charles Reibel, in 1922.[43]

FINANCING RECONSTRUCTION

Government advances were one instrument for moving reconstruction ahead. The day after the Law of April 17, 1919, was passed, the ministry of the liberated regions, giving a broad interpretation to Article 44, on advances, called upon prefects to be liberal when approving them. *Sinistrés* committed to rebuilding became eligible, prior to any definitive evaluation of losses by a cantonal commission, for an immediate advance of 25 percent of their estimated damages and eventual advances not surpassing 75 percent. The total amount of the advances rose significantly from what it had been before April 17.

Once a cantonal commission rendered a final decision on a total indemnity, the *sinistré* exchanged the decision summary for a bond representing the 1914 values of the losses incurred, and if he intended to reconstruct, he received a second bond for the amount of supplementary expenses. Those planning to reemploy their indemnities drew an immediate installment of 25 percent of the actual damages, and they collected further payments upon presentation of proofs of work completed and items purchased. Besides paying in cash, the government offered *sinistrés* the choice of payments in kind.[44]

As the extent and complexity of disbursements in accordance with the Charte des Sinistrés became obvious, a controversy arose over France's finances as a whole. Loucheur, with an eye on prompt damage payments and a quick rebuilding of the economy, agreed with those who encouraged the maximum use of credit possibilities at home and overseas. For monetary policy generally, they believed that there were cer-

43. Charles Reibel to prefects of the liberated regions, Circular No. 185, January 27, 1922, Circular No. 201, February 13, 1921, Circular No. 292, May 30, 1922, all in AJ 24, 136, AN.

44. Grabau, *Industrial Reconstruction*, 53, 65–66. In the summer of 1919, the government reached an agreement allowing a private institution, the Crédit National, to serve as the state's financial agent in distributing funds for indemnities and advances. In meeting financial responsibilities to *sinistrés* from 1919 to 1928, the Crédit National floated eight bond issues that allowed it to distribute close to thirty billion francs in payments. See MacDonald, *Reconstruction in France*, 177; and Grabau, *Industrial Reconstruction*, 82–84.

tain advantages to a depreciated currency. They argued that if the franc appreciated in value, prices would continue to drop and business profits and tax revenues would shrink. When the state's revenues fell, though, its financial obligations would remain high, since approximately half the ordinary budget went to servicing the public debt, which could not be compressed.[45] They saw a partial solution to the financial crisis that sprang from France's wartime debt in the depreciated currency that would let the nation pay its obligations least painfully.[46]

For Loucheur, however, the larger component of the solution lay in expanding production, for he believed that increased exports would dramatically improve France's balance of payments. After his departure from the ministry of reconstruction in January, 1920, he continued to rally the French to production. In the closing lines of a speech he delivered to a group of northeastern industrialists on April 26, 1920, he exhorted, "Let's work, let's work for the best. Let's do our duty, our full duty, each in his own sphere, for the general interest is made up only of the sum of individual interests, and industrialists, in working for themselves, at the same time work to consolidate and safeguard the credit of France, and what is most important of all is that France lives and shines forth eternally in the world."[47]

The ministry of finance was much more conservative. Since it had to meet the country's fiscal requirements while upholding the value of an inflation-threatened franc, it fought to limit spending and even hoped that the franc could appreciate to prewar levels.[48] When Millerand replaced Clemenceau as premier, Frédéric François-Marsal became minister of finance, although he was not a member of parliament.[49] The banking experience he brought to the position set the tone of his ministry's approach. When François-Marsal and Loucheur delivered speeches to the Chamber of Deputies during a budget debate in March, 1920, *Le Temps* wrote, "After M. Marsal, M. Loucheur; after the banker, the entrepreneur. The one has the caution of the banker who reckons with an

45. France had three budgets at the time: the ordinary budget, the extraordinary budget, and a budget based on what France expected to receive from the Germans in reparations.

46. Bonnefous and Bonnefous, *Histoire politique*, III, 214–15; Silverman, *Reconstructing Europe*, 104–105.

47. *Le Progrès du Nord*, April 26, 1920, p. 1.

48. Schuker, *The End of French Predominance*, 35–39.

49. Frédéric François-Marsal was elected to the Senate in 1921.

ever so fleeting, ever so fragile credit, with dreadful consumption, and with self-probing and self-restraining production. The other has the boldness of the businessman who bases his efforts on a sometimes risky credit, paying dearly if necessary to complete things, and whose efforts and creativity spur production. M. Loucheur's speech was a great success."[50] François-Marsal emphasized the harmful effects of fiduciary inflation, consumer extravagance, and excessive imports; Loucheur pointed out that the finance minister had been silent about the reparations anticipated from Germany during 1920. Loucheur emphasized that an imprudent withdrawal of francs from circulation could have an adverse effect on the economy.[51]

In January, 1920, before stepping down as minister of industrial reconstruction, Loucheur had joined Louis Lucien Klotz, the minister of finance, and Tardieu, then serving as minister of the liberated regions, in introducing legislation to provide the government with relief in meeting its financial commitments to the devastated areas. The bill proposed a long-term alternative to the forms of payment set out in the Law of April 17, 1919. Individual *sinistrés* and groups of *sinistrés* were to be eligible for private loans collateralized against their future indemnities provided that their damages amounted to a million francs or more. The government was to guarantee the loans through annuities and an annual interest rate of up to 6 percent on the outstanding balance, and the participation of *sinistrés* was to be voluntary.[52]

In the spring, François-Marsal, concerned about the treasury's ability to meet its obligations to *sinistrés*, superseded the proposal of January with one that was broader in its impact and less attractive to beneficiaries. The new bill substituted ten-year bonds for cash in most initial indemnity payments, lengthened the maturity date of the bonds for advances in excess of three thousand francs, and made participation obligatory for those affected. In addition, François-Marsal's revision required participation in the program of annuity payments by all with indemnities above four million francs, and it reduced the annual rate of interest it would pay to 5 percent. In the bill's preamble François-Marsal broached the possibility that annuitants might use their credit with the

50. *Le Temps*, March 31, 1920, p. 3.

51. France, *Annales de la Chambre: Débats*, March 29, 1920, pp. 633–39.

52. France, *Journal officiel: Chambre des Députés, documents parlementaires* (1920), Projet de loi No. 169, January 13, 1920, p. 80.

state to contract loans with private lenders, but the bill's articles were not explicit on that.[53]

In the storm of opposition that erupted in parliament, Loucheur and others attacked the new bill for failing to give satisfaction to the "rightful claims of the *sinistrés*." A large number of deputies, with Loucheur in the van, offered a counterproposal more generous to claimants in the forms of payment it allowed, all of them voluntary.[54] François-Marsal in late June reacted by submitting a gentler version of the government's bill, but since it preserved the feature of compulsory participation, it did little to placate opponents.[55]

In the end, the only change in methods of payment in the Law of July 31, 1920, concerned the program of payments through annuities, which was made voluntary. A condition for participation in the program was a minimum indemnity total of a million francs. Payments were to be in equal installments over periods ranging from fifteen to thirty years, and *sinistrés* could meet the minimum indemnity requirement by presenting a group's, or even a whole town's or commune's claims together. The indemnities could serve as collateral for immediate reconstruction loans. A ceiling of three billion francs was placed on the combined indemnity value that could be covered in this way during the 1920 budget year, and an interest rate of 6 percent was to be paid on outstanding annuity balances. In December, departments became one of the classes of confederated entities eligible to participate.[56]

The victory of the deputies from the liberated regions must have been particularly satisfying to Loucheur, for parliament adopted a program essentially like the one he had supported when he was minister of industrial reconstruction. Loucheur hoped that the government would energetically support the program that had been enacted. In October, he tried to get François-Marsal to follow his lead in encouraging cities in northeastern France to avail themselves of the advantages that lay in annuities. But the finance minister was hesitant, apparently because the

53. *Ibid.*, Projet de loi No. 684, April 12, 1920, p. 638.

54. *Ibid.*, Projet de loi No. 1055, June 12, 1920, pp. 1621–22. Ninety deputies sponsored the bill, with Loucheur's name at the head of the list.

55. Rapport fait au nom de la Commission des Régions Libérées par M. Philippoteaux, No. 1282, Chambre des Députés, July 9, 1920, in BB 30, 1582, AN.

56. France, *Journal officiel: Lois et Décrets*, August 1, 1920, pp. 10945–46, January 1, 1921, p. 6. The inclusion of departments was a part of the Law of December 31, 1920.

government's 1921 budget proposal, with its special provisions for the liberated regions, augured a large deficit. He told Ogier in December that the government would have to borrow heavily in capital markets to cover projected outlays and that this would put it in direct competition with *sinistrés* who wanted to borrow money in the private sector because of the annuities program.[57] He did little to promote the program before leaving the finance ministry in January, 1921.

Loucheur was convinced of the importance of reconstruction to economic revival,[58] and when he assumed his ministerial post in 1921, he devised a plan to meet the situation financially despite the budget constraints. That included developing the annuities loan program established by the Law of July 31, 1920; reducing substantially the amount *sinistrés* could collect for coefficients;[59] appealing to the new minister of finance, Paul Doumer, for 800 million francs to settle accounts on work performed in the liberated regions during 1920; and encouraging indemnification through payments in kind.[60]

Loucheur embarked on an intensive publicity campaign to encourage the use by industries, cities, and departments of government annuity payments to back loans from nongovernment sources. On February 5, he announced that the mining industry intended to float a collective loan during the latter half of March and that the sugar, brewing, and metallurgical industries planned to follow suit. He also told of several financing projects by cities and departments that he anticipated. Several days later he emphasized the importance of the loans in an appearance before the Senate's commission on the liberated regions, and in mid-February he conducted his promotional drive on a trip to the liberated regions.[61] Some of the group loans that Loucheur envisaged in February began to solidify during the spring. The mining industry floated its loan, for 800 million francs, at the beginning of April, and it was quickly ab-

57. *Le Progrès du Nord*, October 16, 1920, p. 1; Frédéric François-Marsal to Emile Ogier, December 7, 1920, in Series A, Documents soumis à des conditions spéciales de sécurité, Subseries I A, Cabinets Ministériels, Carton 386, MF.

58. He emphasized this in a newspaper interview in November, 1920. See *Le Progrès du Nord*, November 17, 1920, p. 1.

59. For a definition of *coefficients*, see above, pp. 212–13.

60. Minutes, Commission des Régions Libérées (Chambre), February 10, 1921, in XIIe Législature, A-66, AANV; *Le Temps*, February 5, 1921, p. 6.

61. *Le Temps*, February 5, 1921, p. 6; *Le Progrès du Nord*, February 13, 1921, p. 1, February 14, 1921, p. 1, February 16, 1921, p. 1.

sorbed by the public, even oversubscribed.[62] Several days later the city of Albert successfully floated a loan for 25 million francs.

But when the cities of Reims and Verdun decided to issue loans, Loucheur and Doumer reacted differently. In early June, Loucheur was insisting that the two municipal issues proceed as scheduled despite Doumer's reservations. The finance minister, who faced a particularly difficult financial situation in the late spring, talked of priorities in floating loans and apparently considered suspending municipal offerings out of fear that they might limit public interest in national loans. Rumors circulated about an imminent cabinet crisis, and the city council of Verdun threatened to resign in the event of an injunction against the city's loan. Loucheur prevailed in the latter part of June, with the government authorizing Reims to issue a loan of 120 million francs and Verdun one for 60 million.[63]

When Morgan, Harjes et Cie., the J. P. Morgan affiliate expected to participate in the loan, demurred, Loucheur took the matter up directly with Herman Harjes, president of the company. According to Harjes, Loucheur vowed "that he would never shake me by the hand again, that he would never bow to my wife when he saw her in the street and that he would have absolutely nothing more to do with the firm unless we allowed our name to appear on the circular!"[64] Harjes yielded, and the loan issue moved ahead. The glass, sugar, metallurgical, and electrical-energy industries all obtained financing through the government-backed program, as did the municipality of La Bassée. The city of Soissons received authorization to seek an 80-million-franc loan in Canada.[65]

But the Nord, seeking 300 million francs, apparently experienced difficulties at the ministry of finance during the fall of 1921, for Loucheur had to intervene personally with Doumer to secure a loan-issuance date

62. Flyer Announcing the Issuance of the Mining-Industry Loan, April 1, 1921, in B, 34014, MF.

63. MacDonald, *Reconstruction in France*, 186–87; Minutes, Commission des Finances (Chambre), June 15, 1921, in XIIe Législature, Carton A-25, Commission des Finances, Procès-verbaux, AANV; Rough Draft of Letter to the director of the Banque de Paris et des Pays-Bas, June 20, 1921, in B, 39889, MF; Presidential Decree Authorizing Loan for the City of Reims, June 20, 1921, in B, 39889, MF.

64. Silverman, *Reconstructing Europe*, 225.

65. Conventions de paiement par annuités (Loi du 31 Juillet 1920), in B, 33978, MF; Emprunts des sinistrés par souscription publique, *ibid*.

of January, 1922. Even then, a segment of the banking consortium associated with the loan suddenly withdrew from the transaction. As a result, the department had to settle for an initial loan of 150 million francs in early 1922; they floated the other half of the loan they wanted a year later.[66]

All told, the amount raised through collective loans in 1921 came to 2.835 billion francs ($212,375,459), slightly under the three-billion-franc ($224,735,935) limit placed on them.[67] In the annuities program as a whole, close to 3.8 billion francs ($284,666,000) was raised in loans, just under the 4-billion-franc ($299,647,913) limit the law allowed. In November, 1921, Loucheur introduced legislation to reduce the amount qualifying an individual or group for the program from a million to 200,000 francs.[68]

Even before Loucheur became minister of the liberated regions, many contended that coefficients, which at the end of 1920 averaged between five and six times the estimated value of damaged property in 1914, were much too high, if not scandalous. Ogier was conscious of the problem but confessed in March, 1920, that he had found no effective means to control their rise.[69] In November, Ogier's undersecretary of state, Georges Leredu, suggested careful study before taking major corrective measures.[70] Behind the ministry's hesitancy lay a fear of outrage over alleged injustice.

Casting aside his predecessor's trepidations, Loucheur announced that he would reduce coefficients to somewhere between 3 and 3.5 times

66. Morain, *La Reconstitution du Nord,* 179–94, ADN.
67. The average exchange rate during Briand's ministry—January 16, 1921, to January 12, 1922—was 13.349 francs to one dollar. That is the exchange rate for determining the dollar equivalents cited.
68. Emprunts des sinistrés par souscription publique (totals for 1921), in B, 33978, MF; Conventions de paiement par annuités (Loi du 31 Juillet 1920), 1921, *ibid.*; Projet de loi No. 3345 (Chambre), November 15, 1921, in BB 30, 1582, AN; MacDonald, *Reconstruction in France,* 185.
69. MacDonald, *Reconstruction in France,* 180–82; Minutes, Commission des Régions Libérées (Chambre), February 10, 1921, February 1, 1922, March 10, 1920, in XIIe Législature, A-66, AANV.
70. Leredu at that time stated his opposition to fixed coefficients and warned that establishing a maximum also contained pitfalls; if it was too low, it would result in injustices for *sinistrés,* and if it was too high the result would be high prices. See Minutes, Commission des Régions Libérées (Chambre), November 17, 1920, in XIIe Législature A-66, AANV.

1914 values. The moment was opportune, for a business depression that had begun the previous fall was causing deflation in early 1921, and Loucheur continued to benefit from the slowdown during the remainder of the year. His action came when there was a strong belief that prices would fall by policy, under the François-Marsal Convention, an agreement made between the finance minister and the governor of the Bank of France in April, 1920. That agreement obligated the state to repay its 27-billion-franc debt to the bank at a rate of two billion francs a year, beginning at the end of 1921.[71]

Loucheur knew that the success of his maneuver would depend partly on a sizable drop in the price of construction materials. But he realized that for that he needed cheap coal. Sagging coal prices on the world market and a decision by the government in late February to terminate a wartime coal surtax worked to his advantage.[72] Loucheur probably knew that elimination of the surtax was imminent when, in late January, he spoke out about the relationship between cheap coal and affordable building materials. And he probably invoked the government's intentions during a meeting with industrialists in early February, since he was able to extract a pledge of sharp price decreases from at least one of their number: the Comité des Forges committed itself to lowering the price of girders from 140 francs to somewhere between 65 and 70 francs. Loucheur hoped other industries would follow suit, but price agreements did not come easily. In late March, he reached understandings with the brick and cement industries on uniform pricing formulas for their products significantly below those in place at the end of the preceding year. To assure compliance, he publicized the new rates widely and threatened to take legal action against speculators.[73]

Loucheur also compelled some industrial *sinistrés* to accept lower

71. Minutes, Commission des Régions Libérées (Chambre), February 10, 1921, *ibid.*; Schuker, *The End of French Predominance*, 35–36; Eleanor Dulles, *The French Franc, 1914–1928* (New York, 1929), 136–39.

72. Maier, *Recasting Bourgeois Europe*, 224; *Le Progrès du Nord*, March 1, 1921, p. 1; *L'Usine*, February 19, 1921, p. 33. Elimination of the surtax was part of the government's virtually total dismantlement of the remaining wartime controls at the end of February, 1921.

73. *L'Usine*, January 29, 1921, p. 37; Minutes, Commission des Régions Libérées (Chambre), February 10, 1921, in XIIe Législature, A-66, AANV; *Le Progrès du Nord*, February 6, 1921, p. 1; Louis Loucheur to prefects of the liberated regions, Circular No. 856, March 30, 1921, in AJ 24, 136, AN; France, *Annales de la Chambre: Débats*, April 19, 1921, p. 1470.

coefficients for work already done on their properties when the original rates seemed excessive. For work not yet undertaken, he succeeded in winning the industrialists' acceptance of coefficients averaging 3.25 times the values of 1914. In early February, anticipating lower materials prices, he directed administrative agents to seek temporary delays in completing cases of individual *sinistrés'* claims unless a coefficient multiple of 3 to 3.5 was accepted. In addition, he issued a notice recommending that the cantonal commissions and their technical advisers not exceed a coefficient multiple of 3.25. He traveled to the liberated regions in mid-February, in part to explain his policy on coefficients to the *sinistrés*.[74]

Loucheur's announcement about coefficients caused a great stir among those affected, and even after his visit in February there was widespread uneasiness about its impact on the settlement of claims. In mid-February, *Le Temps* argued in favor of giving the *sinistrés* whatever they needed, regardless of Loucheur's notions about coefficients. Criticism in the press intensified during the spring, and the debate within parliament became heated. At one point, the senator Guy de Lubersac attacked the minister's use of the term *thieves* of those demanding a coefficient multiple greater than 3.[75]

Loucheur remained committed to lower coefficients, even though in September he accepted a multiple of 3.85 for the construction of workers' housing in the Somme. In November, although he told a group in the department of the Ardennes that he supported a multiple of 3.5, he added that if that could not be achieved, at least the aim should be for one as low as possible.[76] At the end of May, 1921, he announced that overall there had been a 20-percent drop in multiples so far that year. In early

74. Minutes, Commission des Régions Libérées (Chambre), February 10, 1921, in XIIe Législature, A-66, AANV; France, *Annales de la Chambre: Débats,* May 31, 1921, p. 1451; *Le Progrès du Nord,* February 13, 1921, p. 1, February 14, 1921, p. 1, February 16, 1921, p. 1; MacDonald, *Reconstruction in France,* 203; *Le Temps,* February 16, 1921, p. 2, February 18, 1921, p. 1, February 20, 1921, p. 4.

75. Minutes, Commission des Régions Libérées (Chambre), February 10, 1921, in XIIe Législature, A-66, AANV; *Le Progrès du Nord,* June 24, 1921, p. 1; *Le Temps,* February 17, 1921, p. 1; France, *Annales de la Chambre: Débats,* May 31, 1921, pp. 1463–64. Senator Guy de Lubersac was also president of the General Confederation of Reconstruction Cooperatives.

76. *Le Temps,* September 25, 1921, p. 2, November 23, 1921, p. 3; *Le Progrès du Nord,* November 23, 1921, p. 1.

1922, a multiple of 4 was in place in the department of the Nord, still well below levels prevailing shortly before Loucheur became minister. But some who had accepted a coefficient multiple of 3.25 discovered later that it fell short of meeting their reconstruction costs, as the prefect of the Somme reported. Loucheur's successor, Reibel, admitted the problem in an appearance before the Chamber's commission on the liberated regions in February, 1922, but added that the state had no choice except to let the awards stand. Loucheur was able to stretch state funds by promoting low coefficients, but his policy had a reverse side of compensating some claimants inadequately. In early 1922, some members of parliament contended that even a coefficient multiple of 4 was shortchanging those who accepted it.[77]

The state still owed approximately 800 million francs to builders for work done in the liberated regions during 1920, and its delays in payment were causing a crisis of confidence among bankers and contractors. Shortly after assuming office, Loucheur began negotiations with Doumer for settlement of the debt, but it was not until July that the two men agreed on a formula that shifted 950 million francs' worth of unused credits from the 1920 budget year to 1921.[78] Loucheur at first wanted to submit the transfer to parliament for ratification, but since he could not gain a hearing from the Chamber's finance commission before parliament adjourned, he decided to seek a presidential decree. In anticipation of its issuance, he on July 23 gave instructions to the prefects in northeastern France to begin preparatory work for paying the overdue sums. No decree was issued, however, and the government had to submit a bill to parliament, whose approval was secured before the year's end, but only after Loucheur had persevered through difficult negotiations with the ministry of finance and proceeded through channels he had tried to bypass.[79]

Article 46 of the Law of April 17, 1919, stated that one way the govern-

---

77. France, *Annales du Sénat: Débats*, May 31, 1921, p. 1450; *L'Echo national* (Paris), May 11, 1922, pp. 1–2; Minutes, Commission des Régions Libérées (Chambre), February 1, 1922, in XIIe Législature, A-66, AANV.

78. On May 31, 1921, Loucheur told the Senate that the government was in arrears to contractors for a sum that had risen to close to a billion francs. See France, *Annales du Sénat: Débats*, May 31, 1921, p. 1460.

79. Minutes, Commission des Régions Libérées (Chambre), August 10, 1921, November 16, 1921, in XIIe Législature, A-66, AANV; Loucheur to prefects of the liberated regions, Circular No. 1046, July 23, 1921, in AJ 24, 136, AN; Minutes, Commission des Fi-

ment could discharge its financial commitment to indemnify war losses was through payments in kind, so long as claimants were agreeable. Before the end of 1919, the ministry of the liberated regions had created a system to make state-owned merchandise and materials available to recipients of advances in the form of certificates of transfer (bons pour cession). Loucheur made it known in early 1921 that he wanted to liquidate the state-owned and -warehoused supplies as rapidly as possible, and he took steps throughout the year to do that.[80] No reliable statistics are available, however. Still, early in 1921 he placed a rough value of 1.5 billion francs on what the state had in warehouses, and it seems reasonable to suppose that he distributed a large part of that. Payments in kind were a way not only of making settlements within a tight budget but also of controlling coefficient levels. Nevertheless, along the way some— particularly in the building-supplies industries—contended that the state was engaging in harmful competition with them.[81]

WIESBADEN NEGOTIATIONS

A major breakthrough regarding German payments in kind came in the spring of 1921, after a crisis caused by the failure of Allied and German representatives to agree on a plan for reparations payments. During the London conference in early March, Prime Minister Lloyd George and Premier Briand found the Germans' attitude so unreasonable that, deciding upon military and economic sanctions, they sent troops to occupy three German cities on the right bank of the Rhine and established

---

nances (Chambre), November 18, 1921 (including Projet de loi No. 3063, July 8, 1921), in XIIe Législature, Carton A-19, Commission des Finances, Procès-verbaux, AANV; Journal officiel: Lois et Décrets, December 18, 1921, p. 13766 (Law of December 17, 1921).

80. Morain, La Reconstitution du Nord, 198, ADN; Edmond Michel, Les Dommages de guerre de la France et leur réparation (Paris, 1932), 578; Loucheur to prefects of the liberated regions, Circular No. 839, March 18, 1921, Circular No. 879, April 5, 1921, Circular No. 920, April 26, 1921, Circular No. 780, February 14, 1921, all in AJ 24, 136, AN; Ministère des Régions Libérées, Bulletin des régions libérées, March 5, 1921, pp. 76–77; Loucheur to prefects of the liberated regions, Circular No. 14, September 3, 1921, Circular No. 46, October 4, 1921, both in AJ 24, 136, AN.

81. La Journée industrielle, November 23, 1921, p. 2.

a tariff barrier between the occupied zone and the rest of Germany.[82] In late April, the Reparation Commission announced that the total German bill was 132 billion gold marks. Immediately afterward, Allied leaders again met in London, where they formulated the London Schedule, calling for annual remittances of two billion gold marks, plus 26 percent of Germany's export revenue, about an additional billion marks per year. In the German domestic crisis that followed the Allies' threat to enforce acceptance of the schedule by occupying the Ruhr Valley, the centrist Joseph Wirth, who became chancellor, acceded to the Allies' terms just before the six-day deadline of the ultimatum expired. Germany thereby committed itself to the policy of fulfilling the Treaty of Versailles, including paying reparations.[83] Walther Rathenau, named Germany's minister of reconstruction in May, 1921, and soon extremely influential in the Wirth government, decided to offer generous payments in kind as a way of meeting his nation's obligations. The German provision of materials for French reconstruction would not only stimulate Germany's economy but also help heal the wounds of war in northeastern France. Rathenau probably also believed that success in the negotiations might evoke French goodwill in drawing the Upper Silesian frontier between Germany and Poland, which was imminent. Whatever his motives, he in a speech on June 2 emphasized Germany's interest in paying part of its reparations through the direct reconstruction of northeastern France. Shortly thereafter, he let the French ambassador in Berlin know that he wished to begin negotiations with Loucheur as quickly as possible.[84]

The French government clearly wanted to talk, but leaders in Paris worried about the reactions of other Allied powers and understood that a part of domestic public opinion remained hostile to German payments in kind. Loucheur told a foreign ministry official on June 5, "Personally, I think it is certainly worthwhile for our country to enter into talks, but whoever undertakes them will receive nothing but blows at home—which is to say that I am not thrilled about volunteering to participate in

82. Felix, *Walther Rathenau*, 8–18; Jacques Bariéty, *Les Relations franco-allemandes après la première guerre mondiale* (Paris, 1977), 68–72.

83. Felix, *Walther Rathenau*, 18–24.

84. Bariéty, *Les Relations franco-allemandes*, 83–84, 87–88; Felix, *Walther Rathenau*, 67–68; Telegram Charles Laurent to foreign ministry, June 4, 1921, in Unclassified Documents, R.C. B/84/3/VII Wiesbaden, MAE.

them! But if the president considers it necessary, we could accept a conversation at Wiesbaden, where we have important French government offices that would allow us to play the host."[85] Although Loucheur foresaw the problems, he understood that success promised distinct advantages for France. Substantial payments in kind would help relieve the strains on the French treasury in handling damage claims and thus accelerate reconstruction. They would also facilitate general economic recovery and help in limiting the size of indemnity coefficients.[86]

Rathenau and Loucheur held three sets of meetings at Wiesbaden during the summer and fall. They first met on June 12 and 13 for more than ten hours and reached a general understanding on the outline of an accord. In the weeks that followed, technical representatives from the two sides sat in Berlin and Paris to iron out the details. On August 26 and 27, Loucheur and Rathenau met in Wiesbaden again and initialed a draft agreement.[87] All they needed was the final approval of their governments.

To make German deliveries in kind less objectionable to French industry, Loucheur and other French negotiators sought concessions from Germany in bilateral trade talks. The French already enjoyed most-favored-nation status with Germany under the Treaty of Versailles, but French officials felt the benefits of that were still unrealized. In the July trade meetings, they were insistent upon an end to what they viewed as discrimination against French products and upon guarantees that the Germans open their markets. Their hope was that improved trade opportunities for France in Germany might counterbalance the influx of German payments in kind for the liberated regions. But the talks bogged down, and France scored no breakthrough on trade.[88]

85. Louis Loucheur to addressee unknown (probably Philippe Berthelot), June 5, 1921, in Unclassified Documents, R.C. B/84/3/VII Wiesbaden, MAE. Loucheur cites such a letter in his diary. See his *Carnets secrets*, 84–85.

86. Bariéty, *Les Relations franco-allemandes*, 82–83.

87. Telegram (sender's name illegible) to embassy (country not identified) in Paris, June 13, 1921, in Unclassified Documents, R.C. B/84/3/VII Wiesbaden, MAE; Loucheur, *Carnets secrets*, 85–92; State Department Translation of French Government Memorandum to Charles Evans Hughes, August 9, 1921, in Commerce Papers, State Department, Secretary of State, Charles E. Hughes, HHPL; Memorandum I, August 27, 1921, in Series Papiers d'Agents, Alexandre Millerand Papers, Vol. 13, MAE; Felix, *Walther Rathenau*, 77.

88. Pourparlers en vue de l'établissement d'un régime commercial franco-allemand, July 8, 1921, July 9, 1921, July 11, 1921, in F 12, 8860, AN; Memorandum for Commerce Minister Providing Summary of Negotiations for July 8–9, 1921, *ibid.*; French chargé

In spite of the impasse, the two governments moved ahead on payments in kind, and at the final meetings between Loucheur and Rathenau in Wiesbaden, on October 6 and 7, the accords were officially signed. French *sinistrés* were to be free to purchase materials in Germany with their indemnity credits. A private French agency would collect orders for transmittal to a private German agency, which, under guarantee by the German government, would distribute the orders to German industries in both the occupied and unoccupied zones. The German government was to pay the industries for the products shipped to France and would receive credit toward its reparations obligations. An explicit statement to the effect that materials procured by this method could be used only for reconstruction in the liberated regions was inserted in the agreement to assure that France would not be inundated with German products.

The Germans pledged that over the life of the agreement, which was scheduled to run from October 1, 1921, to May 1, 1926, they would provide payments in kind with a maximum value of seven billion gold marks. Depending on the volume of deliveries, Germany's payments in kind were to give it a maximum annual credit varying from 35 to 45 percent of France's reparations from it in any year. But regardless of how much the Germans delivered, no more than a billion gold marks could be applied to the reparations account with France annually. The value of any materials above that threshhold would have to be credited to Germany's obligation toward France in the ten years following the expiration of the deliveries program, until which time the amounts involved would earn 5-percent interest. This complicated arrangement was designed to allow the French continued access to a significant share of German cash payments each year, and to prevent payments in kind from raising the French share of total Allied reparations above its 52-percent ceiling (see above, 176n11).

On October 7, Loucheur and Rathenau also signed some accessory accords, one of them dealing with coal. Loucheur managed to win a German commitment sufficient to improve the general condition of the French economy. The German concession to provide reparations coal at

d'affaires in Berlin to French foreign minister, August 9, 1921, *ibid.*; Philippe Berthelot to French high commissioner at Coblenz, July 16, 1921, in Unclassified Documents, R.C. B/84/3/VII Wiesbaden, MAE; Foreign ministry to Pierre de Margerie, July 28, 1921, in Unclassified Documents, R.C. B/84/3/VII Wiesbaden, MAE.

the German domestic price plus shipping constituted a prospective tonic to French industry, for since 1919 Germany had insisted that such deliveries take place at the price of German export coal, which was much more expensive than that reserved for the domestic market. The concessionary price was considerably less than the French were paying the British and Americans at the time.[89] Other signs pointed toward closer Franco-German relations, as well. At the end of September, the Allies terminated the internal German tariff they had imposed in March. And Briand in early October was thinking broadly in terms of a Franco-German rapprochement, as he intimated to the German ambassador in Paris.[90]

The negotiations that brought an agreement on payments in kind with Germany generated opposition at home and abroad. In July, Loucheur met with a group of industrialists and parliamentary members from the Ardennes who wanted clarifications and emphasized the injury German deliveries would do to their businesses.[91] In the fall, L'Usine sharply attacked the treaty in a series of articles appearing over several weeks.[92] Various producers of construction materials joined in the assault. Letters of protest rained down on Loucheur, and some French chambers of commerce put out strongly worded statements.[93]

The strongest criticism abroad was by Great Britain. Having suffered little physical damage during the war except to its merchant fleet, Britain had already received replacement tonnage from Germany. The British therefore had no continuing need of payments in kind, and they feared the effects that payments in kind to other countries could have on Britain's economy, particularly on coal exports. The British strongly preferred that German reparations payments be in cash.[94] In

89. Supplément au Bulletin quotidien du 28 octobre 1921, No. 94, in Alexandre Millerand Papers, 13; Jeanne Brémontier, "Les Accords de Wiesbaden: Réparations et Restitutions," Le Parlement et l'Opinion, XIX–XX (1921), 250–60; Bariéty, Les Relations franco-allemandes, 84–85, 88; Weill-Raynal, Les Réparations allemandes, II, 24–52, III, 829–30. The coal in question was that which passed through the ports of Rotterdam, Anvers, and Gand.

90. Bariéty, Les Relations franco-allemandes, 86.

91. L'Usine, July 9, 1921, p. 1.

92. Ibid., September 3–December 10, 1921. The articles appeared regularly throughout the fall months and were on the front page of the newspaper.

93. Ibid., November 12, 1921, p. 3, October 8, 1921, p. 5, December 24, 1921, p. 1, December 31, 1921, p. 1.

94. Bariéty, Les Relations franco-allemandes, 78–81.

mid-July, they argued that a Franco-German agreement involving sizable amounts of German materials would not only create a heavier burden on the defeated power than had been agreed but would also give France an implicit priority over other reparations creditors. The Wiesbaden accords needed the approval of the Reparation Commission, where the British set up roadblocks and mobilized Belgian and Italian opposition. To support the conclusion that the agreement would so burden the German economy that it would almost certainly be unable to sustain cash payments at the level set by the London Schedule, the British cited the depreciation of the mark and the trouble the Germans were already having in meeting their cash obligations.[95]

Loucheur guardedly shared Britain's concerns about Germany's ability to pay, although the solution he proposed would not have passed muster across the Channel.[96] In a memorandum to the Quai d'Orsay on September 10 he complained about halfhearted, ineffectual measures by the German government to shore up its finances. If economic collapse occurred in Germany, he believed, "it would be a fraudulent bankruptcy." He recommended that the French and British join together to take matters in hand, for he saw that if something drastic was not done to strengthen Germany's finances, the Wiesbaden agreement would be at risk.[97]

The final blow to closer Franco-German cooperation came in mid-October on the question of Upper Silesia. Despite Rathenau's generous terms with France on coal, which he offered partly with the design of enlisting its backing for Germany's claim to most if not all of Upper Silesia, including the region's coal-producing basin, the French remained loyal to the Poles. When, on October 20, the League of Nations issued its verdict leaving two-thirds of the territory in German hands but giving Poland most of the coal basin, the Germans were outraged.[98] Since the French had been conspicuous in their sympathy for Poland's territorial

95. Sir Milne Cheetham (British chargé d'affaires in Paris) to Aristide Briand, July 16, 1921, in Alexandre Millerand Papers, 18; Aristide Briand to Sir Milne Cheetham, July 21, 1921, *ibid.*; Bariéty, *Les Relations franco-allemandes*, 88–89; Weill-Raynal, *Les Réparations allemandes*, II, 52–56.

96. See Trachtenberg, *Reparation in World Politics*, 216–36.

97. "La faillite de l'Allemagne" (memorandum), September 10, 1921, in Alexandre Millerand Papers, 18.

98. In March, 1921, in a plebiscite, 717,122 people in Upper Silesia voted in favor of Germany and 483,154 declared themselves for Poland.

aspirations, the Germans focused much of their indignation on them, reverting to a resentment against, by their lights, the main source of the "dictated peace." The Wirth government went through a reshuffling, and in both France and Germany government leaders began to distance themselves from the accords they had signed with such high expectations. In the end, the Wiesbaden accords never took effect, although Raymond Poincaré, who replaced Briand as premier in January, 1922, tried for several months to breathe life into them. But even he had some reservations. He told the Chamber's finance commission in February, 1922, that circumstances required a Wiesbaden agreement in which France worked in concert with the other Allies.[99]

Loucheur had proved his effectiveness as a negotiator by arriving at an agreement that included safeguards for the domestic industries affected. But he had accepted an administrative apparatus that was cumbersome and complex, leading skeptics to wonder how well the system would have worked in practice. Even he had expressed serious reservations to Rathenau about the proposed national centralizing agencies. But a more serious miscalculation was his accession to the Germans' demand that the Reparation Commission approve the accord. That afforded the forum for delaying and undermining implementation. For all practical purposes, Allied misgivings ended Loucheur's hopes that German deliveries in kind would make construction materials more plentiful and relieve some of the strain on the French treasury.[100]

THE FINAL WEEKS: REPARATIONS AND INTER-ALLIED DEBTS

Toward the end of 1921, Loucheur devoted considerable attention to reparations in his meetings with the British, but he also used his talks with them to address debts between the Allies. France had borrowed heavily in Britain and America to finance the war, and at the armistice it owed seven billion dollars to other Allies. Though other states also owed it

99. Bariéty, *Les Relations franco-allemandes*, 87–88, 91–95; Minutes, Commission des Finances (Chambre), February 21, 1922, in XIIe Législature, A-25, AANV.

100. Minutes, Commission des Finances (Chambre), February 21, 1922, in XIIe Législature, A-25, AANV; Trachtenberg, *Reparation in World Politics*, 217; Morain, *La Reconstitution du Nord*, 211–16, ADN; Bariéty, *Les Relations franco-allemandes*, 85.

money, it was the largest single Allied debtor.[101] The burden weighed heavily on French finances in the postwar years, and France was eager to reduce it in order to stimulate economic recovery.

In December, 1921, the questions of reparations and inter-Allied debts became entwined as Allied leaders began to foresee a German default. Numerous indications appeared that Germany would not meet the reparations payments scheduled for January and February, 1922, and that Berlin was on the verge of asking for a partial moratorium. On December 5, Sir Robert Horne, the British chancellor of the exchequer, spoke out in Manchester for a moratorium as a way to prevent financial collapse in the Reich. On the same day, Lloyd George invited Loucheur to London for discussions.[102] The French, though ready in early December to pursue a tougher line against the Germans than were the British, were not prepared to occupy the Ruhr. Nor were they eager to break with Whitehall over reparations when the British opposed instituting, as the French wished, an effective system of Allied controls over German finances, on the ground that such controls would violate German national sovereignty.

Loucheur not only favored controls but readied a far-reaching program of economic stabilization to present in London. On the eve of his departure, he outlined his plan to a small group of foreign-ministry officials, including Briand. Borrowing in part from the ideas of others in the French bureaucracy, he argued for a stabilization of the German currency, the floating of a German loan, and the cancellation of debts and reparations owed to Britain.[103]

During talks on December 8 and 9, Lloyd George warned Loucheur that military occupation of the Ruhr in the event of German default would mark the end of the Franco-British alliance: "France would go its way, we would go ours." On the other hand, he expressed Britain's readiness to relinquish most of its share in German reparations as well as its claims to war debts—provided the United States agreed to do likewise and to enter on discussions of general economic conditions. Lloyd George's apparent optimism about American consent may explain why

101. Aldcroft, *From Versailles*, 92–93.

102. Carole Fink, *The Genoa Conference: European Diplomacy, 1921–1922* (Chapel Hill, N.C. 1984), 22.

103. Loucheur borrowed from Jacques Seydoux and Alexandre Aron. See Artaud, *La Question*, I, 374–79.

Loucheur discounted the prime minister's condition about American involvement.[104] Loucheur presented his case for setting up controls but failed to win British support.[105]

On December 19, Loucheur returned to London with Briand, carrying a definitive version of Loucheur's program, which became known as the Chequers plan. But by the time they arrived, the plan's fate had already been sealed. The British knew for certain that the United States would make no special arrangements to cancel inter-Allied debts. Britain's economy was in no position to absorb large unilateral write-offs, Lloyd George told the French. As an alternative, he suggested that Britain and France join with Germany to develop the Russian economy, so as to outfit the Reich with a vast export market that would improve its ability to pay reparations. His proposal became one of the focuses of the international economic conference held in Genoa during the spring of 1922. Since Russian economic development was a long-term project, however, and Germany needed financial relief immediately, the British returned to their insistence on a moratorium. Before the second round of talks in London ended, Briand had accepted the principle of at least a partial one.[106]

When Loucheur again broached Allied controls over German finances, the British dug in their heels. They did not wish to give an Allied commission the power to control Germany's finances on the Turkish or Chinese models. Loucheur explained that he did not intend that and suggested a review of the matter by technical specialists, but the draft of a moratorium that two of them submitted referred to only one form of Allied control: a technical adviser satisfactory to both the Reparation Commission and the Reichsbank who would have a veto over increases in the German money supply. Even that limited form of Allied control proved too much for Whitehall. In January, 1922, at a meeting in Cannes to approve arrangements for the moratorium, the British objected to the technical adviser, and Loucheur caved in.[107]

Yet Briand and Loucheur did not come out of the discussions completely empty-handed. Showing some flexibility, the British expressed

104. Loucheur, *Carnets secrets*, 185–88; Artaud, *La Question*, I, 379–80.

105. Telegram Loucheur to French foreign ministry, December 8, 1921, in Alexandre Millerand Papers, 19.

106. Artaud, *La Question*, I, 380–83; Felix, *Walther Rathenau*, 115–17.

107. Trachtenberg, *Reparation in World Politics*, 230–31.

willingness, for instance, to consider a modified version of the Wiesbaden accords. More important, they went on record as open to a treaty of military guarantee, although they wished to limit it to France's eastern frontiers and to avoid broad pledges to each other's interests worldwide. Of course the British were really not giving up very much. The Wiesbaden accords were already on hold, and interests of national security probably would have compelled Britain to aid France against German aggression even without a treaty. In the final analysis, the British gained numerous concessions from the French without substantial cost.[108]

During this period, opposition was growing at home. President Millerand led a contingent disaffected with Briand's reparations policy, and in the midst of the conference at Cannes, Briand had to return to Paris to deal with a cabinet revolt. Deciding that the situation could not be saved, he defended his policy in parliament, then dramatically resigned. Loucheur broke the news of the premier's resignation to Lloyd George at Cannes the same afternoon, that of January 12. Although the conference collapsed, the Germans obtained reparations relief through the Reparation Commission's intervention to grant a temporary moratorium.[109] Loucheur's role as a reparations negotiator was interrupted, for he did not join the Poincaré government.

In the end, Loucheur had more influence and impact on reconstruction than any other government official in the critical years between 1919 and 1921. If reconstruction of the devastated areas was largely complete by 1926, a share of the credit for what one historian calls the "greatest economic achievement of post-war Europe" must go to Loucheur.[110] He was pivotal in the formulation of basic reconstruction policies, and he established a momentum that continued after his departure from the ministry of the liberated regions in January, 1922.

108. *Ibid.*, 231–35.

109. Felix, *Walther Rathenau*, 121–24; Trachtenberg, *Reparation in World Politics*, 235–36.

110. Denis William Brogan, *The Development of Modern France, 1870–1939* (Rev. ed.; 2 vols.; New York, 1966), II, 599.

Struggles to Make a Difference, 1922–1925

Although Loucheur had only two brief stays at a government ministry between early 1922 and the end of 1925, he remained prominent in parliamentary politics. He was a member of the Chamber's finance commission and, later, of the foreign-affairs commission, on which he served as vice-chairman.[1] He was therefore well placed to make his presence felt. Even more consequential was his leadership of the Gauche Radicale, a parliamentary group formed immediately after the national elections of May, 1924. In November, 1925, during a debate in the Chamber of Deputies on France's steadily worsening financial position, a critic accused his group of always having the "whip hand" in the affairs of the Chamber. Loucheur bristled at what he called a "grotesque insult," yet the charge had validity since Loucheur's group of forty-one deputies, in occupying the very center of the Chamber, could be decisive in any government coalition.[2] The "swing" position of the Gauche Radicale gave Loucheur a leverage in his dealings with parliamentary colleagues that he capitalized on as he focused during this period on reparations and inter-Allied debts, economic modernization, and government financing.

REPARATIONS AND INTER-ALLIED DEBTS

Loucheur remained keenly interested in the questions of reparations and inter-Allied debts after the collapse of the Briand government. Those became the responsibility of Briand's successor, Raymond Poin-

1. Schuker, *The End of French Predominance*, 59; Gilles Normand, *Politique et Hommes politiques* (2 vols.; Paris, 1925), II, 289–90.

2. France, *Annales de la Chambre: Débats*, November 19, 1925, p. 202; Jacques Ollé-Laprune, *La Stabilité des ministres sous la Troisième République, 1879–1940* (Paris, 1962), 204–206.

caré. A hardworking, honest, and patriotic man from Lorraine, Poincaré had already had long experience in French politics, including one term as premier (1912–1913) and one as president of the republic (1913–1920). He was expected to take a tougher stand on reparations than Briand did.

On February 20, 1922, Loucheur discussed reparations and inter-Allied debts in a speech at Lyon that sparked controversy in the United States and France. In part he was reacting to passage by the United States Congress of a bill containing harsh repayment terms for nations with debts to the United States.[3] In addressing the European economic crisis, he marshaled the ideas he had discussed with Lloyd George in December. He asked for a British and American cancellation of Allied debts, and a concomitant reduction of Germany's total reparation bill of 132 billion gold marks by close to 50 percent. Recalling the American rejection of such steps in December and the congressional action that entrenched the rejection, Loucheur pointed out that France's economy was too weak to allow for debt payments. Even if France had enough exportable merchandise to meet its obligations to the United States, high American tariffs would be an obstacle, he asserted, adding, "As for me, I want to say out loud that I believe that we will never be able to pay a cent to America. I say this because there are some Americans here who, I hope, will cable my message home."[4] In an interview for *L'Homme libre* a few days later, Loucheur reaffirmed his position. In his view, discussions of France's debt by American senators were merely academic.[5] Loucheur was articulating a feeling that had been generally accepted but publicly undeclared within the French government from the time the war ended. He apparently decided to go public out of frustration with the American government and his belief that frankness could effect a change of heart. As he

3. The bill set up the World War Foreign Debt Commission to negotiate repayment terms with foreign debtors, and it specified that debtor states had to repay their loans within twenty-five years and pay a minimum annual interest rate of 4.25 percent. The congressional action elicited a wave of hostility from the French press in early February; the American press responded with irritation over the French press's reaction. See Melvyn Leffler, *The Elusive Quest: America's Pursuit of European Stability and French Security, 1919–1933* (Chapel Hill, N.C., 1979), 64–65.

4. *L'Echo national*, March 20, 1922, p. 1, from a reprint of Loucheur's speech in *Le Petit Journal*, February 21, 1922. The speech, with these lines deleted, was later printed in booklet form as *La Reconstruction de l'Europe et le Problème des réparations: Discours prononcé à Lyon le 20 février 1922 à l'Association Commerciale, Industrielle et Agricole par M. Louis Loucheur* (Paris, 1922).

5. Artaud, *La Question*, I, 393.

said on February 20, "It never hurts to tell the truth to men as concise and productive as our American friends."[6] The French ambassador to Washington, Jules Jusserand, wrote to Loucheur at once, however, that his directness was counterproductive since it diminished the American goodwill needed to work the problem out in France's favor: "In innumerable letters and telegrams I have invariably expressed the view that on the question of our debt to the United States, time and silence were our best weapons."[7] It soon became obvious that Loucheur had misjudged what American reaction would be.

At first, the Poincaré government maintained a public silence on his remarks, while it tried to pressure him into retracting them. When that did not work, Poincaré, to undo the harm to Franco-American relations and recapture the American goodwill that he hoped would let France postpone indefinitely its debt payment, decided to speak out. On March 15, he told the American press corps in Paris that France intended to fulfill its debt commitments to the United States. Only then did Loucheur adjust his statements of February to coincide with the official position.[8] The episode, not soon forgotten in America, resulted in embarrassment for Loucheur.[9] Smarting, he acquired a reticence on the question, though he remained interested as an observer.

In the early spring of 1923, he took on a temporary assignment as a negotiator on reparations and inter-Allied debts. The importance of his new assignment can be understood only in the light of the situation that existed early in the year. Germany, showing no serious interest in making reparations payments, was arguing for an appreciable reduction in its total reparations obligation and an extended moratorium on payments, without guarantees. The British and French were divided on how to react: the British favored an essentially unguaranteed four-year moratorium, whereas Poincaré held that the absence of guarantees was unacceptable. While the French and British haggled, the Reparation Commission on January 9, 1923, declared Germany in default in its

6. Loucheur, *La Reconstruction*, 17.

7. Jules Jusserand to Louis Loucheur, February 22, 1922, in Louis Loucheur Papers, 10/I–K, HI.

8. Artaud, *La Question*, I, 394–95; *L'Echo national*, March 16, 1922, p. 1, March 20, 1922, p. 1, March 22, 1922, p. 1.

9. Loucheur's newspaper *Le Progrès du Nord* stated in early 1925 that the American people still looked upon Loucheur as the man who said that France would never pay back its loans to their country. See *Le Progrès du Nord*, January 27, 1925, p. 1.

reparations coal shipments. Using the commission's decision as a pretext, Poincaré gave orders for a military occupation of the Ruhr, and on January 11, French and Belgian troops moved into the region to force compliance with the Treaty of Versailles. The British protested but as of late March had not taken a clear stand on what to do.[10] Poincaré, concerned about the attitudes of the British government, sent Loucheur on an unofficial mission to London.

The instigation of Loucheur's trip has been ascribed to the French president Alexandre Millerand, who some believed was thinking of having Loucheur replace Poincaré as premier. Yet Loucheur recorded in his diary that Poincaré was responsible for the mission, and the Belgian ambassador to France attested to it. But, Loucheur had urged talks with the British right after France entered the Ruhr; he was troubled by the costliness of the struggle and believed that quick common action by the French and British was the only way to save the situation. It appears that Loucheur himself had in the first place suggested a secret trip to London and received the backing of both Poincaré and Millerand.[11]

In London, Loucheur presented an ambitious scheme that left the prime minister, Andrew Bonar Law, and the chancellor of the exchequer, Stanley Baldwin, both Conservatives, somewhat startled. Loucheur wanted to see Germany receive a loan of 500 million gold marks underwritten by a consortium of German industries to stabilize its finances. It would make annual reparations payments of 2 to 3.5 billion gold marks financed by international loans totaling 40 billion gold marks, collateralized by customs and railroad receipts as well as by a 25-percent participation of the consortium of lenders in the shares of German industries. Germany would also take over the Allied debts to the United States, but all other inter-Allied debts would be canceled. Loucheur projected that Germany could put its finances in order within a year's time and that France would evacuate the Ruhr in rhythm with Germany's fulfillment of reparations commitments. In the interest of French security, Loucheur unveiled the notion of a complete demilitarized, autonomous Rhenish state with an internationally controlled railroad network and police force.

10. Schuker, *The End of French Predominance*, 22–26; Trachtenberg, *Reparation in World Politics*, 289; Sontag, *A Broken World*, 113.

11. McDougall, *France's Rhineland Diplomacy*, 264–65; Loucheur, *Carnets secrets*, 116–18.

Bonar Law, with an air of skepticism, asked on several occasions whether Germany would accept the ideas Loucheur was proposing. The prime minister also took the view, just as Lloyd George had done in late 1921, that Britain could not cancel the debts of other Allies and forgo rights to reparations while still obligated to meet debt commitments to America. He warned that Britain would soon have to arrive at a clear stand on the Ruhr, either on the side of or more actively against France.

Fearing that domestic political pressures would lead the British government to oppose France if the two nations did not reach an understanding, but also believing that Bonar Law wished negotiations with France, Loucheur told Poincaré that the moment was propitious for beginning official talks. He probably overestimated British interest in pursuing the ideas he had laid out, since after he left London, in early April, no further negotiations took place. His unofficial diplomacy drew unwanted publicity in the press and led many to question France's determination to stay the course in the Ruhr. It also excited concern in Belgium that Poincaré was attempting to bypass it. Conveniently remaining outside Paris while Loucheur bore the brunt of the press's reproaches, Poincaré assured the Belgians that France would act only in cooperation with them. It may be that Poincaré, about whom there was a certain restiveness in parliamentary circles, did not wish success for Loucheur at the moment he was being mentioned as the next premier. Poincaré, by outmaneuvering any potential rivals to his power, maintained a firm hold on the government. The episode was a turning point in Loucheur's relations with Poincaré: incensed by the premier's abandonment of him, he never forgave what he considered political cowardice.[12]

During the London reparations conference of July and August, 1924, Loucheur went, on his own initiative, to the British capital and met with the French premier, Edouard Herriot, whose leadership there had failed to inspire much confidence. Herriot was negotiating implementation procedures for a plan that an international committee of financial experts advising the Reparation Commission had recently drafted. The Dawes Plan prescribed a temporary rescheduling of German reparations

---

12. Text of Issues Discussed with Bonar Law, April 4, 1923, in Louis Loucheur Papers, 7/2; Louis Loucheur to Raymond Poincaré, April 4, 1923, April 5, 1923, April 10, 1923 (memo), all *ibid.*; Loucheur, *Carnets secrets*, 116–24; McDougall, *France's Rhineland Diplomacy*, 264–68; Maier, *Recasting Bourgeois Europe*, 404–406; Simone Loucheur,"Histoire familiale," in Simone Loucheur Papers, in family possession, Paris.

payments, an end to the Franco-Belgian occupation of the Ruhr, and an international loan for Germany. Loucheur complained to Herriot about a negotiating process that limited itself to issues that could be settled only through France's sacrifices and that postponed other crucial topics like inter-Allied debts and security. Although Loucheur did not specifically threaten to withdraw his forty-one-member bloc from Herriot's recently formed Left Cartel government—Herriot depended on Loucheur's Gauche Radicale to maintain his left-wing coalition's parliamentary majority—he seemed to intimate that the majority might be in jeopardy if Herriot made further concessions. Whatever the reason, Herriot the next day insisted that the Labour prime minister, Ramsay MacDonald, make a statement on inter-Allied debts before the end of the conference. But MacDonald carefully avoided that issue in his remarks at the last plenary session, on August 16.[13]

Implementation of the Dawes Plan moved ahead after the conference, but a settlement on inter-Allied debts remained as difficult to achieve as ever. During a term as finance minister for two and a half weeks in late 1925, Loucheur negotiated with the United States on debt consolidation. The American government, concerned about the instability of the franc, had in late 1924 proposed to deal with France's war debt on the basis of its "capacity to pay." For the subsequent talks, Joseph Caillaux, who served as finance minister for several months in 1925, even traveled to Washington; although the two sides made some progress, Caillaux left without an agreement, in large part because of France's insistence on a safeguard clause that tied France's payments to the payment of reparations by Germany. By the time Loucheur became finance minister, in late November, the franc was rapidly losing value, and he used the occasion to send the Americans an unofficial proposal that softened some of the rigors France would have agreed to a few weeks before. Loucheur sought a reduction in the size of France's initial annuity payments, a lengthening of the time during which reduced payments would be made, and a decrease in the total France would be required to pay the United States during the life of the agreement.[14] His

13. Loucheur, *Carnets secrets*, 153–54; Sontag, *A Broken World*, 117–18; Schuker, *The End of French Predominance*, 27–28, 371, 374; Artaud, *La Question*, II, 675.

14. Leffler, *The Elusive Quest*, 121–39; Ellen Schrecker, *The Hired Money: The French Debt to the United States, 1917–1929* (New York, 1979), 196–219; Jean Claude Allain, *Joseph Caillaux: L'Oracle, 1914–1944* (Paris, 1981), 324–28; Artaud, *La Question*, II, 786–87.

proposals were apparently an attempt to discover whether the Americans would adhere to their "capacity to pay" principle when France's finances were weakening dramatically. He was aware that Washington had just agreed to generous terms for Italy in debt-consolidation negotiations. If he had high hopes, though, they were soon deflated, when Andrew Mellon, the American secretary of the treasury, decided that Loucheur's proposals did not constitute a basis for negotiation.

Loucheur vacated the rue de Rivoli before he could make revisions, but others continued the bargaining, which finally yielded the Mellon-Bérenger agreement of April, 1926. Its terms were less generous to France than Loucheur had wished, and its failure to include a safeguard clause was particularly galling to many of the French. But at least France had clarified and consolidated its debt obligations to the United States. This agreement, on the heels of a Franco-British debt accord, set the stage for currency stabilization in France, but it took stringent measures by Poincaré, who formed a new government in July, 1926, to stop the slide of the franc. The French parliament waited until 1929 to ratify the Mellon-Bérenger agreement. At the end of 1926, Poincaré announced that France would begin observing its payment provisions even without ratification.[15]

ECONOMIC MODERNIZATION

Loucheur became identified with a group of enterprising modernizers who in the 1920s were called neo-Saint-Simonians even though, like Loucheur, they were not necessarily conscious followers of the Comte de Saint-Simon, the nineteenth-century theorist of productivity and brotherhood. One of the best known of the neo-Saint-Simonians was Ernest Mercier, who in the early 1920s was making a name for himself in the French electrical industry.[16]

Toward the end of modernizing agriculture, Loucheur emphasized an acceleration of fertilizer production. During a Chamber debate in the summer of 1922 he chided parliament for failing to act on bills dealing with the mining of potash in Alsace and the production of nitrate fertil-

15. Leffler, *The Elusive Quest,* 154, 214–15; Schrecker, *The Hired Money,* 230–40; Artaud, *La Question,* II, 786.

16. Kuisel, *Ernest Mercier,* 8–9, 17–21; Wright, *France in Modern Times,* 233–34.

izers. As he canvassed the bill on nitrate fertilizer, he showed his frustration with the inefficiency of the Third Republic, criticizing the methods of the Chamber of Deputies and French governments: "For two years this bill has gone from commission to commission without arriving here. I beg you: Let's bring it to a successful conclusion. Is it the fault of parliament? When I was a part of the government, I got used to having the blame [for] delays transferred to the back of the ministers; I hope you will not mind, my dear minister [of agriculture], if I do the same to you. What I am asking you is to bring these two bills to a successful result."[17] Even after parliament approved legislation at the end of 1923 to deploy a gunpowder factory at Toulouse for the production of nitrate fertilizers, Loucheur remained skeptical about France's production capacity. In February, 1924, he complained that notwithstanding the efforts to inform farmers of the benefits of fertilizers, "we have not succeeded in four years in building the nitrate factories indispensable to this improvement of [agricultural] productivity or in securing a practical system for the working of our Alsatian potash mines." To fill the void while awaiting the construction of French nitrate factories, he urged maximum production in German plants then under French control.[18]

Toward the modernization of communications, Loucheur targeted the postal undersecretariat for criticism during a debate in the Chamber of Deputies at the end of 1922. Under consideration were plans for telephone cables between Paris and several other French cities. Loucheur not only contested the need for a two-year time frame for installing the initial cable, from Paris to Strasbourg, but also questioned the omission of other

17. France, *Annales de la Chambre: Débats,* June 16, 1922, p. 284. Loucheur had already dealt extensively with nitrate fertilizers and nitrogen in 1919. A high point was an agreement in November between his ministry of reconstruction and the German firm of Badische Anilin und Soda Fabrik Aktiengesellschaft by which the German company granted the French government a license to use a patented method for the manufacture of synthetic ammonia, a material employed in the production of nitrogen for explosives and fertilizers. What first struck Loucheur in 1919 about the patented formula was the decisive role it had played in keeping Germany in the war. See France, *Annales de la Chambre: Documents,* 1922, Annex No. 5203, Rapport fait au nom de la Commission des Finances chargée d'examiner le projet de loi comportant approbation et faculté de cession d'une convention en vue de la fabrication de l'ammoniaque synthétique, par Charles Leboucq, December 6, 1922, pp. 84–88, 91–92.

18. Loucheur's Speech "Le Problème Monétaire" at the Ecole Interalliée des Hautes Etudes Sociales, February 12, 1924, in Louis Loucheur Papers, 8/1. The speech was published as a pamphlet in Paris, with no stated publication date.

French cities, like Lyon and Toulouse, from the plans. He commended comprehensive planning for the system, admonishing the postal service to "plan things on a major scale, not on a small one." Contending that "if you do not say it, you will not make it happen," Loucheur maintained that a two-year time limit was feasible for completing virtually all of the most important lines in the nation. The postal undersecretary, representing the government, responded simply that Loucheur's suggestions would be given careful consideration.[19] His comments came in the middle of a campaign to "industrialize" communications, that is, to make the practices of the postal, telephone, and telegraph services conform more closely to those of private industry. In 1923, parliament voted to provide management of the services with budgetary autonomy; other changes were slow in coming, however.[20]

Loucheur regained ministerial rank in March, 1924, when Poincaré, discharging a political obligation incurred when Loucheur assisted in getting a government tax bill moved through the Chamber of Deputies several weeks earlier, named him minister of commerce in a recast government.[21] Loucheur headed the ministry only until June, but he in that short time propelled action toward the creation of a postwar variant of the prewar Superior Council of Commerce and Industry. His idea of such an advisory body—in this case for the ministry of commerce—was not new in the 1920s; several postwar French governments had already formed or restructured consultative councils. Loucheur's proposal for a "superior committee of commerce and industry" reserved almost all the seats for business interests, with only token representation for labor, reflecting the pressure Poincaré's government was under from business interests to provide them with an economic council. On the eve of the national elections on May 11, Poincaré told the Paris Chamber of Commerce that it was only natural that the commerce ministry, like other ministries, have a consultative body attached to it. He offered assurances that Loucheur had suggested just such a council and had begun preparatory work toward constituting it. After the election victory of the Left Cartel, Léon Jouhaux, optimistic about the chances for the plan of the Confédération Générale du Travail (CGT)to set up a broad-based

19. France, *Annales de la Chambre: Débats*, December 27, 1922, pp. 1899–1901.
20. Kuisel, *Capitalism and the State*, 64–65; Walter R. Sharp, "The Political Bureaucracy of France Since the War," *American Political Science Review*, XXII (1928), 318–20.
21. Schuker, *The End of French Predominance*, 59, 116–17.

national economic council, made a strong plea for labor's plan on May 20 in the newspaper *Le Peuple*. Four days later, Loucheur came forward with his proposal for a business-oriented consultative committee, which, according to the conservative press, obviated the need for a national economic council. The CGT, however, was apprehensive that Loucheur's superior committee was nothing more than a preemption of its own plan, adapted virtually to exclude labor participation.[22]

It seems certain that Loucheur hoped to thwart Jouhaux' campaign. He had undermined a proposal by the CGT for a national economic council in 1919 because it granted the envisioned body considerable power to propose and carry out programs, investigate economic problems, and, in essence, oversee production. Even the much watered-down plan of 1924 had aspects that made Loucheur uneasy, the voice it gave labor in the deliberations of the council among them. Jouhaux recommended on May 20 that two of the groups to be represented, business and labor, have eighteen and twelve members respectively. Loucheur wanted to keep a preponderant role for the business community in advising the government on economic matters. But above all, he was chary that a broad-based, Leftist-backed organization might place pressure on the government to make fundamental changes in France's system of economic liberalism. With the imminent seating of a Left Cartel government likely to support such a council, his counterefforts were a last-ditch diversionary tactic.[23]

Loucheur left the commerce ministry before the Superior Committee of Commerce and Industry came into being. Eugène Raynaldy, his successor in Herriot's Left Cartel government, brought the project to fruition. At the same time, the minister of labor, Justin Godart, pushed ahead with Jouhaux' idea of a national economic council. Raynaldy finished his work first, so that the Superior Committee of Commerce and Industry had begun meeting by the time Premier Herriot formally launched the National Economic Council in 1925. The National Economic Council was considerably less than Jouhaux had wanted. But with the inclusion of business, worker, and consumer interests, it was

22. David Arthur Rogers, "The Campaign for the French National Economic Council" (Ph.D. dissertation, University of Wisconsin, 1957), 40, 68–70, 88–90; Edith C. Bramhall, "The National Economic Council of France," *American Political Science Review*, XX (1926), 624.

23. Kuisel, *Capitalism and the State*, 60–61; Rogers, "The Campaign," 68–69, 250–54.

much broader in its representational base than the commerce ministry's consultative committee. Too, it dealt with a wider range of questions, although the government underlined that its role was consultative rather than legislative. Even before it began meeting, Raynaldy was defining certain economic questions as within the purview of only his ministry's committee, but it was not long before the pronouncements of the National Economic Council superseded those of the Superior Committee, which rarely met after 1925.[24]

While Loucheur was at the ministry of commerce, he entered into negotiations to spell out the state's relationship to a national oil company, the Compagnie Française des Pétroles (CFP).[25] The organization of the company had begun the preceding year in response to the weakness of France's petroleum industry. Prior to the war, a small group of private companies had the French oil market to themselves. Averse to risk taking and indifferent to expansion, the companies relied on tariff protection and a market-sharing agreement to reap their profits. By 1914, because they controlled no major crude-oil source and lacked any substantial refining capacity, they depended almost entirely on imported supplies of finished oil products. Anemic entrepreneurship of the sort they practiced became known in France as Malthusianism.[26] The war exposed their inadequacies, especially during the winter of 1917–1918, when oil shortages threatened to shut down the French war machine. After the war, a group of modernizers set out to create a national petroleum industry as independent of foreign supplies as possible. Among them was Loucheur. In April, 1920, Britain and France reached an oil agreement in San Remo, Italy. By its terms, the British agreed to transfer to France confiscated German shares in the Turkish Petroleum Company, which had a concession to develop Mesopotamian oil. The agreement also laid the ground rules for Franco-British collaboration in oil fields throughout the world. When in 1923 the British requested that the

24. Kuisel, *Capitalism and the State,* 83; Rogers, "The Campaign," 33–40.

25. Much here on the Compagnie Française des Pétroles is based on Kuisel's *Ernest Mercier,* 21–44. See also André Nouschi, "L'Etat français et les Pétroliers anglo-saxons: La Naissance de la Compagnie Française des Pétroles, 1923–1924," *Relations internationales,* No. 7 (1976), 241–59.

26. Malthusians were a potent force in the French economy during the interwar years. Recent scholarship, however, has challenged but not completely undermined the view that ultraconservative business practices were a causal factor in the relative decline of the French economy—especially in the 1930s.

French designate a buyer of the German shares, Premier Poincaré proposed creating a powerful privately owned French oil company rather than a mixed company, that is, a company combining private and government ownership. The premier shrank from direct government participation in the venture because of strong business opposition and the risk inherent for the already shaky French treasury. He asked Loucheur to take charge of organizing the CFP, but when Loucheur declined, he turned to Ernest Mercier.

In 1924, at the time Loucheur was named minister, formalities were under way to turn the sequestered German shares in the Turkish Petroleum Company over to the new private company. Loucheur was disturbed to discover that the transfer was occurring in the absence of a contract detailing the state's rights in the company. In addition, after the Left Cartel's election victory in May, the Poincaré government was anxious to move swiftly to solidify the CFP lest the Left Cartel government insist on a mixed company. Loucheur, along with Frédéric François-Marsal, the minister of finance, acted as a government negotiator in concluding a hurried agreement with Mercier. The compact, which ended up serving as a kind of company constitution, gave the state two seats on the board of directors and priority to as much as 80 percent of the CFP's oil. Faced with a fait accompli, Herriot's Left Cartel, which took power in June, let the agreement stand.

Although other battles followed in the succeeding years as France ramified its policy of petroleum independence, the agreement in 1924 was an important step toward its objectives. The convention gave the CFP its structural guidelines and official standing at the same time that it protected the interests of the state. It also opened the way for the company's next phase of development, which required four years of intricate negotiations with foreign oil interests to work out terms on the oil concession in the Mosul region of Mesopotamia.

At the end of the 1920s, Mercier and the government designed a new instrument to govern relations between the CFP and the state. In a reversal of policy, the government decided that the CFP should be a mixed company in which the state held a 25-percent share. Since the new convention entailed a financial commitment by the state, however, parliamentary approval proved necessary. In the long, acrimonious debate centered in the Chamber of Deputies, the Left joined those opposed to the agreement, arguing in favor of a state monopoly. In an effort to appease the critics, the government made a number of concessions, including an increase in the government's share to 35 percent. On March 27, 1931, the Chamber of Deputies approved the mixed company. Mercier, who was pleased to have avoided a state monopoly, wrote Loucheur a letter crediting him with bringing about the parliamentary victory: "It was a good fight; you led it, and you won it!"[27]

PUBLIC FINANCE

In January, 1924, France's financial condition, already precarious for some time, was deteriorating rapidly. The franc began to fall precipitously on currency markets, causing panic within the government. A succession of postwar governments had dealt with France's wartime and reconstruction costs primarily by borrowing rather than by increasing taxes. The common belief in the early years after the war was that Germany would eventually pay for damages so that no large tax increases were necessary. Not before early 1923 did the government propose a significant rise, and then it did so only reluctantly; the measure encountered stiff resistance in the finance commissions of both the Chamber and Senate, with the result that no action was taken in either house. The government continued borrowing to cover the costs of both reconstruction and normal operations.

By the end of 1923, French investors were no longer as willing to purchase government bond issues as they had been previously. Transfusions from abroad were scanter, too. When, at the end of the year, the French treasury asked foreign banking houses to float loans to state rail lines and the Crédit National, the banks' answer was that the government needed to reform its financial policies first.[28] Once France saw its occupation of the Ruhr fail to extract reparations payments from Germany, it became doubtful that the complete satisfaction of German debts would occur any time soon, if at all.[29]

In general, Loucheur showed a strong disinclination to tax in-

27. Kuisel, *Ernest Mercier*, 43. A commercial success, the CFP provided France with nearly half its crude-oil imports by the end of the 1930s. See Kuisel, *Capitalism and the State*, 68.

28. For more details regarding the Crédit National's role in postwar France, see above, 218n44.

29. Kuisel, *Capitalism and the State*, 71–72.

creases. In 1920, when the government introduced a turnover tax as a quick way to raise money, he warned prophetically that what some viewed as a cure-all might very well lose favor over time to other possible taxes.[30] Yet he conceded that "at the present time, it is necessary to take whatever is nearest at hand."[31] Accordingly, he voted for the tax after a lengthy debate in the Chamber. But as early as 1923, he and others were questioning its usefulness, given the "brutal" effect it was having on the cost of living. They called on the government to devise a plan that might allow its elimination.[32]

Loucheur spoke about the alternative to new and higher taxes during a Chamber debate in November, 1922. He supported tighter enforcement of the income tax, to stop its being a "sucker's tax."[33] He also favored reducing the interest the government paid on national defense bonds, a form of floating debt with maturity periods running from one month to one year. The popularity of such bonds for short-term investment had to be sustained in order to finance France's deficits, but Loucheur believed that the law of supply and demand did not hold in servicing the public debt, since France was operating without competition within national limits: "The money paid by the state of necessity returns to the state. Sometimes there is astonishment at the large number of treasury bonds and national defense bonds subscribed to. But that money cannot go anywhere else. I have heard it said that it will go to industry. First of all, so much the better! Through the channel of industrial commerce it will soon return to the banks and from there to the Bank of France or the public treasury." In Loucheur's eyes, the treasury erred after the war when it opened the "faucet of high-interest-bearing defense bonds."[34] In 1921, he had recommended to the Chamber's

30. That is exactly what happened in the later 1920s; the tax was extremely controversial throughout the decade.

31. Carl Shoup, *The Sales Tax in France* (New York, 1930), 21–22.

32. France, *Journal officiel de la République française: Chambre des Députés, débats parlementaires*, April 29, 1920, pp. 1528–29; Shoup, *The Sales Tax*, 30; France, *Journal officiel: Chambre des Députés, documents parlementaires* (1923), Annex No. 6675, November 30, 1923, p. 448.

33. The term Loucheur used was *l'impôt des poires*. See Schuker, *The End of French Predominance*, 70.

34. France, *Annales de la Chambre: Débats*, November 7, 1922, p. 339. National defense bonds were first offered in September, 1914, in small denominations—a hundred and a thousand francs—for maturity periods of three months, six months, and a year, at 5-

finance commission that the government reduce the interest rate on the one-year defense bonds from 5 percent to 4.5 percent, and in early 1922, Charles de Lasteyrie, the finance minister, had done just that.[35] In November, Loucheur was demanding a more dramatic reduction, from 4.5 percent to 3 percent. Besides saving the government money, the drop, he expected, would make longer-term government bonds, which were then losing their market value, more attractive, since they paid 6 percent. He believed the French would continue to buy the defense bonds even at a lower return, since the bonds had the advantages of security and easy liquidity. Loucheur argued that his "cheap money" approach, which was to include ending the deflationary François-Marsal Convention, would not only help the government meet its bond and budget commitments but also make French industry more competitive internationally.[36]

Loucheur's recommendations were a practical application of the *circuit fermé*, or "closed circle," theory regarding national defense bonds in French finance. According to it, the movement into and out of such bonds—the outstanding amount of which totaled an enormous 60.8 billion francs in October, 1922—was a natural circulation containing no danger. Renewals were virtually automatic, and new subscriptions would quickly compensate for money withdrawn. Consequently, there was no genuine risk of a demand for massive repayments.[37]

Critics, however, reasoned that if people's needs mounted in consequence of business volume and price trends, renewals would not be automatic. There was the danger, too, that if prices rose, people could easily withdraw funds from defense bonds to meet the changed situation, and thereby not only make the price increases permanent but also fuel further inflation. And in February, 1923, after a business upturn, rising prices, and the greater relative yield of longer-term bonds had cut the

percent interest. The bonds quickly became a popular investment. One-month maturities were first authorized in 1918. See Eleanor Dulles, *The French Franc*, 94, 185; and Haig, *The Public Finances*, 227–29, 240.

35. Germaine Martin, *Les Finances publiques de la France et la Fortune privée, 1914–1925* (Paris, 1925), 344.

36. France, *Annales de la Chambre: Débats*, November 7, 1922, pp. 338–43. For more information on the François-Marsal Convention, see above, p. 225.

37. Eleanor Dulles, *The French Franc*, 186, 248–50.

sales of national defense offerings, the treasury raised its interest rate on one-year defense bonds to 5 percent.[38]

When France's finances began to unravel in early 1924, the Poincaré government advanced the idea of a 20-percent increase in existing taxes (the *double décime*) as a way of stabilizing the franc. Aware that the proposal of a tax rise on the eve of a national election would face a rebuff in many political quarters, Poincaré deftly maneuvered to strengthen his majority. To ease the legislation through the Chamber's finance commission, he held the bait of cabinet posts in a reshaped government before the commission's two most influential members, Maurice Bokanowski and Loucheur. The legislation moved to the Chamber floor for debate, which lasted for five wearying weeks.[39]

The 109 articles afforded opponents ample opportunity to slow down the enactment process of what Poincaré considered an emergency measure. Almost immediately leftist adversaries shifted attention from the government's bill to scandals and abuses in the liberated regions and to the possibility that, by correcting them, the treasury might recover large sums, maybe enough to moot Poincaré's tax bill. Since Loucheur had been minister of the liberated regions in 1921, he could not escape the debate; he defended his ministerial record by pointing to the steps he had taken to eliminate fraud and other abuses. He also gave his support to the reevaluation of approximately 450 dossiers involving large settlements but warned his colleagues against seeking an extensive review that might take years to complete. At one point the Socialist deputy Albert Inghels suggested that every *sinistré*'s dossier be evaluated again. By the end of this phase of the debate, the Chamber had decided on reevaluating about twenty-five thousand dossiers and had separated the text pertaining to the liberated regions from the rest of Poincaré's bill.[40]

The tax debate concluded with an all-night session on February 22 and 23. Loucheur cast his vote against the completed bill, because he believed it would result in an increase in the cost of living and make French exports less competitive. But the Chamber voted to 312 to 205 in

38. *Ibid.*, 250–53; Georges Lachapelle, *Le Crédit public* (Paris, 1932), 136–40, 155–56; Schuker, *The End of French Predominance*, 39–41; Martin, *Les Finances publiques*, 345–53.

39. Schuker, *The End of French Predominance*, 57–61.

40. *Ibid.*, 83–84; France, *Annales de la Chambre: Débats*, January 29–31, 1924, pp. 312–35, 339–58, 361–77; François Albert, "Chronique politique," *Revue politique et parlementaire*, CXVIII (1924), 314–20.

favor, and the legislation moved on to the Senate, which unenthusiastically voted its approval on March 14. The *double décime*, which shortly thereafter became law, combined with a loan from J. P. Morgan and Company to firm up the value of the franc, and for a while at least, France's financial situation stabilized.[41]

In the national elections of May, which returned Loucheur to the Chamber of Deputies, the Left Cartel was the victor. Among the campaign promises of the coalition was the abolition of the controversial turnover tax and instead either the imposition of a capital levy, that is, a special tax on wealth, or the consolidation of debts by forcing holders of government bonds with short maturity periods and high interest rates to accept long-term bonds—securities with maturities of from fifteen to thirty years—at low rates of return. But many moderate supporters of the Left Cartel, as well as the parties of the Right, preferred raising indirect taxes and the costs of services the state provided, such as those under the postal ministry. Their opposition to a capital levy or debt consolidation was powerful, and looking toward the "tightrope act" of holding the two wings of the Left Cartel together, Premier Herriot, whose own knowledge of finance was limited, named Etienne Clémentel as finance minister.

The Left Cartel's financial manifesto came in Clémentel's 1925 budget proposal, which, though giving a bit more attention to direct taxes than previously, broke the coalition's sensational campaign promise of eliminating the turnover tax. Because of the budget's extraordinary complexity, it moved through parliament slowly, undergoing a number of modifications.[42]

The Left Cartel faced equally hard decisions about monetary policy. Ceilings on fiduciary circulation and on advances from the Bank of France to the treasury hampered the government's ability to handle its debt. Officials of the Bank of France, with strong support in parliament, believed that the ceilings were an effective check on inflation and refused to alter them. Some permanent officials at the finance ministry,

---

41. France, *Journal officiel: Chambre des Députés, débats*, February 22, 1924, p. 1033; *Le Petit Journal*, February 18, 1924, p. 3; Schuker, *The End of French Predominance*, 108–15, 124.

42. Kuisel, *Capitalism and the State*, 73; Robert M. Haig, *The Public Finances of Postwar France* (New York, 1929), 100–110, 115–16, 256–58; Shoup, *The Sales Tax*, 33; Schuker, *The End of French Predominance*, 132–33.

however, had concluded that because of the government's large floating debt, a deflationary course was no longer realistic. Shortly after the new government took power, they encouraged it to work for a higher currency ceiling and a revision of the François-Marsal Convention. But Herriot and Clémentel accepted the views of the bank and adhered to the orthodoxy of their predecessors. In view of the large face amount of short-term bonds—bonds with maturities ranging from beyond one year up to fifteen years—that became redeemable in 1925 and the considerable number of defense bond subscriptions that the treasury had to keep up in the same year, their decision limited the government's flexibility in addressing a potentially explosive situation. The decision also made starkly evident the basic incompatibility between the left-wing and moderate groups supporting the Left Cartel government.[43]

In a speech to the Chamber of Deputies on February 17, 1925, Loucheur voiced his thoughts on public finance, including, unsurprisingly, the turnover tax. In spite of his repugnance toward the levy, the government's resolve to maintain it for the time being met with his approbation. At the same time, though, he suggested that parliament look into a 5-percent payroll tax as an alternative. He acknowledged that such an assessment appeared "very democratic" to him.[44] Aware that the government was close to its 41-billion-franc limit on the currency in circulation, he ventured that there were ways for the treasury to meet the obligations before it apart from raising the ceiling on fiduciary circulation, with the inflationary side effects which that would entail. For one thing, he deplored what he saw as a hoarding of bank notes, on the grounds that it was disrupting France's self-contained monetary system (the *circuit fermé*), with harmful consequences for the government bond market and interest rates. He called on his colleagues to join in waging a propaganda war against hoarders, to prod them into letting funds reenter the market of active exchange. As another expedient to keep the currency issued below the 41-billion-franc limit, he suggested that certain circulating drafts underwriting purchases of raw materials abroad that were then made out in francs be drawn up in dollars and pounds and discounted abroad instead;

---

43. Schuker, *The End of French Predominance*, 36, 38–39, 132–40; Maier, *Recasting Bourgeois Europe*, 494–99; Haig, *The Public Finances*, 256–60. Some confusion existed in the 1920s about whether fifteen-year bonds constituted long-term or short-term debt. On that, see Haig, *The Public Finances*, 259–60.

44. France, *Annales de la Chambre: Débats*, February 17, 1925, p. 856.

that, he believed, would free up between 1 and 1.5 billion francs. He also recommended securing a 200-million-dollar loan outside France— although he was vague about how to do that—and inaugurating a pay-in-advance income-tax scheme that gave discounts to participants. And, as on other occasions, he underscored the part France's exports could play in helping the nation achieve financial stability.[45]

Loucheur continued to believe that France's financial crisis could be resolved without painful tax increases, but some of the remedies he supported were of questionable effectiveness, as the Herriot government learned when it tried the pay-in-advance tax plan, with disappointing results.[46] Not long after Loucheur's speech, the Left Cartel government began to disintegrate. At the beginning of April, Clémentel, whose political affiliation was with the Gauche Radicale, resigned as finance minister rather than sponsor a capital levy to lighten the treasury's problems. Only a few days later, the Bank of France sealed the doom of a government it mistrusted by disclosing its own falsification of currency-circulation figures to cover up government infractions of the fiduciary ceiling. The government lost a Senate vote of confidence on April 10 and resigned.[47]

From Clémentel's resignation to Loucheur's arrival at the rue de Rivoli in late November, there were three finance ministers, none of whom was able to put France's financial house in order. The situation turned steadily worse. The budget for 1925 did not become law until mid-July of that year, and even though it showed a surplus on paper, it was not balanced; furthermore, the delay in passing the budget and the resultant postponement in sending out demand notes for taxes slowed the tax yield in the latter half of the year. An internal loan launched by the treasury in July to help fund redemptions of bonds maturing before year's end was an outright failure. The government hoped to obtain 15 billion francs from the loan, but raised only about 6 billion francs, and its halfhearted efforts at concealing the insufficient result did little to reassure the French public. On top of that, the failure of negotiations in Washington on France's war debt precipitated a sharp drop in the value of the franc.[48]

45. *Ibid.*, 854–62.

46. Maier, *Recasting Bourgeois Europe*, 497.

47. Haig, *The Public Finances*, 114–19; Kuisel, *Capitalism and the State*, 73; Maier, *Recasting Bourgeois Europe*, 497–98.

48. Haig, *The Public Finances*, 111–12, 118–24; Eleanor Dulles, *The French Franc*, 181–85, 352–54; Maier, *Recasting Bourgeois Europe*, 498–500.

The gravity of the situation by mid-November convinced Loucheur at last that drastic tax measures were necessary to deal with the crisis. The government then in power, headed by Paul Painlevé, took a tough stand by supporting a capital levy as well as a forced consolidation of short-term bonds, the amortization of which was rescheduled to begin in 1928 and extend over 25 years. When it was Loucheur's turn to speak during the Chamber's debate on those proposals, he argued for doing everything possible "to meet the obligations of the state." Recognizing the strong opposition there was to the government's program, he offered an alternative that, in addition to imposing three billion francs in new taxes to balance the budget, would have collected five billion more per year for seven years in a capital levy aimed at amortizing the government's short-term treasury bond obligations. Loucheur virtually stated, however, that he would support the government if his alternative failed to generate support and no one else came up with something that did.[49]

The Chamber did not pursue Loucheur's idea, but throughout Painlevé's brief second government in 1925, from October 29 to November 22, Loucheur worked closely with the Socialist party to formulate an acceptable financial stabilization package. He even won praise from his wartime colleague at the armaments ministry, Albert Thomas, who wrote him in early December, "I was delighted, during the second Painlevé cabinet, to feel that you were in agreement with my socialist friends for the realization of a total plan."[50] Loucheur's cooperative spirit was intact on November 22, when he voted in the Chamber for the government's plan of forced consolidation. Nevertheless, because of a few critical moderate defections, the government was defeated and Painlevé resigned.[51]

Aristide Briand, Senator Paul Doumer, and Herriot all tried, unsuccessfully, to form a new government, but Briand, in a second attempt, succeeded on November 29. To fill the post of finance minister, Briand

49. Haig, *The Public Finances*, 125; France, *Annales de la Chambre: Débats*, November 19, 1925, pp. 202–206.

50. Albert Thomas to Louis Loucheur, December 1, 1925, in Fonds Thomas, Relations et Informations, France, Vol. 2, Correspondance: Lettres et Démarches à Paris/Chemise Loucheur, BIT. Thomas served as the first director of the International Labor Office during the 1920s.

51. France, *Journal officiel: Chambre des Députés, débats*, November 22, 1925, pp. 3915–16; Haig, *The Public Finances*, 124–26; *Le Temps*, November 23, 1925, p. 6, November 24, 1925, p. 1.

considered both Doumer, whose preference was to rely primarily on an increase in indirect taxes, a policy rejected by the left wing of the Left Cartel, and Loucheur, who Briand believed would be effective in courting the left-wing vote. When Briand offered the post to Loucheur, he accepted without hesitation. The decision created a certain amount of anxiety in conservative circles, however, because of Loucheur's collaboration with the Socialists.[52]

The most immediate problems for the new minister of finance were balancing the budget and meeting the government's payments for a sizable redemption of short-term treasury bonds—bonds with three-, six-, and ten-year maturities—on December 8. Even before he accepted the post, he had a bill ready to deal with both. To ease the budget deficit, which was due in large part to slow tax collection for the 1925 budget year, Loucheur wanted to require the payment of outstanding direct taxes for 1925 before the end of December. Although the meager inflow of tax revenues did not owe to negligence by the taxpayers, since passage of the budget had not come until July, Loucheur was willing to let them bear the brunt of the funding burden. His proposal was that failure to pay by the end of January, 1926, would result in a surcharge of 10 percent. That by itself, Loucheur predicted, would produce a comfortable surplus for 1925. In the potentially disruptive matter of the bond maturities of December 8, Loucheur again was willing to shift hardship to the taxpayers. He sought a stiff retroactive surtax on certain portions of the income tax, to be payable by March 1, 1926. In addition, he wanted permission to negotiate an increase of six billion francs in advances to the state from the Bank of France, to be repaid with revenue from the surtaxes.[53]

Consideration of Loucheur's emergency taxes took place in the Chamber of Deputies in an emotionally charged all-night session on December 2–3. In the face of the sharp criticism by opponents, particularly those fearing inflation, the government seemed headed for defeat until Briand stepped to the tribune and made an impassioned plea: "For the first time I cling to power; for if I am overthrown grave injury will have

52. Haig, *The Public Finances*, 126; Edouard Julia, "Chronique politique," *Revue politique et parlementaire*, CXXV (1925), 487–88; Bonnefous and Bonnefous, *Histoire politique*, IV, 103–104; Edouard Julia, "Chronique politique," *Revue politique et parlementaire*, CXXVI (1926), 122.

53. France, *Annales de la Chambre: Documents*, 1925, Annex No. 2128, pp. 147–48; Haig, *The Public Finances*, 126–27; Eleanor Dulles, *The French Franc*, 191.

been done your country."[54] Arguing that he too was opposed to inflation, Briand nonetheless insisted that Loucheur's remedies were the only way out of France's immediate crisis. The premier's appeal worked; his government won in the vote, saving the state from bankruptcy.[55]

An earlier government had in July introduced the budget for 1926, claiming it was balanced, but Loucheur declared that it was not. Anyway, the treasury needed additional funds to meet bond maturities in 1926. On December 8, Loucheur thus presented a jolting array of tax increases for parliamentary approval. He described his goal as the halt of an inflationary spiral that, left unchecked, could lead to disaster. Noting that on four occasions in 1925 the government had had to raise the ceiling for advances from the Bank of France, by a combined total of 17.5 billion francs, he blamed again the hoarding of bank notes that a lack of confidence in government bonds engendered, as well as a shortage of working capital for business purposes. Since the exchange of notes for bonds had not occurred in sufficient volume, the government was driven to increasing the limits on advances, and the consequence was permanent inflation. Loucheur believed that if the government wanted to combat that, it could no longer rely on borrowing and would have to depend on taxes to meet the "totality of state expenses." He warned that the increased cost of living resulting from inflation represented a levy "on all citizens" that was "far more considerable than what we want to request in order to stabilize the situation and buttress the value of the franc."[56]

To balance the 1926 budget, Loucheur asked for increases in taxes and in charges for government services totaling 5.6 billion francs. Out of that, 3 billion francs were to come from higher rates in income taxes. He also sought a twenty-franc capitation tax and increases in postal rates and tobacco prices, as well as rises in indirect taxes, such as those on alcohol and automobiles, and an extension of the turnover tax to exports. But that was not all. To raise money for the amortization fund he wanted to set up to reduce the public debt, he called for a new tax "on the first sale of a house or a business"[57] and for special taxes on gifts and

54. Quoted by Eleanor Dulles in *The French Franc*, 192.

55. *Ibid.*, 191–92; France, *Annales de la Chambre: Débats*, December 2, 1925, pp. 342–84.

56. Projet de loi No. 2180, Chambre des Députés, December 8, 1925, in B, 39897, MF; Haig, *The Public Finances*, 128–29.

57. *Le Petit Journal*, December 9, 1925, p. 1.

inheritances. He projected that those taxes would generate 2.2 billion francs annually exclusively for the fund. On December 10, he submitted legislation to parliament to reduce tax evasion and tax fraud.[58] The stiff measures Loucheur backed in 1925 were in distinct contrast to his position on taxes in 1924 and earlier. But when faced with the revenue crisis France was undergoing, he showed the same pragmatic flexibility he had demonstrated on many occasions in his government service. His position on the turnover tax illustrates his adaptability. He expressed reservations when it was introduced in 1920, recommended a substitute for it in 1923, grudgingly accepted its continuation in early 1925, and pushed for its expansion to exports after becoming finance minister in late 1925.

Opponents of Loucheur and his fiscal remedies struck quickly and hard. Loucheur wrote in his diary that the press attacks were "violent— from the Left and the Right."[59] In the corridors of parliament, questions resurged about his activities as a "war profiteer"—a label that he once more immediately and vigorously denied.[60] In the Chamber finance commission, his proposed exactions received a hostile reception. Discussion had barely begun when the commission's Socialists, with whose party Loucheur had just weeks before collaborated, joined other members in moving to send virtually all of his program back to the ministry of finance. On December 15, he resigned as finance minister.[61]

France's crisis worsened after Loucheur's resignation. The franc, which was worth slightly less than four cents in December, 1925, again became the target of speculation and fell to two cents by the following summer. The French public hurried to change their bonds and savings into inflation hedges like jewelry and real estate. Storekeepers raised prices in tandem with the rate at which the franc depreciated on currency markets. And instability reigned at the helm of the finance minis-

---

58. *Ibid.*; France, *Annales de la Chambre: Documents,* 1925, Projet de loi, Annex No. 2180, December 8, 1925, pp. 296–306; France, *Annales de la Chambre: Documents,* 1925, Projet de loi, Annex No. 2181, December 8, 1925, pp. 306–307; *Le Petit Journal,* December 11, 1925, p. 1.

59. Loucheur, *Carnets secrets,* 157.

60. France, *Journal officiel: Chambre des Députés, débats,* December 3, 1925, p. 3933. Loucheur compiled a set of documents to support his public denials of war profiteering and then made arrangements for one of his chief antagonists on the question, the deputy Gabriel Castagnet, to look at them in private. See Louis Loucheur Papers, 1/2.

61. *Le Petit Journal,* December 12, 1925, p. 1, December 15, 1925, pp. 1, 3, December 16, 1925, p. 1; Haig, *The Public Finances,* 130.

try as four more ministers came and went between Loucheur's departure and the latter part of July, 1926. By then France was at the edge of monetary collapse.[62]

With time running out, parliament turned to the financially conservative Poincaré, and his return to power halted the financial panic. Parliament, with Loucheur voting in favor as well, granted him decree power. Unencumbered by parliamentary obstructions, Poincaré swiftly implemented a series of measures, including increases on certain direct taxes and virtually all indirect taxes; on the other hand, he lowered inheritance taxes and the income taxes of the wealthy. The franc began to appreciate, and the budget yielded a surplus. Poincaré was heralded as the "savior of the franc." With the return of financial stability, France experienced an economic upturn that continued for the rest of the decade.[63] Whatever Loucheur's missteps, he at least deserves credit for his courageous disclosure that the only way out of the economic crisis was through a rigorous tax program.[64]

62. Kuisel, *Capitalism and the State,* 74; Haig, *The Public Finances,* 130–61.
63. Kuisel, *Capitalism and the State,* 74; Haig, *The Public Finances,* 161–71.
64. See Eleanor Dulles, *The French Franc,* 385–86.

II

VICTORIES AND DEFEATS
THE FINAL YEARS

The mid-1920s were a turning point for France. In the fall of 1925, it, along with several other states, joined with Germany in agreements that ushered in a period of "good feelings" in European diplomatic relations. After Poincaré saved the franc in 1926, economic prosperity took hold. The middle years of the decade saw certain French modernizers, concerned about the crisis of the franc, persistent industrial backwardness, and growing signs of social unrest, launch initiatives. In late 1925, Ernest Mercier organized the Redressement Français to encourage the adoption of a wide range of modernizing reforms.[1] Loucheur was also in the forefront of the reformers, and in September, 1925, he put forward the idea of an international economic conference within the framework of the League of Nations as a step toward the modernizing goal of European economic integration. After he became minister of labor in 1928, he continued his efforts at reform by working in behalf of legislation to improve France's social and economic fabric. Loucheur's political prominence proved capable of influencing outcomes in a range of matters critical to the general campaign for modernization.

THE WORLD ECONOMIC CONFERENCE

Loucheur believed that close cooperation with other European states in areas like production and trade was vital to strengthening France's eco-

---

1. Kuisel, *Ernest Mercier*, 45–50.

nomic position internationally. The most striking of his efforts toward encouraging such cooperation was his sponsorship of an international economic conference in Geneva in 1927.

Long before he began developing his idea for a conference, he demonstrated interest in a particular form of cooperation: international industrial cartels. He had tried, unsuccessfully, in 1919 to assemble a steel cartel that encompassed France, Germany, Luxembourg, and Belgium (see above, pp. 165–66, 178). In the mid-1920s, he was associated with a group of French politicians and businessmen who believed that arrangements with Germany in several basic industries were essential to the economic well-being of France. The Dawes Plan, which took effect in the fall of 1924, gave Germany a chance to surpass France in postwar recovery. The markets provided by French reconstruction were starting to dry up, and provisions of the Treaty of Versailles that gave France a unilateral most-favored-nation advantage in its trade with Germany and that allowed for duty-free exports of products from Alsace and Lorraine to Germany were about to expire. These men were convinced that without the protection of cartels, a number of French industries would be unable to compete with their German counterparts.[2]

Loucheur's belief in the need for economic cooperation extended to trade policy, where he wanted to curtail the economic nationalism that took concrete shape in high tariffs and import and export restrictions. He had already criticized America's policy of high duties in the early 1920s, and by 1925 he saw that the increasingly restrictive trade policies in Europe were a shackle on economic growth.[3]

Loucheur had the long-range goal of fashioning a European economic organization capable of vying with the United States. His ideas were not fully mature in 1925, but he knew the general direction in which he wished to move. He saw that a failure to rationalize industry—to mechanize production and consolidate industries into larger units—would lead to disaster, since America already had an economically efficient system.

2. Edward David Keeton, *Briand's Locarno Policy: French Economics, Politics, and Diplomacy, 1925–1929* (New York, 1987), 39–51, 122–23; Ervin Hexner, *The International Steel Cartel* (Chapel Hill, N.C., 1943), 66–67; Sauvy and Hirsch, *Histoire économique*, II, 137; Ernst Trendelenburg to Eugène Raynaldy, February 3, 1925, in F 12, 8863, AN; Report of Louis Pradel, President of Lyon Chamber of Commerce, on the Franco-German Accord, October 6, 1927, in F 12, 8867, AN.

3. Loucheur, *La Reconstruction*, 16; "Conférence Internationale Economique" (memorandum), September 11, 1925, in Series Société des Nations, Vol. 1194, MAE.

When, in September, 1925, he presented a proposal for a world economic conference to the League of Nations on behalf of the French delegation, he explained his reasoning: "The causes of war are undoubtedly manifold. They are often political, sometimes ethnical. But I think everyone in this Assembly will agree that one of the most frequent causes of the scourge of war in the past has been the economic struggle between different countries."[4] It was in part because of the strong current of economic nationalism that prevailed in the world, with its potential for leading "to very serious trouble in the future," that Loucheur believed a conference imperative. He explained that he did not seek the signing of international conventions there; instead he wanted the meeting to enunciate principles that would let international producers negotiate the agreements themselves under government supervision.[5]

Shortly after that, Loucheur went before the Second Committee of the League and elaborated on some of his ideas in another speech. Again he stressed the need to find solutions to the economic discord that came from not dealing with production on a multinational scale, and he showed his willingness to bend on principles if necessary: "With respect to state intervention in industrial concerns, I am deeply *anti-étatiste*. I have very little confidence in the virtues of the interventionist state. But, having seen large conflicts close up, having tried my hand in all branches of production and human activity, I have had the chance to realize that at certain moments states must put a brake on the excesses of individualism and that there must even exist a kind of statute on the necessary relations between the state and production." Without making any specific proposals, he left no doubt that he considered a harmonization of production and consumption and a "rational economic system" desirable. He also emphasized the importance of combating what he called a European "race for high tariffs that is comparable to the prewar armaments race."[6]

In December, the League Council set up a preparatory committee

4. Allyn Young and H. Van V. Fay, *The International Economic Conference*, World Peace Foundation Pamphlets, Vol. X, No. 4 (Boston, 1927), 375–76. Loucheur first attended the League of Nations as an alternate French delegate at the session during the fall of 1924, and he continued to serve as a French representative to the League until 1929. See Décret du 30 août 1924 (France), in Section No. 26, Document No. 38352, Dossier 36175 (1924), LNA; *L'Europe nouvelle*, November 28, 1931, pp. 1587–88.

5. Young and Fay, *The International Economic Conference*, 375–76.

6. Provisional Minutes of the Ninth Meeting, Deuxième Commission, Société des Nations, September 22, 1925, in Series Société des Nations, 1194, MAE.

for the economic conference. Although Loucheur was not on the committee, which met in the spring and fall of 1926, he affected its decisions by virtue of his role as the father of the conference and through his presence on other bodies. One of those, the Second Committee of the League, discussed the work of the preparatory committee in the fall of 1926. Another was an interministerial committee of the French government established to formulate policy guidelines for France's representatives to the preparatory committee. The preparatory committee aligned itself with Loucheur in making trade policy and the international aspects of production in certain branches of industry focal points of the conference. It put agriculture on the program as a third major topic. Loucheur opposed making the conference a meeting of world economic experts chosen by the League. He, along with others, wanted the conference to be more than an "academy of economic experts" issuing conclusions of an essentially theoretical nature. He believed that the results would have practical value and would influence the economic policies of governments only if the participating governments named their own delegates. Although the delegates would not come as government representatives, there could be consultation that enabled each government's economic views to come out in what its delegates said. The preparatory committee accepted that line of thinking for the selection of conference delegates.[7]

Loucheur's efforts received a boost at the end of September, 1926,

7. Minutes, Réunion d'une commission interministérielle, November 16, 1925, *ibid.*; Minutes, Réunion interministérielle, February 26, 1926, in Series Société des Nations, 1195, MAE; Note pour les membres français du comité préparatoire de la Conférence Economique Internationale, April 12, 1926, in Series Société des Nations, 1195, MAE; Rapport sur la première session du comité, comité préparatoire de la Conférence Economique Internationale, May 1, 1926, in Series Société des Nations, 1196, MAE; Procès-verbal de la séance, comité du conseil chargé de la préparation de la Conférence Economique, June 8, 1926, in Series Société des Nations, 1197, MAE; Note pour la direction politique, September 17, 1926, in Series Société des Nations, 1197, MAE; Rapport de la Deuxième Commission à l'Assemblée, Société des Nations ("Travaux du comité préparatoire de la Conférence Economique Internationale"), Loucheur, Rapporteur, September 20, 1926, in Series Société des Nations, 1197, MAE; "Travaux du comité préparatoire de la Conférence Economique Internationale" (memorandum), September, 1926, in Series Société des Nations, 1197, MAE; Rapport au conseil sur la deuxième session du comité, comité préparatoire de la Conférence Economique Internationale, Société des Nations, November 25, 1926, in Series Société des Nations, 1197, MAE; Louis Loucheur, "La Conférence économique de Genève," 38–39.

when steel producers from France, Germany, Belgium, Luxembourg, and the Saar signed, with the tacit support of their governments, an agreement to form a cartel. Intended to curb production, it established a system of quotas for crude steel. The agreement became possible only after the German government decided, in response to pressure from Foreign Minister Briand, to encourage German producers to settle for relatively low quotas. The German steel cartel took a few months to accede, but when it did, the way to an international cartel was open.[8] Loucheur expressed the hope that even more important producers' agreements would occur, and he pointed to the international economic conference as having the specific purpose of generating guidance toward that end, but he also cautioned that safeguards were needed for consumers. He accordingly suggested the formation of a superior committee made up of economists, consumers, and producers.[9] He also recognized the need for a "kind of economic tribunal" to arbitrate about matters arising from the later inclusion of steel producers from other countries in the cartel.[10] In Germany, the foreign minister, Gustav Stresemann, expressed his government's official opinion by calling the steel accord a "landmark of international economic policy the importance of which cannot be overestimated," adding that he hoped the agreement would serve as a model for international collaboration in other industries.[11]

French officials worked in 1926 on the supposition that the proposed conference would be the first step toward the formation of an economic league of nations. Loucheur and other members of the interministerial committee preparing for the meetings of the preparatory committee acted on that assumption, and Briand endorsed their objective two months later. But when Loucheur at a committee meeting of the League of Nations in June mentioned that the proposed conference could lead to other economic conferences and perhaps eventually to a permanent economic league, the British delegate, Austen Chamberlain, evinced aversion to the idea.[12]

8. Hexner, *The International Steel Cartel*, 70–79; Keeton, *Briand's Locarno Policy*, 186.

9. C. J. Gignoux, "L'Entente internationale de l'acier," *Revue économique internationale*, IV (November, 1926), 220, 222.

10. Louis Loucheur, *Le Problème de la coopération économique internationale* (Paris, 1926), 12.

11. Hexner, *The International Steel Cartel*, 221–22.

12. Compte-rendu de la réunion interministérielle du 26 février 1926 chargée de la préparation de la Conférence Economique Internationale, in Series Société des Nations,

By November, 1926, preparations for the conference were far enough along to make its convocation a virtual certainty. Loucheur began explaining his conceptions regarding Europe's long-term economic organization in greater detail. Speaking to a group of Austrian businessmen in October, he spoke favorably of organizing Europe's and even the world's principal industries along horizontal lines, with each industry headed by a central committee sitting in Geneva with authority to adjust production monthly and allot it among producers in participating states according to the terms of the industry's cartel agreements. According to Loucheur, each committee would be like an "orchestra conductor" responsible for "making the required harmony prevail." One effect he foresaw was a dramatic decline in national protective tariffs. He also claimed that "horizontal" agreements would better prepare participants to deal with commercial challenges from major competitors in noncartel states. Aware that such a system of cartels contained a negative potential for consumers and working conditions, he recommended that an international entente establish a control system protected from the "muddleheaded interference by states." Referring to that arrangement as a variety of "practical socialism," he believed that the League of Nations, with the consent of countries participating in the cartels, could serve as the enforcement agency needed.[13]

The last steps toward bringing the conference under the official sponsorship of the League were completed before the end of the year. The preparatory committee held its second round of meetings in November and agreed on a conference agenda; it also reached decisions regarding the date of the conference as well as the assembly's composition, which involved the categories of states to be invited, the method of delegate selection, and the maximum number of delegates each state could send. It submitted its recommendations to the League Council, which passed a resolution of acceptance on December 9, 1926.[14]

Loucheur in early 1927 promoted the economic conference through lectures and newspaper interviews. He emphasized the virtues of inter-

1195, MAE; Aristide Briand to Léon Jouhaux, Daniel Serruys, and Henri de Peyerimhoff, April 21, 1926, in Series Société des Nations, 1196, MAE; Note pour Monsieur Berthelot, June 8, 1926, in Series Société des Nations, 1197, MAE; Minutes, Committee of League Council, June 8, 1926, in Series Société des Nations, 1197, MAE.

13. Loucheur, Le Problème de la coopération, 9–12.

14. Young and Fay, The International Economic Conference, 394.

national cartels, but he more than once made reference to the possibility of a European economic or even political union. In late February, he told an audience at the University of Brussels that issues related to a European customs union would be discussed at the conference and that the European delegates should keep in mind the "possibility of at least the beginning of a United States of Europe."[15] He repeated the themes in a speech to a group of German businessmen in April, adding that the formation of industrial cartels should precede tariff reductions.[16]

The World Economic Conference convened on May 4, 1927, and lasted until May 23. Representing fifty countries, including such League nonmembers as the U.S.S.R. and the United States, 194 delegates participated. Loucheur attended as the head of a French delegation that included men of influence like Léon Jouhaux, of the CGT, and Daniel Serruys, the director of trade agreements at the ministry of commerce. At the outset of the conference, the assembled delegates bestowed on Loucheur the honor of being the first vice-president of the conference.[17]

Loucheur once again made it clear in a speech delivered early in the conference that he viewed the key to Europe's economic future as lying in producers' ententes organized horizontally. He emphasized the challenge of America's growing economic power, pointing out, for example, that the United States, besides enjoying a vast domestic market for its products, was steadily increasing exports to other countries and was doing so "at the expense of Europe." Loucheur stressed that the creation of cartels would make Europe more competitive by reducing cost prices at the same time that it provided for real increases in salaries, enabling the postwar continent to regain the "consumption power of prewar Europe." In an attempt to satisfy critics who saw dangers in such producers' organizations, he was more specific than before on how to control them: he suggested that Geneva become an "information and observation station" wielding publicity to arouse the public against abuses by the cartel. He added that it should be left to the League Coun-

15. Carl Pegg, *Evolution of the European Idea, 1914–1932* (Chapel Hill, N.C., 1983), 81.

16. *Ibid.;* Anne Orde, *British Policy and European Reconstruction After the First World War* (Cambridge, Eng., 1990), 319.

17. *Eighth Yearbook of the League of Nations: Record of 1927,* World Peace Foundation Pamphlets, Vol. XI, No. 2 (Boston, 1928), 196; Guillain, *Les Problèmes douaniers,* 24; Telegram Clauzel to foreign ministry, May 4, 1927, in Series Société des Nations, 1199, MAE.

cil to decide eventually whether a permanent body was needed to deal with problems arising from the cartel system.[18]

Loucheur's hopes for the conference rested primarily on the industrial committee, since it was to make recommendations about international producers' ententes. But despite the efforts of cartel proponents, including Loucheur, in its membership, the committee turned out to be less than a forum of support for cartels. Committee members from several smaller states, like Norway, Switzerland, and Finland, were either outspoken in their opposition or deeply concerned about implications. The German representative questioned the potential of cartels for trade liberalization, and delegates from labor unions expressed concern about increased unemployment and the need for public regulation.[19] Because of the committee's desire to present a unanimous report, it issued vague formulas based on compromise. It acknowledged that for "certain specific branches of production," cartels could provide important advantages for producers, consumers, and the community at large, but it also reviewed the dangers and pitfalls inherent in cartels. The report concluded that "the phenomenon of such agreements . . . does not constitute a matter upon which any conclusion of principle need be reached, but a development which has to be recognised and which . . . must be considered as good or bad according to the spirit which rules the constitution and the operation of the agreements, and in particular according to the measure in which those directing them are actuated by a sense of the general interest."[20] The decision of the report was a big disappointment to Loucheur.

The French also experienced problems in the conference's commerce committee, where Loucheur was a member as well. On May 9, France's chief spokesman, Serruys, presented a set of draft proposals concerning trade and tariffs. The foundation of his tariff-reduction provisions was "counterbalancing" duties—duties high enough to counter better production conditions or a more favorable system of prices in the primary country of competition. The French resolutions were so carefully crafted that many at the conference felt they could be used to jus-

18. Loucheur, *Carnets secrets*, 158–63.

19. Robert W. D. Boyce, *British Capitalism at the Crossroads, 1919–1932: A Study in Politics, Economics, and International Relations* (Cambridge, Eng., 1987), 121.

20. League of Nations, *Report and Proceedings of the World Economic Conference Held at Geneva, May 4th to 23rd, 1927* (2 vols.; Geneva, 1927), I, 49–50; Guillain, *Les Problèmes douaniers*, 117–18.

tify almost any tariff policy. Walter Layton, a British delegate, responded the next day that British opinion might support protection should the conference fail to take stronger measures than Serruys'. Since many countries depended on Britain as an export market, Layton's remarks caused consternation. Loucheur defended Serruys' position on May 11, but Serruys soon began to make concessions. He backed away from his support for the principle of conditional most-favored-nation treatment. The committee's unanimous report recommended that governments reach long-term trade agreements based on unconditional most-favored-nation status. The report also called for the states to act individually to simplify customs rates and to end disguised forms of protection. It recommended collective action as a way of dealing with tariff problems in general.[21]

Loucheur was not a member of the agricultural committee, the other major committee at the conference to make recommendations. Among the topics it canvassed were a number having to do with agricultural cooperatives and the development of credit.[22] In the end, the conference was an embarrassing setback for the French. At the core of the defeat was Loucheur's failure to come away with an endorsement for horizontal cartels. The conference resolutions generally favored a return to a liberal economic order internationally and the removal of obstacles to free trade. That was not what the protectionist-minded French had hoped for.[23]

There were signs in 1927 and 1928 that a more liberal system of trade relations might be at hand in Europe. In the summer of 1927, France and Germany, after more than three years of negotiations, signed a comprehensive commercial accord in which each granted the other general and unconditional most-favored-nation status. The two states announced that reaching an agreement would have been much harder "if the Parties had not been able to rely upon the principles laid down by the World Economic Conference and to benefit by the atmosphere created by its

21. Guillain, *Les Problèmes douaniers*, 24–29; Boyce, *British Capitalism*, 120–21; *Times* (London), May 11, 1927, p. 13, May 12, 1927, p. 13, May 18, 1927, p. 15.

22. Rapport et Projet de résolutions présentées par la Deuxième Commission à l'Assemblée, Société des Nations, September 21, 1927, in Series Société des Nations, 1201, MAE.

23. Guillain, *Les Problèmes douaniers*, 112–18; Ulrich Nocken, "International Cartels and Foreign Policy: The Formation of the International Steel Cartel, 1924–1926," in *Internationale Kartelle und Aussenpolitik*, ed. Clemens A. Wurm (Stuttgart, 1989), 79–80.

discussions."[24] After the Franco-German accord, a series of bilateral commercial agreements resulted in much tariff consolidation and in some cases a reduction in duties. The League's Economic Consultative Committee, set up to monitor the progress of the conference's program, reported at its meeting in May, 1928, that although tariffs overall were higher than at the time of the conference, the protectionist trend in Europe had slowed considerably. The committee judged that European commercial relations in general had undergone "some improvement during the year."[25]

The chances for forward movement in industrial organization seemed limited in view of the conference's recommendations, but Loucheur was determined to move ahead. In an article he wrote for a German newspaper during the summer of 1927, he again outlined his ideas on organizing European industries horizontally. He described his goal as an "economic union of European states that will consider and regulate all economic problems from the point of view of the common interest of the participating nations." He used the occasion to compliment Germany on the progress it had made to organize national trusts, adding that industrial concentration at the national level should occur prior to the formation of cartels at the international level.[26]

Other events involving Loucheur also occurred in 1927 and 1928 to advance the movement for a European economic union. On the very eve of the World Economic Conference, Aristide Briand, who like Loucheur was an exponent of European economic cooperation, had decided to associate himself more fully with the Paneuropean Union. Launched in the early 1920s by a young Austrian count, Richard N. Coudenhove-Kalergi, the Paneuropean Union had done much to propagate the idea of European unity. After Loucheur's election as president of the group's French section on May 2, Briand held an impressive reception for the organization's leaders, at which he told them of his readiness to serve as its honorary president. It was a striking way of demonstrating his support not only for the general concept of Euro-

24. Martin Hill, *The Economic and Financial Organization of the League of Nations: A Survey of Twenty-Five Years' Experience* (Washington, D.C., 1946), 50n13a.

25. Boyce, *British Capitalism*, 132; Guillain, *Les Problèmes douaniers*, 35–38; Hill, *The Economic and Financial Organization*, 50–51.

26. Copy of Loucheur's Article in the *Bergwerks-Zeitung*, August 29, 1927, in Albert Thomas Papers, Relations et Informations, France, Vol. 2, Correspondance: Chemise Loucheur, BIT.

pean unity but also for Loucheur's more immediate campaign to organize Europe economically.[27]

In late August, Loucheur used the Twenty-Fourth Conference of the Interparliamentary Union to continue his campaign for greater European economic cooperation. During a debate on a European customs union, he, as a member of the French delegation, argued that a Paneuropean economic confederation was attainable if a solution to problems of national security could be found. He urged the delegates to work on both economic and security matters concurrently. The delegates in the end passed a resolution calling for the gradual phasing-out of customs in Europe.[28]

Beyond the events involving Loucheur, other developments at the end of the 1920s enhanced the prospects of a European economic union. Beginning in the spring of 1928, apprehension about American economic power intensified. A number of Europeans developed the view that the Kellogg-Briand Peace Pact was a wedge by which American industrialists could penetrate European markets.[29] Several months later, Etienne Clémentel, then chairman of the Senate's finance commission, voiced what many of the French thought when he attacked the way America wanted to sell but not buy in Europe: "Unless the United States pursues a different trade policy, the States of Europe may be compelled to move to the verge of a customs union in order to defend themselves."[30] There was also a spreading sentiment within French business circles for closer cooperation with Germany, and in talks with German diplomats, French industrialists pressed for more marketing cartels.[31]

Briand, aware of that sentiment and anxious to counter foreign pressures in disarmament and reparations, decided to move ahead with a plan for a European union. He met with Gustav Stresemann in late June, 1929, and cited the menace of American economic power in order to argue the urgency of a European economic group of which France and Ger-

27. Pegg, *Evolution of the European Idea*, 28–29, 82–83; Richard N. Coudenhove-Kalergi, *Crusade for Pan-Europe: Autobiography of a Man and a Movement* (New York, 1943), 114–18.

28. Pegg, *Evolution of the European Idea*, 82–87.

29. *Ibid.*, 100–101. The Kellogg-Briand Peace Pact, which was signed by sixty-five nations, outlawed war.

30. *Ibid.*, 115–16.

31. Keeton, *Briand's Locarno Policy*, 311–12.

many could be the nucleus.[32] Although Stresemann declined to make a commitment, he professed an understanding of Briand's thinking. Buoyed by Stresemann's words and eager to bolster his own newly formed government, Briand revealed more details in July about his plans for European union and promised to present his proposals publicly before long.[33] On September 5, in a speech to the Assembly of the League of Nations, he suggested a European union as a vaguely conceived European economic organization. Stresemann, in a speech to the Assembly on September 9, spoke of Germany's readiness to consider plans for greater economic cooperation in Europe. And at a luncheon of the League, Stresemann and Arthur Henderson, the British foreign secretary, both showed their regard for Briand's idea, although they cautioned against undertaking a project that diluted national sovereignty. Briand's hopes were compromised, however, when Stresemann died and the New York stock market crashed.[34]

Whatever enthusiasm remained for Briand's idea faded when, in the late spring of 1930, the French foreign ministry released a detailed memorandum on a European federal union. To many, the plan the ministry advanced, by including guarantees of Europe's existing frontiers, appeared to be just another attempt to entrench France's definition of security, which consisted largely of guaranteeing the status quo. Such was the view in Germany, where the government showed little support. The British and Italian replies were also at bottom negative.[35]

Loucheur continued to insist that the first priority in organizing Europe should be horizontal producers' ententes. Speaking before the Economic Consultative Committee in the spring of 1929, he lamented the preceding twelve months' trend toward tariff protection and argued that customs barriers would reach higher levels still if the international disorder in production persisted. He challenged the committee to back a "logical plan" to organize Europe industrially and then agriculturally so that each nation's producers would be protected by something other

---

32. *Ibid.*, 311–14.

33. Briand's eleventh—and last—government was in power from July 29 to October 22, 1929.

34. Keeton, *Briand's Locarno Policy*, 315–20, 325–26; Bonnefous and Bonnefous, *Histoire politique*, IV, 360–63; Pegg, *Evolution of the European Idea*, 119–20.

35. Sontag, *A Broken World*, 137; Pegg, *Evolution of the European Idea*, 140–42, 149–52.

than customs barriers.[36] At the Assembly sessions of the League in the fall of 1929, he reiterated his ideas about cartels and on behalf of the French delegation introduced a proposal for another world economic conference. He probably hoped that at the conference he could win support for his producer-based scheme, but instead of pursuing his idea, the League scheduled a customs truce conference for 1930.[37] That conference did convene but failed to produce an agreement about a tariff truce. Loucheur contended that the failure was further evidence that progress on tariff reductions could not precede the reorganization of production. He criticized the League of Nations' attitude toward producers' ententes as burdened with "too great a mistrust of them, which has not yet disappeared. It is depriving itself of one of the most effective ways of achieving the goals it has set for itself."[38]

To compound Loucheur's frustrations, problems arose with the international cartelization that already existed. The International Steel Cartel, created in 1926, began to come apart shortly after its formation, primarily because German producers, spurred by strong consumer demand, were soon exceeding their quotas. They resented paying fines on their excess production, since by that they were in effect subsidizing competitors. Their cartel partners, meanwhile, resented the lost exports that the Germans' violations caused. After a failed attempt at compromise, the discontented German participants renounced the agreement in May, 1929. The cartel, which suffered also from a weak demand for steel in the months thereafter, was dissolved in 1931. A successor organization, launched in 1933, included a greater number of states and functioned more effectively, but it too collapsed, after the outbreak of war in 1939.[39]

In spite of disappointments, Loucheur pushed ahead with his campaign in behalf of greater economic unity in Europe. He presented his program of European economic rationalization and coordination at

36. Minutes, 2nd Session, Quatrième Séance, Comité Consultatif Economique, May 7, 1929, in C.C.E./2nd Session/P.V. 4 (I), LNA.

37. Draft Resolution Proposed by the French Delegation, September 10, 1929, in Series Société des Nations, 1201, MAE; Senator Victor Boret to Aristide Briand, September 20, 1929, ibid.; Keeton, Briand's Locarno Policy, 325; Pegg, Evolution of the European Idea, 121.

38. Loucheur, Preface to Guillain's Les Problèmes douaniers, v–vi.

39. Ervin Hexner, International Cartels (Durham, N.C., 1946), 206–10; John Gillingham, Coal, Steel, and the Rebirth of Europe, 1945–1955: The Germans and French from Ruhr Conflict to Economic Community (Cambridge, Eng., 1991), 21–44.

Coudenhove-Kalergi's Second Paneuropean Congress in May, 1930. Later he visited several eastern European states, where he attempted to rally support for the principle of economic cooperation in general and Briand's European union in particular. But states were increasingly resorting to high tariffs and other devices of economic nationalism to deal with the effects of the depression. By the end of 1931, virtually all the leaders in the European movement had given up the notion that a European union would occur any time soon. Even though Loucheur's efforts fell short of their purposes, his ideas made an important contribution to the movement for European integration in the latter 1920s and foreshadowed the founding of the European Coal and Steel Community in 1951.[40]

AT THE LABOR MINISTRY, 1928–1930

Shortly after the national elections of 1928, in which Loucheur was reelected as a deputy from the Nord (Avesnes), Premier Raymond Poincaré called on him to serve as minister of labor and health. Seeing that the post could offer new opportunities for him to carry forward his long-standing commitment to the general welfare of workers, Loucheur demanded, as a condition of acceptance, assurances that the government would support both his efforts to obtain credits for a sizable housing program and his preparations to implement a recently passed social insurance law.[41] On June 1, he assumed his new responsibilities. Soon thereafter, he discovered that his ministry had insufficient authority to deal with labor conflicts quickly and decisively; consequently, he added to his legislative agenda in January, 1929, a bill aimed at enlarging his ministry's role in the settlement of labor disputes. As Loucheur moved ahead on housing, social insurance, and dispute settlement, he acted in accordance with a conception he laid before the Chamber of Deputies in January, 1929, regarding the state's role in such matters:

40. Pegg, *Evolution of the European Idea*, 143–45, 164–65; Loucheur, *Carnets secrets*, 168; John Gillingham, "Coal and Steel Diplomacy in Interwar Europe," in *Internationale Kartelle und Aussenpolitik*, ed. Clemens A. Wurm (Stuttgart, 1989), 100.

41. Albert Thomas to Louis Loucheur, June 4, 1928, in Fonds Thomas, Relations et Informations, France, Vol. 2, Correspondance: Chemise Loucheur, BIT. Loucheur's title was changed in November, 1928, to minister of labor, health, and social provision. See Bonnefous and Bonnefous, *Histoire politique*, IV, 392–95.

I am telling you, gentlemen, that in the face of the immensity of the movements of the modern economic world, in the face of their complexity, it is folly to imagine that the state can remain indifferent. . . .

The role of the state is to participate in industries when they take on the appearance of national industries, without ever assuming the management of them. Its role is to defend the rights of all, whether they are producers or workers. Its role—and perhaps it has done this only insufficiently, in fits and starts, when conflicts arose—is to force the diverse elements of production into harmony, without which nothing is possible.[42]

THE LOI LOUCHEUR

Housing was a subject to which Loucheur had given considerable attention earlier in the decade. He cosponsored a major housing bill in 1920 only to see it languish in the Senate (see above, pp. 209–10). In early 1923, he was the leading member of an ad hoc committee that studied ways to stimulate private construction of middle-income housing and that recommended such measures as liberal tax exemptions, the use of standardized materials, and the creation of departmental or interdepartmental lending agencies for the purpose. Some of the committee's ideas were incorporated into a government bill, but the measure never made it to the floor of the Chamber of Deputies. In December, 1924, Loucheur, reacting to government financial restraints, suggested in the Chamber of Deputies that twenty-five thousand inexpensive housing units go up annually for ten years instead of the fifty thousand that had been called for each year in the Bonnevay-Loucheur proposal.[43] Again there was no action taken on his recommendations, though at the time, according to one estimate, there was a shortage of fifty thousand housing units in

42. France, *Annales de la Chambre: Débats,* January 22, 1929, p. 138.
43. Rapport fait au nom de la Commission de l'Hygiène, de l'Assistance, de l'Assurance et de la Prévoyance Sociales, par Paul Strauss (Sénat), No. 614 (annex to the minutes of July 5, 1928), in B, 39896, MF; Annex to the Minutes, Commission d'Assurance et de Prévoyance Sociales (Chambre), February 5, 1926, in XIIIe Législature, Carton A-11, Commission d'Assurance et de Prévoyance Sociales, Procès-verbaux, AANV; France, *Annales de la Chambre: Débats,* December 26, 1924, pp. 1508–10.

Paris and a half million for all of France outside the liberated regions.[44] Loucheur's newspapers also kept the housing crisis in the eye of the public. In late 1925, for instance, *Le Petit Journal* ran a series that highlighted the deplorable living conditions of many in France.[45]

An early sign of the generally receptive feeling toward housing within the Chamber of Deputies had been its unanimous vote of November, 1921, to undertake the first stage of the Bonnevay-Loucheur housing bill. In 1926, the National Economic Council released the first report after its formation, which was devoted to housing. The report called for the construction of 200,000 units, as well as the creation of a national housing bank "to facilitate the construction, conversion, and improvement of buildings for use as housing in the whole of the country."[46] Two years later, Mercier's Redressement Français published a study that also recommended the adoption of a state-supported program to construct inexpensive housing.[47] The governments of the early and mid-1920s, nevertheless, had shown little interest in making a large infusion of state funds into housing programs, because of the costs of reconstruction and the state's shaky financial position. The Bonnevay-Loucheur bill in November, 1921, after the Chamber's favorable action, had gone to the Senate's finance commission, where, partly because the finance ministry opposed its provisions, it was allowed to die. The government's basic approach continued to be rent controls. Some legislative steps had been taken to improve the position of landlords, but the legal protection of tenants remained considerable in the mid-1920s and rental prices were still well below where increases in the overall cost of living would have pegged them. The Law of April 1, 1926, instituted a phaseout of lease extensions on rental properties built before 1914, however. By its terms those paying the lowest rents would be protected the longest—until 1931. The law thus reinforced a private-sector emphasis on the construction of expensive housing.[48] This is not to say that the

44. Bureau International du Travail, *Les Problèmes*, 137. The estimate was in a study by the federal tenants' commission of the Communist party published in *L'Humanité* in December, 1923.

45. *Le Petit Journal*, December 13–18, 1925, pp. 1–2.

46. Conseil National Economique, Rapport sur le problème du logement, January 7, 1926, in F 12, 8801, AN.

47. That is, Lévêque and Ricard's *Une Politique du logement*.

48. Sauvy and Hirsch, *Histoire économique*, II, 268–72. Parliament reversed its 1926 legislation three years later. According to a law of June 29, 1929, the phasing-out of remain-

governments of France completely ignored the need to construct low-cost housing. Even before the war several housing laws dealing with low-cost housing had been passed; these, combined with certain post-war laws that modified the earlier legislation, had been codified in the Law of December 5, 1922, providing an operational framework for government action during the 1920s. What was lacking was a significant financial commitment from the government. Only forty thousand low-cost units went up between 1923 and 1927, that is, an average of eight thousand lodgings per year. France's construction rate lagged well behind that of other European countries like Britain, Germany, and Belgium.[49]

On June 28, Loucheur presented parliament with a housing bill that he asked to have dealt with on an emergency basis. The bill called for the construction of 200,000 low-cost dwellings and 60,000 moderately priced rental units, by the end of 1933. In the spirit of the so-called Ribot Law of 1908, the bill identified as the special goal of the low-cost program the construction of dwellings "destined to become the property of low-income persons and in particular of workers living principally from their salaries."[50] Loucheur estimated that the program would cost 1.4 billion francs a year, with the state providing 850 million francs toward that amount in subsidies and loans, and communes, departments, and other sources supplying the rest. Accordingly, the bill provided for state loans to companies building low-cost housing, to real estate credit soci-

---

ing lease extensions on pre-1914 properties was delayed, and even where extensions on buildings predating 1914 had expired, rent controls were reintroduced. This was the last significant legislative act on rents before World War II.

49. Henri Sellier and A. Bruggeman, *Le Problème du logement: Son influence sur les conditions de l'habitation et l'aménagement des villes* (Paris, 1927), 99; André Houille, *La Question des habitations à bon marché en France* (Paris, 1932), 26–27; *Le Temps*, July 1, 1928, p. 1; Rapport fait au nom de la Commission de l'Hygiène, de l'Assistance, de l'Assurance et de la Prévoyance Sociales, par Paul Strauss (Sénat), No. 614 (annex to the minutes of July 5, 1928), in B, 39896, MF; France, *Annales de la Chambre: Débats*, December 26, 1924, p. 1509; Jean Bastié, *La Croissance de la banlieue parisienne* (Paris, 1964), 298–99.

50. *Le Temps*, June 30, 1928, p. 4. The Ribot Law of 1908 set up real estate credit soci- eties (*sociétés de crédit immobilier*) that received loans from a state-sponsored bank, the Caisse des Dépôts et Consignations, at an annual interest rate of 2 percent. The initial amount of 100 million francs was allocated on the understanding that the societies would place the money at the disposal of individual low-income workers for the purpose of buying a home. See Georges Risler, *Better Housing for Workers in France* (Paris, 1937), 9–12.

eties, and to public low-cost housing bureaus at an interest rate of 2 percent instead of the prevailing 3.5 percent.[51] But Loucheur avowed his intention to reserve the better part of the funds for the real estate credit societies, which, in contrast to the other two agencies, specialized in making loans to individuals. Loucheur also recommended that existing laws limiting state subsidies to the construction of nonsalable collective housing for large families be modified to allow most of the money to go to disabled workers, war veterans, and the heads of large families for buying individual housing. He maintained that with these and other provisions enacted, the purchase of individual dwellings would be within the reach of French workers.[52]

Loucheur projected that the capital needed to complete the program for moderately priced rental housing was 4.2 billion francs, of which the state would provide 900 million francs in loans at a reduced interest rate of 4 percent. The state planned to make 300 million francs available for 1928 and 1929 together, and 150 million for each of the program's four remaining years. To qualify for state assistance, contractors had to be capable of down payments of 20 percent on their projects. Loucheur's bill included other inducements to encourage this form of construction, such as the possible assumption by communes and departments of a small fraction of contractors' mortgage payments on the amounts not borrowed from the state.[53]

One challenge to the bill came in the Chamber of Deputies, where the Socialists introduced a counterproposal that, in line with recommendations in the housing report of the National Economic Council in 1926, provided for a powerful state-operated national housing office rather than a program that they called individualistic and *propriétiste* in character. The proposal was defeated in a Chamber vote, by 420 to 142.

Once the Chamber passed Loucheur's bill, at the end of a session

51. Companies specializing in low-cost housing (*sociétés des habitations à bon marché*) were authorized under a housing bill in 1894 to obtain low-interest loans from the Caisse des Dépôts et Consignations for building purposes. By a housing law of 1912, public low-cost housing bureaus were granted the same loan prerogatives as the low-cost housing companies. See Risler, *Better Housing,* 5–12.

52. *Le Temps,* June 29, 1928, p. 4; France, *Journal officiel: Chambre des Députés, débats,* July 3, 1928, pp. 2226, 2228.

53. *Le Temps,* June 30, 1928, p. 4; Ministère du Travail et de l'Hygiène, *Bulletin du Ministère du Travail et de l'Hygiène,* XXXV (October–December, 1928), "Chronique législative: Chambre et Sénat," 483.

that lasted late into the night of July 3–4, the legislation moved to the Senate, where strong objections arose against an autonomous *société nationale de l'habitation*. In Loucheur's plan, that agency was to determine suitable housing designs, coordinate the acquisition of widely used building materials—especially through payments in kind—and oversee the general application of the housing law. In contrast to the Chamber of Deputies, the more conservative Senate saw the agency as a scarcely veiled instance of *étatisme*, since the state was to be the company's majority stockholder. With Loucheur's reluctant consent, the upper house deleted the articles pertaining to the company from the bill it passed on July 7. All the bill's other principal provisions remained intact, and on July 13 the bill became law.[54]

Loucheur's next task was to assure that the Loi Loucheur, as the legislation came to be known, functioned successfully. Building on administrative entities and procedures already in place, Loucheur put together the necessary system. In late July, he set up a technical committee to select standardized designs for individual and collective dwellings, to determine the most efficient and cost-effective ways to apply the law, and to lay down procedures for using German payments in kind, should they become available. By the latter part of August, Loucheur had three more committees in place, to formulate guidelines for low-cost housing, housing in rural areas, and moderately priced dwellings. In October, he established priorities for the construction of low-cost housing, and he sent to prefects a voluminous document filled with ministerial explanations about the housing law. In spite of the organizational task he faced in July, he could announce in a speech to the Chamber on December 21 that the administrative framework was in place and that the period of application was under way.[55]

---

54. Ministère du Travail et de l'Hygiène, *Bulletin du Ministère du Travail et de l'Hygiène*, XXXV (October–December, 1928), "Chronique législative: Chambre et Sénat," 483–89; "Chronique politique," *Revue politique et parlementaire*, CXXXVI (1928), 301–303; France, *Journal officiel: Chambre des Députés, débats*, July 3, 1928, pp. 2226–29; *Le Temps*, July 9, 1928, p. 1; Rapport fait au nom de la Commission de l'Hygiène, de l'Assistance, de l'Assurance et de la Prévoyance Sociales, par Paul Strauss (Sénat), No. 614 (annex to the minutes of July 5, 1928), in B, 39896, MF; Projet de loi, textes proposés par la Commission des Finances, Sénat, in B, 34023, MF; Projet de loi, adopté par la Chambre des Députés, adopté, avec modifications, par le Sénat, July 1928, in B, 34023, MF.

55. *Le Temps*, August 1, 1928, p. 3, August 8, 1928, p. 3, August 26, 1928, p. 4, October 22, 1928, p. 3, October 27, 1928, p. 1; Minutes, Commission d'Assurance et de Prévoyance

One way Loucheur tried to control construction costs was by securing promises from manufacturers not to raise prices unless the price of coal increased. He obtained commitments from the steel and cement industries in the summer of 1928, although his means of assuring compliance were limited. In addition, he promoted the use of modern building techniques. Stigmatizing the building trades in 1928 as the "most backward industry in France," he badgered builders to modernize their methods.[56] In the fall of 1929, as a part of his campaign but also as a demonstration of how rapidly the building industry had progressed technologically, he mounted a housing exposition in which construction methods used in fulfilling the Law of July 13 were on display.[57]

Loucheur's efforts were not enough to prevent construction costs from climbing rapidly between 1928 and 1930, however, largely because of the steep rise in housing construction that the Loi Loucheur brought about. Building costs in the department of the Seine, for example, shot up by 26.5 percent in those years, and concern grew in parliament that accelerating costs might stand in the way of completion of the law's building program. But that did not happen; construction costs began to ebb in 1931, and parliament voted sufficient funds to ensure continuation.[58]

The Loi Loucheur had a conspicuous but not controlling effect on French housing. No precise count of low-cost dwellings constructed during this era is available, but one inquiry concludes that for the years of the Loi Loucheur (late 1928–1933) and the Law of December 5, 1922 (1923–late 1928), the number completed or nearly completed was 240,000. Since 40,000 low-cost homes were built from 1923 to 1927, one can infer that by January, 1934, the goal of building 200,000 low-cost homes under the Loucheur program was well toward realization.[59] It

Sociales (Chambre), November 30, 1928, in XIVe Législature, Carton A-10, Commission d'Assurance et de Prévoyance Sociales, Procès-verbaux, AANV; France, *Journal officiel: Chambre des Députés, débats,* December 21, 1928, p. 3833.

56. Minutes, Commission d'Assurance et de Prévoyance Sociales (Chambre), November 30, 1928, in XIVe Législature, A-10, AANV.

57. *Le Progrès du Nord,* December 22, 1928, p. 1; *Le Temps,* November 4, 1929, p. 4.

58. Houille, *La Question,* 151–55; Bastié, *La Croissance,* 298–99; Minutes, Commission d'Assurance et de Prévoyance Sociales (Chambre), November 30, 1928, in XIVe Législature, A-10, AANV.

59. Jean Coutard, *Les Habitations à bon marché: Leur but, leur organisation, leurs résultats* (Paris, 1938), 138.

was while the housing law of 1928 was in effect that the government's interwar financial participation in housing construction was greatest. The government, in application of Ribot's public-housing law of 1908, paid out 1.2 billion francs, or 120 million francs a year, on construction during the period 1919–1928. But to fulfill the terms of the Loi Loucheur, it spent 8.2 billion francs, or 1.64 billion francs a year, between 1929 and 1933. In the last interwar years (1934–1939), government expenditures fell back to an annual average of 300 million francs, or 1.8 billion francs in all.[60] Despite the increased government financing in the law of 1928, Loucheur's program in the end proved too modest to meet France's housing demands. France still had a major housing problem at the close of the 1930s.[61]

SOCIAL INSURANCE

The passage of the Law of April 5, 1928, was a social legislative turning point that set in motion the administrative action and parliamentary debates that made French social security a reality in 1930. Work on the legislation started in 1920 when Paul Jourdain, an Alsatian serving as labor minister, began framing a bill that his successor presented to the Chamber of Deputies in 1921. That the German system of social insurance was already in full force in the newly acquired provinces of Alsace and Lorraine was a major determinant of the government's resolve to institute a system covering the entire country. The Chamber's welfare commission conducted a lengthy inquiry, and it was only in 1924 that a social insurance bill passed in the lower house. The bill went to the Senate, where further inquiries and debates delayed a vote until 1927. The bill the Senate approved went back to the Chamber with substantial revisions. The Chamber's welfare commission began new hearings but soon concluded that, after eight years of discussion, the time for action had come; it therefore recommended acceptance of the Senate's version. On the understanding that corrective legislation could be introduced in the next legislature, the Chamber on March 14, 1928, accepted the bill, 477 to 2.[62]

The law, designed primarily for industrial and agricultural workers,

60. Bastié, *La Croissance*, 298–99.

61. *Ibid.*, 300; Evenson, *Paris*, 218–19, 232.

62. Bonnefous and Bonnefous, *Histoire politique*, IV, 246–47; Paul H. Douglas, "The French Social Insurance Act," *Annals of the American Academy*, CLXIV (1932),

provided insurance benefits for retirement, sickness, and incapacity, with supplemental benefits for maternity and death. According to its terms, coverage was mandatory for workers earning less than a specified salary, with employers and employees each making contributions of 5 percent of a worker's pay to a local insurance fund. Workers were to have the right to select their own fund and to participate in the direction of its affairs. The state's role was to be limited to general supervision; the system was to be decentralized and rely largely upon private initiative.[63]

Enthusiasm for the social-insurance legislation was far from unanimous. Agricultural groups contended that it placed too heavy a financial burden on the farming community. Many industrialists were unhappy with the increased costs they faced. Medical doctors objected to what they claimed was state interference with their profession. Even the Communist party opposed the legislation, because it required workers to contribute 5 percent of their wages. It was in an atmosphere of bitter controversy that Loucheur became responsible for the law's fate.[64]

Since the law was not scheduled for full implementation until February 5, 1930, his immediate assignment was to put together the necessary administrative framework. In 1928, his principal concern was readying the law's public administrative regulations. With what some considered an impossible deadline of April, 1929, Loucheur persevered, and when the regulations were published on time, he unabashedly referred to the accomplishment as a "veritable tour de force."[65]

To facilitate oversight of the new social-insurance system, Loucheur in late 1928 announced plans to purchase sophisticated machinery for compiling statistics and classifying an anticipated twelve million in-

---

211–12; Rapport fait au nom de la Commission d'Assurance et de Prévoyance Sociales (Chambre), par Edouard Grinda, 1928, in Unclassified Documents, Une Loi de 1928 sur les assurances sociales, Carton 6, AN; *Le Temps,* March 16, 1928, pp. 1, 3; Henri Hatzfeld, *Du paupérisme à la sécurité sociale: Essai sur les origines de la sécurité sociale en France, 1850–1940* (Paris, 1971), 146–47.

63. Rapport fait au nom de la Commission d'Assurance et de Prévoyance Sociales (Chambre), par Edouard Grinda, 1928, in Unclassified Documents, Une Loi de 1928 sur les assurances sociales, 6, AN; Ministère du Travail et de l'Hygiène, *Bulletin du Ministère du Travail et de l'Hygiène,* XXXV (January–March, 1928), 78–80.

64. Bonnefous and Bonnefous, *Histoire politique,* IV, 246–47.

65. Minutes, Commission de l'Agriculture et Commission d'Assurance et de Prévoyance Sociales réunies (Chambre), May 30, 1929, in XIVe Législature A-10, AANV.

formation cards. He also announced plans to construct a new building for the ministry of labor. The ministry's social-insurance offices were to be in the new structure, and space was to be added later to house other departments of the ministry then scattered in eight buildings. In disclosing his plans, he told the Chamber's welfare commission, "The physical organization [of the social-insurance program] must be very good. I attach great importance to the provision of offices. That the French administration sometimes uses former kitchens and bathrooms is one of the reasons the departments of ministries do not always function very well. I am going to try to change methods; I want the organization to be excellent from a physical point of view."[66] Through modern technology, much of the social-insurance complex, whose construction began in the spring of 1929, was finished by the end of the year.[67]

But Loucheur's most difficult task in the months prior to the scheduled date for applying the law was dealing with its critics. Loucheur, agreeing that the agricultural interests were in large part justified in their objections, introduced modifying legislation in March, 1929, to ease the law's effects on them. He also made a concession to French industrialists in the same bill by including a clause granting them equal representation with workers on the boards of directors of insurance funds that the workers themselves set up. The law of 1928, by contrast, had guaranteed workers the right to elect all the board members and to hold a majority of the seats. Loucheur's bill failed to restore calm, however; instead, it became a new issue in the debate, which only heightened. The CGT protested Loucheur's proposed change in the composition of administrative boards, and the labor movement in general campaigned vigorously against it during the spring. Loucheur's bill also produced a strong negative reaction among agriculturalists. One of their leaders used the occasion to condemn the law of 1928 generally, referring to it as a "kiss of death" for the national economy.[68]

As the spring progressed, Loucheur, under pressure from industrialists, began to feel reservations about applying in a single stroke that part

66. Minutes, Commission d'Assurance et de Prévoyance Sociales (Chambre), November 30, 1928, *ibid.*

67. *Le Progrès du Nord,* November 20, 1929, p. 1; *Le Temps,* December 15, 1929, p. 1.

68. The man (named de Vogue) who used the phrase was president of the Société et Union Centrale des Syndicats des Agriculteurs de France. See France, *Annales de la Chambre: Documents* (1930), Rapport par Edouard Grinda et Etienne Antonelli, Annex No. 3187, April 9, 1930, pp. 516, 550.

of the law mandating a combined employer and employee insurance contribution of 10 percent of a worker's salary. By the end of May, he was talking about how a sudden increase in costs would temporarily harm France's export industries and cause even more difficulty for agriculture, and shortly after that he stated his intention to introduce a bill reducing the law's financial burden on agriculture. On June 20, he announced that the legislation he was framing "would contain a clause by which industries only progressively became subject to the expenses of the law."[69] Thus, in July he sent the Senate a new modifying bill, which became a focal point for parliamentary and public discussion during the fall and winter of 1929–1930. At first, Loucheur's bill was "left blank"; only in September were its details filled in. Because of labor's sharp objections to equal representation for industrialists on the governing boards of the insurance funds, Loucheur dropped that idea. On the other hand, the new bill gave special attention to farmers. For agricultural employers, one of the most basic modifications of the law of 1928 was the bill's proposed reduction in the combined employer and employee contribution to 2 percent of salary. To offset the reduction in private contributions, the legislation called for a scaling back of insurance coverage— only the retirement program was to be mandatory—and for financial infusions from the government. To help industry, the bill proposed moving toward the combined employer and employee contribution of 10 percent in stages, with 6 percent required the first year, 8 percent the second, and 10 percent the third.[70] But in early December, Loucheur responded to pressure by introducing amendments that altered the financial arrangements yet again. He replaced the three-stage phasing-in of employer and employee contributions in industry and commerce with an average single rate of 8 percent, and he also increased the state's financial obligation to the agricultural program.

In the Senate, Loucheur's bill and amendments went to the commission on public health and welfare, whose members wove together a modifying text of their own. Their bill, announced on December 27, accepted an 8-percent contribution rate for industry and commerce until 1935. But for the special agricultural program, they went well beyond

69. France, *Annales de la Chambre: Documents* (1930), Rapport par Edouard Grinda et Etienne Antonelli, Annex No. 3187 April 9, 1930, p. 551.

70. *Ibid.*, 552; Newspaper Clipping from *L'Ami du peuple*, December 12, 1929, in F 7, 13939, AN.

Loucheur and reintroduced the principle of obligatory sickness insurance, with the state assuming a considerable share of the increased costs. It was projected that the state's supplemental costs for the agricultural system would be 674 million francs per year.[71]

Opponents of the act of 1928 attacked parts of the modifying legislation as being either unacceptable or inadequate. *Le Temps*, a leading voice of the opposition, published almost daily articles to undermine public confidence in the law, and in early January, 1930, remarked that in the wake of the multiple proposals for modification, the law had lost "all moral authority."[72] Organizations representing industry, agriculture, and medicine added to the growing confusion and discontent by demanding fundamental changes in the modifying bill and in some cases continuing to question the soundness of the act of 1928 itself.

The controversy reached a climax during January and February. In spite of giving repeated assurances that full implementation of the law would begin as scheduled—on February 5, 1930—Loucheur knew at New Year's that the deadline was impossible to meet. In mid-January, he modified his pledge to say that the law would be "effectively applied" on that date and that full application would occur as soon as the registration of participants had been completed.[73] His announcement was unsettling to proponents and opponents alike of the legislation. Foes launched a new flurry of maneuvers to bring about the demise of the law. *Le Temps* called it the "crazy law" and used such terms as *mess* and *jumble* in describing the state in which parliament had left it.[74] In parliament, Loucheur's decision generated a storm of protests culminating in a call on January 23 for an interpellation of the government on the law. Loucheur, who responded for the government, reproached opponents for unleashing a "fiery campaign, terrifying the public," and accused some of the critics of hyprocrisy, saying that they were people "who begin by claiming to be partisans of the law but who at the same time are each day trying to destroy it." But he also affirmed

71. France, *Annales de la Chambre: Documents* (1930), Rapport par Edouard Grinda et Etienne Antonelli, Annex No. 3187, April 9, 1930, pp. 551–52; *Le Temps*, September 7, 1929, p. 3, November 7, 1929, p. 1, November 9, 1929, p. 1, December 6, 1929, p. 4, December 28, 1929, p. 5, December 29, 1929, p. 1.
72. *Le Temps*, January 8, 1930, p. 1.
73. *Ibid.*, January 13, 1930, p. 1.
74. *Ibid.*, February 8, 1930, p. 1.

the government's readiness to have a full-scale debate, which was set for early February.[75]

Adding to Loucheur's problems in the new year was a debate over the financial provisions in the modifying bill. In a letter on January 15, the minister of finance, Henry Chéron, joined by Loucheur, criticized the financial arrangements for agriculture in the text of the bill the Senate's commission on public health and welfare had framed. The two ministers complained that the commission's amendments, besides raising the contribution of the state onerously, profoundly modified the character of the original law by committing the state to an annual supplementary infusion for agricultural workers that was not permanently fixed. As a result, they warned, the bill's revised text increased budget expenditures and aroused fears of "even heavier costs in the future."[76]

On January 24, Chéron, whom Loucheur privately described as a "nervous person of unequaled touchiness," appeared before the Senate's finance commission to pursue the matter.[77] Reiterating the government's acceptance only of fixed total infusions for the insurance funds, he disclosed that the state would provide 540 million francs for the general program and a supplementary 275 million francs for the agricultural program. The commission members had no objection to Chéron's first figure, which they had examined and accepted in Loucheur's bill, but they were skeptical about the supplement for the agricultural program: the amount Chéron mentioned was far less than the 674 million francs the proposal from the Senate's commission on public health and welfare projected as the state's contribution. Chéron answered that the text of the bill should conform to the state's budgetary capability, and not budgetary demands on the government to a text that neglected to set limits.[78] It appeared that the divergence between Chéron's position and the finance commission's would cause new delays. But the very next day Paul Doumer, the president of the Senate, convened a conference at the Luxembourg Palace to close the gap. In attendance were four government ministers, including Loucheur and Chéron, as well as the chair-

75. France, *Annales de la Chambre: Débats,* January 23, 1930, pp. 103–106.

76. France, *Annales de la Chambre: Documents* (1930), Rapport par Edouard Grinda et Etienne Antonelli, Annex No. 3187, April 9, 1930, p. 552.

77. Louis Loucheur to Simone Loucheur, August 22, 1929, in Simone Loucheur Papers, in family possession, Paris.

78. *Le Temps,* January 27, 1930, p. 1; Newspaper Clipping from *Le Matin,* January 25, 1930, in F 7, 13939, AN.

men and reporters of seven of the Senate's commissions concerned with the bill. Chéron defended the position he had taken the preceding day, only to find Loucheur pressuring him to bend. An irritated Chéron eventually agreed to raise the government's allocation to the agricultural insurance plan by twenty-five to thirty-five million francs. By the end of the conference that day, the participants were in general harmony on a revised text that was in line with the financial prudence of Chéron.[79]

It was reported in the press that the finance minister was so incensed at the conduct of his ministerial colleague Loucheur that he offered his resignation to André Tardieu, then the premier. According to the reports, Tardieu not only resisted the offer but called Loucheur to London for discussions.[80] What the two men said is unknown, but Loucheur pronounced his full support for Chéron's stand on the finances of the insurance law after he returned to Paris.

The full-scale debate in the Chamber that the government had accepted took place on February 7. Tardieu's return from a naval conference in London underscored the gravity of the occasion. The debate, which lasted until 3:30 in the morning, began with two interpellations: Gustave Guérin, a member of the conservative Union Républicaine Démocratique, contended that the government had acted illegally in proceeding with the enrollment of workers while a revised text for the law was still under consideration. The Socialist Paul Ramadier rebuked the government for not implementing the program fully on February 5, as the law of 1928 required. Loucheur responded for the government that worker registration was the "normal and regular beginning" of the law's application and that it was a "considerable step forward." He countered opponents' predictions that the law would increase the chance of moral decay, create an extremely complicated administrative apparatus, cause deep economic damage, and beget an imbroglio of unsound finances. But the decisive statement of the day came from Tardieu, who vowed that all the remaining steps toward the system's full effectuation, including the vote of a definitive version of the law and the registration of

79. Newspaper Clipping from *Le Matin*, January 26, 1930, in F 7, 13939, AN; *Le Temps*, January 26, 1930, p. 8, January 27, 1930, pp. 1, 3, January 28, 1930, p. 4, January 29, 1930, p. 1, January 31, 1930, p. 3.

80. Newspaper Clipping from *La Victoire*, January 29, 1930, in F 7, 13939, AN; Newspaper Account in *L'Indépendant* (Perpignan), January 29, 1930, *ibid*. The text of the newspaper article was sent to Paris by Charles Emmanuel Brousse.

workers, would be completed by July 1. The government prevailed, 315 to 257.[81]

The Chamber debate was Loucheur's final action of consequence on social insurance as labor minister. The Tardieu government collapsed over another matter on February 17. Loucheur remained at his post in a government that the Radical-Socialist Camille Chautemps headed from February 21 to February 25, but when Tardieu formed a new government in early March, he replaced Loucheur with Pierre Laval. The new cabinet, by abandoning the policy of fixed subsidies for the social-insurance system and accepting state financial participation without any antecedent setting of a maximum, assured rapid passage of the modifying legislation in parliament. The relevant Senate commissions had completed their work by then, and the measure was before the full Senate for deliberation. By the end of April, both the Senate and the Chamber had accepted a definitive text.[82]

In final form, the social-insurance law of 1928–1930 put the initial combined employer and employee contribution rate in industry and commerce at 8 percent rather than 10 percent. It included a system for agriculture with a combined contribution rate of 2 percent; to help underwrite the agricultural program's costs, the government consented to provide large subsidies. The government also assumed the burden of subsidizing the costs of participant incapacity in the program's first years. In contrast to all earlier drafts of the legislation, which had embodied the principle of considerable autonomy for the system, that of 1930 gave the ministry of labor administrative control over it.[83]

Although Laval, not Loucheur, presided over the full implementation of the system in the summer of 1930, it was Loucheur who conducted the negotiations that reconciled discontented groups to a revision of the law of 1928, who developed the administrative apparatus needed to supervise the law, and who defended the law most vigorously when a sustained assault was launched against it. Loucheur's role was prominent enough that some of his contemporaries attributed the law's paternity to him. That notion later found its way into some historical

81. France, *Annales de la Chambre: Débats*, February 7, 1930, pp. 460–96.

82. Bonnefous and Bonnefous, *Histoire politique*, V, 14–16; France, *Annales de la Chambre: Documents* (1930), Rapport par Edouard Grinda et Etienne Antonelli, Annex No. 3187, April 9, 1930, p. 553; Hatzfeld, *Du paupérisme*, 150–53; *Le Progrès du Nord*, March 23, 1930, p. 1; *Le Temps*, March 7, 1930, p. 1, March 24, 1930, p. 1, May 2, 1930, p. 4.

83. Douglas, "The French Social Insurance Act," 220.

literature, but Loucheur denied the bloodline.[84] Still, his name is as closely associated with the law as that of anyone.

LABOR DISPUTES

Shortly after Loucheur's arrival at the ministry of labor, a series of strikes made him anxious to prevent other management-labor confrontations from degenerating into strikes, and if strikes occurred, to minimize their length. But he discovered that the means available to the ministry for dealing with labor disputes were limited. Loucheur had no authority to impose arbitration on the parties to a conflict, nor did he have a license to require the two sides to engage in direct talks. What the minister could do was monitor the confrontation through government instrumentalities and, when no negotiations were under way, offer the services of his office to bring the two sides into contact. If one of the parties rejected his offer, however, he had no direct way of combating the resistance. He could bring the weight of the government to bear more dramatically, as through the intervention of the premier's office, but that was the exception rather than the rule.

Loucheur did influence the outcome of a conflict that developed in 1928 in the textile industry of the Nord. The three major labor unions in the area—the conservative Confédération Française des Travailleurs Chrétiens (CFTC), the Socialists' Confédération Générale du Travail (CGT), and the Communists' Confédération Générale du Travail Unitaire (CGTU)—fought for a wage increase from textile manufacturers by invoking the report, in May, of a government-established cost-of-living commission for the Nord. The commission's findings showed the cost of living to have risen 5.7 percent above what it had been in October,

84. Jacques de Launay, as editor of Loucheur's *Carnets secrets*, leaves the impression that the 1928 law came from Loucheur. He refers to it as a *loi Loucheur* and affirms that it was Loucheur who secured final passage of it in the spring of 1928. But the 1928 measure cannot legitimately be called a *loi Loucheur*, and Loucheur was not the key person behind its passage in the Chamber of Deputies in 1928. Fred Kupferman, in his biography of Pierre Laval, carries de Launay's theme to the point of calling Loucheur the father of the law. For Loucheur's remarks regarding the paternity of the law, see Minutes, Commission de l'Agriculture et Commission d'Assurance et de Prévoyance Sociales réunies (Chambre), May 30, 1929, in XIVe Législature A-10, AANV. See de Launay's comments in Loucheur's *Carnets secrets*, 146–48; and see Fred Kupferman, *Pierre Laval* (Paris, 1987), 71.

1927, the time of the previous report. The cost-of-living commission, comprising owners, workers, and bureaucrats, was one of many the government had formed in 1920 to operate regionally. The commissions' estimates were dubious, however, in part because the conflicting motives of the labor representatives and the owners led each to defend figures that served their own pocketbooks better than they did accuracy. The commissions also employed haphazard methods of calculation in reaching their conclusions.[85] In the fall of 1928, even Loucheur admitted that the commissions' results were "so contradictory that they were absolutely absurd" and "prejudicial to the workers."[86] It is not surprising that the textile workers' appeal to a commission's report to justify a wage increase led to a showdown.

The textile plant owners of the Nord, organized into a powerful association generally referred to as the Consortium, responded through the Consortium's chief administrator, Désiré Ley. Ley, whose contempt for labor unions was well known in the region, bluntly repulsed the unions' demand, arguing that a Consortium study showed the commission's cost-of-living figure to be grossly exaggerated. During the summer of 1928, Ley's hostility reached such a pitch that he gave notice that he would no longer receive representatives from the CGT, the one union that still had access to him. While the CGTU threatened a general strike and began planning its launch, the CGT took its case to Loucheur. At the union's behest, Loucheur approached the Consortium, which sent two representatives—one of them Ley—to meet with him on August 30. Citing a law of 1884 that recognized the right of labor to organize, as well as the government's general policy of support for direct contact between the two sides in a labor dispute, Loucheur importuned the Consortium to grant the CGT leaders of the Nord an interview. In a following letter, Loucheur even proposed the labor ministry as the site for the meeting. Ley's response on behalf of the Consortium was emphatic refusal.[87]

The labor troubles intensified. At the forefront of the agitation was the CGTU, which on September 20 proclaimed a general strike in Halluin, a city where the union had considerable strength. In the ensuing

---

85. Sauvy and Hirsch, *Histoire économique*, II, 183–85.

86. Angel Marvaud, "Le Conflit du textile dans le Nord," *Le Musée social*, March, 1929, pp. 81–87, in Subseries F 22, Ministère du Travail, Carton 191, AN. The quotation from Loucheur is on p. 86.

87. Report Entitled "La Grève d'Halluin," with Attached Note (indicating that the report goes to January 1, 1929), Ministère de l'Intérieur, in F 7, 13917, AN.

days the strike spread to other cities, and by the end of the month approximately 30,000 workers out of a textile force of 200,000 were involved.[88] Ley predicted that "the workers would return to the factories on their knees."[89]

Neither the CGT nor the CFTC joined the Communist union's strike; instead they concentrated on reestablishing direct communication with the Consortium. Leaders in both unions warned Loucheur and Premier Poincaré about the growing crisis and pleaded for government intervention.[90] Loucheur met with another CGT delegation on September 22 and afterward informed Ley that the CGT disclaimed responsibility for articles in the press the Consortium's administrator had used to justify his refusal to enter into unmediated contact with the union. At the same time, the labor minister was working behind the scenes to arrange a meeting between Poincaré and a delegation of industrialists from the Nord that excluded Ley. Fearing that Poincaré might offer to arbitrate the dispute, thereby putting the factory owners in an extremely awkward position whether or not they assented to the offer, Ley in early October agreed to meet with union leaders not only from the CGT but also from the CFTC. But he decreed that under no circumstances would he examine the question of a wage increase with them. The reestablishment of direct relations was enough to defuse the crisis, and by the latter part of October factory operations had returned to normal virtually everywhere in the Nord.[91] Loucheur's tactics brought the two sides together, but his success came only after the crisis was almost out of hand and had drawn the premier himself close to the fray.

Several bills about binding procedures to settle labor disputes had failed to make it through parliament before, but Ley's intransigence

88. Marvaud, "Le Conflit du textile dans le Nord," 81–83, in F 22, 191, AN.

89. Report Entitled "La Grève d'Halluin," with Attached Note, Ministère de l'Intérieur, in F 7, 13917, AN.

90. Louis Blain to Louis Loucheur, October 4, 1928, in Series M 619, Grèves 1886–1939, Carton 79A, ADN. Blain was the general secretary of the CFTU.

91. Fernand Motte to Louis Loucheur, September 26, 1928, in F 22, 191, AN; prefect of the Nord to Loucheur, September 26, 1928, in F 7, 13917, AN; Commission Intersyndicale de l'Industrie Textile de Roubaix-Tourcoing, Circular No. 288, from Désiré Ley, September 28, 1928, in F 22, 191, AN; "Téléphone par M. Hudelo," October 4, 1928, in F 22, 191, AN; Désiré Ley to the prefect of the Nord, October 8, 1928, in F 7, 13917, AN; Louis Blain to Louis Loucheur, October 15, 1928, in F 22, 191, AN; Report Entitled "La Grève d'Halluin," with Attached Note, Ministère de l'Intérieur, in F 7, 13917, AN.

dramatized the need for action. Socialist deputies and leaders of both the CGT and the CFTC exploited the occasion to press for such legislation. At the beginning of October, Jouhaux reported to the national committee of the CGT that, at his urging, Loucheur had made a commitment to introduce a bill by the terms of which "the owners would be obligated to enter into relations with workers' organizations."[92]

Loucheur saw the bill that he presented in January, 1929, as an extension of the law of 1884 legalizing labor organizations. According to Loucheur's proposal, if a labor dispute arose and no work stoppage had taken place, either party could require the other to grant an interview. If no agreement resulted, the labor minister or the appropriate prefect could step in and compel the two sides to meet again. If strikes or lockouts ensued, the labor minister, the prefect, or either of the disputing parties could insist on yet another round of conversations. Throughout the process, the disputants could have representatives from labor organizations or employer groups present to assist them if they chose. The bill said nothing of binding arbitration. Overall, it was similar to a proposal the CGT had advanced in its publication *L'Atelier* in November, 1928.[93]

In Loucheur's campaign in behalf of the legislation, his general argument, such as before the Chamber's commission on commerce and industry in March, rested on the way striking workers had previously returned to their jobs as soon as owners and labor representatives had come together in face-to-face discussions. The problem, as Loucheur saw it, was in propelling the parties to that point, since the minister of labor lacked the authority to do much: "The labor minister, responsible for assuring labor peace in this country, is currently without any means of action. The industrialist to whom I appeal can tell me, after listening to me, 'I'm sorry, I don't agree with you.' And he leaves." Loucheur contended that had a law of "obligatory conversation" been in place during France's rash of walkouts, "we would not have had the strikes we have experienced."[94]

The bill provoked considerable opposition. Conservative opponents groused that the legislation was aimed primarily at owners, "as if the

---

92. Marcel Tardy, "Le Règlement amiable des conflits collectifs du travail," *Revue politique et parlementaire,* CXXXVIII (1929), 435–43.

93. *Ibid.*, 425–26; France, *Annales de la Chambre: Débats,* January 22, 1929, p. 140.

94. Minutes, Commission du Commerce et de l'Industrie (Chambre), March 20, 1929, in XIVe Législature, Carton A-34, Commission du Commerce et de l'Industrie, Procès-verbaux, AANV.

danger came from their side and not from the labor side." They worried about the legitimacy the Communists' CGTU would gain if owners had to deal with it. In February, Le Temps claimed that Loucheur's legislation entailed binding arbitration and questioned the wisdom of that at a time when, in its view, the approach was failing in other countries.[95] The Communists, too, argued against the bill. During the debate in the Chamber of Deputies in June, the Communist spokesman described it as contrary to the interests of the working class because it effectively deprived workers of their power to strike; furthermore, the Communists believed that it would lead to a system of binding arbitration and resisted putting the fate of workers in the hands of agents representing owners and a bourgeois government.[96]

Nevertheless, there was overwhelming support for Loucheur's bill in the Chamber of Deputies, provided that it was slightly amended. Loucheur's main concern was to obtain passage without amendments that might turn the workers against the legislation. One proposed amendment would have required the party with a labor grievance to meet with the other side before any work stoppage could take place. When Loucheur warned that the stipulation infringed upon the workers' right to strike and would "raise up the entire working class against the law," its sponsors withdrew it. Another amendment would have barred representatives of labor unions from being present at the initial meeting between workers and their employer over a dispute. Loucheur pointed out that the bill already specified that union officials could attend the first meeting only if the workers in the dispute formally requested their presence. He added that "when the workers formally request the presence of men who can defend them and enlighten them, who are the heads of their professional organizations, we should give them this satisfaction." Allowing workers that option at the very outset of the conciliation process was, in Loucheur's words, a "question of justice." Again the labor minister obtained an amendment's withdrawal without a vote. On June 25, the Chamber, including the Socialists, passed the bill by a vote of 575 to 12.[97]

The bill lingered in the Senate for several years. Not until March,

95. Tardy, "Le Règlement," Revue politique et parlementaire, CXXXVIII (1929), 429, 444–45; Le Temps, February 20, 1929, p. 1.

96. France, Annales de la Chambre: Débats, June 18, 1929, pp. 349–56.

97. Ibid., June 21, 1929, pp. 369–70, 376–79, 424–29, 435.

1935, did the Senate pass a modified version, but even after that the measure did not become law. In the wake of the electoral victory of the Popular Front in 1936, it was overtaken by an effort to devise legislation for the conciliation and arbitration of disputes. The result was the Law of December 31, 1936, which went beyond Loucheur's bill by requiring mandatory arbitration when other prescribed procedures failed.[98]

Seeing the state's commitment to social reform as insufficient, the Left had in January, 1929, launched an interpellation of the government's social and economic policy. One speaker accused the government of "skimpy deeds" in social legislation. Responding for the government, Loucheur presented an overview of how governments of the Third Republic had acted to improve workers' conditions, and he cited his government's efforts to move forward. At one point Loucheur, reviving an idea found in his railroad bill of 1920 (see above, p. 207), suggested the issuance of union-held "labor shares" as a way for workers to participate in profits: "When through the application of the dividends that will be assigned to [labor shares], they can become capital shares, you will have achieved, as in the question of small peasant property, worker ownership of industrial property itself." But the minister warned that changes like that could be attained only "step by step. Those who want to go too fast are certain to fail." Loucheur's set of proposed reforms failed to win the support of Radicals, Socialists, and Communists, who opposed the government in a vote of confidence at the end of the debate. The government won, however, 327 to 262.[99]

In February, 1930, during deliberations on social insurance, the Socialist Léon Blum exhibited the leftist opposition's dominant attitude when he remarked that a government that could find money for the defense of France's frontiers should also be able to finance social needs. At the conclusion of this debate, too, the same three parties of the Left opposed the government in a vote of confidence.[100] The leftist opposition arose partly from simple politics but also from Loucheur's adherence to middle-of-the-road solutions to social and economic problems. However zealous he was about providing workers with benefits, he believed in moderate, steady

98. Paul Pic, "De l'accord de Matignon à la loi du 31 décembre 1936 sur l'arbitrage obligatoire," *Revue politique et parlementaire*, CLXXI (1937), 446–74; Bonnefous and Bonnefous, *Histoire politique*, VI, 84–86.

99. Bonnefous and Bonnefous, *Histoire politique*, IV, 319–22; France, *Annales de la Chambre: Débats*, January 22, 1929, pp. 135–40.

100. Bonnefous and Bonnefous, *Histoire politique*, V, 7–10.

doses, since his interest was in adjusting, not overwhelming, France's socioeconomic system. One of his goals was to absorb workers more completely into the existing economic system and thereby reduce the likelihood of social upheaval. But he also believed that his measures would occasion a more economically productive society. His general approach to workers was similar to that favored in the 1920s by other neo-Saint-Simonians, including active followers of the Comte de Saint-Simon and modernizers like Ernest Mercier.[101] They advocated high wages for workers and encouraged employers and employees to act collectively in a capitalist system that emphasized production. They also, despite a diversity of views, in the main sought to give workers a greater stake in private enterprise through devices like profit sharing and called on the state to play a more positive role economically.[102]

REPARATIONS, ECONOMIC DEPRESSION, AND LOUCHEUR'S DEATH

Domestic considerations were at the heart of Loucheur's work at the labor ministry, but he did reemerge as a negotiator on reparations in 1929 and 1930 at two international conferences at The Hague. Enlisted by Briand, the foreign minister, he in August, 1929, attended the first Hague conference, where his chief contributions bore on payments in kind. At this round of meetings the British attacked the Young Plan, which was intended to replace the Dawes Plan, in force from 1924. Formulated by a committee of experts appointed in early 1929, the new plan reduced considerably the amount Germany would pay in reparations, but it also gave France advantages in the distribution of payments. Philip Snowden, the British chancellor of the exchequer, heaped ridicule on the proposal at the conference, laying claim to a larger share of Germany's payments for Britain. The British also objected to the plan's openness to payments in kind, for they held that reparations shipments from Germany had adversely affected Britain's economy, particularly its coal exports. The British representative on payments in kind professed fright at what he viewed as the plan's still-substantial figures in that regard. Loucheur contended that German payments in kind had little impact on the British economy, and he dwelled on the prejudice a marked reduction in

101. On neo-Saint-Simonianism, see above, p. 244.
102. Kuisel, *Ernest Mercier*, 69–70.

such payments would cause countries dependent on them.[103] But Snowden's relentlessness almost brought the conference to rupture. Loucheur bitterly predicted in a letter to his daughter that "the stupid stubbornness of this man from Yorkshire will in the end give him fewer results than a negotiation conducted in confidence and with courtesy."[104] In a session that began at 5 P.M. on August 27 and lasted late into the night, Briand made enough minor concessions to Snowden to satisfy the British on reparations, and the conference ended with Germany, France, and Britain signing a final protocol that included acceptance in principle of the modified Young Plan.[105]

Loucheur was also part of the French delegation that went to The Hague in January, 1930, to work out the details of the understandings reached in August. Loucheur's primary role there was as chairman of some difficult negotiations over reparations concerning Hungary, on the one hand, and Romania, Czechoslovakia, and Yugoslavia, on the other. Hungarian magnates were claiming compensation, under the terms of their defeated country's 1920 peace treaty, for lands lost after the war to agrarian reform in Romania, Czechoslovakia, and Yugoslavia.[106] These nations argued that the treaty article in question did not apply to lands taken for agrarian reform. Though a special committee organized at the first Hague conference had worked on the disagreement until the end of December, 1929, it failed to break the deadlock. After several weeks of painstaking talks once Loucheur entered the negotiations, the squabbling states agreed to the Accords of Paris of April 28, 1930. Loucheur had managed to put together a compromise the central feature of which was an autonomous "agrarian fund." Money from several sources, including France, Italy, and Britain, was to be used to settle with Hungarians who had had foreign real estate expropriated. After the resolution of that issue, the states of central Europe were willing to assent to the Young Plan.[107]

103. *Le Progrès du Nord*, August 16, 1929, pp. 1–2.

104. Louis Loucheur to Simone Loucheur, August 28, 1929, in Simone Loucheur Papers.

105. Weill-Raynal, *Les Réparations allemandes*, III, 489–523, 874–76; Vincent Pitts, *France and the German Problem: Politics and Economics in the Locarno Period* (New York, 1987), 328–32.

106. Hungary signed the harsh Treaty of Trianon with the Allies on June 4, 1920. See Sontag, *A Broken World*, 9–10, 62.

107. Weill-Raynal, *Les Réparations allemandes*, III, 572–86; France, *Annales de la Chambre: Débats*, March 24, 1931, pp. 2011–14.

The conference at The Hague in 1930 was the setting for Loucheur's last active participation in reparations negotiations, but he remained an interested observer upon them and upon negotiations about the related problem of inter-Allied debts through the closing months of his life. In his final public analysis of the situation, in late September, 1931, he contested Germany's allegation that "tribute" to France was responsible for the German economic and financial crisis. Loucheur placed most of the blame for Germany's financial collapse during the summer on its attempt earlier in the year to form a customs union with Austria. He also criticized America, for insisting on payment of the inter-Allied debt while levying high tariffs during the 1920s. Because European states had found it exceedingly difficult to make payments in kind to discharge their debts to the United States, the chief results were the accumulation of gold in America and the impoverishment of Europe. Loucheur was unimpressed by the United States' one-year moratorium on foreign debts, including reparations and inter-Allied payments, announced by President Herbert Hoover in July, 1931: "Today, at the initiative of the United States, Germany benefits from a moratorium; but will it be able to pay more easily in six months than today? For that, it would have to discover gold mines in the Rhineland."[108] The generally optimistic Loucheur's pronouncements were unusually bleak. He was aware that the policies he had helped forge more than a decade before had collapsed.

France's economy, too, was in jeopardy in 1930 and 1931. Alarmed at how rapidly the economies of other countries were deteriorating, the French looked to blunt the effects of the Great Depression at home. In December, 1930, Loucheur accepted the post of minister of the national economy, commerce, and industry in a government that the senator Théodore Steeg formed. Loucheur's jurisdiction, which combined the ministry of commerce with a just-budding undersecretariat for the formulation of national economic policy, was a halfway house on the way to what Loucheur hoped would be a powerful national economics ministry controlling general economic policy and administering the departments of commerce, agriculture, and public works.[109] That ministry

108. Louis Loucheur, *La Situation économique en Europe: Discours prononcé par M. Loucheur, à Pavilly, le 23 septembre 1931* (Paris, n.d.), 1–6.
109. Joseph Avenol to Louis Loucheur, December 16, 1930, in Series Papiers d'Agents, Joseph Avenol Papers, Vol. 36, MAE; Loucheur, *Carnets secrets*, 170; Bonnefous and Bonnefous, *Histoire politique*, V, 49–60.

never came to be, however, and even the more modest scheme of enhanced responsibilities for the ministry of commerce did not outlast the Steeg government, which fell in the latter part of January, 1931.

Loucheur had little time to do much as minister of the national economy, but he did join other ministers in seeking passage of a portion of a "national retooling" plan that Tardieu had introduced a year earlier as the centerpiece of his government's "prosperity policy." The plan, which was little more than a typical public-works program, had encountered stiff resistance in parliament and was still being discussed in the Chamber when the Tardieu government was overturned in early December. Loucheur and his colleagues succeeded in obtaining passage of their bill in the Chamber just a few days before the Steeg government collapsed.[110]

In the summer of 1931, as the depression began to take hold in France, Loucheur and a number of other deputies presented a resolution to the Chamber calling on the government to move expeditiously to see the entire national retooling scheme enacted. Because of the rising concern of many politicians regarding France's crumbling economic situation, most of the appropriations that Tardieu had sought in 1929 received legislative approval before 1931 was over. By 1931, however, the thrust of the program was no longer to renovate the economy but to limit unemployment.[111]

Aptly, Loucheur's address on the economic situation in September, 1931, had the curbing of unemployment as a central theme. He envisioned an active role for the state in the effort but made clear that he opposed public ownership. He called for the signing of conventions with other European nations to regulate working hours in major industries and thus keep production and consumption in balance. He warned against raising customs duties, since that would elicit retaliation from other countries. Rather, he suggested import quotas in industries that needed them—such as textiles, a recent devaluation of the pound having made that industry more vulnerable to competition from across the Channel. He also urged parliament to act swiftly on the national retooling plan to modernize France's economic infrastructure.[112]

Loucheur believed that government interventionism was needed

110. Projet de loi, texte adopté par la Chambre des Députés, January 17, 1931, in B, 34024, MF; France, *Annales de la Chambre: Débats,* January 17, 1931, pp. 42–45.

111. France, *Journal officiel: Chambre des Députés, documents parlementaires* (1931), Proposition de résolution, Annex No. 5500, July 3, 1931, pp. 1248–49; Kuisel, *Capitalism and the State,* 90–92.

112. Loucheur, *La Situation économique,* 8–11.

for the recovery and was acceptable as long as the state acted within a basically liberal framework. Yet his remedies had a defensive cast, to protect home markets and preserve jobs. And in the end, import quotas and cartelization turned out to prolong France's economic stagnation. Loucheur was ready to bestow upon the state an enlarged role in coordinating and overseeing the economy by outfitting a powerful national economics ministry. Such a ministry might have proved effective in the economic crisis, but the possibility was not pursued. The governments of the early 1930s, working through traditional ministerial channels, put together poorly conceived and piecemeal efforts that lacked consistency and imagination.[113]

In June, 1931, Loucheur learned he had a serious heart condition. His physician instructed him to limit his activities, and his daughter Simone tried to persuade him to resign his seat in the Chamber of Deputies and consider running for a seat in the Senate. His answer was an emphatic no. He used part of the summer to rest, but in September he told his daughter that he could not retire from his heavy schedule, "for you know that without [work], I would be depressed."[114] Loucheur's daughter has described her father as caught in the "battle of such an energetic nature against a heart that could no longer stand the strain."[115] Against the advice of his physician and family, he traveled to Copenhagen with several agriculturists in early November to observe new methods in dairy farming. In mid-November, relying on a promise from Edouard Herriot, he anticipated a seat on the Chamber's foreign-affairs commission, only to learn that Herriot had had himself put on the commission instead. That was a bitter blow for Loucheur, but politically the last he sustained. He suffered a massive stroke on November 18 and received extreme unction the same evening. Four days later, with his family at his side, he died peacefully at the age of fifty-nine.

Loucheur's funeral, which he himself had planned a month earlier, took place on November 26. It began in dreary weather with the celebration of mass at the small Parisian church of St. Pierre de Chaillot; the church overflowed with mourners. The ceremony ended in sunlight at

113. Kuisel, *Capitalism and the State*, 93–98; Wright, *France in Modern Times*, 364–66.

114. Louis Loucheur to Simone Loucheur, September 10, 1931, in Simone Loucheur Papers.

115. Simone Loucheur, "Histoire familiale," in Simone Loucheur Papers.

Montparnasse Cemetery, where Premier Laval joined the mourners for Loucheur's interment.[116]

Fernand Bouisson, president of the Chamber of Deputies, commented at Loucheur's death that whenever, during the 1920s, Loucheur entered a government, "it was, if time permitted him to do so, to undertake some major task."[117] This was certainly true at the ministry of labor, and Loucheur's sense of mission was also evident at the League of Nations, in his labors in behalf of European economic union. One post that Loucheur desired in the 1920s but never obtained was the premiership. He was frequently viewed as a strong contender, but there was a stumbling block in parliament's reluctance to entrust the premiership to a former industrialist with an engineering degree. No interwar premier had his sort of background. Most had studied law or the humanities. That Loucheur never led a government of his own attests to the political limitations of the Third Republic. Had he lived on in good health, it seems likely that he would have regained ministerial rank, with the depression as his "major task."[118]

116. *Ibid.*
117. Fernand Bouisson, "Eloge funèbre de M. Loucheur prononcé par M. Bouisson," in *Louis Loucheur,* without recorded editor (Les Moulineaux, n.d.), 12.
118. For comments—both laudatory and disparaging—about Loucheur and his political activities by his contemporaries, see Normand, *Politique et Hommes politiques,* I, 135–46; Hamp, "Louis Loucheur," 377–85; *Ceux qui nous mènent* (Paris, 1922), 213–22; Etienne Fournol, *Le Moderne Plutarque* (Paris, 1923), 177–204; Albert Inghels, *Le Panama des régions dévastées* (Paris, 1924), 7–12; and Léon Daudet, *Termites parlementaires* (Paris, 1930), 157–73.

CONCLUSION

The years of Louis Loucheur's public career were at the end of an era for
the Third Republic. When Loucheur entered the government, in 1916, the
republic was locked in a war of unprecedented dimensions that tested the
system to its limits. Once the Republic achieved victory in the Great
War, many of the French were anxious to return to what they considered
normal, recapturing prewar liberal values to the greatest extent possible.
Economically their desire realized itself in a rapid dismantling of wartime
government controls and a return to old business habits in many sectors.
The wisdom of restoring liberal ways seemed confirmed as France experienced steady industrial growth in the 1920s, reaching a production-level
index rating of 140 in 1929–1930, as compared with a base rating of 100 in
1913. In some circles, however, there was a strong feeling that France
needed economic and social modernizing. The neo-Saint-Simonians were
anxious to rationalize French industry, to make it more productive and
efficient. And the enthusiasm for modernization at the national level
spread to the international sphere in the mid- and late 1920s, with efforts
directed at European economic cooperation. But the Great Depression,
whose impact was felt in France in 1931—the year Loucheur died—
undermined the modernizers' efforts by evoking measures that generally
favored weak and inefficient producers.[1]

In the front ranks of the modernizers was Loucheur, an early French
technocrat. After succeeding as a private munitions manufacturer, he
was called into the government during the war, and he brought a set of

---

1. Wright, *France in Modern Times*, 357–58, 364–66; Kuisel, *Ernest Mercier*, 86–88;
Kuisel, *Capitalism and the State*, 93–98; Tom Kemp, *The French Economy, 1913–1939: The
History of a Decline* (London, 1972), 99–114.

technocratic values with him. As a government minister he established ambitious production programs, and to achieve them, he not only promoted mass production, a rationalized use of resources, a moderate approach toward labor, and careful quality control but he also took on increased ministerial responsibilities, believing that he could thereby administer more effectively. He recruited like-minded assistants but often experienced resistance from politicians and bureaucrats with priorities in conflict with his own. Misunderstandings and conflicts continued to the end of the war.

Though in general a supporter of economic liberalism, Loucheur was unhesitant about using the state to coordinate and oversee economic activities in which he thought it could assist, such as in the purchase and distribution of critical raw materials. His advocacy of state intervention on a large scale undoubtedly stemmed from the wartime emergency, but it was also a consequence of his pragmatism. He was willing, too, to see the state direct aspects of the international economy, as in the carefully organized system of inter-Allied economic cooperation he helped devise in response to the German campaign of submarine warfare.

Through his efforts at home and abroad, Loucheur made a decisive contribution to the Allied victory over the Central Powers in 1918. He proved that a technocratic businessman could marshal an economy for war production in exceedingly difficult circumstances. His wartime achievements gradually fell into obscurity, however, in part because he was preceded as armaments minister by Albert Thomas, whose contributions to munitions production have drawn more attention than his. Yet it was Loucheur who was the key organizer of France's war industry during the last two years of the conflict, especially after Thomas' departure in September, 1917. In many ways the years of Loucheur's service posed more serious problems of raw materials and armaments manufacture than those when Thomas was alone in charge.

At the end of the war, Loucheur, having seen rents in the French economic fabric, was impatient for economic renovation, but he was thwarted by those desiring a return to prewar patterns. Internationally, where he hoped for the continuation of Allied controls on raw materials, the wartime system of cooperation began to crumble. Loucheur, amenable to according private initiative preponderance in the postwar economy, embraced a policy that restricted the state's economic role. Two results of that were his dissolution of wartime consortiums for raw materials and his gradual loss of interest in converting state arsenals to civilian purposes. Still, he viewed the state as affording useful instruments for some of his postwar plans, especially in coal and metallurgy. For a strong postwar surge, he saw the desirability of obtaining plentiful supplies of coal from Germany, as reparations. He also hoped that by controlling coal prices he could stimulate iron and steel production and make France competitive in international markets. He appreciated the urgency of the task, since France, in acquiring the metallurgical potential of Lorraine, was suddenly to be thrust into second place worldwide in iron and steel output. In that connection, he used the might of the state to promote industrial ententes within the metallurgical industry and backed off only in early 1919, when he had to contend with resistance from small producers, sharp attacks within parliament, and a press campaign directed against him personally. Loucheur made special financial arrangements with steelmakers for the metal needed to develop France's merchant marine. He encouraged the establishment of producers' consortiums, or *groupements,* in the devastated regions, to help industrialists there reestablish themselves economically, though he left specific plans for renovation to the industrialists themselves. He called for state participation in the ownership of mines through a *régie intéressée,* a form of organization he employed again in 1920 when he introduced legislation to revitalize France's railroads.

Loucheur also tirelessly attempted to persuade the French to look anew at their economic culture. He emphasized efficiency before the Chamber of Deputies in February, 1919, and during the election campaign of 1919 he urged a receptivity to bold economic ideas. Loucheur's quest was for a production-oriented society operating within the framework of a dynamic French economy. His drive toward modernization acquired a political dimension in 1919. At the personal level was his decision to run for a seat in the Chamber of Deputies, since by the fall of 1919 it was apparent that he could not continue as a government minister without the political sanction of the voters. Loucheur may have hoped that other modernizers would follow his example of standing for office. At least *La Journée industrielle* hinted at that in 1919 when it commended the election of industrial figures capable of tapping France's economic potential effectively. But Loucheur himself never mounted a systematic campaign to transform the composition of the French parliament toward technical expertise, although he worked closely with members seeking economic renovation throughout the 1920s.

The end of, arguably, the most critical phase in Loucheur's postwar efforts in behalf of modernizing France's economic liberalism came when he ceased to be minister of industrial reconstruction, in January, 1920—just as he attained the position of an elected official in the Chamber of Deputies. He had reason to feel disappointment that more had not been accomplished in 1919, but his efforts at economic renewal had not been completely in vain. Some consolidation in the coal and steel industries took place in the early 1920s as a sequel to his tentatives, and his wartime partner, Schneider-Creusot, played a part in that progress.[2] In the devastated regions, too, modernization occurred, through persuasion rather than the state's dictate. The way the Office of Industrial Reconstruction introduced electrification for industry there illustrates the approach. Because of Loucheur's reliance upon private enterprise in building what the war had left in ruin, however, industrial renovation in the liberated regions turned out to be uneven and unsystematic. Still, it is certain that Loucheur helped set the tone for the trends toward modernization by his reconstruction work of 1919.

He was not long without a cabinet post after stepping down as the minister of industrial reconstruction, for his managerial skills were again needed in 1921—this time at the ministry of the liberated regions. Although he continued to encourage the use of modern methods, his overriding concern in 1921 had to be to accelerate the speed at which reconstruction was carried forward. Giving top priority to the settlement of claims for war damages, he rapidly increased the number of dossiers processed. His success was a turning point for reconstruction, even if problems continued to plague the ministry's management of it after his departure in early 1922. But one unintended outcome of his policies was a shortchanging of some claimants in their settlements.

Loucheur remained a leading political advocate of modernization through the 1920s. He showed his pragmatism by qualifying his economic liberalism where he judged state intervention necessary for the well-being of the nation. In the development of the Compagnie Française des Pétroles, which finally emerged with combined private and state ownership to move France toward virtual oil independence, he played a determining role; he also supported state participation in the development of French fertilizer production. At the international level,

2. Brelet, *La Crise de la métallurgie*, 54–59; Grabau, *Industrial Reconstruction*, 168–69.

he fathered the World Economic Conference of 1927 with a view toward achieving a concentration in basic European industries and toward engineering tariff reductions. He even spoke in favor of an eventual European economic union.

Loucheur's modernizing objectives included improved conditions for workers in France's capitalist system. As early as 1920 he introduced legislation committing the government to the construction of a large number of housing units, mostly for workers. Though the bill was effectively killed in the Senate, his tenacity paid off in 1928 with parliamentary passage of another housing bill that he sponsored. More moderate than the legislation he wanted in 1920, it was the vehicle for the largest financial commitment that the French government made in the interwar years to housing intended primarily for workers. In addition, as labor minister, Loucheur was at the center of the legislative debate over and the preparatory measures for the implementation of the social-insurance law of 1928–1930. Humanitarianism was an impulse Loucheur felt, but he was also concerned to absorb French workers more completely into France's economic structure in order to give them a greater stake in the system. When, in early 1929, he talked about the issuance of labor shares of stock that could be converted into capital shares, he was again trying to enfold the workers' interests within interests of larger scope. His introduction, in 1929, of a labor mediation bill, was also for technocratic as well as compassionate ends.

Loucheur, aware that Germany would eventually outstrip France economically and convinced that the preservation of peace in Europe hung on economics, concluded that French security lay in cooperation and conciliation with the republic's recent enemy. He inclined to moderation on reparations at the Paris peace conference and in direct economic negotiations with the Germans after the signing of the Treaty of Versailles. But political constraints at the end of 1919 negated his efforts. He renewed his bold attempts in negotiations with Germany at Wiesbaden in 1921, but they too came short of the outcome he desired.

Despite Loucheur's perspicacity, he, like numerous other politicians, was slow to reckon with France's financial crisis. Preferring to avoid tax increases in the early 1920s, he belatedly accepted the evidence that they were the only solution. But when as minister of finance he tried to shepherd some harsh measures through the Chamber of Deputies in late 1925, he ran into resistance from the Chamber's finance commission that forced his resignation. Nevertheless, he helped France through a financial emergency by succeeding with a preliminary tax measure that enabled the government to meet payments on maturing bonds in early December.

At the beginning of the 1930s, France still lagged behind other advanced industrial nations in crucial ways. The number of firms of one to five employees had been reduced by 25 percent between 1901 and 1931 and the number of large firms doubled, but there were still 400,000 small firms in 1931 as against only 1,100 large ones.[3] Perhaps Loucheur was partly to blame for the deadlock between the dynamic and static sectors of the economy, for his direct moves toward modernization never touched more than a small segment of the French economy. He left much of the decision making in private hands without any state supervision, with the result that changes often occurred slowly. But his technocratic orientation anticipated ideas and policies that were incorporated into France's administrative system after World War II, and his exertions for economic renovation at home and economic cooperation in Europe prefigured other changes that have transformed France since 1945. Even though Loucheur's public career was checkered, his contributions to France have been manifold. And in his professional luster there was the herald of the new class of "manager technicians" who were to have extraordinary influence in the economic life of France.

3. Kuisel, *Capitalism and the State*, 84–85.

BIBLIOGRAPHY

ARCHIVAL SOURCES

Archives de la Préfecture de Police, Paris
    Series B A, Carton 1375.
Archives de l'Assemblée Nationale, Versailles
    XIIe Législature
        Cartons A-19, A-25, Commission des Finances, Procès-verbaux.
        Carton A-66, Commission des Régions Libérées, Procès-verbaux.
    XIIIe Législature
        Carton A-11, Commission d'Assurance et de Prévoyance Sociales, Procès-verbaux.
    XIVe Législature
        Carton A-10, Commission d'Assurance et de Prévoyance Sociales, Procès-verbaux.
        Carton A-34, Commission du Commerce et de l'Industrie, Procès-verbaux.
Archives du Département du Nord, Lille
        Morain, Alfred (préfet). *La Reconstitution du Nord dévasté au 1er septembre 1923: Exposé présenté au Conseil Général.* Lille, 1923.
        Series M 619, Grèves 1886–1939, Carton 79A.
Archives du Ministère des Affaires Etrangères, Paris
        Series A, Paix, 1914–1920, Vols. 90–92.
        Series Guerre, 1914–1918, Grande Bretagne, Vol. 551.
        Series Papiers d'Agents.
        Joseph Avenol Papers, Vol. 36.
        Alexandre Millerand Papers, Vols. 13, 18, 19.
        André Tardieu Papers, Vol. 42.
        Series Société des Nations, Vols. 1194–97, 1199–1201.
        Series Y, Internationale, 1918–1940, Vols. 151, 152, 154, 155, 191.
        Series Z, Europe, 1918–1929.

Belgique, Vol. 124.
Grande Bretagne, Vols. 94, 96.
Unclassified Documents, R.C. B/84/3/VII Wiesbaden.
Archives du Ministère des Finances, Paris
Series A, Documents soumis à des conditions spéciales de sécurité.
Subseries 1 A, Cabinets Ministériels, Carton 386.
Series B, Série générale, constituée par les documents de l'Administration Centrale, Cartons 15617, 33978, 34014, 34023, 34024, 39889, 39895–97.
Subseries F 30, Administration Centrale du Ministère des Finances, Cartons 1500, 1501.
Archives du Sénat, Paris
Commission des Affaires Etrangères, Procès-verbaux, 1919.
Archives Nationales, Paris
Subseries AJ 24, Office de Reconstitution Industrielle des Départements Victimes de l'Invasion, Cartons 128, 135, 136.
Series AP, Archives Privées.
Subseries 94 AP, Albert Thomas Papers, Cartons 21, 51, 57, 63, 86, 87, 112, 113, 121, 133, 170, 176, 233, 275, 343, 362, 367, 370.
Subseries 130 AP, Jacques Louis Dumesnil Papers, Cartons 7, 12.
Subseries 313 AP, Paul Painlevé Papers, Cartons 104, 107, 171.
Series BB, Ministère de la Justice.
Subseries BB 30, Versements disparates de 1904 à 1961, Cartons 1580, 1582.
Series C, Procès-verbaux des Assemblées Nationales, Chambre des Députés, Cartons 7498–7503, 7557, 7559–61, 7769, 7771.
Subseries F 7, Police Générale, Cartons 13366, 13367, 13917, 13939.
Subseries F 12, Ministère du Commerce et de l'Industrie, Cartons 7657, 7662, 7664, 7666, 7673, 7681, 7683, 7785, 7786, 7799, 8023, 8075, 8801, 8860, 8863, 8867.
Subseries F 22, Ministère du Travail, Carton 191.
Unclassified Documents, Une Loi de 1928 sur les assurances sociales, Carton 6.
Service Historique de l'Armée de Terre, Vincennes
Series N 1872–1919.
Subseries 3 N, Comité de Guerre, Cartons 2, 3.
Subseries 6 N, Fonds Clemenceau, Cartons 103, 147, 149, 152.
Subseries 10 N, Ministère de l'Armement, Cartons 2, 3, 29, 37.
Public Record Office, London
Cabinet Office.
CAB 23/, Records of the Cabinet, Minutes of Cabinet Meetings, Conferences of Ministers, 2, 4, 25.
Foreign Office.
FO 368/, General Correspondence, Commercial, Vol. 2114.
FO 371/, General Correspondence, Political, Vol. 3751.

FO 382/, General Correspondence, Contraband, Vols. 1680, 2078 (File 1398), 2079 (File 1398), 2484.
Ministry of Transport.
MT 25/, Ministry of Shipping, 20/52422/1918.
Ministry of Munitions.
MUN 5/, Historical Records Branch, 1901–1943.
Bureau International du Travail, Geneva
Fonds Thomas, Relations et Informations, France, Vol. 2.
Housing, Carton W 8/4/1/22.
League of Nations Archives, Geneva
Section 26, Document No. 38352, Dossier 36175 (1924).
C.C.E./2nd Session/P.V. 4 (I).
Herbert Hoover Presidential Library, West Branch, Iowa
Commerce Papers, State Department, Secretary of State, Charles E. Hughes.
Records of the American Commission to Negotiate Peace, 1918–1931, Microfilm 135.
Supreme Economic Council Documents (Bound typescript), Vol. 3.
Hoover Institution on War, Revolution, and Peace, Stanford, California
Louis Loucheur Papers, Boxes 1, 2, 7–12.

PERSONAL PAPERS

Simone Loucheur Papers, in family possession, Paris.

PUBLISHED DOCUMENTS

France. *Annales de la Chambre des Députés: Débats parlementaires.* 1916–22, 1924, 1925, 1929–31.
———. *Annales de la Chambre des Députés: Documents parlementaires.* 1925, 1927, 1930, 1931.
———. *Annales du Sénat: Débats parlementaires.* 1917, 1921.
———. *Journal officiel de la République française: Chambre des Députés, débats parlementaires.* 1920, 1924, 1925, 1928.
———. *Journal officiel de la République française: Chambre des Députés, documents parlementaires.* 1920, 1923, 1925, 1931.
———. *Journal officiel de la République française: Lois et Décrets.* 1918, 1920, 1921.
Groupement des industries de l'armement no. 10 pour l'approvisionnement du charbon. N.p., 1917.
League of Nations. *Report and Proceedings of the World Economic Conference Held at Geneva, May 4th to 23rd, 1927.* Vol. I of 2 vols. Geneva, 1927.

Ministère des Régions Libérées. *Bulletin des régions libérées.* 1920, 1921.
Ministère du Commerce, de l'Industrie, des Postes et Télégraphes, des Transports Maritimes et de la Marine Marchande, Direction des Etudes Techniques. *Rapport général sur l'industrie française, sa situation, son avenir.* Vol. I of 3 vols. Paris, 1919.
Ministère du Travail et de l'Hygiène. *Bulletin du Ministère du Travail et de l'Hygiène.* 1928.

INTERVIEWS

Huvelin, Paul, July 20, 1977.
Loucheur, Simone, June 17, 1977.

FRENCH NEWSPAPERS

Paris
    L'Action française, 1919.
    La Bataille, 1919.
    L'Echo national, 1922.
    Le Figaro, 1917.
    L'Humanité, 1917.
    La Journée industrielle, 1918, 1919.
    Le Petit Journal, 1917, 1919, 1922, 1924, 1925.
    Le Temps, 1917–21, 1925, 1928–30.
    L'Usine, 1917–21.
Lille
    Le Progrès du Nord, 1919–21, 1925, 1928–30.

FRENCH PERIODICALS

L'Europe nouvelle, 1918, 1919, 1931.
Revue politique et parlementaire, 1924–26, 1928, 1929, 1937.

BOOKS, ARTICLES, AND DISSERTATIONS

Aldcroft, Derek H. *From Versailles to Wall Street, 1919–1929.* Berkeley and Los Angeles, 1977.
Allain, Jean Claude. *Joseph Caillaux: L'Oracle, 1914–1944.* Paris, 1981.
Armitage, Susan. *The Politics of Decontrol of Industry: Britain and the United States.* London, 1969.
Arrigon, Louis Jules. *Industrial France and the War.* Paris, n.d.

Artaud, Denise. *La Question des dettes interalliées et la Reconstruction de l'Europe, 1917–1929.* 2 vols. Lille, 1978.

Baker, Ray Stannard. *Woodrow Wilson and the World Settlement.* Vols. I and II of 3 vols. Garden City, N.Y., 1922.

Bariéty, Jacques. *Les Relations franco-allemandes après la première guerre mondiale.* Paris, 1977.

Baruch, Bernard. *American Industry in the War.* New York, 1941.

Bastié, Jean. *La Croissance de la banlieue parisienne.* Paris, 1964.

Beau de Loménie, Emmanuel. *Les Responsabilités des dynasties bourgeoises.* Vol. III of 4 vols. Paris, 1954.

Bernard, Philippe. *La Fin d'un monde, 1914–1929.* Paris, 1975.

Binion, Rudolph. *Defeated Leaders: The Political Fate of Caillaux, Jouvenel, and Tardieu.* New York, 1960.

Bonin, H. *La Reconstitution des houillères du Nord de la France.* Paris, 1926.

Bonnefous, Edouard, and Georges Bonnefous. *Histoire politique de la Troisième République.* 2nd ed. Vols. II–VI of 7 vols. projected. Paris, 1967–1986.

Bouisson, Fernand. "Eloge funèbre de M. Loucheur prononcé par M. Bouisson." In *Louis Loucheur,* without recorded editor. Les Moulineaux, n.d.

Boyce, Robert W. D. *British Capitalism at the Crossroads, 1919–1932: A Study in Politics, Economics, and International Relations.* Cambridge, Eng., 1987.

Bramhall, Edith C. "The National Economic Council of France." *American Political Science Review,* XX (1926), 623–30.

Brelet, M. *La Crise de la métallurgie: La Politique économique et sociale du Comité des Forges.* Paris, 1923.

Brémontier, Jeanne. "Les Accords de Wiesbaden: Réparations et Restitutions." *Le Parlement et l'Opinion,* XIX–XX (1921), 250–60.

Brogan, Denis William. *The Development of Modern France, 1870–1939.* Rev. ed. Vol. II of 2 vols. New York, 1966.

Bruun, Geoffrey. *Clemenceau.* Hamden, Conn., 1962.

Bureau International du Travail. *Les Problèmes du logement en Europe depuis la guerre.* Geneva, 1924.

Burnett, Philip, ed. *Reparation at the Paris Peace Conference from the Standpoint of the American Delegation.* 2 vols. 1940; rpr. New York, 1965.

Ceux qui nous mènent. Paris, 1922.

Chevrier, Jean Michel. "Le Rôle de Loucheur dans l'économie de guerre, 1914–1918." Thèse de maîtrise, Université de Paris X (Nanterre), 1972.

Churchill, Winston. *The World Crisis, 1916–1918.* Vol. II of 2 vols. New York, 1927.

Clémentel, Etienne. *La France et la Politique économique interalliée.* Paris, 1931.

Coffman, Edward M. *The War to End All Wars: The American Military Experience in World War I.* New York, 1968.

Coudenhove-Kalergi, Richard N. *Crusade for Pan-Europe: Autobiography of a Man and a Movement.* New York, 1943.

Coutard, Jean. *Les Habitations à bon marché: Leur but, leur organisation, leurs résultats.* Paris, 1938.

Czernin, Ferdinand. *Versailles, 1919.* New York, 1964.

Daudet, Léon. *Termites parlementaires.* Paris, 1930.

Derfler, Leslie. *President and Parliament: A Short History of the French Presidency.* Boca Raton, Fla., 1983.

Douglas, Paul H. "The French Social Insurance Act." *Annals of the American Academy,* CLXIV (1932), 211–48.

Doukas, Kimon A. *The French Railroads and the State.* New York, 1945.

Dulles, Eleanor. *The French Franc, 1914–1928.* New York, 1929.

Dulles, John Foster. "The Reparation Problem." *New Republic,* XXVI (March 30, 1921), 133–35.

Dutacq, François. *La Ville de Lyon et la Guerre.* Paris, 1924.

Eighth Yearbook of the League of Nations: Record of 1927. World Peace Foundation Pamphlets, Vol. XI, No. 2. Boston, 1928.

Etevé, Albert. *La Victoire des cocardes.* Paris, 1970.

Evenson, Norma. *Paris: A Century of Change, 1878–1978.* New Haven, 1979.

Falls, Cyril. *The Great War.* New York, 1961.

Felix, David. *Walther Rathenau and the Weimar Republic: The Politics of Reparations.* Baltimore, 1971.

Ferro, Marc. *The Great War, 1914–1918.* Boston, 1973.

Ferry, Abel. *Carnets secrets, 1914–1918.* Paris, 1957.

Fink, Carole. *The Genoa Conference: European Diplomacy, 1921–1922.* Chapel Hill, N.C., 1984.

Flu, Henri. *Les Comptoirs métallurgiques d'après-guerre.* Lyon, 1924.

Fohlen, Claude. *La France de l'entre-deux-guerres, 1917–1939.* 2nd ed. Paris, 1972.

Fontaine, Arthur. *French Industry During the War.* New Haven, 1926.

Fournol, Etienne. *Le Moderne Plutarque.* Paris, 1923.

Fraser, Geoffrey, and Thadée Natanson. *Léon Blum: Man and Statesman.* Philadelphia, 1938.

French, David. *British Economic and Strategic Planning, 1905–1915.* London, 1982.

Gignoux, C. J. "L'Entente internationale de l'acier." *Revue économique internationale,* IV (November, 1926), 211–22.

Gillingham, John. "Coal and Steel Diplomacy in Interwar Europe." In *Internationale Kartelle und Aussenpolitik,* edited by Clemens A. Wurm. Stuttgart, 1989.

———. *Coal, Steel, and the Rebirth of Europe, 1945–1955: The Germans and French from Ruhr Conflict to Economic Community.* Cambridge, Eng., 1991.

Girardet, Philippe. *Ceux que j'ai connus*. Paris, 1952.

Girault, Gabriel. *Le Comité des Forges de France*. Paris, 1922.

Giros, Alexandre. "Allocution prononcée par M. Alexandre Giros." In *Louis Loucheur*, without recorded editor. Les Moulineaux, n.d.

Godfrey, John F. *Capitalism at War: Industrial Policy and Bureaucracy in France, 1914–1918*. Leamington Spa, Eng., 1987.

Grabau, Thomas W. *Industrial Reconstruction in France After World War I*. New York, 1991.

Griffiths, Richard. *Marshal Pétain*. London, 1970.

Guillain, Robert. *Les Problèmes douaniers internationaux et la Société des Nations*. Paris, 1930.

Haig, Robert M. *The Public Finances of Postwar France*. New York, 1929.

Haight, Frank Arnold. *A History of French Commercial Policies*. New York, 1941.

Hamp, Pierre. "Louis Loucheur." *Revue hebdomadaire*, n.s., No. 22, May 28, 1921, pp. 373–85.

Hardach, Gerd. *The First World War, 1914–1918*. Berkeley and Los Angeles, 1977.

―――. "La Mobilisation industrielle en 1914–1918: Production, planification et idéologie." Translated by Dora Fridenson and Evelyne Shalgian. In *1914–1918: L'Autre Front*, edited by Patrick Fridenson. Paris, 1977.

Hatry, Gilbert. "Les Délégués d'atelier aux usines Renault." In *1914–1918: L'Autre Front*, edited by Patrick Fridenson. Paris, 1977.

Hatzfeld, Henri. *Du paupérisme à la sécurité sociale: Essai sur les origines de la sécurité sociale en France, 1850–1940*. Paris, 1971.

Hayes, Carlton J. H. *France: A Nation of Patriots*. New York, 1930.

Hexner, Ervin. *International Cartels*. Durham, N.C., 1946.

―――. *The International Steel Cartel*. Chapel Hill, N.C., 1943.

Hill, Martin. *The Economic and Financial Organization of the League of Nations: A Survey of Twenty-Five Years' Experience*. Washington, D.C., 1946.

Homberg, Octave. *Les Coulisses de l'histoire: Souvenirs, 1898–1928*. Paris, 1938.

Horne, Alistair. *The Price of Glory: Verdun, 1916*. New York, 1963.

Houille, André. *La Question des habitations à bon marché en France*. Paris, 1932.

Hurwitz, Samuel. *State Intervention in Great Britain: A Study of Economic Control and Social Response, 1914–1919*. New York, 1949.

Hymans, Paul. *Mémoires*. Edited by Frans van Kalken and John Bartier. Vol. I of 2 vols. Brussels, 1958.

Inghels, Albert. *Le Panama des régions dévastées*. Paris, 1924.

Jeanneney, Jean Noël. *François de Wendel en République: L'Argent et le Pouvoir, 1914–1940*. Paris, 1976.

Jones, Adrian. "The French Railway Strikes of January–May, 1920: New Syndicalist Ideas and Emergent Communism." *French Historical Studies*, XII (1982), 517–38.

Keeton, Edward David. *Briand's Locarno Policy: French Economics, Politics, and Diplomacy, 1925–1929.* New York, 1987.

Kemp, Tom. *The French Economy, 1913–1939: The History of a Decline.* London, 1972.

Kindleberger, Charles P. *The World in Depression, 1929–1939.* Berkeley and Los Angeles, 1975.

Kuisel, Richard. *Capitalism and the State in Modern France: Renovation and Economic Management in the Twentieth Century.* Cambridge, Eng., 1981.

———. *Ernest Mercier: French Technocrat.* Berkeley and Los Angeles, 1967.

———. "Technocrats and Public Policy: From the Third to the Fourth Republic." *Journal of European Economic History,* II (1973), 53–99.

Kupferman, Fred. *Pierre Laval.* Paris, 1987.

Lachapelle, Georges. *Le Crédit public.* Paris, 1932.

Lamont, Thomas W. *Across World Frontiers.* New York, 1951.

Landes, David. *The Unbound Prometheus: Technological Change and Industrial Development in Western Europe from 1750 to the Present.* London, 1969.

Launay, Jacques de. *Major Controversies of Contemporary History.* Trans. J. J. Buckingham. Oxford, 1965.

Launay, Louis. *M. Loucheur.* St. Cloud, France, 1925.

Leffler, Melvyn. *The Elusive Quest: America's Pursuit of European Stability and French Security, 1919–1933.* Chapel Hill, N.C., 1979.

Lévêque, Jean, and J. H. Ricard. *Une Politique du logement.* Paris, 1928.

Liddell Hart, B. H. *The Real War, 1914–1918.* Boston, 1964.

Lloyd George, David. *The Truth About Reparations and War-Debts.* London, 1932.

———. *War Memoirs.* Vols. IV and V of 6 vols. Boston, 1934–36.

Loucheur, Louis. *Carnets secrets, 1908–1932.* Edited by Jacques de Launay. Brussels, 1962.

———. *Le Commandement unique: Comment il fut réalisé à Doullens, le 25 mars 1918.* Lille, 1928.

———. "La Conférence économique de Genève." *Revue économique internationale,* II (April, 1927), 36–43.

———. Preface to *Les Problèmes douaniers internationaux et la Société des Nations,* by Robert Guillain. Paris, 1930.

———. *Le Problème de la coopération économique internationale.* Paris, 1926.

———. *La Reconstruction de l'Europe et le Problème des réparations: Discours prononcé à Lyon le 20 février 1922 à l'Association Commerciale, Industrielle et Agricole par M. Louis Loucheur.* Paris, 1922.

———. "Réparations et Sécurité." *Revue de Paris,* January 15, 1924, pp. 241–54.

———. *La Situation économique en Europe: Discours prononcé par M. Loucheur, à Pavilly, le 23 septembre 1931.* Paris, n.d.

————. *Tramways départementaux de la Creuse: Propositions de MM. A. Giros et Loucheur, avril 1911.* Auxerre, 1911.

Loucheur, Louis, and Laurent Bonnevay. *Proposition de loi no. 1336: Annexe au procès-verbal de la séance du 22 juillet 1920.* N.p., 1920.

Lucas, Pascal Marie Henri. "L'Evolution du matériel militaire pendant la Grande Guerre (suite)." *Revue d'études militaires,* XXIII (April 1, 1935), 15–29.

MacDonald, William. *Reconstruction in France.* London, 1922.

McDougall, Walter A. *France's Rhineland Diplomacy, 1914–1924: The Last Bid for a Balance of Power in Europe.* Princeton, 1978.

————. "Political Economy Versus National Sovereignty: French Structures for German Integration After Versailles." *Journal of Modern History,* LXI (1979), 4–23.

Maier, Charles S. *Recasting Bourgeois Europe: Stabilization in France, Germany, and Italy in the Decade After World War I.* Princeton, 1975.

Mantoux, Paul. *Les Délibérations du conseil des quatre, 24 mars–28 juin 1919.* Vol. I of 2 vols. Paris, 1955.

Marcesche, Henri. *Le Charbon: Elément de réparations et de négotiations dans le traité de Versailles et les accords qui l'ont suivi.* Lorient, 1933.

Marks, Sally. *Innocent Abroad: Belgium at the Paris Peace Conference of 1919.* Chapel Hill, N.C., 1981.

Marshall, S. L. A. *World War I.* 1964; rpr. Boston, 1987.

Martin, Germaine. *Les Finances publiques de la France et la Fortune privée, 1914–1925.* Paris, 1925.

Mayer, Arno. *The Politics and Diplomacy of Peacemaking: Containment and Counterrevolution at Versailles, 1918–1919.* New York, 1967.

Mercier, Ernest. *Albert Petsche, 1860–1933.* Paris, n.d.

Merlin, Yves. *Les Conflits collectifs du travail pendant la guerre, 1914–1918.* Dunkerque, 1928.

Mermeix [pseud.]. *Au sein des commissions.* Paris, 1924.

————. *Le Combat des trois: Notes et Documents sur la conférence de paix.* Paris, 1922.

Michel, Edmond. *Les Dommages de guerre de la France et leur réparation.* Paris, 1932.

Mordacq, Jean Jules Henri. *Le Ministère Clemenceau: Journal d'un témoin.* Vol. I of 4 vols. Paris, 1930.

Motte, Fernand. "Discours." In *Louis Loucheur,* without recorded editor. Les Moulineaux, n.d.

Nocken, Ulrich. "International Cartels and Foreign Policy: The Formation of the International Steel Cartel, 1924–1926." In *Internationale Kartelle und Aussenpolitik,* edited by Clemens A. Wurm. Stuttgart, 1989.

Normand, Gilles. *Politique et Hommes politiques.* 2 vols. Paris, 1925.

Nouschi, André. "L'Etat français et les Pétroliers anglo-saxons: La Naissance de la Compagnie Française des Pétroles, 1923–1924." *Relations internationales,* No. 7 (1976), 241–59.

Ogburn, William F., and William Jaffe. *The Economic Development of Post-War France: A Survey of Production.* New York, 1929.

Olivier, Maurice. *La Politique du charbon, 1914–1921.* Paris, 1923.

Ollé-Laprune, Jacques. *La Stabilité des ministres sous la Troisième République, 1879–1940.* Paris, 1962.

Orde, Anne. *British Policy and European Reconstruction After the First World War.* Cambridge, Eng., 1990.

Oualid, William, and Charles Picquenard. *Salaires et Tarifs: Conventions collectives et grèves.* Paris, 1928.

Papayanis, Nicholas. "Collaboration and Pacifism in France During World War I." *Francia,* V (1977), 425–45.

Pedroncini, Guy. *Pétain: Général en chef, 1917–1918.* Paris, 1974.

Pegg, Carl. *Evolution of the European Idea, 1914–1932.* Chapel Hill, N.C., 1983.

Peschaud, Marcel. *Les Chemins de fer pendant et depuis la guerre, 1914–1920.* Paris, n.d.

Picard, Roger. *Le Mouvement syndical durant la guerre.* Paris, 1927.

Pinot, Robert. *Le Comité des Forges de France au service de la nation.* Paris, 1919.

Pitts, Vincent. *France and the German Problem: Politics and Economics in the Locarno Period.* New York, 1987.

Poincaré, Raymond. *Au service de la France.* Vol. IX of II vols. Paris, 1932.

Reboul, Frédéric. *Mobilisation industrielle.* Vol. I of 2 vols. Paris, 1925.

Redmayne, Richard A. S. *The British Coal-Mining Industry During the War.* Oxford, 1923.

Renouvin, Pierre. *The Forms of War Government in France.* New Haven, 1927.

Risler, Georges. *Better Housing for Workers in France.* Paris, 1937.

Rogers, David Arthur. "The Campaign for the French National Economic Council." Ph.D. dissertation, University of Wisconsin, 1957.

Ropp, Theodore. *War in the Modern World.* Rev. ed. New York, 1966.

Salter, James Arthur. *Allied Shipping Control: An Experiment in International Administration.* Oxford, 1923.

Sardier, Georges. *Le Ravitaillement en charbon pendant la guerre.* Paris, 1920.

Sauvy, Alfred, and Anita Hirsch. *Histoire économique de la France entre les deux guerres.* Vols. II and III of 3 vols. Paris, 1984.

Schaper, B. W. *Albert Thomas: Trente Ans de réformisme social.* Translated by Louis Dupont. Paris, 1957.

Schrecker, Ellen. *The Hired Money: The French Debt to the United States, 1917–1929.* New York, 1979.

Schuker, Stephen A. *The End of French Predominance in Europe: The Financial Crisis of 1924 and the Adoption of the Dawes Plan.* Chapel Hill, N.C., 1976.

Sellier, Henri, and A. Bruggeman. *Le Problème du logement: Son influence sur les conditions de l'habitation et l'aménagement des villes.* Paris, 1927.

Sharp, Walter R. "The Political Bureaucracy of France Since the War." *American Political Science Review,* XXII (1928), 301–23.

Shoup, Carl. *The Sales Tax in France.* New York, 1930.

Silverman, Dan. *Reconstructing Europe After the Great War.* Cambridge, Mass., 1982.

Sontag, Raymond J. *A Broken World, 1919–1939.* New York, 1971.

Soutou, Georges. "Der Einfluss der Schwerindustrie auf die Gestaltung der Frankreichspolitik Deutschlands, 1919–1921." In *Industrielles System und politische Entwicklung in der Weimarer Republik,* edited by Hans Mommsen *et al.* Dusseldorf, 1974.

Suarez, Georges. *Briand: Sa vie, son oeuvre.* Vol. IV of 5 vols. Paris, 1940.

Tardieu, André. *The Truth About the Treaty.* Indianapolis, 1921.

Trachtenberg, Marc. *Reparation in World Politics: France and European Economic Diplomacy, 1916–1923.* New York, 1980.

U.S. War Office. *Handbook of Artillery, Including Mobile, Anti-Aircraft, and Trench Matériel.* 1920.

Vandel, Jean. *Les Chemins de fer français depuis la guerre, 1919–1924.* Paris, 1925.

Watson, David Robin. *Georges Clemenceau: A Political Biography.* New York, 1974.

Weill-Raynal, Etienne. *Les Réparations allemandes et la France.* 3 vols. Paris, 1947.

Wright, Gordon. *France in Modern Times.* 2nd ed. Chicago, 1974.

Wurzburg, Frederic. "The Politics of the Bloc National." Ph.D. dissertation, Columbia University, 1961.

Young, Allyn, and H. Van V. Fay. *The International Economic Conference.* World Peace Foundation Pamphlets, Vol. X, No. 4. Boston, 1927.

INDEX

Taxes, 1, 200, 250–61 *passim*, 251*n*30, 306, 307; and reparations, 160
Taylor, F. W., 11
Le Temps, 47, 74, 186, 226, 286, 294
Thomas, Albert, 12, 90; and French armaments production, 13–29 *passim*, 33, 34–44 *passim*, 52, 54, 56, 64, 104, 303; trip of, to Russia, 30, 40; and labor relations, 65–66, 70; comments of, on Loucheur, 133, 134, 257; and nationalization of railways, 206
Transportation, 35, 76, 97, 98, 100–101, 104, 182, 200; priorities in, 84, 92–93; wartime damage to, 99, 146. *See also* Railways
Treaty of Versailles, 150, 159, 172, 173–82, 204, 211, 229, 230, 241, 263, 306
Turkey, 6, 176
Turkish Petroleum Company, 248, 249

Union Républicaine Démocratique, 288
United States: imports of steel from, 35, 36–37, 37*n*31, 40, 41, 42, 43, 76, 78, 79, 99–100, 101; imports of grain from, 39, 43; imports of iron from, 82, 103; and

coal emergency, 95–96, 193–95; forces of, in France, 98; price-control program of, 102; post-war policies of, 152, 154, 158–59, 163–64, 166, 263; and peace treaty, 168, 176; and reparations, 235–36, 239; Allied debts to, 239–40, 242, 243, 256, 298
Upper Silesia, 229, 233–34, 233*n*98
L'Usine, 74–75, 194, 199, 232
U.S.S.R. *See* Russia

Verdun, battle of, 16, 17
Viollette, Maurice, 40, 47, 48, 49
Viviani, René, 6, 21, 46

Waterloo, battle of, 166
Weil, Colonel, 90
Wendel, François de, 197
Wiesbaden negotiations, 228–34, 237, 306
Wilson, Henry, 88
Wilson, Woodrow, 150, 153, 156, 165, 166, 167, 169; Fourteen Points of, 163, 167
Wirth, Joseph, 229, 234
World Economic Conference, 262–75, 306

Young Plan, 296, 297